Songs of the Shaman

Songs of the Shaman

The Ritual Chants of the Korean *Mudang*

Boudewijn Walraven
Centre for Japanese and Korean Studies
Rijks Universiteit Leiden

KEGAN PAUL INTERNATIONAL
London and New York

First published in 1994 by
Kegan Paul International Ltd
UK: P.O. Box 256, London WC1B 3SW, England
USA: 29 West 35th Street, New York, NY 10001-2299, USA

Distributed by
John Wiley & Sons Ltd
Southern Cross Trading Estate
1 Oldlands Way, Bognor Regis
West Sussex, PO22 9SA, England

Columbia University Press
562 West 113th Street
New York, NY 10025, USA

The publishers gratefully acknowledge the assistance of The Korea Research Foundation
in the publication of this volume.

Printed in Great Britain by T J Press, Padstow, Cornwall

British Library Cataloguing in Publication Data
Walraven, Boudewijn, 1947-
 Songs of the Shaman.
 1. Korea. Shamanism. Rituals. Use in songs
 I. Title
 291.62

 ISBN 0-7103-0403-X

Library of Congress Cataloging in Publication Data
Walraven, Boudewijn, 1947-
 Songs of the shamen: the ritual chants of the Korean *mudang* / Boudewijn
Walraven.
      p.   cm.
 Includes translations of several muga.
 Includes bibliographical references and index.
 ISBN 0–7103–0403–X
 1. Shamanism – Korea.   2. Korea – Religious life and customs.
 3. Songs, Korean – Korea – History and criticism.   I. Title.
 BL2236. S5W35 1991
 299 .57 – dc20   90-42659
                                                                        CIP

Contents

Abbreviations

For full bibliographical details consult the Bibliography.

AA: Akamatsu Chijō, Akiba Takashi, *Chōsen fuzoku no kenkyū* (2 volumes: I and II).

CCM: Kim Yŏngjin, *Ch'ungch'ŏng-do muga*.

Cheju sajŏn: Hyŏn Yongjun, *Cheju-do musok charyo sajŏn*.

Han'guk siga: Kim Sŏnp'ung, *Han'guk siga-ŭi minsokhak-chŏk yŏn'gu*.

HKMT: *Han'guk kubi munhak taegye*.

HMCCP: *Han'guk minsok chonghap chosa pogosŏ*.To refer to individual volumes, the abbreviation *HMCCP* is followed by the name of the province which is the subject of that volume.

HSC: *Sim Ch'yŏng chyŏn*, publ. by Hyangminsa.

Kasa chŏnjip: Kim Sŏngbae a.o., *Kasa munhak chŏnjip*.

Kasa sŏnjip: Yi Sangbo, *Han'guk kasa sŏnjip*.

KIM: *Sim Ch'ŏng kut* text in *THM*, (Kim Yŏnghŭi).

KTG: Kim T'aegon, *Han'guk muga chip* (four volumes: I, II, III, IV).

Kwanbuk muga: Im Sŏkchae, Chang Chugŭn, *Kwanbuk chibang muga* (two volumes: I and II).

Minyo chip: Im Tonggwŏn, *Han'guk minyo chip* (six volumes: I, II, III, IV, V, VI).

MSr: Chang Chugŭn, *Kankoku no minkan shinkō, ronkō-hen*.

MSs: Chang Chugŭn, *Kankoku no minkan shinkō, shiryō-hen*.

Munhwajae IV: "Sŏngju p'uri", recorded by Ch'oe Kilsŏng.

Namwŏn kosa: Kim Tonguk a.o., *Ch'unhyang chŏn pigyo yŏn'gu*.

NSC: Chang Chiyŏng, *Hong Kiltong chŏn . Sim Ch'ŏng chŏn*.

PAM: *Sim Ch'ŏng chŏn* text in *Han'guk siga*, (Pak Yongnyŏ).

PC: *Sim Ch'ŏng ka* text in Chŏng Pyŏnguk, *Han'gug-ŭi p'ansori*.

PH: *Sim Ch'ŏng ka* text in *Han'guk kubi munhak sŏnjip*.

Pulgyo kasa: Yi Sangbo, *(Han'guk) Pulgyo kasa chŏnjip*.

PY: *Sim Ch'ŏng ka* text in Yi Ch'angbae, *Han'guk kach'ang taegye*.

PYM: *Sim Ch'ŏng kut* text in *KTG* I, (Pyŏn Yŏnho).

Sangyong ŭibŏm: *Pulgong chaesik sangyong ŭibŏm*.

SC: The story of Sim Ch'ŏng.

Shinka ihen: Son Chint'ae, *Chōsen no shinka ihen*.

Sijo sajŏn: Chŏng Pyŏnguk, *Sijo munhak charyo sajŏn*.

Sin Chaehyo: Kang Hanyŏng, *Sin Chaehyo p'ansori sasŏl chip*.

SSC: *Sim Ch'ŏng ka* text in *Sin Chaehyo*.

THM: Ch'oe Chŏngnyŏ, Sŏ Taesŏk, *Tonghaean muga*.

WSC: *Wanp'anbon Sim Ch'ŏng chŏn*.

YIM: Texts of the *Sim Ch'ŏng kut* performed by Yi Kŭmok (see below).

YIM I: *Sim Ch'ŏng kut* text in Sin Tongik, "Muga 'Sim Ch'ŏng chŏn'".

YIM II: *Sim Ch'ŏng kut* text in Yi Kyŏngbok, *Sim Ch'ŏng kut yŏn'gu*.

YIM III: *Sim Ch'ŏng kut* in *HKMT* 7-7.

Preface

I first read *muga* as a student at Leiden University, when the Korean shaman songs collected by Akamatsu and Akiba -together with their other writings on Korean shamanism- were about the only material available to me for studying the *mudang* and their rituals. I soon discovered that reading *muga* was not exactly the easy way to enter into this subject; even native speakers of Korean were often unable to explain the texts. A grant from the Ministry of Education of the Republic of Korea gave me the opportunity to study at Seoul National University and there to pursue my interest in the *muga* as a source for the study of Korean shamanism. In the process I had to face the question to what extent and in what manner the *muga* should (and indeed could) be so used. At the same time I found that one key to the understanding of the *muga* was a deeper knowledge of the various genres of traditional literature, and this again led to the decision to examine the place of the *muga*, as a source for the study of shamanism, by tracing the relationship of the songs to such literary genres as *sijo*, *kasa* and *p'ansori*.

This book is the revised version of the doctoral dissertation that was the result of these investigations. It falls into three parts: the first two chapters provide a brief, basic introduction, the next four chapters deal with various problems of a general nature, and the last section consists of three chapters in each of which a particular *muga* is examined. Two of these have been translated in extenso. These three chapters add the necessary flesh to the bones of the argument of Chapters III-VI. Chapter IX, which deals with a song describing some of the most important aspects of the life of the Korean shaman, also adds detail to the more general description of the *mudang* in Chapter I.

It is my hope that the book will provide the groundwork for a better understanding of the *muga* and their significance for Korean shamanism. Much, however, remains to be done. It would be fruitful if more individual songs or types of songs were to be made the subject of further studies, and, above all, the songs should be studied in the concrete social setting of the rituals of which they form so important a part. Only then can their full meaning be appreciated. An awareness of the historical character of the *muga* and of their literary form and context, to which this book may contribute, will, I am convinced, be of value for such studies.

It is stressed throughout that the *muga* have changed with the times, as has shamanism itself. This is a continuing process. In recent years, Korea has developed in amazing fashion, and at least some of the *mudang* have adapted to the times, seeking new forms of performance and new audiences. Certain *mudang* perform on stage, in Korea as well as overseas, or they appear on television, acquiring the status of media personalities. In 1993, one prominent shaman published a novel entitled *Mudang*, which is sold with two cassette tapes of *muga*. All this should not be dismissed as loss of authenticity. Rather it is evidence arguing the vitality of *mudang* and *muga*. These new developments are no less worthy of study than the so-called ancient traditions. It goes without saying then, that my conclusion that the *muga* are not in all respects as ancient as some would have us believe, is in no way a disparagement of their value. Many of them are are fascinating, whatever their origins, and used in the right way, *muga* may tell us a great deal about the meaning and history of Korean shamanism, with all the changes it has known through time.

This study would have been impossible but for the enormous amount of work done by the collectors of *muga*, chiefly Korean scholars, to all of whom I am greatly indebted. Several of them, moreover, have been so kind as to give of their time to answer my questions and further my understanding of the *mudang* and their songs. Many other Korean scholars, at one time or another, have done what they could to guide me, and for this, too, I am most grateful, as I am to the Korean Traders Scholarship Foundation, which enabled me to do fieldwork. The list of individuals who have helped me is far too long to even think of mentioning each by name. Indeed I should like here to express my appreciation to all those from whom I have learned, be it in Korea, in Holland or elsewhere, and whether they have formally been my teachers or not: to shamans, scholars, relatives and friends. But allow me to express my special gratitude to my mentor Frits Vos, who introduced me to *muga*, and on whom I have always been able to call for advice, encouragement and friendship.

I The *Mudang,* their Rituals and their Gods

The mudang

Muga literally are the songs of the *mudang*. In these pages *mudang* will be used as a general appellation for members of a class of professional religious specialists who act as mediators between the world of the supernatural and the world of man, although perhaps a majority of them do not call themselves *mudang*, but *munyŏ*, *mansin*, *miji*, *tan'gol*, *simbang*, *hwaraengi* or yet other names.[1] Both in daily usage in Korean and in academic treatises, however, these people are commonly called *mudang*. Not only does the word *mudang* originally refer to women, most of the religious mediators of this kind are female, and therefore any unspecified *mudang* will be referred to as "she." Men who follow this profession are often called *paksu* or *paksu mudang*.

Both westerners and Korean academics often call the *mudang* a shaman. Whether this is correct depends first of all on one's definition of shamanism. If shamanism is primarily a "technique of ecstasy", as Eliade insists, many *mudang* cannot be called shamans.[2] L. Vajda in his article "Zur phaseologischen Stellung des Schamanismus" has described shamanism as a complex of phenomena, which taken one by one may exist outside shamanism, but only in conjunction constitute something which really deserves the name of shamanism.[3] He enumerates eight constituents, which certainly are not all present in so-called Korean shamanism. Much looser definitions are used by American anthropologists. William P. Lebra, for instance, defines a shaman as a religious practitioner "who has 1. recognized supernatural powers which are utilized for socially approved ends or goals, and 2. the capacity to enter (and withdraw from) culturally defined trance states (i.e., spirit possession)."[4]
Still another definition is given by A. Hultkrantz:

"The central idea of shamanism is to establish contact with the supernatural world by the ecstatic experience of a professional and inspired intermediary, the shaman. There are four important constituents of shamanism: the ideological premise, or the supernatural world and the contacts with it; the shaman as the actor on behalf of a human group; the inspiration granted him by his helping spirits; and the extraordinary, ecstatic experiences of the shaman."[5]

The definition of Lebra, with its "culturally defined trance states", includes the *mudang*, while that of Hultkrantz may do so, if ecstasy is not understood in the meaning Eliade gives to the term and if the helping spirits do not have to be exactly the same as in Siberian shamanism.[6]

Whether Korean shamanism is real shamanism, is of little importance for the purposes of this study. For convenience the terms "shaman" and "shamanism" will be used occasionally, but these terms are not supposed to imply a complete identity with shamans and shamanism elsewhere. Many earlier writers have used the terms in similar fashion and therefore they are justified by tradition, if not by theoretical considerations.

Recently several books and articles have appeared in Western languages, which describe the *mudang* and their beliefs and for that reason in this chapter only a very brief survey will be presented of the nature of the activities of the *mudang*.[7]

The beliefs of the *mudang* are supposed to be connected historically to the religion of the peoples who inhabited the peninsula before Korean culture on a large scale underwent the influence of China. In the oldest sources, the *Samguk sagi* (Records of the Three Kingdoms) and the *Samguk yusa* (Remnants of the Three Kingdoms) shaman-like figures repeatedly appear in the records of the ancient states of Koguryŏ, Paekche and Silla.[8] Originally, "shamanism" was the main *Weltanschauung* of these states, but this changed with the introduction of Chinese culture, which brought with it Buddhism, Confucianism and Taoism. From that time on, shamanism became more and more the religion of the lower classes in general, and of women irrespective of class, although it can be argued that even masculine upper-class thinking was often moulded by the patterns of the native religion. In fact, some scholars are of the opinion that up to the present day shamanism has been a major influence on every form of religion in Korea, including Christianity.[9]

An early source for the study of the *mudang* is a poem by the Koryŏ statesman and poet Yi Kyubo (1168-1241). It is called "The Old *Mudang*" and clearly expresses the contempt of the literati for "superstitious nonsense." On the other hand, it proves that certain basic forms of modern Korean shamanism had already been established at that time. The *mudang* in this poem claims that gods descend in her, she speaks with a strange thin voice (the voice of a spirit), dances ecstatically, predicts good and bad fortune and has a room in her house displaying the pictures of the deities she serves, the most prominent among them probably being Chesŏk, a god that is still widely revered. Unfortunately, the poem does not refer to songs sung during the rituals.[10]

Not all connections between the ruling class and the *mudang* were severed when shamanism lost its privileged position. *Mudang* not only kept up a relationship with the women of the palace, they were also employed by the government to assist in ceremonies to pray for rain.[11] Nevertheless, especially during the Chosŏn dynasty, the government frequently took repressive measures against the *mudang*. The Dutch sailor Hendrik Hamel, for instance, witnessed in 1662 the destruction -on the King's orders- of shrines in which the gods of the *mudang* were revered.[12]

When Korea was opened to the outside world, shamanism was an "underdog-religion", scarcely regarded as a religion at all by the literate, and this remained so. Confucianist contempt for the *mudang* was succeeded by or combined with Christian and materialistic/rationalistic bias against the popular religion. Only after the liberation from Japanese occupation in 1945, and then only very slowly and in limited circles, it was realized that the *mudang* were bearers of important elements of Korean traditional culture.[13] In scholarly circles "shamanism" has acquired a certain respectability in recent years. It is regarded by many as an essential part of traditional Korean culture, as the most important element of the "roots" of the modern Korean. Appreciation for shamanism in this respect is not always accompanied by any knowledge of what Korean shamanism really is and does not imply a complete acceptance of the *mudang*. There is considerable tension between the interest in shamanism as something "truly Korean" and the contempt still felt by some scholars -not all- for the "superstitiousness" of the actual *mudang*. Academic interest in the *mudang* has, nevertheless, influenced government policies. Some *mudang* have received official recognition as "Human Cultural Assets" and the authorities make efforts to preserve some of their festivals. In 1983, for instance, the Seoul City Government decided to revive a shamanistic ritual performed to console the spirit of a famous Yi dynasty general, Nam I (1441-1468), who was executed in the prime of life, when he fell victim to a conspiracy of his enemies.[14] This festival was originally a local festival, similar to the village festivals held regularly in all parts of Korea in the past.[15] One should be aware of the fact, however, that the decision was not prompted by love of shamanism *per se*. The aim of the festival, according to the press report, will be to provide the citizens of Seoul with opportunities for recreation and to impart a sense of history. In the countryside the New Village Movement, which was launched by President Park Chung-hee, has led to the abolition of many village festivals. This movement not only advocated the consolidation of farm land and the changing of straw roofs for slate roofs, it also propagated the "rationalization" of ritual expenditures. A *muga* refers to the tension between the New Village Movement (*Sae-maŭl undong*) and the organisation of a village festival.[16]

> While the New Village projects had started,
> Whether they had money or not,
> While they had to change the roofs, improve the roads
> And tidy up the houses, too,
> And while they had no money,
> Having used all,
> Still collecting bit by bit, little by little,
> All the families,
> Intending to transfer it to the Guardian Deity of
>   the Village,
> Exerted themselves.

In spite of some improvement, the attitude of most people toward the *mudang* is ambivalent at best.[17]

There are two main types of *mudang*: "possessed" *mudang* into whose bodies the gods "descend" during their ceremonies, i.e. those who have become *mudang* after an illness that is interpreted as a summons by the gods to start a *mudang* career, and, second, "hereditary" *mudang* who have been born in *mudang* families. Geographically, the former are said to be more numerous in the Central and Northern region, the latter in the South. The "divine illness" of the first group greatly resembles the illness preceding the initiation of Siberian shamans.[18] Both groups serve gods and ghosts during elaborate ceremonies -usually called *kut*-, during which they sing and often dance to the accompaniment of a drum and other instruments (gongs, cymbals, oboes, etc.), played by their assistants. *Kut* have three main purposes: first, bringing good luck in various forms (a good harvest, a good catch of fish, success in business, a male heir etc.), second, soothing the souls of the deceased and guiding them to the world of the dead, and finally, the curing of illness. These ceremonies have different names according to the region, but they are commonly called *chaesu kut*, *chinogi kut* and *pyŏng kut*, respectively.[19] The *kut*, the full-scale ceremony, undoubtedly has received more attention from students of Korean shamanism than all other activities of the *mudang* together. Yet, these other activities are far from negligible. According to Cho Hung-youn besides the holding of *kut*, the *mudang* occupy themselves with fortune-telling, manufacturing amulets (*pujŏk*), the performance of small-scale rituals (*ch'isŏng*) and meetings with their clients.[20] If the *kut* would be the only form of contact between a *mudang* and her clients, this contact would necessarily be rather infrequent, because of the relatively high cost of the *kut*. In the relationship between *mudang* and client, activities other than the *kut* are of the greatest importance; a close bond between the two would be unthinkable if contacts were limited to the elaborate and expensive *kut*.[21]

For a study of the *muga*, however, one cannot avoid concentrating on the *kut*, as almost all *muga* are sung to accompany this type of ceremony. In general, *ch'isŏng* does not include song and dance. The verbal component of *ch'isŏng* rituals often consists of the recitation of sutras.[22] There may be some exceptions, such as a brief song in which the Mountain God is entreated to stop a baby's crying, [23] but without any doubt the vast majority of all *muga* texts collected so far are connected with some form of *kut*.

To hold *kut* in their traditional, elaborate form requires certain skills and special knowledge. Hereditary *mudang* receive instruction from their fathers and mothers, and sometimes from other relatives who are *mudang*. When they marry into another *mudang* family -as frequently happens- they may also learn from their in-laws. The possessed *mudang* forms a pseudo-family relationship with an established *mudang*, who is called her "divine mother" (*sin-ŏmŏni*) and acts as her teacher. The apprentice is called *sin-ttal*, "divine daughter." Details about the way in which the new *mudang* learn their craft will be given in Chapter III.

This study only deals with the *mudang* who have such special knowledge; these are the performers and the creators of *muga*. It should be noted, however, that besides the two types of *mudang* mentioned above, there are a considerable number of shamanistic practitioners who do not sing *muga*. In many cases they have a background similar to that of the possessed *mudang*: protracted illness regarded as *sinbyŏng* (divine illness), which only can be cured by accepting the summons of the gods. These people, because they cannot find a *sin-ŏmŏni* or do not have the aptitude to learn the songs, or perhaps just because they do not feel the need (this type of *mudang* has hardly been studied), perform without the elaborate ritual of the traditional *mudang*. The basics of ritual that cannot be dispensed with, they often borrow from Buddhism.[24]

Still another category of kindred practitioners is formed by the exorcists, the *p'ansu*. These recite so-called "shamanistic scriptures", *mugyŏng*, which are often written in pure Chinese and are of Buddhist or Taoist origin. The pantheon of the *mugyŏng* has little in common with that of the *muga*; there is a quite amazing lack of integration.[25] In this study the *mugyŏng* will not be examined.

The structure of the ceremonies

Because the *muga* only function within the entirety of the ceremonies, the latter should be examined more in detail. The structure of the ceremonies will be illustrated through the *chaesu kut*. The *chinogi kut* qua form may be regarded as an extension of the *chaesu kut* and the *pyŏng kut* is usually quite simple. Therefore the *chaesu kut* is best suited to serve as an example. In theory it is divided into twelve parts: each devoted to a specific god or to a group of deities or spirits. In practice, the number of parts is rarely exactly twelve; there may be as many as twenty-four. Many authors use the term *kŏri* to refer to any one of the constituent parts of the *kut*, but according to Cho Hung-youn, *kŏri* should not be used for those parts of the ceremony in which there is no dancing and relaying of the words of the gods.[26] Confusingly, in some regions, especially on the East Coast, *kut* is used to refer to the smaller parts of a ceremony as well as to the whole: so the *Kyemyŏn kut* there corresponds to a *kŏri* in Central Korea and is part of the larger ceremony called *Pyŏlsin kut* as well.

At the beginning and the end of a ceremony there are always rituals for the less important gods and spirits. Usually one starts with rites to rid the place of noxious influences which might annoy the more important deities who will be invited to participate later.[27] In the very last *kŏri*, usually called *Twitchŏn kŏri*, food is offered to inferior gods and ghosts. Both the opening and the concluding parts of the *kut* are performed outside, not in the house or shrine where the more important rituals take place. Another feature the parts at the beginning and the end have in common is that the *mudang* does not wear a special costume. For the *kŏri* devoted to the more important gods, the *mudang* changes into special robes belonging to the deity whom she is going to impersonate.[28]

The middle *kŏri* have a more or less fixed structure of their own. They start with an invitation to the god(s) to descend to the place where the *kut* is held (*ch'ŏngbae*). Then there are songs to entertain the gods (*noraekkarak* or *t'aryŏng*); there may be a song describing the origin of the god. At a certain moment, during some frenzied dancing, the god takes possession of the *mudang*. She stops dancing and the god now speaks through the mouth of the *mudang*; this is called *kongsu*. Usually, *kongsu* is not found in the *kut* of hereditary *mudang*, which is logical as the hereditary *mudang* do not know possession. It is rather surprising, therefore, that some hereditary *mudang* do have *kongsu* in their ceremonies.[29] One might suppose that the contents of *kongsu* differ from *kut* to *kut* and have nothing in common. This is not the case; *kongsu* usually follow traditional patterns. *Kongsu* again is followed by "entertainment" offered to the god as an expression of gratitude. At the end of the *kŏri* the *mudang* invokes the blessing of the god.[30] In practice, the order

of some of the parts may differ and some may be left out, but basically these
are the elements of a *kŏri*: the invocation to invite the god, the songs sung to
please him, messages of the god to the believers, and the entreaties for divine
blessings.

Between songs, the *mudang* dances to the accompaniment of a drum
shaped like an hour-glass (the *changgo*), which is played by an assistant.
Other instruments frequently used are gongs in various sizes, cymbals and the
p'iri, the Korean oboe.

Traditional *mudang* never perform alone. They not only need assistants to
take care of the musical accompaniment, but also to take their turn in
performing the various *kŏri*. The most senior *mudang* will do the most
important parts, the junior *mudang* or the *sin-ttal* sing and dance for the less
important deities. Many *mudang* specialize in specific parts.[31]

A complete ceremony takes a day and a really big *kut* can last three or four
days. *Kut* on such a scale are seldom seen nowadays; the modern trend is
rather towards simplification of ceremonies. The duration of individual *kŏri*
is from about half an hour to four hours. The length of the songs and dances
is not fixed; these can be stretched or shortened as the situation demands.
When there are many clients wanting to hear the words of the gods, even the
kongsu part of a *kŏri* may last a considerable time.

The gods of the mudang

A list of the parts of a *chaesu-kut* makes a natural link to the preceding
section and will serve to introduce the most important gods of the *mudang*.[32]

1.   *Pujŏng*. This means "uncleanliness", which fits the purpose of this part:
      to get rid of all kinds of unclean spirits which might spoil the following
      parts of the *kut*. But *Pujŏng* is personified as a deity. This is most
      obvious in a *muga* from Osan[33], in which the honorific suffix *-nim*
      (which always follows names of persons) is added to Pujŏng and which
      explains who were his father and his mother. Among the spirits
      addressed in the song are the *yŏngsan*, ghosts of people who have died
      an untimely death, because of accident, illness or violence. Also
      invoked are the *sangmun*, unclean spirits which spring from the defile-
      ments of death.

2.   *Kamang-kŏri*. Kamang are a class of ancestral gods of a rather uncer-
      tain nature. According to Cho Hung-youn, Kamang refers to gods
      revered as founders of shamanism, and also to ancestors of believers or
      to the shamans of these ancestors.[34] According to Laurel Kendall, one

of the Kamang, the so-called Ch'o Kamang ("First Kamang") is "... a spirit of suicides, violent deaths, and deaths far from home."[35] The ideas of the *mudang* about their deities are not infrequently so vague, that it is difficult to give a concise description of a god or even a class of gods.

3. *San-manura*. San-manura is another name for the Mountain God (San-sin). Veneration of sacred mountains was not only a part of the popular religion, the government, also, took part in it. The founder of the Chosŏn dynasty, for instance, honoured sacred mountains by bestowing titles of nobility on them.[36]

4. *Pyŏlsang kŏri*. Pyŏlsang are deified kings, princes and generals.[37]

5. *Chesŏk kŏri*. Chesŏk is the God of birth. The name is borrowed from Buddhism; it is the Korean pronunciation of the Chinese characters used to write the name of the Indian god Sakro devānām Indra. The association with Buddhism is retained in the costume of Chesŏk (that is, the costume which the *mudang* wears during this *kŏri*), which includes a *kokkal*, a head covering for monks and nuns.[38]

6. *Ch'ŏnwang chung t'aryŏng*. This is devoted to the Heavenly Kings (Ch'ŏnwang) of Buddhism (in the *muga* represented as monks, *chung*), who assist as guardians of the Dharma. It is actually an appendix to the preceding part and not often found separately.

7. *Hogu kŏri*. Hogu are, according to Cho Hung-youn, the souls of girls who were sent to China, during the period of Mongol domination in the 13th and 14th century, as part of the tribute Korea had to pay. According to Akiba and Akamatsu they are spirits of smallpox. The *muga* for this *kŏri* in the collection of Akiba and Akamatsu contains nothing to corroborate this proposition. Nevertheless, the Hogu definitely seem to be linked with smallpox (cf. names as Hogu pyŏlsŏng-mama for the god of smallpox).[39]

8. *Malmyŏng kŏri*. Malmyŏng are deified *mudang* of the past or ancestor spirits in general.

9. *Kunung kŏri*. Kunung are deified warriors.[40] Many of the gods of the *mudang* are represented as fierce warriors, brandishing swords and halberds.

10. *Taegam kŏri*. Taegam originally was an appellation of government officials. The *mudang* use this word as a suffix to the names of a whole group of gods, but also separately for gods of this class. A Taegam is primarily a god of wealth and fortune. Gods of the Taegam class are commonly regarded as extremely greedy and overbearing, but they are also amusing in their own way and the *Taegam kŏri* is often most entertaining. The following fragment from a Taegam *muga* gives something of the flavour of this *kŏri*.

> Do you know what kind of Taegam
> Is our Taegam?
> He is a Taegam who in the days of yore
> Would have *sijo* and drinking songs sung to him,
> With a *kisaeng* sitting in his lap.[41]

In one *kut* I have witnessed, the *mudang* who acted the part of Taegam greedily drank pig's blood, which gruesomely stained her lips. Keeping some of it in her mouth, she amused and frightened the spectators by threatening to spit it in their faces.

11. *Ch'angbu kŏri*. *Ch'angbu* means actor or husband of a *mudang*. These husbands often act as assistant to their wives, especially in the southern provinces. Spirits of the great *ch'angbu* are revered by the *mudang* as guardian deities or as gods of singing and dancing. This is comparable to the veneration of *mudang* of the past, in the *Malmyŏng kŏri*.[42]

12. *Twitchŏn kŏri*. This is a *kŏri* for a variety of less important gods and ghosts. Cho Hung-youn subdivides this *kŏri* in no fewer than eleven parts.[43] In the *muga* collection of Akiba and Akamatsu, the gods addressed in the song for this *kŏri* are Kŏllip (said to be a kind of servant to other deities,[44] but who are also guardian spirits of the *mudang*[45]) and further gods of the Taegam group, Sŏnang (a group of local tutelary gods), and the *yŏngsan*, earlier invoked in the *Pujŏng* part of the ceremony.

An important god who has not been included in the above *chaesu kut* is Sŏngju the god of the house, to whom we devote Chapter VIII. Other gods connected with the house but not here included are Chisin, the deity of the earth, the god who guards the gate, and the female spirit who is in charge of the outhouse. The latter is sometimes called Puch'ul kaksi, "Miss Squatting-board." According to one *muga* her hair is fifty-five feet long[46] and according to another song "in one hand she receives faeces, in the other she receives urine."[47]

In a small shrine on the slopes of Mt. Inwang in Seoul, the Kuksadang, which is rented by *mudang* to hold their *kut*, there are pictures of the following gods:

a.   Ch'angbu (cf. part 11 of the *chaesu kut*)

b.   Kwakkwak sŏnsaeng, "Master Kwakkwak". Kwakkwak seems to be a corruption of Kwak Pak, the Korean pronunciation of Kuo P'u, the name of a scholar from Eastern Chin, who was well versed in the theory of the Five Elements, geomancy, astronomy and divination. Works written or compiled by him were apparently much read in Korea.[48]
Such learned diviners, who originally had nothing to do with shamanism, often are mentioned in the *muga* as "ancestors" of exorcists.[49] They are sometimes venerated during the *Twitchŏn kŏri*.[50]

c.   Pyŏlsang. According to Clark[51], one the deities of this class, the ghost of Crown Prince Changhŏn (1735-1762), who was accused of plotting against his father, King Yŏngjo (r. 1724-1776) and locked up alive in a rice chest, was one of the most popular gods in the vicinity of Seoul. The *mudang* call him Twiju Taewang, "the Great King of the Rice Chest."

d.   Sansin, the Mountain God.

e.   A Kunung (a deified warrior).

f.   Ch'oe Yŏng changgun. General Ch'oe Yŏng (1317-1389) was one of the most important figures of the last days of Koryŏ. He was murdered by a rival, the founder of the Chosŏn dynasty, Yi Sŏnggye (1335-1408). Ch'oe Yŏng combines two characteristics possessed by deities revered by the *mudang*: he belongs to the group of famous warriors, and he died a violent death, like Crown Prince Changhŏn or the anonymous *yŏngsan* spirits. General Nam I is another example of a warrior who died a tragic death and became an object of veneration for the *mudang*.

g.   Hogu (cf. the seventh *kŏri* of the *chaesu kut*).

h.   Kang-bi, "Royal Consort Kang", second wife of Yi Sŏnggye (the first king of the Chosŏn dynasty).

i.   T'aejo. T'aejo is the posthumous name of Yi Sŏnggye himself.

j.   Muhak Taesa. "Grand Preceptor Muhak" (1327-1405), a Buddhist monk who acted as advisor to Yi Sŏnggye.

k.   Sambul Chesŏk. Chesŏk is often represented as a trinity of three Buddhas (Sambul). The god in charge of childbirth is also called Samsin (which may be translated as "three gods", although it is uncertain whether this is the real meaning). One often speaks of Samsin halmŏni, "Grandmother Samsin", imagining this deity as a single figure (although different families have different Grandmothers Samsin; the problem of the individuality or singularity and plurality of shamanistic gods is complicated and will be discussed later).

l.   Naong. A famous monk from the reign of King Kongmin (1330-1374) of the Koryŏ dynasty.

m.   Ch'ilsŏng. The seven stars of the Big Dipper, venerated as deities who protect children, and as such closely related to Chesŏk. The worship of Ch'ilsŏng is sometimes cited as an example of Taoist influence on Korean shamanism, but the cult of Ch'ilsŏng is found in many Buddhist temples.[52] Worship of Ch'ilsŏng is also hinted at in the poem "The Old *Mudang*" by Yi Kyubo.

n.   Yongwang. The Dragon King. According to some *muga* as well as to certain literary sources, there are separate Dragon Kings for the Eastern, Southern, Western and Northern Seas. Dragon Kings are not only gods of the sea, but also gods of water in general. Near the Han River, at Kwangnaru, there used to be a shrine dedicated to the Dragon King.[53]

o.   Min-bi, "Royal Consort Min." She is better known as Queen Min (1851-1896). She was a great patroness of the *mudang*. The Japanese murdered her for political reasons.

Among these gods there are some who are venerated throughout the country, like Chesŏk, Ch'ilsŏng and Yongwang, and some who are only worshipped in and around Seoul, where the ceremonies of the *mudang* were much influenced by their relations with the "Inner Court", the women of the Palace.

Most *mudang* also have a place within their own homes where they worship the gods who are of the greatest importance to them. This room is called *sindang*. A certain *paksu mudang* venerates in his *sindang* pictures of the following deities:

- Taesin halmŏni, "Great-God Grandmother", a deified *mudang* which he equated with the Ur-*mudang* Pari kongju, the Abandoned Princess, who is the heroine of a famous narrative *muga*.

- Sambul Chesŏk, the Three Buddha's Chesŏk, represented in the painting as three Buddhist monks.

- Ch'ilsŏngnim, the Seven Stars (see above), depicted as seven anthropomorphic figures.

- Puch'ŏnim Hubul, the future Buddha: Maitreya.

- Sansin harabŏji, "Grandfather Mountain God", depicted (as is customary) as an old man accompanied by a tiger.

- Ch'oe Il changgunnim. Ch'oe Il is the same as Ch'oe Yŏng, the famous general of the last days of Koryŏ.

- Paengma sinjang, the Divine General on the White Horse, who sometimes is thought to be Hong Kyŏngnae (1780-1812), the leader of a rebellion which was bloodily suppressed in 1811-1812.

This *paksu mudang* also worshipped Pyŏlsangnim, whom he identified with Crown-Prince Changhŏn, the "Rice-chest King", but he "for no special reason", was not represented by a picture.[54]

The categories of gods found in this *sindang* are typical: a deified *mudang*, a *mudang*-ancestor (*mujo*), figures of Buddhist origin, the Mountain God, famous warriors of the past and a person of royal blood whose life ended in tragedy.

One important class of gods, which has been mentioned only in passing, is that of the Sŏnang or Sŏnghwang. Sŏnghwang is the Korean pronunciation of Ch'eng-huang, the Chinese god of the walls and moats of a city.[55] In Korea, however, Sŏnang (as it is usually pronounced) is a tutelary deity, usually a *deus loci*, who, when associated with a mountain, is hard to distinguish from the Mountain God. Often Sŏnang is the protector of a village. The place where Sŏnang is worshipped is called Sŏnangdang, "Hall of Sŏnang", but in spite of this name in many cases there is no building at all, the actual object of worship being a heap of stones or an old tree.[56] With fishermen one finds the worship of pae-Sŏnang, "Boat-Sŏnang", protectors of their fishing boats, who are frequently imagined to be female.[57]

A relatively large amount of space has been devoted to the pantheon of the *mudang*. This is because the pantheon shows some important aspects of Korean shamanism. First of all, Korean shamanism is open to outside influences; it easily absorbs elements of Buddhism and Taoism, for instance. In the pantheon there always is place for new additions. Among the deities listed above, there were several who were deified after their death in the 18th or 19th century. Many "new" gods are deified humans, but gods may be created in the most curious ways. One deity with a peculiar origin is Kangnim Toryŏng ("Young Master Kangnim"; *toryŏng* is an old-fashioned appellation for a young man, a bachelor), who acts as a messenger for the King of the Underworld. Yi Nŭnghwa has suggested that his name comes from a Sino-Korean Buddhist prayer formula: *kangnim toryang, su ch'a kongyang*, "descend to this *toryang* (*bodhi-mandala* or place of enlightenment) and receive this offering."[58]

Korean folk belief shares this openness of the pantheon with forms of popular religion elsewhere. Among the Buryat the souls of those who were killed during the suppression of the Paris Commune were worshipped when Soviet propaganda brought their stories to Central Asia.[59]

In the second place, the pantheon of the *mudang* reflects the history and diversity of Korean culture. It is evident that Korean shamanism, although it is not a religion with a highly developed systematic theology, is not just a primitive belief, an elementary form of religious life which stands outside of history. It has absorbed all kinds of native and foreign elements and changed with the times. It is important to be aware of this fact when one studies the *muga*.

One may think of the pantheon as a mishmash, an amorphous and inconsistent collection of vaguely defined deities. This impression is confirmed when one reads in *muga* from Cheju Island about "Master Chu", that is the Chinese philosopher Chu Hsi (1130-1200), as the son of Sŏkkamoni (= Sākyamuni) and Sŏkka Yŏrae (the Tathāgata Sākya, i.e. Sākyamuni!).[60] Nevertheless, certain patterns are discernable: the high and mighty are venerated -such as kings and queens-, persons with great religious (or perhaps one should say magico-religious) prestige -such as the monk Muhak-, persons who were redoubtable warriors -such as Ch'oe Yŏng and Nam I-, great predecessors within certain occupations (shaman, musician/actor, fortune-teller) -such as the Ch'angbu, Kwakkwak and Taesin halmŏni-, gods related to nature -such as Sansin and Yongwang-, and persons who have died an unusual, violent death. The last category is certainly not the least important.[61]

Several of the gods mentioned fit more than one category, Ch'oe Yŏng and Nam I, as warriors and figures who died a tragical death, and Queen Min, as a royal personage and a victim of murder, for instance.

The bewildering pluriformity of the Korean pantheon, with its superficial absurdities, inconsistencies and vaguenesses, should not deflect attention from the fact that there are fundamental patterns, which are more easily understood when seen as such and which provide a better basis for cross-cultural comparisons.

II *Muga* and *Muga* Collections

The term *muga* is of rather recent origin and probably was first used by Akamatsu and Akiba. Son Chint'ae, the first systematic collector, used *sin'ga*, "songs of the gods." In North Korea, Hong Kimun uses *mudang sori*, which is equivalent to *muga*, but puristically avoids Sino-Korean.[1]

There are *muga* of many different kinds and of different origins. Some are narrative, some descriptive, some lyrical, some dramatic in nature and some have the character of invocations or prayers. As for their origins, it would seem that hardly any form of literature can with certainty be said to have had no share in the creation of shaman songs (see Chapter VI).

As long as the *mudang* sing it as a regular part of their rites, no song should *a priori* be rejected as a *muga*. That its origin is non-shamanistic, does not disqualify a song as a *muga*. Very little would remain of certain *muga* if they were to be stripped of all elements that could be considered as alien, but they are "*mudang*'s songs", none the less. The *Chosang-antang kut*, for instance, which was recorded in Osan by Akiba and Akamatsu is almost completely built up out of Buddhist elements and a folk-song.[2] From sixty-six lines, forty-eight are Buddhist in character, thirty-four of them actual Buddhist formulae in pure *hanmun* (i.e., Chinese written by Koreans and pronounced in the Korean fashion). Twelve of the lines have no (explicit) references to Buddhism and the greater part of these make up a specific kind of folk-song, a pall-bearers' song.

In the same way in which it facilitates the acceptance of new gods, the openness of folk-religion facilitates the adoption of new *muga*. Among the Buryat a song, made up by the local youth to mock a girl who was killed after an illicit love affair, in the end acquired the status of a shamanistic hymn.[3] In

Korea, too, songs sometimes changed status. One example, that of the "Tale of Sim Ch'ŏng", will be treated in a separate chapter.

The term *muga* is usually taken to include all utterances of the *mudang*, whether sung, chanted or spoken, as long as they are part of the *kut*. Only some of the more recent collections, however, record everything that is said, although the spoken parts often are very important if one wants to understand what a ceremony is about.

The length and complexity of *muga* may differ greatly. Some songs are nothing but simple prayers, not exceeding a few lines, while the narrative songs may take three, four or five hours to sing in their entirety. Specimens of the longer *muga* will be discussed in separate chapters; here three examples will be given of the briefest *muga*: a prayer for the pureness of the water in a well, a prayer that a nursing mother may have enough milk for her baby and a *muga* from a death ritual. Uncomplicated as these songs are, they are more than simple requests, bald statements of specific wishes. In the first two, the Dragon Kings, associated with Buddhism, are mentioned; in the first song, they are the gods being invoked, in the second they appear in a parallelistically repeated simile. The use of the same elements for different purposes, as well as the repetition is characteristic of *muga* style. In this respect the short prayer *muga* -which in other ways are quite different from the lengthy narrative songs- do not constitute a category of their own.

The first song was collected by Son Chint'ae from a *mudang* from Tongnae-gun in Southern Kyŏngsang Province.[4]

> Words offered to the Gods of the Wells
>
> In the East, Dragon King of the East Sea!
> In the West, Dragon King of the West Sea!
> In the South, Dragon King of the South Sea!
> In the North, Dragon King of the North Sea!
> Please partake freely of the offerings
> And grant that this drinking water
> Will be good to taste,
> Will be good to look at!

The second song is from a male shaman from Osan; this text was collected by Akiba and Akamatsu.[5]

> Prayer for Mother-milk
>
> Deity who takes care of breastfeeding,
> Grandchild of Samsin (= the God of Childbirth, B.W.)!

> Please help us, make the milk flow
> As [the water] gushing out of the well of the Dragon King
>   of the East Sea,
> Gushing out of the well of the Dragon King of the South Sea,
> Gushing out of the well of the Dragon King of the West Sea,
> Gushing out of the well of the Dragon King of the North Sea,
> Like [the water] of the Dragon Pool of the Sasil Dragon King in
>   the Centre (The meaning of Sasil is unclear, B.W.)
> So that [milk] will be left after feeding,
> So that [milk] will be left after it has been
>   squeezed out.[6]

The last song to be translated in this chapter is part of a *chinogi kut*. When the ritual is almost finished, the ghost of the deceased person speaks to his or her relatives through the mouth of the *mudang*.[7]

> Ay, sad, sad it is!
> The body that was alive yesterday
> Has become a ghost, become a spirit
> Why is it, that I belong to the shades?
> Today I go to Paradise, to the Ten Kings [of the Underworld]
> My kind and dutiful daughters-in-law and descendants!
> Because you all have made a great effort,
> I will help you, I will support you.
> I will help you to pass the three years of mourning for me nicely,
> To pass the three months after my death comfortably.
> I will see that you, my descendants precious as gold,
> Will rise high, will be honoured.
> I will give you gain and I will give you growth.
> Don't worry, thanks to all my descendants
> I go to Paradise,
> And become a cherished child of the Lord Buddha
> I will go to Paradise, flying up steadily,
> I will go to the Ten Kings.

Traditional Korean mourning lasted for three years (actually two years and two months, but Koreans always speak of the three years of mourning). After three months a ritual was held that meant the end of ritual wailing for the deceased.[8] This song not only illustrates that the descendants expect protection from their deceased relatives, it also betrays anxiety with regard to the intentions of the dead, through the emphatic assurance that there is no need to worry.[9]

Muga collections

In a survey of *muga* collections up to 1978 Kim T'aegon counted a total of 627 collected *muga*, excluding songs which had not been published in books.[10] The vast majority of these *muga* were collected after 1945; eighty-six only dated from before the Liberation. Even when one takes into account that publications in periodicals were deliberately omitted, this survey is not complete. Missing are, for instance, Kim Yŏngjin's collection of Ch'ung-ch'ŏng Province *muga* (*CCM*) and Chang Chugŭn and Ch'oe Kilsŏng's book about a *mudang* from Yangju in Kyŏnggi Province, which is not primarily a *muga* collection, but nevertheless contains twenty-three *muga* texts.[11] Considering that the number of *muga* published in periodicals is not negligible[12] and that since 1978 several new publications have appeared, the total number of recorded *muga* now will be close to one-thousand.

There are some early songs which are regarded by many as pre-modern *muga*; first of all, a number of songs in the 13th c. history *Samguk yusa*. Of these the "Song of Ch'ŏyong" (*Ch'ŏyong ka*) has had most attention devoted to it.[13] It is doubtful, however, if these songs can truly be equated with the *muga* recorded in this century, for we do not know whether they really were sung by *mudang* during their rituals. In any case, there are but a few of them; there is not a large corpus which may be contrasted with that of the modern *muga*. Therefore, and because of their doubtful status as *muga*, no attention will be paid to these songs in this study.

There are also a number of songs in the *Siyong hyangak po* (a music book of the Chosŏn period of uncertain date), which probably rightly deserve the name of *muga*. This work is generally estimated to date back to before the 17th century: Kim Tonguk has assigned it to the late 15th century.[14] Some of the songs are undoubtedly for gods venerated by the *mudang*, but next to nothing is known about the occasions when they were performed. They are also extremely brief; most likely only the first stanzas of the text were recorded, the real purpose of this book being to set down the music, not the words of the songs.

Apart from the shamanistic songs in the *Siyong hyangak po*, some fragments of *muga* were recorded in *ko-sosŏl* (novels or tales) and *p'ansori* ("one-man opera"). In a traditional novel, *Hŭngbu chŏn* (The Story of Hŭngbu), for instance, there are two fragments of Sŏngju *muga* and a song in which General Ch'oe Yŏng appears.[15] Sin Chaehyo's *Pyŏn Kangsoe ka* ("The Song of Pyŏn Kangsoe", a *p'ansori* libretto) contains a song for warding off evil influences and a song for the spirits of the dead.[16] Moreover, *mudang* themselves sometimes transcribed *muga* or had others write them down, as will be shown in the discussion of the transmission of the *muga*.

Modern *muga* collecting began with Son Chint'ae, who in 1930 published the first scholarly collection, *Chōsen shinka ihen*, "Collection of the Remnants of the Divine Songs of Korea" (henceforth abbreviated to *Shinka ihen*). The *muga* in this volume were collected from 1923 onward. The Korean text is given with a translation in Japanese. The value of this book is diminished by the fact that little information is given about the informants, while the *muga* are neither presented in the context of the complete repertoire of one *mudang*, nor in the context of a complete ceremony. Nevertheless it is a precious source of information. Son was a conscientious scholar and he collected interesting *muga* from the North and from Kyŏngsang Province, regions where prior to the Liberation no other *muga* were recorded. The Japanese translation adds an interpretation to the text, which is lacking in most modern collections; these usually present the text of the *muga* with a few notes only. Later Son published other *muga* in periodicals, in a triple presentation: the original version in dialect, a version in standard Korean with some Chinese characters added and a Japanese translation. Like other early collectors, Son had to write down the songs from dictation, as he had, as yet, no modern recording equipment at his disposal. In one case being confronted with a tired and inebriated shaman returning from a ceremony, he was not able even to do that and had to be satisfied with taking down the outline of the story of a narrative *muga*.[17] Texts taken down from dictation cannot be expected to be the same as texts actually recorded during a ceremony. There is no response from the audience (which may considerably influence the form and the duration of the *muga*) and the singer who dictates may find it difficult to keep the rhythmic structure intact.[18] On the other hand, dictation may facilitate the elaboration of certain passages.

All this diminishes the importance of Son's records but it should be pointed out that recording *muga* in completely natural surroundings is almost impossible even with modern equipment because the din of the music usually drowns out part of the words. Therefore, even now *muga* are often recorded under more or less artificial conditions, if not dictated, then sung with minimal accompaniment in quieter surroundings than the scene of the average *kut*. A text recorded in this way can be checked against a recording made during a real performance.[19] The difference between the collection of Son Chint'ae and modern collections made with the help of tape recorders is, therefore, less than one might assume. In these matters, it is important to what extent the *muga* have fixed texts or are improvisations on traditional patterns. This will differ from *muga* to *muga*, but in many cases the texts seem to be fixed to a rather high degree; then the differences resulting from "artificial conditions" during the recording will be less serious.

The second collection was made by the Japanese scholars Akamatsu and Akiba, and published in the first volume of their *Chōsen fuzoku no kenkyū*

(Studies of the Shamanistic Customs of Korea), which was published in 1937 (*AA*). To a large extent this collection is not the work of Akamatsu and Akiba themselves, but of their Korean collaborators. In their Preface the two Japanese express indebtedness to several persons who have assisted them, one of these being Son Chint'ae. According to the only surviving assistant, Yu Hongnyŏl -today a well-known historian, then still a student- the Korean language competence of Akiba and Akamatsu was very limited. Akiba takes most of the responsibility for the collecting of the *muga*, but the actual work was done by Koreans; certainly in the more remote regions like Cheju Island, Akiba and Akamatsu were not even present. Local people (primary-school teachers) were asked to collect the songs and although this can be said to be an improvement over the method of information gathering of Murayama Chijun, the author of *Chōsen no fugeki* (Korean Shamans), who made use of the nation-wide network of policemen to collect his data, the abilities and methods of Akiba's and Akamatsu's collaborators will have varied.[20] The collector (or collectors) of the Cheju *muga* clearly did not send the texts as they were sung; all the Cheju *muga* are presented in standard language. The original Cheju dialect of the songs, which is virtually unintelligible to speakers of standard Korean, apparently was translated by the people who recorded the *muga*. The curious result is that the Cheju Island *muga* in *AA* are easier to understand than the other *muga*; translation becomes interpretation and leads to the elimination of ambiguities. Nevertheless, the Cheju *muga* in this collection are quite valuable. They are all narrative *muga* of which at least the plot easily survives translation. It is likely, if not as obvious as in the case of the Cheju *muga*, that the songs of other regions, too, have been adapted to a certain extent.

It is often pointed out that the translations into Japanese in *AA* contain many mistakes. One of the critics is Hong Kimun, a well-known linguist who now lives in North Korea, but who came originally from Ch'ungch'ŏng Province. There as well as in Seoul, he observed the ceremonies of the *mudang* and he recorded some *muga* himself, which, however, he lost.[21] Apart from his criticism that the Japanese translation and the notes contain numerous errors, Hong has two other objections.[22] The first is that the anti-Japanese feelings, which according to him, were frequently expressed in the *muga*, cannot be found in *AA*; these must have been expurgated. *Muga* also often contained praise of the Yi Kings; this, too, seems to have been left out, as being offensive to the Japanese. Son Chint'ae's collection, which was published in Japan, has no anti-Japanese or pro-Yi passages, either. Secondly, some of the informants, in Hong Kimun's opinion, did not represent truly traditional shamanism. In particular, he criticizes the Seoul *mudang* Pae Kyŏngjae (whom he had known himself) as being an opportunist; he accuses her of catering too much to the taste of the times.[23] Her songs, as recorded in

AA, hardly contain any narrative songs explaining the origin of gods (*ponp'uri*). This, again according to Hong, goes against tradition. As far as he had been able to observe, even in the Seoul area -where, at least in recent times, narrative *muga* are rare- *ponp'uri* were an element of almost every part of the *kut*. If this is true, it is of interest for two reasons: it tells us something about an older stage in the history of the *muga*, when narrative songs were more numerous than today, and it furnishes another piece of evidence of the *muga*'s changing with the times. If Pae Kyŏngjae did indeed adapt her songs to changing circumstances, this does not, in my eyes, diminish her qualifications as an informant. One should not be bound by antiquated folkloristic conceptions, according to which folklore and folk beliefs are regarded as "survivals" which are pure in the measure in which they retain the forms of a distant, mythical past.

The collection of Akiba and Akamatsu does not contain much information about the *mudang* who acted as informants. Detailed explanations of the rituals to which the songs belonged can be found in the second volume of *Chōsen fuzoku no kenkyū*, but only relative to the *muga* of Seoul and the surrounding area.

Apart from publications in periodicals, after the liberation in 1945 no *muga* collections appeared until the middle of the 1960's, when the Ministry of Culture and Information published several collections in mimeographed form (directly responsible was the Bureau for Cultural Preservation, Munhwajae kwalliguk). First the most remote areas were covered. In 1965 a collection of Cheju Island *muga* by Hyŏn Yongjun and Kim Yŏngdon: *Cheju-do mudang kut nori* appeared. In that year and in 1966 Im Sŏkchae and Chang Chugŭn published no less than three volumes with *muga* from the Northern Provinces (Hamgyŏng-do and P'yŏngan-do): *Kwanbuk chibang muga* I, II and *Kwansŏ chibang muga*. As informants Im and Chang had to use *mudang* from these regions who had fled to the South, where they continued their activities, usually with a clientèle with the same regional background. In the first chapters of these collections the most important facts about the informants and their rituals are related. The songs were recorded on tape and then transcribed as faithfully as possible, leaving mistakes, inconsistencies and dialect forms uncorrected. The recordings were not made during an actual séance.

In 1966 Kim T'aegon published his first book, *Hwangch'ŏn muga yŏn'gu* ("A Study of Yellow Springs *Muga*", i.e. of *muga* used for death rituals), which contains four versions of the narrative Pari kongju *muga*, as well as a study of the contents and background of this kind of song. Between 1971 and 1980, the same author published four volumes of a work entitled *Han'guk muga chip* (KTG I, II, III, IV), in which he presents the repertoire or part of the repertoire of a great number of *mudang* from various regions. The texts (recorded with the help of a tape-recorder), are preceded by brief introductions and annotated, although rather sparingly.

Kim T'aegon usually presents all the *muga* that belong to one ritual from the repertoire of one *mudang*, but this does not mean that in his collection one can find all the *muga* sung during one actual ritual, because *mudang* take turns during a séance and one *mudang* does not -and probably could not- sing all the songs herself.

More background detail is given in the mimeographed study of a Kyŏnggi-do *mudang* by Chang Chugŭn and Ch'oe Kilsŏng: *Kyŏnggi-do chiyŏk musok* (1967), another publication of the Bureau for Cultural Preservation. The information in this book is of importance for the study of the way in which the *mudang* acquire the texts of their songs.

A new stage in the recording of *muga* was reached with the publication of *Tonghaean muga* (*THM*), "Muga from the East Coast", compiled by Ch'oe Chŏngnyŏ and Sŏ Taesŏk. The texts include not only the songs proper, but also spoken explanations, incidental remarks and audience reactions and enable the reader to catch the atmosphere of the *kut*. It is a pity that this collection, which has a substantial introduction, does not contain all the *muga* of a whole ceremony, although -as the compilers point out-the omitted *muga* (rather simple songs without narrative content, mainly prayers) may be found in the first volume of Kim T'aegon's *Han'guk muga chip* (KTG I).

In the meantime, collecting of Cheju *muga* continued. In 1968 Chin Sŏnggi published *Namgug-ŭi muga* (*Muga* of Cheju), which offers several versions of the same *muga* as performed by different *mudang*. In this book Chin collected *muga* which had been published earlier in mimeographed form in three volumes under the title *Cheju-do muga chip*.

Muga from Chŏlla Province, in the south-west of the peninsula, appeared in 1970 in a collection made by Im Sŏkchae, under the somewhat misleading title *Chŏlp'o muak* (Shamanistic Music of Chŏlp'o).

In 1973 followed two volumes by Chang Chugŭn, published in Japan, one descriptive and analytic and one containing the texts of *muga*. In spite of the title, *Kankoku no minkan shinkō* (Folk Beliefs of Korea), these books are about Cheju Island. Chang presents original texts in Cheju dialect and Japanese translations (the text volume, *shiryō hen*, will be referred to as *MSs*, the volume with descriptions and analyses, *ronkō hen*, as *MSr*).

Cheju-do musok charyo sajŏn (Dictionary of Material Related to the Shamanistic Customs of Cheju Island), compiled by Hyŏn Yongjun and published in 1980, is an impressive work, a true *magnum opus*. It contains more than 800 pages of very fully annotated *muga* and definitely has unlocked the treasury of Cheju Island *muga* (abbreviated to *Cheju sajŏn*).

Also helpful is *Namgug-ŭi musok sŏsa-si* (A Shamanistic Narrative Poem of Cheju), recorded by Chin Sŏnggi, which presents the text of one very long narrative *muga*, *Segyŏng ponp'uri*, with line by line annotations (1980).

Returning to the mainland, mention should be made of a collection of *muga* from Ch'ungch'ŏng Province: *Ch'ungch'ŏng-do muga* (*CCM*), published by its compiler Kim Yŏngjin in 1976. This is an interesting collection, because in Ch'ungch'ŏng Province the distinction between shamanistic practitioners who sing *muga* and reciters of *mugyŏng* is not very sharp. The same people use *muga* as well as *mugyŏng*.[24] More *muga* from Ch'ungch'ŏng Province are included in *Kut-kwa mudang* (*Kut* and *mudang*) by Yun Kwangbong and Yi Kangnyŏl, which appeared in 1987. This collection contains evidence that recently the *muga* of the centre, Seoul, have influenced shaman songs in other parts of the country.

A new approach was attempted in 1990 by Sŏ Taesŏk and Pak Kyŏngsin, who in their book *Ansŏng muga* (*Muga* from Ansŏng) not only appended detailed notes to the texts, but also systematically included comments by the informant, a male shaman, which facilitates the interpretation of the songs.

A considerable number of *muga* have also appeared in two important serial works: *Han'guk minsok chonghap chosa pogosŏ* (*HMCCP*), "Reports of a Comprehensive Survey of Korean Folklore", published by the Bureau for Cultural Preservation, and *Han'guk kubi munhak taegye* (*HKMT*), "Outline of Korean Oral Literature", published by the Academy of Korean Studies. In these works, the *muga* are usually presented with only the merest background information.

When one surveys the body of collected *muga* -there are more than were mentioned above[25]- the total number of collected *muga* is impressive, but there still is need for studies which will elucidate the meaning of the texts. The recorded *muga*, to a large extent, are still virgin territory which awaits exploration. Kim T'aegon has made the narrative *muga* more accessible by a free rendering of the contents of a substantial number of them in his book *Han'gug-ŭi musok sinhwa* (Shamanististic Myths of Korea). The most substantial contribution so far has been made by Sŏ Taesŏk, with his *Han'guk muga-ŭi yŏn'gu* (Studies of Korean *muga*). Except for Kim T'aegon's *Hwangch'ŏn muga yŏn'gu*, which was mentioned above, there is no other booklength study of the songs of the *mudang*. There are articles to be sure, and parts of books devoted to the interpretation of the *muga*, but only rarely do these discuss textual problems and details in the songs. They mostly treat the narrative motifs, mythological themes and the general background of the *muga*.

Muga in translation

The translator is forced to confront problems which the collector may ignore. When a *muga* is translated from Korean into Japanese, the translator still can avoid committing himself on certain points, as both languages allow ambiguities in the same areas. Translation into a language like English, however, brings with it inevitable choices, for instance between singular and plural, which in Korean and Japanese may be left unspecified. When properly done, therefore, translations may contribute considerably to our understanding of the *muga*. Even if a translation is imperfect -as it generally will be- it may serve to make scholars reflect upon problematic aspects of the texts.

Translations into Japanese are most numerous, all the *muga* in the collections of Son Chint'ae and Akiba and Akamatsu having been translated into that language, as have the songs in Chang Chugŭn's *Kankoku no minkan shinkō*.

Translations into Western languages are rare. The *AA* version of the Pari kongju *muga* has been translated into French with copious notes by Park Byeng-sen.[26] Other *muga* from the collection of Akiba and Akamatsu, belonging to the twelve-*kŏri kut* of Seoul, have been translated into English by Lee Jung-Young, but unfortunately in so unscholarly a manner that the translation is more likely to mislead than to instruct.[27] Perhaps it is of value as proof that the *muga* are not easily understood even by native speakers of Korean.

Four brief Cheju *muga* have been translated by Alan Heyman in a volume called *Folk Culture in Korea*.[28] A longer, narrative Cheju *muga* (*Sŏgwi ponhyangdang ponp'uri*), has been translated into German -in prose form- by Vos.[29] A translation of again another Cheju *muga*, *Illwe-tto ponp'uri* is part of the article "The Deity of the Seventh Day" by the present author. Heyman has also published a translation of a *muga* for the Gods of smallpox, the Sonnim (literally "Guests").[30] Abbreviated prose versions of *muga* in English can be found in a volume entitled *The Folk Treasury of Korea*, edited by Chang Tŏksun, in cooperation with Sŏ Taesŏk and Cho Hŭiung. This book contains six *muga*, collected before and after the Liberation, from Hamgyŏng Province, P'yŏngan Province, Kyŏnggi Province and Cheju Island.[31]

Finally, two narrative *muga* from *KTG* I (about Pari kongju and Chesŏk) have been abridged and rendered into English by Lee Tae-dong: "Princess Pari" and "A Shamanistic Deity Epic (Chesŏk)."

III   The Transmission of the Songs

How are *muga* transmitted from one generation to another? Is it even correct to speak of the transmission of *muga*, or are only the elements which may be combined to make a *muga* transmitted? To what degree are the texts fixed, to what extent are they improvised? Secondary literature that tries to answer these questions, although not wholly lacking, is scarcer than one would expect.[1]

In this chapter these problems will be investigated on the basis of available literature, an examination of some recorded *muga*, observations made during actual performances, and conversations with *mudang*.

As stated earlier, the *mudang* transmit their lore mainly in two ways: within the family as part of the family inheritance, or within a pseudo-family relationship, that between *sin-ŏmŏni* and *sin-ttal*. In the capital the *sin-ŏmŏni/sin-ttal* relationship may be part of the larger frame-work of one of three existing "*mudang* schools", each of which has a separate tradition, also with regard to the *muga*.[2] Hereditary *mudang*, who from birth have close contacts with other *mudang*, understandably experience fewer difficulties in the process of learning their craft than possessed *mudang*, who have to find a *sin-ŏmŏni* and are usually somewhat older when they begin to learn. In either case, however, the singing of *muga* is an important part of what is transmitted, even though a *mudang* may claim that she did not have to learn the *muga* because the gods made them flow from her lips spontaneously.[3] Such statements should probably be interpreted as meaning that the *mudang* follows traditional patterns that are so familiar to her that she is not aware of them and experiences her "inspired utterances" as completely natural.

An interesting case with regard to the problem of the *muga* that are not acquired through an ordinary learning process, is furnished by Cho Hung-

youn, who has given us a valuable description of the making of a famous
paksu mudang from Seoul, Yi Chisan.[4] One song was taught to Yi Chisan by
a goddess who appeared to him in a dream. The text of the song, as given by
Cho turns out to be almost identical to parts of a *muga* collected by Akiba and
Akamatsu.[5] Yi Chisan's text is as follows:[6]

Namsan-ŭn ch'ŏnnyŏnsan-iyo	1
Han'gang-ŭn mannyŏnsu-ra	2
Namsan-e tallae-rŭl k'aesŏ	3
Han'gangsu hŭrŭnŭn mur-e ssitko ssisŏ	4
kŭ tallae mas-i choha	5
hwaryu chaengban-e sŏryŏ tama	6
Nara-nim-kke chinsang kalkka	7
Uri-do sŏngju-nim mosigo tongnak t'aep'yŏng	8

(South Mountain is a Thousand-Year Mountain,
The Han River is a Ten-Thousand-Year River.
We will gather wild garlic on South Mountain
And wash it, wash it
In the streaming waters of the Han River.
So good is the taste of that garlic,
We shall offer it to our King
Filling trays of red sandalwood,
Serving our Sage Ruler (Sŏngju)
Rejoicing with Him in an Age of Great Peace.)

The older *muga* reads as follows (numerals refer to the corresponding lines in
the song of Yi Chisan):

Namsan-ŭn ch'ŏnnyŏnsan-iyo	1
Han'gangsu-nŭn mannyŏnsu-ra	2
....	
uri-do kŭmju-nim mosigo	
tongnak t'aep'yŏng	8
Namsan-e tallae-rŭl k'aeyŏ	3
Han'gangsu hŭlli ssisŏ	4
kkot kŏrin hwaryu changban-e	
ŏrisŏri koeyŏ tŭlgo	6
kŭ tallae mas-i chosowa	5
chinsang kalkka	7

In other words, the divinely revealed text is thoroughly traditional. This becomes even more apparent when one observes that this song contains elements from traditional poems in the *sijo* form: the juxtapositon of Namsan and Han River (*Sijo sajŏn*, Nos. 379 and 384), and the whole of line 8 (*Sijo sajŏn*, No. 406, a poem from the the oldest anthology, the *Ch'ŏnggu yŏngŏn*, "Songs of Green Hills," of 1728; cf. also No. 385).[7]

Probably, statements claiming that the songs come forth spontaneously are also made by *mudang* who, for whatever reason, have never been able to learn the traditional lore. One collector of oral literature met a possessed *mudang* in Kyŏngsang Province, who could not reproduce more than one, very short *muga* for him. She told the man, however, that she sings spontaneously when she is possessed. In a normal state of mind she could think of no other songs.[8] This type of *mudang* is very close to the type which has no traditional lore at all.

In general, *mudang* often say that one reason it takes a long time to become a full-fledged shaman, is that it is so difficult to learn the songs. Some *mudang* will relate how they coach their *sin-ttal*, when these have to learn the *muga*.[9]

To a certain degree at least, the form of the *muga* is fixed; the songs are not newly created by each *mudang* and not completely different each time they are performed. So much is clear from even a casual examination of the texts. In fact, even *kongsu* utterances -supposedly the words of the gods directly spoken to individual worshippers through the mouth of the *mudang*-follow traditional patterns.

A   The landscapes we saw in the past
      where have they gone?
      The waters we saw in the past
      where have they gone?
      ....

B   This human life of ours-
      Even if we die having lived for eighty years,
      If we deduct days of illness
      and days of sleep,
      Worry and sorrow,
      We do not live even forty years,
      Such is our life!

This is from the *kongsu* of a possessed *mudang*.[10] These lines -in the *muga* spoken by the ghost of a deceased relative- are thoroughly traditional; they are also found in *ko-sosŏl* (A), and in poems (*kasa*) that sing of the transience of human life (B).[11] This traditional character of such *kongsu* passages is not exceptional.[12]

It is difficult to say whether in the past every new *mudang* could find a senior *mudang* to teach her the *muga*, but it is a fact that in modern times even *mudang* who have a *sin-ŏmŏni*, may receive little aid from her after their initiation and have to look elsewhere for instruction, just as those who do not have a *sin-ŏmŏni* at all.[13]

Because *mudang* do not work alone, a new *mudang*, provided that she is accepted as an assistant, always has other models besides her *sin-ŏmŏni*. A male shaman from Seoul, whom I met one month after he had been initiated (after having suffered from *sinbyŏng* for fifteen years), and who was still in the middle of the process of learning the *muga*, told me that he did not intend to learn them all from his *sin-ŏmŏni* or from any one person, but would look around to see who was best for a particular song and imitate that *mudang*. Even a *paksu mudang*, it should be noted, usually has a divine mother; *paksu mudang* wear a woman's skirt under their other costumes when they perform and many of them act in a feminine manner. He also stated that it was not necessary to know all the songs because *mudang* work together; they can participate in a *kut* even though knowing only a few songs. Indeed, one often hears it said that only the more experienced *mudang* master the longer narrative *muga*, such as the song about the Abandoned Princess, Pari kongju.

There are great differences in the number and length of songs known by individual *mudang*. The repertoire of some *mudang* would take only a relatively short while to sing in its entirety, but with others even the singing of one song may last two, three or four hours.

Usually a *muga* is sung by one *mudang* alone, but the musicians often assist her with cries of encouragement and occasionally they join in the singing. On the East Coast, in some *muga*, the drummer sings a phrase, after which the *mudang* sings a line. The drummer repeats the phrase, while the *mudang* sings a new line and so they continue. The drummer constantly repeats the same words, the lines of the *mudang* change all the time.[14] In such songs the task of the drummer is to give support, he is not an independent singer. In parts of the *kut* with a theatrical element, such as one often finds at the end of a ceremony, the contributions of the drummer are of greater importance, when he takes part in humorous dialogues.

When more than one *mudang* participates in the singing, there is usually one who sings the song itself, while the others sing refrains or encouragements. Only certain folk-songs or popular songs, such as are often inserted in the *kut* by the East Coast *mudang*, are sung by two or three persons together. If *muga* were regularly sung by several *mudang* at a time, this would, of course, demand a fixed text, which all the participants would have memorized beforehand.

Possible forms of transmission

A further examination of the transmission of the *muga*, and the function of memorization and improvisation in this process, may begin with a listing of the major possibilities with regard to transmission. In theory, there are -at least- four possibilities.

I   *Muga* are handed down orally in their entirety, word-for-word, from one generation of *mudang* to another. There is a fixed text, which hardly changes at all. When it changes, it is unintentionally, because of carelessness or lack of mnemonic power.

II   *Muga* are transmitted orally by successive generations and each *mudang* changes the inherited texts, quite apart from unintentional changes due to forgetfulness etc.

III   There is no transmission of texts; what is transmitted is a poetic language (themes and plots included), which enables the *mudang* to create the actual *muga* during the *kut*. Each performer may develop this inherited language to suit his taste and needs.

IV   The *muga* have a fixed form, which is transmitted by means of writing.

The first possibility is the least realistic. Exact oral transmission over a long period of time is exceedingly rare. The *Rgveda* is said to have been handed down orally in its original form for hundreds of years, but -if true- this is a most exceptional case. On the whole, the concept of unchanging oral literature is rejected today.[15] Exact memorization of very long texts is, of course, not impossible. In the Far East, learning the Classics by heart was part and parcel of a proper education. Nevertheless, it is difficult to imagine continuous exact reproduction of a text where there is no written canon, or no special class of guardians of the tradition, fully dedicated to preserving the purity of the texts. For the *muga* neither of these conditions obtained. *Sin-ŏmŏni*, no doubt, do not appreciate their *sin-ttal* arbitrarily changing the songs, but the *mudang* do not seem to have a conception of a completely immutable, fixed text.

It is sufficient, moreover, to look at the texts to know that the first theory can have no bearing on the *muga*. The *muga* contain numerous elements that belong to the past, but equally elements that cannot be dated earlier than the twentieth century. Invocations to the ghosts of people who have died an unnatural and untimely death (*yŏngsan*) provide examples of both antiquated and modern elements. Clearly related to the Chosŏn period are the following *yŏngsan*:[16]

> *Yŏngsan* of those whose heads were cut off
> And exposed on a stake at the gate of the barracks,
> *Yŏngsan* of those whose limbs were torn off
> At the cross-roads near the Little West Gate,
> *Yŏngsan* of those who were decapitated posthumously.

These can only be understood within the context of the penal system of the Chosŏn dynasty. More modern are the following *yŏngsan*:[17]

> *Yŏngsan* of those who have been hit by a street-car,
> By a train, by a horse-drawn cart, by an automobile,
> *Yŏngsan* of those who died in a bombing attack,
> *Yŏngsan* of those who died through bullets and swords.

A mixture of traditional and contemporary elements is seen in the following fragment, which was recorded in 1965. It is from a *muga* dedicated to certain deified warriors, the Divine Generals.[18]

> We pray to the Generals
> That the youth of the Great Han (Taehan, i.e. Korea)
> Will prove themselves to be loyal servants to His Majesty (*Nara-nim*)
> That as soon as possible [our country] will be unified
> And several tens of millions of our brethren will dance [for joy],
> [We pray] that the Republic of Korea will be victorious

Elsewhere ghosts are mentioned of persons who were hit by bullets during the Korean War and the Students' Revolt of April 1960.[19]

Even phrases that bring to mind the past are often dateable; these, too, were once modern and do not go back in history as far as the origin of the *mudang*. This can be illustrated with the names of royal palaces in Seoul as they are mentioned in the *muga*.[20] Of course, the lines in which these names occur, cannot antedate the Chosŏn dynasty (1392-1910) and there are reasons to believe that, when the Kyŏngbok Palace is spoken of, this refers to the Kyŏngbok Palace after its restoration in the second half of the 19th century, rather than to the old Kyŏngbok Palace built by the first Yi King in 1395, which was destroyed by fire during the Japanese invasions at the close of the 16th century, and which during the following 270 years lay in ruins.[21]

Theory I is also in conflict with the explicit statement by Pak Yongnyŏ, a senior *mudang* from Kangnŭng, that, although the basic story of the *muga* is retained, each *mudang* adds new words.[22]

Thus, of the four theoretic possibilities, the first can be easily dismissed. The same cannot be said of the remaining three. Unlikely though it may seem in view of the commonly assumed lack of literacy among the *mudang*, some evidence can be found in favour of even Theory IV. Although at first sight they appear contradictory, each of the theories contains a measure of truth. This partial validity is the result of the fact that the method of transmission for *muga* A is not necessarily the same as for *muga* B or C. Theories II and III come closer to actual practice than IV, and, although a true statistical statement is impossible, it is my impression that in the majority of cases it is II, rather than III, which fits the facts.

Before we discuss II and III, however, it is convenient to examine the validity of Theory IV. For the entire period during which *muga* have been collected, there is evidence of the use of written texts. In fact, some of these texts antedate the first scholarly attempts to record the *muga*. The supplement to the *Bibliographie coréenne*, published in 1901, lists under No. 3681 a (printed!) book called *Yŏsŏ ŏnch'ŏm*, which is described as "Formules en langue vulgaire pour les sorcières."[23] Although this book, which is completely in *han'gŭl* (Korean alphabet), contains formulae to be used in divination, and not what we have styled *muga*, it is significant that in the late 19th century a written work existed for the use of the *mudang*. Undoubtedly, there were real *muga* in written form as well. Yi Nŭnghwa, in his "Chosŏn musok ko" of 1927, refers to a book in *han'gŭl* called *Sŏngsin malpŏp* ("Divine Speech"), which contained among other things a narrative *muga* about Pari kongju.[24] An undated manuscript of *Pari kongju* has been discovered by Kim Tonguk.[25] Kim Sŏkch'ul, a *hwaraengi* (male shaman/*mudang*'s husband) from Kyŏngsang Province, keeps a handwritten book dated (according to the traditional sixty-year cycle) the twenty-first day of the Twelfth Month of the year Imja, which cannot be later than 1912.[26] The source which refers to this book, also mentions written *muga* in the possession of other *mudang* from the same region.[27] Kim Sŏkch'ul further keeps a manuscript in which his nephew Kim Yongŏp has recorded the *muga* he learned from his parents and grandparents.[28]

A hereditary *mudang* from Chŏlla Province holds a *muga* collection received from her husband's grandmother. It is dated in the year Chŏngmyo, which most likely refers to 1927.[29]

In Kangwŏn Province, the hereditary *mudang* Sin Sŏngnam owns an undated manuscript with *muga*.[30] Yi Yongu, a shaman from Kyŏnggi Province and a nephew of Yi Chongman (one of the informants of Akiba and Akamatsu, cf. Chapter VI) possesses a book with "scriptures", actually containing *muga* (for the Kunung, for Sŏngju and for other gods), which were written (or perhaps just written down?) for his uncle by a monk from a Buddhist temple. Yi Yongu told a researcher that he freely allowed others to copy it.[31]

Hong Kimun has drawn attention to the existence, in the pre-Liberation period, of written records kept by the *mudang*, which were called *sinssŏk*. The ones he inspected contained "magic texts" (*chumun*), as well as "magic pictures" (*pujak* or *pujŏk*).[32]

Son Chint'ae has recorded that a male shaman in P'yŏngan Province owned a manuscript with *muga*.[33]

At present, in Seoul and vicinity, there is in circulation a book of 96 pages, printed in traditional style, without title, publisher or date of publication. Apart from formulae used in divination, it contains the texts of fifteen *muga*. In 1982, this work was presented to me twice, once by a *mudang* from Kanghwa Island and once by a *paksu mudang* from Seoul. The latter, who claimed to have learned the *muga* without any special effort, obviously had studied parts of the text closely, as he had added corrections in several places. This text can also be found in second-hand bookshops in Seoul and seems to be in considerable demand.

In secondary literature about *mudang*, we find several cases in which *muga* were learned through the written word.[34] According to Murayama Chijun, in his *Chōsen no fugeki* (1932), out of seventeen female and twenty male shamans in Kangwŏn Province, six had learned their lore from written sources.[35]

Although this may sound paradoxical, one should realize that literacy of the *mudang* is not a necessary condition for the use of written texts. A *mudang* only needs to know a person who is willing to read a written text to her. One *mudang* from Kyŏnggi Province, for instance, had another *mudang*'s *muga* copied by a schoolboy and this text was read out to her by her lover.[36]

Learning from a written text should not be supposed to be easier than learning directly from a senior *mudang*. First, the text only provides the words, not the rhythm and the melody, and second, to people who do not read and write much, learning by ear is much more pleasant. "After you have read half a page you become sleepy", a *mudang* said who herself owns a collection of written *muga*.[37] Others, too, even though they are literate and books are available, affirm that it is preferable to learn from senior *mudang*.[38] The use of written texts to learn *muga* is only attractive to *mudang* with a better than average education, or to *mudang* who have no other alternative. In recent years, the tape recorder offers a way out for the last category. This instrument is definitely not used only by academic researchers to record the *muga*. A *mudang* from Kangwŏn Province confessed that she had learned her songs from a recording which she had made of the *kut* of a famous East Coast *mudang*, Yi Kŭmok.[39] The East Coast *mudang* themselves are in the habit of tape-recording their own performances. In Seoul, Pak Tonghŭi, a *paksu mudang*, has in his house commercially produced cassette tapes with songs such as *Taegam nori*, sung by professional female singers. He knows the text of these songs by heart; playing the tapes, he is able to join the singing without a single lapse or hesitation.

Possibly, the tape recorder will diminish the role of written texts in the transmission of the *muga*, but it is an undeniable fact that during the entire period of modern *muga* collecting written texts have been used by some *mudang* to learn the songs. Therefore Theory IV cannot be dismissed as irrelevant to the transmission of the *muga*. It is difficult to estimate how many *mudang* rely on the written word to learn *muga* texts, the more so, because this method can be used in combination with others.

Probably for the majority of *mudang* the process of transmission is rather that outlined in the second and third theory. Theory III is close to what Milman Parry and Alfred Lord have christened "oral composition", which is composition of poetry in performance on the basis of traditional patterns. "Oral poetry", the result of oral composition, therefore, excludes poetry which is orally presented, but made up beforehand, as much as it excludes purely improvised poetry. Oral poets use traditional elements: the formulae. And a formula is defined as "a group of words which is regularly employed under the same metrical conditions to express a given essential idea."[40] The concept of the formula is not only used with regard to lexical items such as the stereotyped *epitheta ornantia* found in epic poetry; according to Lord, "everything in the style is in the category of formula" in oral poetry.[41] Because *muga* abound in formula-like elements -as will be shown in Chapter V- it is tempting to consider the *muga* as oral poetry in the sense in which Parry and Lord have used the term. Nevertheless, it is clear that not all of the *muga* are oral poetry in this sense (e.g., the *muga* learned from books are not) and it is doubtful that any *mudang* relies completely on oral composition. Often *mudang* seem to memorize as well as improvise on traditional patterns. In such cases, Lord refuses to speak of oral composition. He argues that the use of writing or preliminary composition makes a poet unfit to use the technique of oral composition successfully; a "transitional style" he deems impossible.[42] Theory III, however, should not be understood as excluding *a priori* the possibility that a *mudang* who recreates according to traditional patterns, may also memorize *muga* learned either from another *mudang* or from written sources.

A Korean scholar who has tried to apply the insights of Parry and Lord to Korean oral poetry, and to *muga* in particular, is Sŏ Taesŏk.[43] According to him, *mudang* first learn by heart the shorter non-narrative *muga* (invocations, prayer-formulae etc.), familiarizing themselves in this way with the patterns and rhythms of the *muga*, while they also learn Buddhist formulae, folk-songs and other traditional songs that are often inserted into the *muga*. Later in their career, when they have gathered sufficient experience, they then need no special training for the performance of narrative *muga*.[44] These narrative *muga*, according to Sŏ, are the products of oral composition.

I do not altogether want to deny the validity of Sŏ Taesŏk's claim, but it is not true that *all* narrative *muga* are created without special training. The *Sim Ch'ŏng kut* was performed in 1982 at the Tano Festival in Kangnŭng by a *mudang* who had never before publicly performed this *muga*, which lasts several hours. As will be explained in Chapter VII, this was not an improvised performance, and she hád been trained by a senior *mudang*. In the Seoul area, *mudang* recite the text of *Pari kongju* very quickly and monotonously -it reminded me of Buddhist sutra chanting- giving the impression that they are reproducing something which they have learnt by heart. When I recorded on tape a Seoul *mudang*'s version of *Pari kongju*, she said that other *mudang* would be willing to pay a lot of money for such a recording as a help to learning the text, which seems to imply that a more or less exact text is needed rather than the outline of the story (which ought to suffice for a true oral poet). A real oral poet needs to hear a story only once in order to be able to repeat it in his own poetic language. The presence of a *Pari kongju* text among the *muga* in the book which today circulates in Seoul, and in the older book mentioned by Yi Nŭnghwa, together with the existence of this text in the form of a manuscript, confirms the impression that *Pari kongju* is not composed in performance.

In justice to Sŏ Taesŏk it must be said that he seems to be very much aware of the limitations of his statement that narrative *muga* do not need special training. He himself is of the opinion that a particular version of a narrative Chesŏk *muga* was completely memorized.[45] Although he does not say so explicitly, this, of course, makes the applicability of the oral-formulaic theory to the *muga* rather questionable.

Comparisons of several versions of one song by one mudang

To study the part of creative improvisation versus memorization, a comparison will be made between two versions of a number of *muga*, as sung by the same *mudang*. The *muga* that are to be examined, are all from the East Coast, where the most famous teams of *mudang* have been studied more extensively than the *mudang* of any other region. For this area several examples of texts of the same *muga* by the same *mudang* are available. In evaluating the results of the comparisons of the texts of these *muga*, one should not forget that the

East Coast *mudang* display certain peculiarities. Their *kut*, for instance, have a more "artistic" character than that of other regions and are more designed to entertain than performances elsewhere.[46]

A. First, two versions of the *muga* sung during the *Kyemyŏn kut* by Sa Hwasŏn will be compared (the *Kyemyŏn kut* is discussed in detail in Chapter IX).[47] The two texts, recorded with an interval of eight years, are strikingly different. The 1972 *muga* tells of a girl born into a *yangban* family, who is possessed by the gods and against her will becomes a *mudang*. She visits her regular clients to collect rice -as is the custom- but many of them refuse outright or seek a pretext for not giving her anything. Only the fifth family she visits receives her warmly. The 1980 text contains essentially the same story, but in the first part the social discrimination of *mudang* is stressed by means of a rather elaborate sub-story, about the daughter of the protagonist - also a *mudang*- marrying a *yangban* son, who is actually unwilling to accept her as a bride, but is forced to marry because of the magic powers of the mother. After the marriage, the *yangban* husband is able to pass the government examinations with the help of his mother-in-law, but in spite of this, he tries time and again to abandon his *mudang* wife, while he never misses an occasion to show contempt for her mother. In the end he is punished by Heaven for his unseemly conduct. Then the *muga* continues with a story about the sowing of hemp seeds, which was not included in the 1972 version, but is also part of the *Kyemyŏn kut* of another *mudang*, Pak Yongnyŏ. The *mudang* who is the protagonist of the story and is called Chemyŏn halmŏni, makes both her own daughter and her daughter-in-law sow hemp seeds, but because she hates the latter, she roasts the seeds she gives to the daughter-in-law. Birds, however, exchange the seeds, so that in the end the daughter's field remains a barren waste, while the daughter-in-law reaps an abundant harvest. This story is here told in much greater detail than in the version by Pak Yongnyŏ. After the harvest the hemp is used to make a bag to collect rice. Now the visit to the houses of the *tan'gol* (regular clients) can begin. This part of the story is basically the same in both versions of the *muga*. Many clients refuse to give anything but the poorest quality of rice. Then, something strange happens in the 1980 version. The story goes back to the hemp seed episode and from that point on begins again, with different wording and details, however. In one *tan'gol* home, illness of the children more or less forces the family to treat Chemyŏn halmŏni with respect; and with this change of attitude, the children at once recover.

It is possible, in theory, that between 1972 and 1980 Sa Hwasŏn learned a new version of this *muga* by heart, but it is more likely that she never completely memorized it. It would seem that she truly improvises according to traditional patterns. The fact that in the 1980 *muga* she dealt with the same episode twice in different words, points in the same direction. The reason for the repetition itself is unclear. It may have had something to do with the particular circumstances of the *kut* where this *muga* was sung. No information on this subject is available, however. About one thing there can be no doubt: the exact form of the story is of subordinate importance. This should be kept in mind when the interpretation of the *muga* is discussed in the next chapter.

B. From another East Coast *mudang*, Pyŏn Yŏnho, two versions have been recorded of the *muga* sung for the gods who bring smallpox, one in 1968 and one in 1972.[48] In this case, the difference between the two versions is much less marked than in the *Kyemyŏn kut*. Some of the divergencies are caused by the insertion of elements which themselves are rather standardized, and which the *mudang* know by heart, such as a description of several kinds of food (e.g., the *namul t'aryŏng*, a list of vegetable dishes; cf. Chapter V) and the description of the appearance of a monk (*chung t'aryŏng*), which is used here for one of the Sonnim, the gods of smallpox.[49] The resemblances are especially striking in those passages in which the plot of the story is developed. Where the text is similar in both versions, the congruity is such that anything like the process described in Theory III, let alone true "oral composition", is unlikely. Differences are often due to the insertion of elaborations. Examples in the 1972 text are a Buddhist magic formula[50] and a song to express affection for a baby (*sarang ka*).[51]The Buddhist formula which is completely in Koreanized Sanskrit, Pyŏn Yŏnho could not but have learnt by heart, nor can the song, as it occurs elsewhere in her *muga* and in those of others, be called an improvisation. In her rendition of the *Sim Ch'ŏng kut*, Pyŏn Yŏnho relies heavily on a written text (cf. Chapter VII) and the evidence of the two versions of her *Sonnim kut* suggests that she memorizes large portions of the song. Her *Sonnim kut muga* seems to be the result of the process outlined in the second theory.

C. The *Sonnim kut* of Kim Yusŏn, wife of Kim Sŏkch'ul, performed in cooperation with her husband, is also available in two versions, recorded in 1972 and 1978.[52] The order of the scenes and their narrative content is very similar in both versions, but the actual words are quite different. As an example one may cite the descriptions of one of the Sonnim, who in the 1972 version is called Munsu Sonnim and in the 1978 version Munsin Sonnim.[53] A few elements recur in both versions, but the description as a whole is different. In both cases, however, the style is traditional, with characteristic antithetical parallelisms ("in one hand..., in the other hand", "in his left hand ..., in his right hand", etc.).

Remarkable is the addition of another Sonnim in both *muga*. In most of the other *muga* for the Sonnim, there are fifty-three Sonnim; fifty who stay in

China and three who go to Korea. In the 1972 version, first there are said to be a total number of fifty-three Sonnim, of whom three go to Korea, but when the latter are described in detail, there are four of them! In the 1978 version, there are fifty-four Sonnim from the beginning. The number of fifty-four is undoubtedly an innovation; not only do other *muga* always mention fifty-three Sonnim, fifty-three is also a number which occurs in various tales about Buddha images that -like the Sonnim- come from China or another foreign region to Korea. One of these tales can be found in a 14th century Koryŏ source,[54] another is the story of the founding of the Kwanŭm Temple, the well-known cognate of the story of Sim Ch'ŏng.[55] Generalization should be avoided, but this suggests that freedom for improvisations or additions does exist even with regard to matters that easily might be regarded as sacred and inviolable, such as the traditional number of a group of gods.

The text of these two *Sonnim kut* could very well be the result of the process of Theory III. Kim Sŏkch'ul, the husband of Kim Yusŏn, is undoubtedly an able improviser. In June 1982, his team performed in unusual surroundings, the Unesco Building in downtown Seoul, for an audience that consisted of students and professors. Without hesitation he adapted his prayers to suit the occasion. When asked if he had prepared this beforehand, he denied it, saying that the words "just came up." Such evidence from the lips of the *mudang* themselves, should always be tested against other evidence before it can be accepted as proof of genuine improvisation, but in combination with the results of an examination of other *muga* by Kim Sŏkch'ul it seems acceptable. Improvisations in the form of adaptations to the situation in which the *kut* is held, are at any rate quite common. In many songs, at the beginning the name of the locality and the time of the year are mentioned, and these things are, of course, different on each occasion. Also, a fifty-five year old *mudang* from Kyŏngsang Province told a researcher that she modified a song to chase ghosts away according to the kind of ghosts against whom it was directed.[56]

D. The last *muga* to be examined here in two versions is sung during the *Kŏri kut*, the concluding part of a big ceremony. The *Kŏri kut* is largely theatrical in character and contains a great deal of speaking as opposed to song. It includes some dialogues between the main performer and the drummer or others (the usual inclusion of the texts of the *kŏri kut* in *muga* collections, shows that in practice the term *muga* covers more than, literally, the "songs of the *mudang*"). In contrast to the other parts of the ceremony, the *Kŏri kut* is performed by the male members of the East Coast *mudang* teams, whose main task is the musical accompaniment of the *kut*.

The *Kŏri kut* of Kim Yongt'aek, a nephew of Kim Sŏkch'ul, was recorded twice in 1978, in July and November.[57] Kim Yongt'aek was then thirty-three years old. In a *captatio benevolentiae*, he stresses the fact of his relative youthfulness; his seniors excel in the performance of this *muga*, but he, "a young fellow", will have a try once. A little later he says:[58]

> "because in the past my seniors have often performed the ceremony, my ears have seen (*sic*) it all, my eyes have seen it all, my ears have heard it all, and so I will do this *kŏri*, thinking as I go along."

This does not suggest systematic learning of a text or memorization. Indeed, a comparison of the two versions shows that the text is not fixed, although the contents of the scenes that make up the *Kŏri kut* and their order are basically the same in both. Kim Yongt'aek hardly uses Sino-Korean phrases such as one finds in great quantity in the *Kŏri kut* of his uncle, Kim Sŏkch'ul.[59] These Sino-Korean phrases are often combined into larger units ("themes", cf. Chapter V), which are just as traditional as the smaller phrases. The latter are quite different from ordinary language, and have to be memorized by the *mudang*, either as part of the larger units of the themes, or one by one. Presumably, the *mudang* first memorizes these phrases in the context of the larger unit, then, having become thoroughly familiar with them, he progresses to the stage where the smaller elements, the phrases, can be taken out of the original context and employed to create a new text. Kim Yongt'aek, however, seems not to have completed or even reached the first stage. He does know a few traditional phrases, which he uses, for instance, in the invocation to all kinds of inferior ghosts, mostly of the *yŏngsan*-type, but it looks as if he has not mastered the more elaborate phraseology, such as one can find in the *Kŏri kut* of his uncle and of another prominent *hwaraengi* of the East Coast, Song Tongsuk.[60] Kim Yongt'aek knows the plot of the scenes of the *Kŏri kut*, some short enumerations (e.g., one of book titles, cf. Chapter V), some lines to call the spirits, some songs -or fragments of songs- (such as the song which mocks a woman who, in her turn, has made fun of a blind man in one of the scenes), et cetera, but he has to leave a lot to improvisation.

Conclusions to be drawn from the examination of East Coast *muga*

The survey of East Coast *muga* suggests three types of *mudang*:

1. the performer who has memorized only a few traditional elements and has to rely on improvisation for most of the text (Kim Yongt'aek);

2. the performer who has memorized a substantial number of traditional texts, and improvises and recreates comparatively little (Pyŏn Yŏnho);

3. the performer who has memorized a large amount of traditional texts and is able to use the constituent elements of such texts to create something novel (Sa Hwasŏn, Kim Yusŏn, Kim Sŏkch'ul).

Note that in this classification the oral/written distinction plays no role. If one compares these three types of *mudang* as they emerge from an examination of their texts, with the theoretical possibilities listed above, Type 2 fully corresponds to Theory II in those instances when the texts were transmitted orally. This is, however, not always the case with Type 2. Memorization may be based on a written text as well as on direct contact with a teacher. The distinction between oral and written transmission turns out to be of secondary importance. Type 3 is consistent with Theory III but not, strictly, with the oral-formulaic theory, because in the first stage of transmission memorization -which in the oral formulaic theory is radically opposed to oral composition- is of considerable importance.[61] Nevertheless, the performer of Type 3 is able to do something which very much resembles oral composition.

Type 1 does not correspond to any of the categories of the schematic representation of ways of transmission. This is hardly surprising, because here one sees a breakdown of transmission rather than transmission. That Kim Yongt'aek is able to perform the *Kŏri kut* at all, has to do with the theatrical nature of this part of the ceremony, which contains a lot of talking and dialogue. These are easier to improvise than songs. In this context, we may refer once more to Sŏ Taesŏk, who has noted that spoken passages change considerably, while passages that are sung remain quite constant.[62] A *mudang* with the limited kind of knowledge that Kim Yongt'aek possesses, cannot but abbreviate the *kŏri* drastically if he has to perform a whole *kut*. Probably he will have to omit the longer narrative *muga* completely. *Mudang* of this type are quite numerous these days.

The conclusions listed above are based on an examination of the *muga* of the East Coast *mudang*. If one were to concentrate attention on the *mudang* of the Seoul area -who hardly sing any narrative *muga*- the role of memorization of texts would be even more striking. There one observes relatively little change in the texts. The songs to accompany the twelve-*kŏri kut* in *AA* I and *KTG* I are quite similar, the passing of about three decades between the recording of the one and the other notwithstanding. Cho Hung-youn, moreover, has noted that the differences with regard to the *muga* of the three Seoul "schools" of *mudang* are not basic differences, but variations.[63]

The final conclusion must be that several types of transmission exist side by side and that even the songs of one and the same *mudang* have not always been transmitted in the same manner. More detailed study would perhaps show particular emphasis on certain methods according to region, but the evidence is that nowhere are the *muga* created by pure oral composition.

The muga of the past

To conclude this chapter, a word should be said about the study of the transmission of the *muga* in the past. Can it be done? It will be clear that for such an undertaking one needs either a number of historical *muga* or the ways and means for reconstructing the *muga* of earlier periods. The obstacles are formidable. Texts that confidently can be called historical *muga* are almost non-existent. The pieces in the *Siyong hyangak po* are too short to satisfy our curiosity. One might attempt reconstruction by the negative method: by eliminating from the *muga* all more recent elements, but, as will be argued in subsequent chapters, the influence of the popular literature that arose in the late 17th century, and especially flourished in the 18th and 19th centuries, has been so great that is is difficult to imagine what the *muga* looked like before that time.

One could also try to eliminate all "extraneous" elements to reconstruct the "original" *muga*. This will be a quixotic enterprise where the aim is to rid the *muga* of Buddhist elements; in many cases next to nothing will remain after such an operation. Buddhism has been an active force in Korean culture for more than a millennium and a half, and its influence, although sometimes superficial, has touched most areas.

Not only is reconstruction of older *muga* difficult, one might even wonder if there is anything to reconstruct. What positive evidence, for instance, is there to prove that in remote times narrative *muga* existed at all? One may point out that some modern narrative *muga* are similar in structure to myths of nation-founders in the oldest historical sources, and cite the fact that in many cultures shamans are known as singers of tales.[64] This is not direct, hard evidence. One would like to have an unambiguous statement -if not for the pre-Buddhist period (which seems utterly impossible), then for the period prior to 1700- to the effect that a *mudang* sang a song about a certain god. The poem "The Old *Mudang*" by Yi Kyubo (1168-1241) mentions dancing, drumming and something that may be interpreted as *kongsu*, but contains no reference to the telling of a story in song. Other sources of the Koryŏ period furnish evidence that the *mudang* when possessed spoke in strange voices[65], but -as far as I know- keep silent about the existence of narrative *muga*.

An entry in the *Chosŏn wangjo sillok*, the annals of the Chosŏn dynasty (1392-1910), possibly implies that something resembling the narrative *Sonnim kut muga* may have existed in 1537: "Also there are evil *mudang*, who claim that the gods of smallpox have taken possession of them and that life and death of the children who have caught smallpox are all in their hands. They drum and sing heterodox doctrines."[66] The term "heterodox doctrines" (*sasŏl*) seems to refer to more than prayers, invocations or inspired mutterings. That the life and death of children who suffer from smallpox are in the hands of the Sonnim, is the message of the modern *Sonnim kut* as well.

It is not my intention to deny the existence of narrative *muga* in earlier periods entirely. I only want to emphasize that a reconstruction of historical *muga* is almost impossible, as is, for that reason, a study of the transmission of the *muga* in the past. So long as new sources are not discovered, historical study of the *muga* will have to be study of the historical elements of the *muga* of the twentieth century.

IV   The Interpretation of the *Muga*

Muga may be studied for a variety of reasons; for the linguistic information they contain, for instance, or for their literary interest. In this study, two questions are asked with regard to the *muga*: what is their value as a source for understanding popular religion in Korea, and what is the place of the *muga* within Korean literature as a whole? At first sight, it may seem strange to combine these two aspects of the study of the *muga*. The first question pertains to the investigation of the history of religion or the anthropological study of religion, the second is part of the study of cultural or literary history. But to answer the first question, it is necessary to know how the data the *muga* yield should be interpreted and for an interpretation of these the literary context of the *muga* must be taken into account. In fact, the first question cannot be answered until at least a partial answer to the second has been arrived at.

The *muga* do not exist in complete isolation from other forms of literature. As will be shown in Chapters V and VI, there are many links between the songs of the *mudang* and other genres. Many stylistic features, topics and themes of the songs of the Korean shaman are not unique to the *muga*. Korean scholars have proposed a host of theories in which some kind of relationship between the *muga* and other genres is posited. Not all of these theories can be seriously considered -if only because they often are contradictory- but their number alone is sufficient indication that some kind of relationship does exist.

To a large extent the relation between the *muga* and other genres is historical in nature. It is with various forms of traditional Korean literature that the *muga* can be fruitfully compared (cf. Chapters V and VI). A first question, then, is: when did the traditional period of Korean literature end? It seems reasonable to put the close of the traditional period around 1910, when the last Yi monarch abdicated and Korea fell completely under foreign domination. From this time onward, modern poems, stories and novels are published. This does not mean, however, that the production of works in the traditional style completely ceased and it certainly does not mean that traditional literature was no longer enjoyed. The folk-song and the folk-tale are sung and told to the present day, as is proved by a survey of Korean oral literature currently being compiled.[1] Genres like the classical *sijo* (a three-line poetic form), the *kasa* (longer poems) and the *ko-sosŏl* (novels or tales) are no longer living genres in the sense that new specimens are produced in any quantity today, but they continued to be created in the period after 1910 and still found a public. One version of the *kasa* called *Hanyang ka* was published by the firm Sech'ang sŏgwan in 1935, traditional material was used for the creation of new Buddhist *kasa* after 1945[2], and a widely read version of the "classical novel" *Sim Ch'ŏng chŏn* goes back to an edition of the 1920's (cf. Chapter VII).[3] The *ko-sosŏl* were, until quite recently, still available in cheap paperback editions which often reproduced the text as it was printed fifty or more years ago. *P'ansori*, "the one-man opera", or *ch'anggŭk* (musical theatre derived from *p'ansori*) remained quite popular until the Liberation in 1945 and recently have found new audiences. All this means that the contacts between *muga* and other traditional genres do not necessarily have to go back to the period before 1910. On the other hand, it is undeniable that traditional literature, as a whole, has gone into a decline. Within this disappearing tradition, the *muga* may be regarded as belonging to the most viable part.

The basis for an interpretation of the *muga* must be a sound understanding of the relationship between the *muga* and other traditional genres. In interpreting a text -whether it is of a religious nature or not- a knowledge of the historical and social milieu in which the text was produced is of great advantage, but it is just as important to know something about its literary context, about the conscious and unconscious codes which it shares with other texts. Without this awareness, it is easy to draw the wrong conclusions from a passage. To illustrate this, one example taken from *p'ansori* will be presented. This has some relevance for the study of the *muga*, not only because it provides an example of a problem that also may arise in the interpretation of *muga*, but because it can be demonstrated that this passage from *p'ansori* can be better understood when it is seen within a context that encompasses the *muga*.

In a discussion of a fragment from the *p'ansori* libretto of the "Song of Ch'unhyang" (*Ch'unhyang ka*), Marshall Pihl expresses the opinion that the "originality" of the replies of Ch'unhyang shows that she is more than a stock heroine, that she has distinct individual traits. Ch'unhyang wonders when her lover will return:[4]

When the highest peak of Diamond Mountains
Becomes a plain, will then you come?
When the vast waters of the Four Seas
Become land, will then you come?
When horses grow horns, will then you come?
When crows turn white, will then you come?

I believe that Ch'unhyang's answers are nothing but more or less successful variations on a well-known theme, variations that are to be expected in this genre and that in no way deviate from the unwritten rules. Perhaps, in this case, they are slightly spiced with satirical intent, but the satire -if present- is directed rather at the literary form. The answers were not meant to demonstrate to the audience elements of Ch'unhyang's psyche. The genre in general does not aim at individualisation in the psychological sense; so it strives to make the heroines as appealing as possible, while painting the villains in the blackest hues.

If we examine this passage in detail, it should be noted first that women waiting for their lovers are stock figures in the whole of East Asian literature.[5] The particular words with which Ch'unhyang expresses her fear that she will have to wait for ever, are far from original either. On an abstract level this is the type of exaggeration that is also found in *sasŏl sijo* in which a woman wonders why her lover does not come: has he been bound and put into a chest, a chest which was put into a locked room, a room in a closely guarded castle, a castle surrounded by a wall, et cetera.[6] Then, this fragment is but one example of the use of the topos of impossible things, which is frequently encountered in Korean literature. In one of the Koryŏ songs ("Chŏngsŏk ka" in the *Akchang kasa*) this topos is used to pledge loyalty: the persona will be loyal until "roasted chestnuts start to sprout", until "an iron cow eats iron grass", etc.[7]

The actual wording of Ch'unhyang's reply is not unique either. "When horses grow horns" occurs in a *muga* (AA I, 129; for a translation of the fragment in question, see p. 81), in a description of a "time that never was", with other variations on this theme, which in the context cannot be explained as meant to demonstrate individual psychology. As to the blackness of the crow, this is one of the most obvious examples of a condition that is in the nature of things, which makes its reversal as an example of something that is impossible somewhat less than original.[8] The originality of the "Song of Ch'unhyang" lies in the way traditional elements have been deftly fitted into the story. Ch'unhyang's complaint heightens the tension of the narrative, by stressing the fact that she is devoted to her lover and that it is far from certain that she will ever see him again.

What goes for *p'ansori*, goes for the *muga*: a passage will be misunderstood, if interpretation is not based on the conventions of the genre.

What is the purpose of the muga?

Failure to take into account the interaction of *muga* and other literary genres is one possible source of misunderstanding, but there are others. Interpretation should be preceded by reflection about the nature of the *muga*. An outstanding collector of *muga*, Kim T'aegon, has made the following statement: "The *muga* are a comprehensive systematization, directly expressed in words, of all thinking of the *mudang* -from their view of the gods, their view of spirits and ghosts and of the afterlife, to their view of the origins of being; therefore, we may regard them as the Oral Scripture of Korean shamanism."[9] I find it difficult to agree with this statement. The *muga* are not systematic at all, but full of contradictions, as even a casual survey will show.[10] In fact, it would be rather strange, if they were systematic expressions of belief, because the religion of the *mudang* is not the kind of religion that expresses doctrines consciously. In popular religion, contradictions are more acceptable than in religions where theologians reflect on the doctrines.[11] This lack of consistency in popular religion (when viewed as systematic theology) is not unique to Korea. Buryat stories about the origins of the gods reveal contradictions which are reminiscent of those found in Korean songs about the origin of deities (*ponp'uri*).[12] A fine example of the indeterminate character of some gods in popular religion in Japan is furnished by Embree, when he speaks about two of the seven Gods of Good Fortune (*shichi-fukujin*). People in the countryside have widely diverging conceptions of these gods:[13]

"Some say that Daikoku and Ebisu, so often seen together, are a married couple; others say they are father and son, still others call them brothers. Their sex is vague and their representation is not always the same."

The *mudang* has considerable freedom in choosing the words of her songs, because of the vagueness of the conceptions of the supernatural on the one hand, and because of a general absence of social limitations on her powers of imagination. Constraints which might be operative in a small, closed society do not exist for the *mudang*. Tungus shamans who serve one clan, have to memorize faultlessly the names of ancestors of that clan, to use long lists of them in their performances. These lists are important for the identity of the clan and consequently the shaman is not free to add or to omit anything.[14]

In the statement cited above, Kim T'aegon suggests that the *muga* are a kind of oral Bible. This is misleading, not so much because the *muga* are unsystematized theologically -in fact, the Christian Bible itself, in its entirety, is not a systematic expression of beliefs-, but because the Bible is seen by Christians as the foundation of their faith; the text is sacred. The *muga* do not enjoy a like prestige. A movement comparable to Christian fundamentalism, advocating a return to belief in the literal truth of the texts is unthinkable in Korean shamanism. A *mudang* does not necessarily believe what her *muga* say. One *mudang*, from Yangju in Kyŏnggi Province, told researchers that she did not believe in a here-after separate from this world, although such a world is depicted in the "Song of the Abandoned Princess", which is part of her repertoire.[15] The public do not listen to the *muga* as if they were divine revelations; only *kongsu* is regarded as such. Often people pay little attention to the text of the *muga* and primarily show interest when there is divination or *kongsu*.[16] In sum, the most sensible way to regard the *muga* is as "immaterial tools" of the *mudang*, without which she is unable to perform her rites. These tools are as necessary to her as the drum and other paraphernalia. Because they are created by *mudang* and used by *mudang*, the songs reflect the thinking and the attitudes of the *mudang*; as such they are a source for the study of shamanism, but they do not systematically express the beliefs of Korean shamanism.

The adaptability of the muga

Because the *muga* are the tools of the *mudang* rather than the sum of their beliefs, they have the licence to change or omit parts[17] and also to adopt elements from other literary genres. The adaptability of the *muga* is all the greater because the pantheon of the *mudang* is boundless and always can accomodate another god or spirit. When the name of a certain god is mentioned in the *muga*, this may be due to little more than the wish to fill out some literary pattern, to achieve parallelism or to create a fine-sounding alliteration. It does not necessarily mean that this god is of any importance in the rituals of the *mudang*.

There is still another reason why the *mudang* are not too closely bound to the texts of the *muga* as they have learnt them. According to one author, "The very core of magical power in the rites of the *mudang* is found in the *muga*."[18] If this is supposed to mean that there is some inherent magical power in the words of the *muga*, it is difficult to accept without qualification. The *muga* are not magic formulae which only need to be pronounced to be effective. They are always addressed to supernatural beings and try to achieve their ends through an agent. Gods and ghosts are requested to descend to the place where the ceremony is held, requested to enjoy themselves and the *mudang* tries to secure peace and happiness for her clients by propitiation and prayer. There is no indication that it is the power of words *sui generis* that forces supernatural beings to comply. Certain elements in the *muga* may be essential: the invitation to "descend", the songs that are sung to please the gods, the request to partake of the offerings, and the prayers, but all these elements can vary in length. There are long *kut* and short *kut* and one *muga* may be presented in an elaborated or a shortened form. Two factors that influence the length of the ceremonies are the amount of money paid by the clients and the interest shown by the audience.[19]

This is the present state of affairs. It has been suggested that in recent times, because of the increase in human knowledge and the developments of modern medical science, the magical elements in the *muga* have decreased in importance, while the parts sung for entertainment have become more prominent.[20] Because the *muga* we know almost all date from this century, it is hard to test the validity of this hypothesis. One of the *hyangga* in the *Samguk yusa*, the "Song of Ch'ǒyong" (*Ch'ǒyong ka*) is by many scholars regarded as a *muga*. This song was sung by Ch'ǒyong, the son of the Dragon King of the Eastern Sea, when he found his wife in bed with a demon of pestilence, and it made the demon retreat. It may be regarded, therefore, as a magical song to exorcize spirits that cause disease.[21] This is, however, a meagre basis for the assertion that the *muga* in the past were more magical in character. It is not known if the "Song of Ch'ǒyong" really was used by shaman-like religious specialists. To a certain extent, I feel, *Ch'ǒyong ka* has been called a *muga* on the very assumption that *muga* are by definition magical songs. As we have seen, this is not true for the modern *muga*, and whether it was true for the *muga* of the past is precisely the question we are trying to answer.

While it seems impossible, at this stage, to come to a conclusion about the magical nature of the *muga* of the past, this is not to say that the magic power of words *sui generis* was not recognized in Korea. Buddhist *dharani* were recited in the original Sanskrit -even though this was meaningless to the reciter- so as to retain their power, and in the oldest collection of Korean tales, the *Silla Sui chǒn*, there is a story about an incident which is said to have occurred in the reign of Queen Sǒndǒk (r. 632-647). A man fell in love with the Queen and his passion turned him into a fire demon. The Queen ordered a magician to compose an incantation to get rid of him:

> The fire in Chigwi's heart
> Consumed his body and he became a fire-ghost

> Let him be exiled over the ocean,
> Neither appearing here nor being intimate with me.

This text was pasted on walls and gates in Silla as a protection against fire.[22] The existence of such texts may be thought to corroborate the supposition that the *muga* of an earlier age were magical in character, but pleading against this argument is the fact that nowadays the *pujŏk*, charms against evil, which are not completely verbal, but which have verbal elements, and resemble the text pasted on the walls in Silla, exist side by side with non-magical *muga*. One could also point out that in the present century magic texts have been used by the exorcists, the *p'ansu*, who, unlike the *mudang*, try to intimidate and coerce spirits by means of their spells. The contrast between the *mudang* and the *p'ansu* is not absolute, but *mudang* act as true exorcists only in rare cases[23] and the *muga* recorded in modern collections are hardly or not at all used on such occasions. We may conclude, therefore, that magic texts may co-exist with non-magic texts used by religious specialists; the existence of magic texts in the past cannot be taken as proof that the *muga* of the past were necessarily magical in nature. Whatever the character of the *muga* of earlier periods may have been, for the purposes of this study the most important fact is that, if the *muga* of the past were magical texts, they were, in this respect, different from the *muga* of the present.

Although *muga* are not the kind of magic formulae that depend on the power of specific sounds, it is possible to regard them as having magical power in a more general sense. Kim T'aegon describes the *Ch'il kongju muga* (a variant of the story of the Abandoned Princess) as "having the magic power to clear the way to the nether world for the deceased."[24] This opening of the way is symbolized, during the *kut* for the deceased, by actions such as the tearing in two of a length of cloth.[25] A form of magic can also be discerned in a theatrical part of a Cheju Island ceremony. There the story of an agricultural deity, Segyŏng, is followed by a little play, in which a young woman, after being raped bears a son who, because he is too stupid to study, becomes a farmer. As such he reaps an abundant harvest.[26] There is an obvious relation here between human fertility and agricultural fertility. It should be noted in passing that the entertainment value of this rather obscene play is not in conflict with its magical or ritual function. A similar play is found on the mainland, in Kyŏnggi Province, where it follows a *muga* devoted to Chesŏk, a deity who is in charge of agriculture. In this *So-nori kut*, "Cow-play *kut*", a cow appears as the symbol of agriculture in a ceremony which is held for an abundant harvest.[27] In all these instances, any magic power to be detected, is not in the words themselves, but in the whole of the ceremony or in the actions of the *mudang*.

The *muga* do not possess magical power that is inherent in the words of the songs; these rather resemble the "liturgical chants" sung during the séances of Vietnamese mediums, which have been described as follows:[28]

> Tous ces hymnes commencent généralement par une spécification de la divinité (ou des divinités) qu'on implore. Puis on la décrit physiquement, on indique la couleur de ses habits; on dépeint ses gestes, son allure; on raconte ses faits et gestes, sa légende, afin que, au milieu de cette assemblée d'immortels en nombre incalculable, elle sache bien que c'est à elle qu'on s'adresse. On cite les offrandes. On l'invite à descendre sur terre à se réincarner. L'hymne s'achève par les demandes de paix, de bonheur, de longévité, ou par des demandes plus précises. Le médium, durant le chant de l'hymne, mime l'allure de la divinité implorée, s'efforce d'adopter ses gestes, ses travers, son naturel.

This is very similar to the character of the *muga*, in which the gods are approached in a respectful manner. Even the lowliest gods or ghosts (*chapsin* and *chapkwi*) are invited to take their share of the offerings, although the invitation may be couched in impolite, low-level speech, "Eat a lot and off with you!"[29] They are treated as beggars, not as enemies. In one *muga*, the *chapkwi* are warned that a magic formula (*chinŏn*) will be used against them, if they do not leave as they are bidden, which would imply that the *muga* itself is of a different nature.

Because the *muga* are not true magical formulae, the *mudang* is free to embellish and adorn, and can avoid mere mechanical repetition, which is said to increase the efficacy of real magic spells, such as the Japanese *majinai-uta*.[30]

If it is difficult or even impossible to detect in the *muga* magical formulae such as must be reproduced exactly, one does, on the other hand, observe that, in some cases, elements that might be supposed to carry an important religious meaning àre changed. A recurring theme in the story of the origin of most gods is their supernatural birth, which, of course, is an indication of their special status as members of a world that is separate from that of ordinary human beings. In stories of the so-called Tanggŭm-aegi type,[31] a girl (Tanggŭm-aegi) becomes pregnant after meeting a monk, usually by swallowing three grains of rice, which she has received from the monk. In many versions of the story, it is stressed that there is no sexual intercourse between the two. This is to be expected: the three boys the girl will give birth to are not ordinary bastards, but gods-to-be. In one version of the story however, the monk is depicted as a sex-starved old lecher: "After three months, a hundred days on the road/The monk felt lust surging within him!"[32] This, of course, does away with the element of supernatural conception. One may propose various theories to account for this decrease in religious content of this *muga* -it could be attributed to general secularisation, or to the influence of *p'ansori*, where there is a strongly reminiscent description of a lascivious monk in *Pyŏn Kangsoe ka*, or to the influence of the mask plays, where the amorous monk is one of the stock figures. Also, it may not be entirely typical, but the fact remains that in the *muga* we know, such variations are possible and permissible. There is, in other words, no sacred canon of *muga*.

The basis of interpretation

As material for the study of Korean shamanism the *muga* can be mis-interpreted if interpretation is founded on a wrong conception of the nature of the songs. But there is also a more fundamental problem, which concerns the nature of interpretation itself. The same text means different things to different people. What it means to the *mudang*, is not necessarily what it means to her clients, and this may be different again from what the text means to the scholar. When one researcher decides that *wŏnangsae* in a certain song does not mean "mandarin duck" (the usual meaning), but is a corruption of *wŏn wang saeng*, a Buddhist phrase meaning "I want to go [to Paradise] to be re-born",[33] does this imply that interpretation should follow the presumed original meaning? If so, the danger is not imaginary that a meaning is extracted from the *muga* that has reality only within the four walls of the scholar's study. One should try to find criteria to choose between possible meanings. When the informant is available for comment, one could, of course, rely on her explanations. In fact, it would be interesting to have one *mudang* explain in detail the whole of her repertoire. No one, however, has systematically attempted to record the comments of *mudang* on their songs, which is not surprising, as such an undertaking would pose many practical problems and consume a lot of time. Moreover, these comments -however interesting- would not be the last word about the songs. They would constitute only one - possibly rather idiosyncratic- view. To ask the audience for an explanation is not a complete solution either. Again it would be interesting to have a systematic body of comments, but this, too, would be a one-sided explanation.

Illustrative of the difficulties that would arise if one were to follow blindly the opinion of one informant, is a comment made to the *paksu mudang* Yi Chisan by the husband of a senior *mudang*. The latter *mudang*, Pak Haengwŏn, was born in 1873 and although the age of the husband is not given by Cho Hung-youn, to whom we owe this information, one may assume that he, too, grew up in the last days of the old Korea.[34] The comment is about a certain recurring formula in the *muga*, the *ho(e)ngsu-magi* formula, which is recited to ward off noxious influences.

"Die damaligen (that is to say, around 1948, B.C.A.W.) schama-
nistischen Sitten seien so vulgär geworden, dass die meisten Schamanen
während des Stadiums für Ch'angbu sängen, "Irwŏr-e tŭnŭn hongsu,
iwŏr-e makko, iwŏr-e tŭnŭn hongsu, samwŏr-e makko ..."
(Unerwartetem Unglück, das im Januar eindringt, beuge (ich) im
Februar vor; Unerwartetem Unglück, das im Februar eindringt, beuge
(ich) im März vor). Wozu brauchte man einem vergangenen Unglück
vorzubeugen?"

This seems illogical, indeed, but is it really an instance of the degeneration of
shamanistic customs in recent times? I doubt it, for two reasons. First, this
formula has been reported, as cited above, in several sources.[35] One would not
expect such consistency if this version of the formula was nothing but a silly
mistake. Second, the formula is also reported in this form in a literary work
of the 1880's: the libretto of the *p'ansori* play *Pyŏn Kangsoe ka* by Sin
Chaehyo (1812-1884).[36] Sin Chaehyo was something of a folklorist avant la
lettre, who noted down the text of songs to use in his libretti, and we may
assume that the form of the text which he recorded was common in his time.
Therefore one cannot very well say that the "illogicality" of the *muga* is a
recent degeneration; if a degeneration, it goes back to the middle of the 19th
century. It is difficult to solve the problem of the apparent illogicality -one
might perhaps interpret the lines as meaning: "The unexpected evil that (starts
to) enter in January, we stop (from going further) in February", etc.- but
neither is it easy to accept the criticism of the *mudang*'s husband at face
value.

The example given above concerns the opinion of a "layman", a well-
informed layman probably -considering that, as a *mudang*'s husband, he had
ample opportunities to hear *muga*- but still not a religious specialist himself.
Our next example, however, is an explanation of a term in the *muga* by Yi
Chisan, the *paksu mudang* who was the informant of Cho Hung-youn.
According to Yi Chisan, *chungsang* means "ghosts of the people." The context
of a song in which it is used does not confirm this; there *chungsang* is used
to refer to a monk; the *chungsang* in the *muga* wears a monk's robe and a
monk's head-covering.[37]

Not only may the *muga* mean different things to the *mudang*, the audience
and the scholar, it is not uncommon that parts of *muga* do not mean anything
at all to one or more of these. Even the *mudang*, who might be expected to
know best, are not always able to explain details.[38] One *mudang* admitted this
to two *muga* collectors, saying: "These are the words of the ghosts; how could
human beings understand them?"[39]

Undoubtedly, it is even more difficult for the audience to understand all the
details of the texts than for the *mudang*. To a certain extent this is a

consequence of the use of antiquated expressions from older traditional literature; nor is intelligibility advanced by the insertion of Sino-Korean phrases taken from Buddhist liturgical texts. All this does not necessarily spoil the effect of the songs. Wassiljewitsch has reported that in the case of the Evenki shaman songs, too, archaic language is frequently employed. "Aus diesem Grunde verstehen die modernen Ewenken die Texte der Schamanenlieder nicht, die offensichtlich eben deshalb einen tiefen Eindruck auf sie machen."[40] Sometimes the *mudang* add explanations to old-fashioned terms: "Nowadays you have schoolteachers, in the past you had masters of the *sŏdang* (village schools, B.W.)."[41] This is not very common, however, and seems largely to be confined to the East Coast *mudang*.

Given the fact that individual interpretations may differ and that some passages perhaps do not mean anything at all, what should the basis of interpretation be? The answer, briefly stated, is: the context of the corpus of all *muga* and the context of the literature of which the *muga* form one sub-division.

The *muga* may be compared to a language. Words in a language can have a considerable semantic range. Moreover, within a closed group, such as a family or a gang, certain commonly used words carry meanings that to outsiders are not intelligible. In spite of multiple meanings of one and the same word, in spite of idiolects, jargon and slang, however, there is a shared framework, within which specific uses of language function. A word may acquire a special meaning in the mouth of an individual speaker or in a particular context but, nevertheless, it is possible to compile a dictionary, which summarizes the meanings of words. Similarly, one can broadly indicate what a certain passage of a *muga* is about; what it is that is actually communicated by this passage during a specific ceremony, however, is quite another matter. The *muga* form only one part of a ceremony and if one wants to study the text to know more about a specific event as a whole, the other elements cannot be neglected. Yet the study of the texts of the *muga* alone, without reference to the specific occasion when the songs were sung, is not, therefore, useless. It serves as a preliminary to researches concerning the concrete functions of the *muga*, it helps us to understand the basic language of the *muga*.

So long as the context of a *kut* during which a *muga* is sung is not taken into account, interpretation of *muga* must follow general principles which can be deduced from the available corpus of *muga* and -to stress a point made earlier- from related forms of literature which, to a greater or lesser degree, share certain patterns with the *muga*. A knowledge of the general features and circumstances of Korean shamanism also contributes to interpretation.

A very simple example of the importance of the larger context is the interpretation of epitheta prefixed to the names of gods. Suppose one were to attempt to discover the nature of a particular deity by examining all the epitheta used in the *muga* for this god. It is obvious that it makes a great difference whether these epitheta are attached to one deity exclusively, or to many gods. Only after a study of many songs will one be able to know which is the case. Often it will appear that the same epitheta are used for different gods.[42] If certain prefixes are used for many different gods, this cannot but mean that they do not denote individual qualities. In extreme cases one has the feeling that such epitheta are added quite mechanically. A study of the context, therefore, shows that one should be cautious in interpreting epitheta as indications of the individual character of gods.

To come back to the example of the term *wŏnangsae* given above, interpretation on the basis of the wider context implies that the aim is not just reconstruction of the "original meaning" with the help of historical philology. The way in which the word is fitted into the text, and the way in which it is used in other texts should be examined, as well as the question what words might have been used in the same text instead of *wŏnangsae*. The answer to the last question is at least partly dependent on a comparison with similar texts. If "mandarin duck" is an obvious anomaly here and if mandarin ducks do not occur in other *muga*, while words of the same category, i.e. names of birds, are not found either, then the interpretation "I want to be reborn in Paradise" must be preferred. If, however, the mandarin duck heads a list of birds (as it does in the example under discussion) and thus fits in quite naturally and if similar lists often are part of *muga*, then the first interpretation: "mandarin duck", should be favoured. In that case, the remark about the original meaning of *wŏnangsae* makes an interesting footnote, but cannot be accepted as the one and only correct interpretation. In another *muga*, however, *wŏnangsae* appears in a context that makes it obvious that it is a corruption of the opening words of a *gāthā*, a Buddhist hymn.[43] One cannot establish the meaning of a term once and for all; one always needs to consider the immediate and the wider context.

Ambiguities inherent in the language

A daunting problem in interpreting the *muga* is the vagueness of many conceptions, which is added to by the fact that in Korean number is not always expressed. If, for instance, the name of a deity is mentioned, it is often doubtful whether it should be translated in the singular or plural. Also, this makes it difficult to know whether the name is used to refer to a class of gods or to an individual god. Compare the use of the word "father" in English, which may refer to all men who have begotten a child, or to an individual whom we call "Father." In English, it is often the use of the singular or the plural which distinguishes the two meanings. To illustrate the problem that can arise because of this, we may take the case of Sŏngju, the god of the house. In *muga* from all over the country his origin is given as a place near Andong in Kyŏngsang Province.[44] This would lead one to think of Sŏngju as one, but the *muga* also contain passages which imply a plurality of Sŏngju. There are said to be, for example, different Sŏngju for different age groups.[45] This is affirmed explicitly by *mudang*. "Sŏngju", as is the case with many other names of Korean deities, is a general concept with individual manifestations (like "father"). If the context offers no support, it is impossible to know which aspect of the term is meant. The name of another deity, Chesŏk, is the Korean pronunciation of the Chinese character used to render the name of the Indian god Sakro devānām Indra. Sakro devānām Indra clearly is one deity, but Chesŏk appears in various forms. In a *muga* from Osan, one finds a Mountain Chesŏk and a Dragon-King Chesŏk.[46]

Koreans do not seem to be bothered by such ambiguities. Alexandre Guillemoz has noted, that the villagers of the community he studied, never asked themselves the question whether Grandmother Samsin (the goddess of childbirth) was one or many, although in practice they seemed to assume that each house had its own Grandmother Samsin and that these grandmothers could be jealous of each other.[47]

Embree has observed similar phenomena in Japan, where[48]

".. different Kwannon (Avalokitesvara) or different Jizō (Ksitigarbha) etc. are regarded as having different powers and so are in a sense separate individuals but all of the same species. Thus a Jizō-san is always Jizō-san, but this Jizō-san is by no means the same as that Jizō-san."

Such ambiguity is not only found in the popular beliefs of the Far East. In Belgium, the Blessed Virgin of Loreto in Brussels is a patroness of travellers by air, while "another" Virgin, the Virgin of Deerlijk, specializes in answering prayers requesting peace of mind and also has the power to pacify crying babies. The Virgin adored in Beulare (O.L. Vrouw ten Groenen Straten) protects her believers against floods, and the Virgin of Ertvelde may grant a peaceful death.[49] It is the absence of obligatory indication of number in the language -not the existence of ambiguity- that distinguishes Korea from Flanders, and makes it even more difficult for the student of the *muga* - especially the translator- to know whether the singular or the plural is meant and whether a name refers to a class of gods or to one god with a certain individuality.

V Formal Characteristics of the *Muga*

In this chapter the diction of the *muga* will be examined. To say that the *muga* differ in form from prose may seem superfluous, yet one distinguished collector of *muga* has expressed the opinion that the language of the songs is that which was spoken (emphasis added, B.W.) by educated people sixty or seventy years ago.[1] Since it was originally the language of the educated, Sino-Korean expressions are numerous in the *muga*. This brings up the question of how the *mudang*, who on the whole cannot be called well-educated, learned to speak in this way. The explanation for the admittedly high occurrence of Sino-Korean is, in my opinion, rather that the *mudang* make use of a formalized literary language, which was, at least in part, created by others. Whether this literary language belongs to oral or written literature, is another matter. My view on this point is presented in the chapter on the transmission of the *muga*.

The *muga* show too much stylization to be called "spoken language." This will be argued in detail below: here a single example, consisting of no more than sixteen syllables, may suffice. It can be considered fairly representative of *muga* style.

> *naj-imyŏn-ŭn mur-i malkko, pam-imyŏn-ŭn pur-i palga ...*

> [Please grant] that by day the water is clear,
> that by night the lights are bright...

Apart from the fact that this line fits the metre of *kasa* poetry, it shows syntactic parallelism, double semantic antithesis (*nat/pam*, *mul/pul*), parallelistic alliteration (*mur-i malkko* and *pur-i palga*), assonance and rhyme.

The ways in which the *muga* are stylized are, on the whole, not unique to the *muga*. Many of these stylistic features are encountered in other forms of Korean literature, such as *sijo, kasa, chapka, minyo, p'ansori*, mask-plays, traditional prose tales (*ko-sosŏl*) and Buddhist liturgical texts. An examination of the stylistic features of the *muga* as they compare with those of the other forms may serve as the foundation for a study of the complicated relationships between the various genres mentioned in the following chapter, and may ultimately provide an answer to the question which parts of the *muga* are oldest.

It has been said that the most marked formal feature of poetry is repetition.[2] In *muga*, repetition is found in many forms and on various levels: sounds are repeated (e.g. assonance and alliteration, sometimes full rhyme), words are repeated, whole phrases or lines recur (sometimes in exactly the same form, sometimes with variations), the same themes are found over and over again and the same syntactic pattern structures a number of consecutive lines. The terms formula, formulaic expression and theme may conveniently be used to describe the style of the *muga*, even if the oral-formulaic theory as formulated by Parry and Lord, in which these terms play a key role, does not adequately describe the genesis of all or even a majority of *muga*. The Parry/Lord theory has already been mentioned briefly in the discussion of the transmission of the *muga*; now it should be examined more in detail.

The oral formulaic theory and Korean literature.

The theory states that oral poetry is composed in performance with the help of formulae, formulaic expressions and themes, which are all of a traditional nature. In other words, oral tradition is not, as had often been supposed, a process in which a memorized text is handed down, in roughly the same form, for a long time, but it is rather the transmission of the elements out of which an oral poem during performance may be recreated. Parry and Lord have convincingly shown -through their registrations of the songs of Yugoslav singers- that oral composition in this sense is possible and does exist. This does not mean, however, that other forms of oral poetry are unthinkable. In fact, there is a wide range of possibilities with regard to the creation and transmission of oral poetry in a more general sense: i.e. orally delivered poetry.[3] For the transmission of *muga* in Korea, one single explanation, which excludes all others, is out of the question, as has been argued in Chapter III. Nevertheless, in all *muga* there are elements which could be called formulae, formulaic expressions, or themes. The first problem to be addressed is, what the creators of the oral-formulaic theory meant these terms to signify; the second what they can mean in the context of Korean literature in general, and for the *muga* in particular.

A formula, according to Parry is "A group of words which is regularly employed under the same metrical conditions to express a given essential idea."[4] This definition raises some questions -what is "a group of words" (are two words a group?), what is "regularly", what is an essential idea, how can one demonstrate objectively that a phrase is an "expression of an essential idea"-, questions which have not all been answered in Parry's work. Later adherents of the oral formulaic theory have interpreted the original definition very freely and the result, as H.L. Rogers has pointed out, has been that in practice the term formula "becomes a portmanteau, enclosing within its ample capacity many different, and often undefined, sorts of lexical, morphological, and syntactic similarities."[5] This vagueness is partly the result of the lumping together of formulae and formulaic expressions. The latter Lord defined as "a line or half line constructed on the pattern of formulas."[6] Parry called a set of such phrases a "formulaic system", i.e., "a group of phrases which have the same metrical value and which are... alike in thought and words."[7] In his frequency counts, Parry kept the notions of formula and formulaic system carefully apart, but he was not followed in this by many of his adherents.[8] Even in the writings of Lord, the distinction is blurred. "Everything in the style is in the category of formula", Lord has stated.[9] "Everything" includes "characteristic syntax, rhythmic, metric, and acoustic molds and configurations." Parry's definition of the formula clearly referred to lexical units only. Although it certainly is not Lord's intention, his statements might be taken as implying that all poetry in a strictly parallelistic style, some forms of Chinese poetry for example, are a 100% formulaic (and therefore of oral origin).

Criticisms as made by Rogers show that the oral formulaic theory is of doubtful value as an instrument to establish the oral provenance of a text, the purpose for which it has most often been used.[10] Its worth as such is all the more questionable, because it may not be assumed that oral poetry, even if fully conforming to the condition of being composed in performance, contains an equal percentage of formulae or formulaic expressions in all languages. A simple metre may allow oral composition with a smaller number of formulae. For each literature, therefore, the percentage of formulae proving "orality" may be different.[11]

There is evidence, moreover, that formulae, formulaic expressions and themes are also used in considerable quantity in written literature. From a formulaic analysis of the poems of the *Shih Ching*, the ancient Chinese Classic of Poetry, C.H. Wang draws the conclusion that some poems of known authorship (by literate writers) in this collection are not less formulaic than others that are supposed to be oral folk-songs.[12] Similar evidence exists for other literatures.[13]

In view of this lack of reliability of the oral formulaic method with regard to frequency counts, and because it must be seriously doubted that a highly formulaic style is sufficient proof of oral origin, one has to agree with C.H. Wang, who has written: "Perhaps 'oral or not' is not the matter that concerns us. Formulaic composition, perhaps, ..., was once practiced by writing as well as improvising poets. The mode of creation that concerns us is not necessarily oral-formulaic composition, but formulaic composition."[14]

Authors who acknowledge the possibility of formulaic composition by literate authors, usually assume that this is a phenomenon that belonged to a transitional period.[15] In some cases it may indeed be correct to speak of a transitional period, but in others -and I suspect that the Korean case is one of these- it may be misleading, because there the use of formulae in written literature is not a passing phenomenon, but quasi-permanent. If within one society there is an upper-class which is literate, while the remainder of the population is illiterate or semi-literate, in the borderland between high and low culture a literature may be produced which employs "oral" formulae for written poems. This poetry is transitional from the social point of view. Such a situation will more easily arise where a society has a prestigious written language of foreign origin. Members of the literate upper-class, then, will sometimes stoop to borrow from folk traditions when they want to write in the vernacular, the overwhelming prestige of the literary language impeding the formation of a purely upper-class vernacular style. This prestige of the written language, on the other hand, will induce lower-class vernacular poets to borrow elements of that language. The tendency to employ formulaic language will be reinforced, moreover, if vernacular literature, although not orally composed, is mainly intended for oral presentation. The state of affairs described here is, of course, similar to that which existed in traditional Korea.[16]

Among the three types of recurrent elements in oral literature mentioned above, formulae, formulaic expressions and themes, the last is not used for frequency analysis, but to explain how oral poets organize their texts (or their performances), how the smaller units of the formulae and the formulaic expressions are fitted together into larger entities. The concept of the theme can be used for the analysis of formulaic texts without any need to get involved in a barren "oral or not" controversy. Lord, who has elaborated the theory of the theme, has described themes as "repeated incidents and descriptive passages in the songs."[17] And elsewhere: "The theme, even though it be verbal, is not any fixed set of words, but a grouping of ideas."[18] Imperfect adaptation of a theme to a specific song may lead to inconsistency, "the famous nod of Homer."[19]

While some scholars have sharply criticized the oral formulaic theory, others, who basically adhere to its tenets, have considerably modified it. One may regret this, as a possible source of confusion, but to the extent that it is the result of well-reasoned attempts to apply the theory to literatures of different times and regions, it ought to be recognized as of value. Once the idea of an easily applicable universal theory (the idea of the universal "orality" test) is put aside, the value of the theory lies in that it provides a method to describe the way in which language is used in specific, traditional literatures. As Ann Watts has said about Parry[20]: "In fact, it may be thought to be Parry's greatest merit not that he has established a general theory of oral composition -this is still a subject of controversy and probably will remain so- but that he has used the conception of formula and formulaic system to describe convincingly how Homer used language." If one uses formulaic analysis in this way, that is to understand how specific texts are structured, "local adaptation" of the oral-formulaic theory is not only permissible, it is even desirable.

To illustrate that formulaic analysis may be useful even for works of manifestly literary origin, we will examine a *sijo* by the 18th century *sijo*-collector Kim Ch'ŏnt'aek.[21]

Sesang sarămdŭr-a i nae mal tŭrŏ poso

Ch'ŏngch'un-i măeyang-imyŏ paekpar-i kŏmnănkŏtka

Ŏtŏt'a *yuhan-hăn insaeng-i* **ani nolgo ŏiri**

Roughly translated: "Men of this world! Listen to my words/Is youth forever, will grey hairs turn black again?/How, during this limited life of ours, could we not look for pleasure?!" The parts in boldface consist of formulae, recurring phrases in Korean traditional literature, and the phrase in italics is formulaic, which means that an exact equivalent has not been found, but that the phrase belongs to a formulaic system of similar phrases. (The content of the terms formula and formulaic system for Korean literature, will be discussed in greater detail below.)

Text	Supporting evidence
1. *Sesang sarămdŭr-a:*	*Sijo sajŏn*, Nos 1166, 1171
2. *I nae mal tŭrŏ poso:*	*Sijo sajŏn*, No. 1435
	Kasa chŏnjip, pp. 463, 536
3. *Ch'ŏngch'un-i măeyang-imyŏ:*	*Sijo sajŏn*, No. 1435
4. *Paekpar-i kŏmnănkŏtka:*	*Sijo sajŏn*, No. 1435

5. *Ŏttŏt' a yuhan-hǎn insaeng-i:*

Sijo sajŏn, No. 768: *ŏttŏt' a i insaeng-i kǔtch' ŏ kal che*; *Sijo sajŏn*, No. 1181: *ŏttit' a sesok insim-ǔn*; *Sijo sajŏn*, No. 2015: *ŏttŏt' a sesang insa-nǎn*; *Sijo sajŏn*, No. 2181: *ŏjǔbŏ yuhan-hǎn ch' ŏnun-ǔl,*

6. *Ani nolgo ŏiri:*

Sijo sajŏn, No. 1163

This analysis shows that Kim Ch'ŏnt'aek, who is an important figure both as a poet and as a collector of poetry, composed in a formulaic manner: 83.3% of this *sijo* consists of straight formulae, while the remainder is "formulaic" in the sense that it can be recognized as coming from the matrix of a formulaic system. The poem is, therefore, a hundred percent formulaic. This conclusion alone is of some importance. Apparently *sijo* poets of Kim Ch'ŏnt'aek's stature, lettered poets, relied on formulae. Furthermore, the analysis allows us to quantify the first impression most people will receive from this poem: that it is a conventional piece of work. If this analysis is compared with that of other *sijo*, further insights into the manner of *sijo* composition may be expected.

In clarification of how the *muga* are constructed, their metre (an essential element of the formula), their formulae and formulaic systems, and their themes, as well as the phenomenon of parallelism (which could be called a formulaic pattern) will be examined below. Moreover the use of alliteration and rhyme as means to create a poetic diction which -together with the metre- distinguishes the language of formulae from that of ordinary language, will be briefly discussed. Finally there will be a few remarks on wordplay and narrative style.

Metre

In the oral-formulaic theory metre is an important element in the definition of the formula: "a group of words, regularly employed under the same metrical conditions, to express a given essential idea." As metres differ from one genre to another, and from language to language, as an element of definition it is probably the factor that presents the greatest problems when one attempts a comparative application of the theory. The metre of some verse-forms (e.g. the hexameter or the Serbo-Croation decasyllabic) is more demanding than that of others; Old English poetry, for example, has a "natural" metre, close to that of ordinary speech. The more demanding the metre, the greater the need of the

oral poet for oral formulae as convenient ready-made building blocks, and also
-important for the researcher who wants to make frequency counts of
formulae- the easier it is to distinguish formulae from habitual collocations
used in ordinary speech.[22] Korean verse-metre generally is simple and very
close to the rhythms of natural speech and for that reason one may doubt its
usefulness as a touchstone for distinguishing a true formula from a spoken
language cliché.[23]

If Korean metre in general is undemanding and close to natural speech, the
metre of *muga* is still less formalized. As far as a fixed metre is to be
discerned at all, it is similar to that in *kasa* poetry. The metre of *kasa* poetry,
in its turn, is similar to that of *p'ansori* and folk-songs (*minyo*).[24]
Traditionally, *kasa* metre has been described in terms of syllable counts and
is said to consist mainly of groups of three or four syllables. Such a
description leaves one with many "irregularities" and therefore an analysis in
rhythmic groups has come to be preferred.[25] As David McCann has put it:
"Syllable counting is not, as such, a primary constitutive feature of the *kasa*
form. The fundamental constituent element.... (of the *kasa*) and of Korean
verse generally, is the rhythmic group, in both *kasa* and *sijo* the four units out
of which the line is composed. ....it is this unit rather than the syllable, which
is counted in the structuring of the Korean verse line."[26] One line, then,
consists of four groups (each being about four syllables long), with a caesura
in the middle dividing the line into two hemistichs. The notation of *kasa* in
old manuscripts sometimes stresses the hemistichs, by using spaces between
the half-lines[27] and sometimes the lines by writing two hemistichs next to each
other and the following line below on the lower half of the page.[28] Some
groups are longer than others; groups of four syllables are most common, but
groups of two, three, and five or more syllables also occur. If within a
hemistich one group is longer than the other, it will often be the last one.[29]
This, however, is only a tendency, not a rule that cannot be broken. It does
not, therefore, make versification much more difficult and does not mean that
specific rhythmic groups cannot be used in different positions within the line,
in contrast to the constituent parts of, for instance, the hexameter.

In modern *muga* collections little attention is paid to metre, although most
collectors divide the songs into lines, sometimes claiming that these are based
on "natural breath groups."[30] It happens that the same lines, used a second
time, will be "cut up" in a different way. One should not always accept the
division of lines made by the collectors as the basis of versification.[31] Often
there seems to have been no clear principle guiding this division, which is not
altogether surprising in view of the loose metrical structure of the *muga*.
Application of a strict principle would be very awkward because of the
numerous irregularities. In spite of this, it is sometimes possible to bring out

a more regular structure in the *muga*, recorded in the collections, by rearranging the lines.[32]

The relation between verse metre and musical metre will not be examined here, because of the lack of musicological knowledge of the author. At any rate, the style of singing of the *muga* does not require a song to have an exact syllable count. If it proves difficult to fit a text to a certain musical rhythm, syllables can be stretched or added.[33]

Formulae and formulaic patterns in Korean vernacular literature

The formula in traditional Korean literature is best identified with the half-line, "the smallest freestanding prosodic unit: that is a unit which is preceded and followed by a caesura."[34] This is a unit of a convenient size; it is not so small that it might coincide with a mere lexical item (typically, it will consist of about eight syllables), and yet small enough to be handled with ease by both poet and analyst. In many cases even the halves of half-lines are standard units with a recognizable poetic diction, especially when they are Sino-Korean phrases. But here it becomes difficult to draw the line between units of poetic diction and lexical items. The quarter-lines of recognizable poetic diction may be called "half-formulae"; they are of great importance in the creation of formulaic systems.

As long as one uses the classic definition of the formula, "a group of words which is regularly employed under the same metrical conditions to express a given essential idea", certain traditional patterns, in which there is so much variation in the wording that one cannot speak of a (constant) group of words, remain outside the reach of the analyst. To describe these patterns, one needs other concepts, among which that of the formulaic system is the most important. Parry has defined a formulaic system as "a group of phrases which have the same metrical value and which are enough alike in thought and words to leave no doubt that the poet who used them knew them not only as single formulas, but also as formulas of a certain type."[35] This definition contains a subjective, unverifiable element. I will use as a "working definition" a simplification of the definition of Parry: "a formulaic system is a group of phrases which have the same metrical value and which are alike in wording and syntax." What is felt to be "alike" may differ from person to person, but the researcher can objectively demonstrate what he considers to be similar, while it will prove impossible to enter the mind of the poet. It is questionable, moreover, whether traditional poets were sufficiently conscious of their poetic language to know certain phrases "not only as single formulas but also as formulas of a certain type." As with natural language, it is possible to use the "grammar" of traditional poetic language without conscious knowledge of its principles.

Within Korean formulaic systems one can discern several types, and by distinguishing these, an attempt will be made to give the vague and inclusive working definition a more exact content for traditional Korean poetry.

Our formulaic analysis of the *muga* has two purposes. First, it sheds light on the structure and composition of the songs. Second, it contributes to an understanding of the place of the *muga* in Korean literature. To show how *muga* are related to other genres, the examples of both formulae and formulaic systems presented below and in Appendices I and II have been culled from various genres: *muga, kasa, sijo*, mask-dance drama, folk-song (*minyo*) and *p'ansori*. It appears from an examination of these formulae and formulaic systems that formulae and formulaic systems in Korea were not limited to one genre; there was overlapping. Formulaic elements in the *muga* are to a large extent also found in other genres. Formulaic analysis, in other words, is a method to demonstrate the fact that *muga* are part of the continuum of traditional Korean literature.

Formulae
As examples of formulae some phrases may be cited describing the exterior of a house: "*kodae kwangsil nop'ŭn chip*, "a tall house, on a lofty platform, with spacious rooms" and *ne kwi-e p'unggyŏng tara*, "with windbells hung on its four corners". More examples and full references are given in Appendix I.

In many cases the first part of the formula is Sino-Korean and the second pure Korean. This is very common, although other possibilities (pure Korean followed by Sino-Korean, formulae without Sino-Korean) are not excluded. Below, when the formulaic system is discussed, this aspect of the formula will be further examined, together with other particularities of diction.

Formulaic systems
The definition of the formula demands the regular use of the same group of words, with only a minimum of variation allowed. A perusal of the examples of formulae given in Appendix A will, for anyone familiar with traditional Korean literature, bring phrases to mind that are similar, but not quite the same. The concept of the formulaic system makes it possible to describe such phrases, too, as parts of the heritage of traditional patterns. Formulaic systems are substitution sets: lines that belong to one system share one or more

elements, but also have elements which cannot be found in the other members of the set.

Some examples of formulaic systems and the way they function are given below.

A I

1. *tongjisŏttal kin'gin pam-e* ("during the long, long nights of the month of the winter solstice and the twelfth month"); *KTG* IV, 85
2. *tongjittal kinagin pam-ŭl* ("the long, long nights of the month of the winter solstice"); *Sijo sajŏn*, No. 672
3. *tongjittal ch'uun kyŏur-e* ("in the cold winter, in the month of the winter solstice"); *Han'guk siga*, 331
4. *tongjisŏttal sŏrhanp'ung-e* ("in the cold, wind and snow of the month of the winter solstice and the twelfth month"); Ch'oe T'aeho, *Naebang kasa*, 288;*KTG* I, 126; *CCM*, 271

Tongjisŏttal, "the month of the winter solstice and the twelfth month", is in this case the stable element of the formulaic system, which, in each case, is followed by a phrase that in some way or other is related to winter or cold.

A group of words that is the variable part in a half-line within one system, may become the stable part of another system, as a comparison of A I and A II shows.

A II

1. *tongjisŏttal kin'gin pam-e* (= A I, 1)
2. *ch'an sŏri kin'gin pam-e* ("in the long, long nights with cold frost"); *Nongga wŏllyŏng ka*, 52-53
3. *odong ch'uya kin'gin pam-e* ("in the long, long nights, the autumn nights [with the patter of rain on the leaves of] the *odong*-trees; *Kasa chŏnjip*, 439
4. *changjang ch'uya kin'gin pam-e* ("in the long long nights, the autumn nights that are so long"); *Kasa chŏnjip*, 439

In the formulaic systems presented above, one part in each phrase is constant (with only minor variations such as *tongjittal* instead of *tongjisŏttal*), and the other is variable. The variable parts, although not synonymous, have a common semantic element; in A I they are all associated with winter, in A II all with one of the two colder seasons, winter and autumn. Substitution systems such as A I and A II represent a typical form of formulaic system in Korean literature.

One might try to integrate into these systems other verses, which have no common constant element, or which have a different distribution over the half-line of common elements, or a common element which is shorter than in the systems A I and II. For example, can one take *changjang hail kin'gin nar-e* ("on the long, long days, the summer days that are so long")[36] as belonging to A II? If one wants to distinguish between different patterns of resemblance and different levels of abstraction, this is not advisable. Nevertheless, this half-line is certainly related to both A I and A II; first, it could be fitted in into a system that takes A II, 4 as its start. The pattern created would then be: constant-variable/constant-variable, against the constant/variable of A I and variable/constant of A II. In the second place, it could be integrated into a system of the simple variable/constant structure, together with, for instance, *ongnan'gan kin'gin nar-e* ("on the long, long days at the jewelled balustrade").[37] That system (A III) can be said to be related -although the common element is small: *kin'gin-* to all the half-lines of A II, which had as the stable element *kin'gin pam-e*, "in the long, long nights." If what they have directly in common is limited to two syllables, there is a further, semantic relation -albeit one of antithesis, of opposition- between the "days" and the "nights." The relation between A II and A III is a little more abstract than that between A I and A II, but there is good reason to connect A III to A II; in Korean traditional literature substitution or expansion on the basis of a relation of opposition is extremely common. It is a major device for creating new phrases.

For the sake of analysis it is recommendable to take separately formulaic systems with different patterns and those with different levels of abstraction. For a better comprehension of the texts or of the patterns of association of traditional Korean poetry, however, groups of related systems may fruitfully be studied together. To illustrate this, one may ask the question whether *changjang hail kin'gin nar-e* (translated literally: "on the long, long days, the long, long summer days"; one part is Sino-Korean, one pure Korean) has anything in common in its variable element with *ongnan'gan kin'gin nar-e*, "on the long, long days at the jewelled balustrade." At first sight the answer is no; what do summer days and a balustrade have in common? Still, there is a connection and this is discovered when one surveys the verses in related systems. In almost all cases, these verses are used to describe a lonely woman, abandoned by her lover or robbed of her husband by death. In traditional Korean poetry, it was usual to depict such a woman against the backdrop of the ever-changing seasons. The verse *changjang hail kin'gin nar-e* provides an example. Now, what about the jewelled balustrade? In which contexts is this term used? If one looks for verses in which a balustrade is mentioned one finds:

> *nan'gan-ŭi pigyŏ syŏsyŏ* ("reclining against the balustrade"); *Kasa sŏnjip*, 246

and

> *nan'gan-ŭl ŭiji haya* ("leaning on the balustrade"); *Kasa chŏnjip*,
> 439

Upon examination of the context of these verses, both turn out to be part of
a description of a lonely woman! Therefore, *ongnan'gan* and *changjang hail*
do have a common semantic element, even if it is not in the denotation of the
words, but in their connotation.

A more detailed discussion of such connections between formulaic systems
falls outside the scope of this chapter. I would only like to note that the study
of these connections may be a method: 1. to obtain a better understanding of
the meaning of literary works; 2. to form a judgement concerning the
creativity of the author (which may be in the way he arranges traditional
elements, rather than in the originality of his verses); 3. to distinguish whether
a work is in the mainstream of tradition or marginal to it. In the formulaic
systems presented above, one part in each phrase was stable (with minor
variations such as *tongjittal* instead of *tongjisŏttal* allowed), while the other
part was variable. The variable elements, although they carried different
meanings, had something in common semantically. Those in A I were associated with winter, those in A II with either one of the two colder seasons,
winter or autumn. Each half-formula brings with it certain expectations and
usually it is combined with another phrase so as to fulfil these expectations.
But there is no law that a phrase, which does not meet the usual expectations,
cannot be substituted. When this happens, there are two possibilities: this is
either done on purpose, in order to achieve a conscious literary effect, or
because the poet is not fully aware of the tradition. In both cases the poet
moves away from the core of the tradition. It is my impression that the *muga*,
which contain a great number of formulae and formulaic systems also found
in other genres, will show a lower degree of affinity with the mainstream of
the tradition, if their consistency according to the canon of Korean traditional
literature is studied with the help of this method. This is nothing but an
impression, however, and verification will have to wait for the completion of
basic studies concerning this canon.

More examples of formulaic systems and full references are given in
Appendix II.

Themes

The term "theme" refers to a unit with a certain content, not a certain form,
to "repeated incidents and descriptive passages in the songs."[38] Examples of

themes given by Lord are the council, the assembly of an army or of wedding guests, the dressing and arming of the hero, the return of the hero from captivity.[39]

Passages which may be regarded as themes in this sense are numerous in the *muga*, and -as with the formulae and formulaic systems- in many cases these themes are found in other genres, too. Sŏ Taesŏk, I think, has been the first to point out that themes, in the sense of the oral-formulaic school, coincide with the units which Kim Tonguk has christened "interlude songs" (*sabip kayo*).[40] Kim has painstakingly traced these interlude songs in *p'ansori*, noting that some (descriptions of dress, furniture, landscapes, food, etc.) could be traced to the *muga*. Whether this opinion can be accepted as it stands or has to be qualified, will be discussed in Chapter VIII. It is at least certain that several of the interlude songs in *p'ansori* and in novels derived from *p'ansori*, are also found in *muga*.

So the study of themes in traditional Korean literature began in the late fifties (as the study of interlude songs), and in recent years -under the influence of the oral-formulaic school- it has received renewed attention. Nevertheless, no recent work can match that of Kim Tonguk in volume and thoroughness. Is it really necessary, then, to discard the term interlude song (a more literal translation of the Korean would be "inserted song") in favour of theme? Why not retain the terminology of the scholar who made the first contribution in this field? Some arguments can be advanced for preferring the term theme.

The first argument in favour of the use of "theme" is that "interlude song" (as does -*a fortiori*- "inserted song") suggests that a ready-made, unchangeable unit is inserted in a story, while in fact there are, in different versions, variations of one interlude song (as Kim Tonguk himself points out). The second is that the interlude songs are not really "interludes", but often are essential elements in the stories. To appreciate this point, one should note, for instance, how in two traditional stories (*ko-sosŏl*), *Pae pijang chŏn* and *Ong Kojip chŏn*, the theme of the enumeration of different kinds of silk or other cloth is adapted and put to satirical and comical use.[41] A last argument in favour of the term "theme" is that it is wider in meaning than *sabip kayo* as described by Kim Tonguk. Interlude songs, although subject to variation, tend to have similar wording. Themes do not necessarily have more in common than one generalized idea.[42]

The most important themes will be enumerated below. A broad division is made between themes which are mainly catalogues on the one hand, and themes which are more descriptive or narrative on the other. References are given in Appendix III.

I. Catalogues

1.   Animals
2.   Birds (*sae t'aryŏng*)
3.   Books
4.   Fish
5.   Flowers (*kkot t'aryŏng, hwach'o t'aryŏng*)
6.   Food (*ŭmsik t'aryŏng*)
7.   Fruit
8.   Furniture
        This catalogue usually is part of the description of the interior of a
        house.
9.   Games
10.   Gods and ghosts
        Catalogues of gods and ghosts are the natural way to begin *muga* sung
        to call the gods to the place where a ritual is held. This is not the kind
        of catalogue that can easily be used in non-religious literature, but in
        Buddhist invocations and prayers, as well as in *mugyŏng*, such
        enumerations are very common.
11.   Government posts
12.   Medicine
13.   Mountains and rivers (*sanmaek p'uri, P'alto kangsan*)
        Cf. the theme of mountain passes (*kogae t'aryŏng*)
14.   Paintings
15.   Roll-call
        The most common form of roll-call outside the *muga* is that of
        kisaeng.
16.   Ships (*pae t'aryŏng*)
17.   Silks and other fabrics (*pidan t'aryŏng*)
18.   Temples (*chŏl t'aryŏng, chŏl kwanggyŏng p'uri*)
19.   Trees
20.   Vegetables (*namul t'aryŏng*)
        This is really a sub-theme of the theme "food", but it is listed separately
        because it appears in a very distinct form.
21.   Wine (*sul t'aryŏng*), sometimes including an enumeration of wine
        bottles.

Not all enumerations have the same form. Some, such as the catalogue of
books, are just lists without any adornment. In others, however, each item is
preceded by an ornamental phrase. In the latter case the enumeration takes the

form of a song which may be lifted out of the context of a *muga* or a story and sung separately (it is uncertain whether this is how the separate songs originated; a reverse development, from separate song to part of larger wholes, is possible). It is because certain themes take this particular form that the units we have identified with the themes of the oral-formulaic school, in Korean traditional literature have first been described as "interlude songs" and that recent authors use the term *t'aryŏng* (a kind of song) to refer to some themes.

The ornamental phrases preceding the items in the list could be styled epitheta ornantia, but one is tempted to use the Japanese term *makura kotoba*, because often, as with the *makura kotoba*, the connection between modifying phrase and noun is tenuous; similarity in sound, for instance, suffices. An example from a *namul t'aryŏng*:[43]

>   If you go up: early ferns,
>   If you come down: late ferns.

In the translation any connection has disappeared. In Korean, there is an acoustic link:

>   *olla kamyŏn ol kosari-go*
>   *naeryŏ omyŏn nŭt kosari*

Something similar happens in the following line.[44]

>   One penny, two pennies, "shilling" greens
>   *han p'un tu p'un ton-namul*

"*Ton-namul*" is here translated as "shilling greens" to retain the association, which, however, is based on a false etymology: this "*ton*" does not refer to money, but is a corruption of *tol*: "stone." The plant referred to is the *sedum sarmentosum*: *tol namul*.

II. Other Themes
(references in Appendix III)

1.   Auspicious geomantic location (*myŏngdang p'uri*)
Sometimes the relation between the foundation of a dynasty and the location of its capital is emphasized - as a kind of prelude to the description of an auspicious house site. In this way the theme is often connected to passages about the history of ancient Chinese and Korean states, in particular about the foundation of these states (*ch'iguk chapki*). These historical passages, in their turn, often are preceded by the theme of the Creation of Heaven and Earth.
This theme often incorporates that of the Mountains and Rivers (Catalogues, 14).

2.   A beautiful woman

3.   A child growing up
      In narratives a child is often born to parents of a rather advanced age,
      who have prayed to the Buddha or the gods for the blessing of a child
      (Theme 16). When the child is born, it is usually described as very
      handsome and intelligent. Within a few years it learns to read -if it is
      a boy- and in this place the catalogue of books may be inserted. The
      growing up of a child may also be used in a prayer to Samsin, who is
      asked that the children will grow fast and be without illness.
         [Please grant that the children will grow
         fast] as a cucumber swells, as the moon swells
         as an egg-plant swells, as a lotus bud swells,
         [without difficulty, placidly]
         As water in a flat bowl,
         [prettily] as flowers in a flower pot.[45]

4.   Complaint about misfortune (*sinse t'aryŏng, chat'an ka*)

5.   Creation of Heaven and Earth
      Cf. Other Themes 1.

6.   Dress
      This theme can easily be sub-divided according to the various persons
      who wear the particular garments: women, actors, monks, et cetera.
      In most cases the elegance and beauty of the dress is stressed, but a
      variation is the description of someone in rags and tatters.

7.   Examination scene
      The examination scene proper may be followed by a description of the
      festivities after passing the examination (for instance, in *Hanyang ka*,
      a poem about the capital) or by a description of the successful
      candidate on his thriumphant return home.

8.   Explanation of Chinese characters
      A variation is the explanation of the Korean alphabet, *han'gŭl*.

9.   Itinerary (*nojŏnggi*)

10.   Landscape
      Usually a beautiful landscape. Typical is the description of the eight
      sights of the region of the Hsiao and Hsiang Rivers in China (*Sosang*

p'algyŏng), but one also comes across the Eight Sights of the Western Provinces (North-West Korea) and the Eight Sights Beyond the Pass (the Korean East Coast region). Cf. Ch. VII.

Kim Tonguk assumes that the origin of the landscape descriptions in the novel *Namwŏn kosa* is in the passages about the famous mountains in the Eight Provinces (Korea) in the *muga*.[46] This can only be true if one thinks of "origin" as "origin of the theme"; the passage in *Namwŏn kosa* is so full of Sino-Korean that in this form it is most unlikely to have originated in the *muga*. There is no way to verify or disprove the proposition that the theme of the beautiful landscape in abstracto first was used in the *muga*.

This theme is close to that of the Mountains and Rivers (Catalogues, 13) and that of the Auspicious Geomantic Location (Other Themes, 1).

11.   Lullaby (*sarang ka*)

A lullaby is part of almost all versions of the story of Sim Ch'ŏng, whether novel, *p'ansori* or *muga*. Cf. Chapter VII.

This *sarang ka* should not be confused with the "love songs" sung by Ch'unhyang and Yi Mongnyong or Pyŏn Kangsoe and his lascivious spouse!

12.   Magistrate's procession

13.   Monk (*chung t'aryŏng*)

The typical monk in the *muga* and vernacular narratives is on his way to collect alms from devout laymen. The description of the attire of such a monk, however, is also used for Buddhist figures in general. Śākyamuni, too, is portrayed as a mendicant monk in *muga*. When a monk comes to a house, people ask him why he has come, what kind of monk he is, or what kind of special skills he possesses (divination, physiognomy etc.). The predictions made by monks with divinatory talents have an important narrative function in creating suspense; in these stories a prediction is always true, but the suspense is: how will it be realized in spite of efforts to thwart fate? In several *muga*, especially of the Tanggŭm-aegi type,[47] a monk miraculously fathers children who are to become deities. It is because of the various stereotyped aspects of the monk that it makes sense to treat his appearance as a separate theme, instead of dealing with descriptions of his attire as merely a part of the theme of dress.

14.   Pall-bearers' song (*hyangdu ka, sangyŏ sori*)
        Pall-bearers' songs are a separate class of folk-songs, of which
        numerous examples have been collected in Kim Sŏngbae, *Hyangdu ka*
        . Sŏngjo ka.[48]
        The pall-bearers' song can be inserted whenever someone dies in a
        narrative *muga*, but is also well-suited to use as one of the songs for
        the ancestors (*chosang*).
        The Korean pall-bearers' song may be compared with an old Chinese
        bearers' song -probably 3rd c. B.C.- which contains a line that often
        returns in Korean bearers' songs: "Once a man is dead and gone, when
        will he come back?"[49]

15.   Parting (*ibyŏl ka*)
        The *ibyŏl ka* in *Namwŏn kosa* and *Pae pijang chŏn* belong to scenes in
        which lovers are parted. In one *muga* it is part of a song for the
        deceased, but from the wording it is obvious that this parting song, too,
        originally referred to the separation of lovers. It is also full of
        references to Chinese history, as are the other two *ibyŏl ka*. There is
        therefore good reason to assume that this particular form of the theme
        of parting (which as a theme in general is of course universal and
        consequently of little use in tracing the relations between works and
        genres) was not part of the tradition of the *mudang*.

16.   Prayers for a child
        An elderly couple is childless and decides, as a last resort, to pray to
        the gods and perform all kinds of pious acts.
        This is an extremely common theme for *ko-sosŏl* to begin with.

17.   Pregnancy/formation of the child in the womb
        Several sub-themes can be distinguished: a dream in which the
        conception is announced (extremely common in *ko-sosŏl*, e.g., in *Sim
        Ch'ŏng chŏn, Hong Kiltong chŏn* and *Ong Kojip chŏn*, and also
        frequently found in *muga*), a list of precepts to be followed by the
        pregnant woman, characteristic physical complaints of the expectant
        mother (*iptŏt t'aryŏng*), and last but not least, a month-by-month
        description of the development of the foetus in the womb. The latter
        sub-theme is especially prominent in the *muga*, perhaps because it is at
        the same time an example of amplification on the basis of a row of
        numbers. It is not confined to the *muga*, however. It is also found in
        kasa. This sub-theme is similar to the month-by-month description of
        pregnancy in the *Tongŭi pogam* (Precious Mirror of Eastern Medicine,

Vol. I, 72), a work written in Chinese. It might also be compared with some Chinese folk-songs about the ten months of pregnancy.[50]

18.   Prognostication by dreams
Dreams in traditional narratives always have a meaning, even though it may take a specialist to understand what a dream foretells. In some dreams the dreamer receives instruction from a supernatural being.

19.   Sawing song (*t'opchil norae*)
Probably this was first a simple work song. Its introduction into the *muga* may be rather recent; in *KTG* I, 292, it is Hŭngbu, the protagonist of the *p'ansori* play *Pak t'aryŏng*, who wields the saw!

The list presented above is by no means exhaustive; neither have all the sources where a theme can be found, been listed. A whole category which has been omitted, although Sŏ Taesŏk includes it among the interlude songs, is that of Buddhist liturgical texts in Chinese (pronounced in the Korean manner).[51] These are, it is true, frequently inserted in the *muga* and no discussion of the way in which the *muga* are composed would be complete without mentioning them, but they are different from the themes listed above in several respects: the language (Chinese), the fixedness of the texts, and the fact that they appear in the *muga* as Buddhist liturgical texts. The importance of themes in the composition of traditional literature lies precisely in the fact that they are so adaptable: questions addressed to a lover in one text may in another text become questions addressed to an ancestor (*ibyŏl ka*), a list of silks may do service as a list of goods which the believers hope to receive through the blessings of the gods (in Sŏngju *muga*), or it may be an illustration of the amorous foolishness of the man who gives all these things to a scheming female (*Pae pijang chŏn*). Seen as an element of composition, the Buddhist interlude songs have a smaller range of usefulness than such themes.

Parallelism

Parallelism is a form of repetition (either syntactic or semantic), and as such, has something in common with formulae and formulaic systems, which are based on complete or partial repetition. It may be regarded as a kind of formulaic pattern.

In traditional Korean literature, parallelism is of importance in two ways. First, there is the parallelism of the members of formulaic systems, secondly, there is the parallelism between lines or half-lines of one text. The former is a device to build a formulaic line or half-line, the latter a device to construct a poem or a song.[52]

Parallelism within one text is frequently encountered in the *muga*, as well as in other genres. One author asserts that in the *muga* parallelism is used as a means to make the songs longer,[53] but this is certainly not the only function of parallelism in Korean shaman songs. Parallelism, which is often found in folk literature, aids improvisation as well as memorization, and has, of course, a rhetoric effect. If one asks why the *mudang* use parallelism in their songs, one should also be aware of the fact that in some cases the *mudang* borrowed from folk-songs or literary works that already contained it.

Parallelism in the *muga* is frequent, but it is not obligatory as it is, for instance, in the songs of the Indian Toda where each sentence occurs in a paired distribution with another sentence.[54] Nevertheless, the tendency to use parallel sentences is very strong, as appears from the first twenty-four half-lines of a *muga* for the Ancestors.[55] Of these twenty-four hemistichs, ten are parallel to adjoining half-lines and five to half-lines that are one half-line removed (if the analysis were made in full lines, they would be in adjoining lines), two half-lines, which are not parallel to other half-lines, have internal parallelism, and, finally, five half-lines have parallels at some distance elsewhere in the song. Of these five half-lines, one has also an adjoining parallel. Altogether there are only three half-lines out of twenty-four that in no way share in the parallelism.

The analysis was carried out in terms of half-lines, although there also were parallelisms on the level of the line and that of the quarter-line. The half-line was chosen, because at that level parallelism is most marked. Many parallels are only between half-lines, not between whole lines and often a division into lines would leave one parallel half-line hanging loose, as in the following example:[56]

> *param-i pura t'aep'ung pada-na*
> *pi-ga wasŏ ujung pada-na*
> *nun-i wasŏ sŏlchung pada-na*
> "Whether it is a stormy sea when the wind blows,
> whether it is a pluvial sea when it rains,
> whether it is a nival sea when it snows"[57]

In the following paragraphs the most important parallelistic phenomena will be illustrated with examples. Additional illustrations can be found in the *muga* translations of Chapters VIII and IX.

Common forms of parallelism

Parallelism has been described as "a type of repetition ..... in which one element is changed, the other ..... remaining constant."[58] In some cases, the constant element is semantic in nature, for instance, when the two halves of a formula are roughly or exactly synonymous, as so often happens.

> *yennal put' ŏ chago irae-ro*[59]
> "Since the days of the past, from olden times"
> *hae-ga chyŏsŏ ilmol hanŭnde*[60]
> "The sun set, the sun sank down"

Semantic parallelism of this kind is found in Korean in even smaller units, some of which are also used in ordinary speech.

> Hanyang *sŏul*, "Hanyang, the capital"[61]
> *sara saengjŏn-e*, "while living, during one's lifetime"[62]
> *p'alto yadŭpto-e*, "in the Eight Provinces (bis)"[63]

Typical of this kind of parallelism is the use of Sino-Korean in one part and of pure Korean in the other part.

In many cases the constant element is more syntactic than semantic in character, although frequently some semantic element is retained. In syntactically parallel sentences, one often finds a common basic idea used to structure these lines. Of this kind of parallelism several kinds can be distinguished.

I

Often the idea which is at the basis of two parallel verses is a binary semantic opposition: high/low, heaven/earth, night/day, front/ back, sweet/sour, water/fire, big/small, man/woman, etc.[64]

> Preparing sour wine,
> Preparing sweet cakes[65]

Here syntactic parallelism is combined with semantic antithesis.

> When it is night, the moon is bright,
> When it is day, the water is clear.[66]

> Looking up, ten-thousand gorges and thousand peaks,
> Looking down, piled up boulders and steep cliffs.[67]

> Living under water,
> Floating on the water.[68]

The high/low opposition is very common. Cf. *Sijo sajŏn*, Nos. 771 and 1135.

> At ebb tide playing in the Eastern Sea,
> At high tide entering the Western Sea.[69]

Here one sees a double opposition, ebb tide/high tide, and East/West, just as in a *sijo* by Yun Sŏndo (1587-1671): *Sijo sajŏn*, No. 894.

To demonstrate that parallelism based on binary oppositions is not a characteristic of the *muga* alone, it is sufficient to count the number of such parallelisms in the celebrated *sijo*-cycle *The Fisherman's Calender* by Yun Sŏndo, where they are used fifteen times in forty poems. One poem of an even earlier period, *Sindo ka*, "The Song of the New Capital", by Chŏng Tojŏn (?-1398) uses parallelism based on the front/back opposition.[70]

> In front, there is the Han River,
> At the back, there is Samgak Mountain.

Another example:[71]

> (Her) father who had gone to stay under heaven,   AX
> (Her) mother who had gone to stay under the earth   ax

This again combines two fundamental oppositions: father/mother, and heaven/earth. Pairs of antonyms are represented schematically by A and a, and X and x.

> Even if the first part was good,   AX
> The last part was bad.   ax
> Even if the last part was good,   aX
> The first part was bad.[72]   Ax
>
> In the East, entering,   AX
> In the West, going out,   ax
> In the West, entering,   aX
> In the East, going out[73]   Ax

These two examples are from one *muga*. Therefore, the half-lines of each are not only parallel to other half-lines in the same fragment, but the pattern of their parallelism is also exactly repeated, as can be seen in the schematic representation. Here one sees the use of a particular form of parallelism as a formulaic pattern structuring more than one part of a *muga*.

II
Special uses of antithetical parallelism

> Bestowing [long] life on your way in,
> Bestowing happiness on your way out,
> Blessing them with boundless bliss[74]

This is a specimen of a special parallelistic phenomenon, which in Chinese is called *hu-wen*, "reciprocal phrasing."[75] These lines do not mean that long life is only given on the way in and happiness on the way out. They rather ask for happiness and long life at all times, whenever the house is entered and whenever the house is left. One might compare this phenomenon with bisyllabic Sino-Korean compounds such as *changdan*, which literally means "long" and "short", but has the generalized meaning of "rhythm/measure/(relative) length."

Another example of reciprocal phrasing in the *muga* is the following:[76]

> Bestowing long life on infant sons,
> Bestowing happiness on infant daughters

Parallelism is sometimes combined with a feature that is seen in two lines from the *Siyong hyangak po.*[77]

> "Great Country" is also "Small Country",   Aa
> "Small Country" is also "Great Country".   aA

"Great Country" in these paradoxical lines refers to a god, Taeguk. The paradox may be seen as giving expression to the mysterious nature of the deity. Parallelism and antithesis are often found in other genres of vernacular literature (as they are, of course in Korean poetry and prose in Chinese), but this use of antithetical parallelism to express a paradox seems to be typical of the *muga*. From a more formal point of view, these half-lines show a chiastic pattern, which is also found in modern *muga*.

> Whether one buys new timber for an old house,   Aa
> Whether one buys old timber for a new house[78]   aA

The next example strongly suggests that this chiastic pattern is used for its own sake only.[79]

> With the water of the upper rice fields
> they irrigated the lower rice fields,
> With the water of the lower rice fields
> they irrigated the upper rice fields.

These examples may also be regarded as instances of *Kettenbau* (or "terrace lines"), a term used when a new line begins with a repetition of the word that was used last in the preceding line.[80]

If one sees that the formal characteristics of the half-lines from the *Siyong hyangak po* quoted above are often used in modern *muga* and that this pattern is sometimes used to achieve a rhetorical effect rather than to express a fact, it becomes easier to imagine how these paradoxical lines came into being. Their purpose may indeed be to emphasize the mysteriousness of the deity, but if one assumes that the chiastic pattern was already in common use at the time when the *Siyong hyangak po* was compiled, it becomes less of a mystery how the author of this song came to express this idea the way he did.

III

Sometimes there is not a binary, but a tripartite opposition:

> In upper Songdang Village: Kŭmbaekchu,
> In middle Songdang Village: Saemyŏngju,
> In lower Songdang Village: Sorosŏch'ŏnguk paramun[81]

A poetic formulaic pattern may be stronger than reality or "theology." Chang Chugŭn has pointed out with regard to a *muga* recorded by him, which contains these same lines, that the verses are not in accordance with the facts; there are, in fact, three villages called Songdang, but in the middle one (Sae-Songdang), no deity named Saemyŏngju is worshipped.[82] Note the alliteration between the name of the village and the name of the deity in the second line.

One brief *muga* from Cheju Island is almost completely built on a framework of threes. It speaks of upper, middle and lower fishermen, of upper, middle and lower boats, of upper, middle and lower diving girls and of upper, middle and lower clients of the *mudang*.[83] Perhaps upper, middle and lower here, too, refers to three sub-divisions of a village, but one should not exclude the possibility that this song only follows a conventional pattern and is not related to factual realities.

IV

Not only binary oppositions,or tripartite divisions can be used as a framework
for parallelism. Any fixed set, whether it has four, five or more members, will
do: points of the compass (four or five, depending whether the centre is
included), the Confucian Five Bonds, the Eight Provinces of Old Korea, a row
of numbers, the four seasons or the twelve months of the year. In the
following fragment this framework is the concept of the Confucian Five
Bonds (*oryun*).[84]

> (Prayer to Samsin)
> [Please grant that the children]
> will be loyal servants to the state,
> be filial sons to their parents,
> love their brothers,
> live in harmony with their relatives,
> be true to their friends.

In this fragment the relationship with the relatives, which is not part of the
Five Bonds, is substituted for that between husband and wife, which, in view
of the age of the children for whom blessings are asked, is a logical
adaptation.[85]

Below the cardinal points of the compass are used as a frame:[86]

> Chickens of the East, chickens of the South,
> Chickens of the West, chickens of the North,
> You, cluck-cluck chickens!

The directions of the compass are used in this manner in one of the oldest
remaining narrative texts in Korean, the *Wŏrin sŏkpo* (a description of the life
of the Buddha in several reincarnations, dating from 1459), in the story of
Prince Allakkuk[87], but also in Korean Buddhist liturgical texts in Chinese.[88]
They are frequently mentioned in association with the colours that correspond
-according to a tradition accepted from China- with the primary points of the
compass.

> In the East, the Blue-Emperor-Divine-General,
> In the South, the Red-Emperor-Divine-General,
> In the West, the White-Emperor-Divine-General,
> In the North, the Black-Emperor-Divine-General[89]

In some of the *muga* in which the points of the compass provide the framework for parallelism, this literary pattern shows itself capable of creating deities. The *mudang* venerate Ch'ilsŏng, literally the "Seven Stars", the brightest stars of the constellation Ursa Major (cf. Ch. I). In full, these stars are called Puktu Ch'ilsŏng, the "Seven Stars of the Northern Peck." The presence of *puk* (North) in Puktu Ch'ilsŏng is sufficient to trigger off a complete parallelistic row: Tongdu Ch'ilsŏng, Namdu Ch'ilsŏng, Sŏdu Ch'ilsŏng, Puktu Ch'ilsŏng (*tong*, *nam* and *sŏ* mean East, South and West).[90] Tongdu Ch'ilsŏng and Sŏdu Ch'ilsŏng are non-existent. There is a constellation called Namdu (the "Southern Dipper"), but it has six stars not seven. "Namdu" is also used as another name for Puktu (strange as it may sound). Our only conclusion can be that three new deities enter the pantheon thanks to the literary convention of parallelistic expansion on the basis of the four cardinal points of the compass.

The following lines combine the points of the compass, not with the Five Colours, but with a row of numbers.[91]

> The Eastern granary is filled with
> one thousand one hundred and eleven sacks,
> The Southern granary is filled with
> two thousand two hundred and twelve sacks,
> The Western granary is filled with
> three thousand three hundred and thirty three sacks,
> The Northern granary is filled with
> four thousand four hundred and forty four sacks.[92]

An example of parallelism based on a numerical row is seen in a *kut* for the Sonnim (the gods of smallpox), where the unfortunate son of impious parents has to suffer for the lack of hospitality of his father and mother.[93] A henchman of the Sonnim attacks him with a sledgehammer.

> When he hit him once
> The high ceiling lowered.
> When he hit him twice,
> The low ceiling heightened.

In another *Sonnim kut*, the successive stages of the illness are described: the first and the second day the patient feels ill, the third and the fourth day the pocks appear, on the fifth and the sixth day the black scabs fall off, etc.[94] Parallelism based on a numerical row also may accompany the theme of the growing up of a child. The infant is described as walking at one, learning to speak at two, learning to write at three, learning good manners at five.[95] In one *muga*, there is yet another variation on this use of the numerical row. All possible forms of infantile naughtiness are enumerated: one year old the baby hits her mother's breast, two years old she pulls her father's beard, three years old she spills grain, and so on until the age of nine.[96]

Such frameworks as the points of the compass and rows of numbers may be viewed in several ways. One could say that they are aids to oral composition in the orthodox sense. The more standard, traditionalized associations such a frame has (as, for instance, the association of certain colours with certain points of the compass), the easier it will be to improvise on given patterns. But such frames may also be thought of as aids to memorization. Irrespective of the fact whether a text is orally composed or memorized, the frames have a literary effect: they serve as foils to variations, which would never stand out so clearly without the background of the traditional frame.

Occasionally the frameworks described above are more than just a device to create parallelism between lines; in some instances they are a peg for whole themes. A clear example is the theme of the "Paintings of the Four Walls", found in *Hwangje p'uri* (a *muga* for the god Sŏngju, translated in Chapter VIII) as well as in *ko-sosŏl* such as *Ch'unhyang chŏn*; this is constructed on the framework provided by the cardinal points of the compass.

V

There are still other frames for parallelism. Sometimes it is based on a series of questions: is it A, is it B, is it C?[97] In Chapter IV a passage from the *p'ansori* libretto *Ch'unhyang ka* was quoted, in which she wondered when her lover would return. These lines are a good illustration of the process of expansion by parallelistic elaboration. Similar in structure is a fragment of an East Coast *muga* for the dead, in which the singer repeatedly asks why the deceased cannot come to this world anymore.[98] Is it because the water is too deep, because of illness, because his horse is lame, or because there is too much snow? Each of these reasons for not coming is preceded by a phrase which, in contrast to the questions themselves, is almost completely in Sino-Korean. Each full line, therefore, consists of a Sino-Korean half-line, followed by a purely Korean half-line: a typical pattern. One of the introductory phrases is from a poem by T'ao Ch'ien or T'ao Yüan-ming, 365-427) and is found also in a *sijo*, with a similar function![99] This poem is addressed to an absent lover: "Did you not come because there is too much water, spring water having filled all the pools?", followed by a second line: "Did you not come because the mountains are too high, summer clouds so numerous around the strangely shaped peaks?"[100]

The hero of a *muga* for Sŏngju, who lives in exile on an uninhabited island, sees a ship approaching.[101] Is it a ship that passes by, is it a trading ship, is it a ship with military supplies, is it a ferry, is it Li Po's ship loaded with wind and moon (poetry), is it the boat in which Yen Tzu-ling[102] sat angling, is it the boat in which Su Tung-p'o (1037-1101) enjoyed the scenery of the Red Cliffs, and many more questions he asks himself. Even in the context of a narrative *muga* that is as realistic as the average fairy tale, this is not assumed to be a realistic description of the thoughts of the protagonist; it is a formal game: how many fanciful elaborations can one make by offering diverse and complicated suggestions for the answer to one simple question, "What kind of ship is that?"[103]

Another parallelistic sequence consists of a series of negative answers to a question: "What is this? It is not A, it is not B, it is C."[104] Such negative descriptions do not necessarily begin with an explicit question. In *Sim Ch'ŏng chŏn* a monk approaches:[105]

> It was not Sŏngjini,
> Who played with Eight Heavenly Maidens
> On a stone bridge in the spring wind.
> It was not Samyŏngdang,
> Whose shaven head indicated that he had escaped the dusty world,
> But whose remaining beard showed him to be a real man.
> A monk from the Dream Cloud Temple
> Was on his way to his almsgivers.

Sŏngjini is the hero of the novel *Kuunmong*. Samyŏngdang (1544-1610) is a historical figure, a monk who, like Sŏsan Taesa (1520-1604) played a leading role in the resistance against the Hideyoshi invasions.

Similar is the following passage in a *muga* for Sŏngju.[106]

> A monk comes down!
> It was not a monk who frequents the houses of laymen to beg,
> Clanging a small gong
> It was a monk collecting alms, from the Dream Cloud Temple
> at Samgak Mountain near Seoul.[107]

Related, too, is the frame which consists of repeated suggestions and rejections.[108]

When you say, "Let's go over the mountains",
We cannot go because the wind is too strong.
When you say "let's go along the path through the gorge,
We cannot go because it is too heavy for us.

Sin Chaehyo, 542-543, has a similar pattern.

Parallelism as the basis of fanciful elaboration
Above an example was given of new deities engendered by a parallelistic pattern. In other instances parallelistic patterns are used in a kind of wordplay, in lines which are not at all needed to provide information, and whose only purpose is the fanciful application of the pattern.[109]

Calling the front (*ap*)-boatman at the Yalu (Ap-nok) River
Calling the back (*twi*)-boatman at the Twinnok River

Here parallelism is based on the false etymology of *ap* in the Korean name of the Yalu River: Ap-nok (which according to McCune-Reischauer romanization should be spelt: Amnok). There is, of course, no Twinnok River.
Imaginative elaboration of a parallelistic pattern is also seen in the following lines.[110]

[Please grant that]
Water luck comes flowing in,
Snake luck comes crawling in,
Weasel luck comes jumping in,
Human luck comes walking in.[111]

Introductory phrases to parallel lines
Many parallelistic passages are introduced by an isolated sentence, a line that does not parallel any other line. One example is the line that introduces the description of the monk cited above: "A monk comes down!" The following lines, which, incidentally, contradict a popular Christian conception, contain another example.[112]

When you want to go to the world of Paradise,
If you take the narrow road,
It is the road to Hell,
If you take the wide road,

It is the road to Paradise.

Alliteration and rhyme

In the whole of Korean traditional poetry rhyme and alliteration are optional; their use is never obligatory as it is in certain poetic genres elsewhere. Nevertheless, they are used in Korea -especially alliteration- and to good effect, as the following poem by Yun Sŏndo shows.[113]

> *moeh-ăn kilgo kilgo, mur-ŭn mŏlgo mŏlgo*
> *ŏbŏi kŭrin ttŭd-ŭn mank'o mank'o hago hago*
> *ŏdŭisyŏ oe kirŏgi-năn ulgo ulgo kanăni*

> Long, long are the mountain ranges,
> Broad, broad are the waters.
> Great, great, strong, strong
> Is my longing for my parents.
> Somewhere a lone goose flies,
> Crying, crying.

An example of rhyme in the *muga* is *nanari tadari pinŭn mar-i* ("the prayers she said day after day, month after month").[114] Alliteration is seen in *tong-e tongsan ttŭnŭn hae-ga* ("the sun which rises over the Eastern hill")[115] and *Tongdusan-e Tongduch'ŏn-e Tongsuja-rŭl ch'aja kara* ("Go and look for Tongsuja at Tongdu Mountain in Tongduch'ŏn!").[116]

Variations through rhyme
Sometimes new words are created through making a rhymed variant of an existing word. Such a word is always used in conjunction with the existing word. E.g., *injŏng sajŏng*; *injŏng*, which means "human feelings/charity/-benevolence", in the *muga* stands for money given to the gods, especially the money offered to the Messengers of the Underworld who have come to escort a dead person. *Sajŏng* is a variation created with the help of rhyme.[117] Hyŏn Yongjun calls such phrases *choun'gu*, "rhyming phrases."[118]

The process of the formation of such phrases is similar to that of the exclamation *ŏlssigu chŏlssigu* (used to express enthusiasm) and some onomatopoetic expressions used in daily speech: *ŏppak chappak* ("disorderly"), *ŏjŏng pŏjong* ("loiteringly"), *ulgŭt pulgŭt* ("many-coloured"), et cetera.

Wordplay

Some examples of wordplay have already been given. In another kind of wordplay a row of numbers is skillfully inserted into succeeding lines. These numbers are not necessarily all real numbers, some may be just homophones which because of the context of the other numbers acquire an extra meaning as numerals. On the East Coast such wordplay is found in an enumeration of famous warriors in the *Kunung kut*.[119] This type of wordplay is common in *p'ansori*. There is an example in Sin Chaehyo's *Pyŏn Kangsoe ka* in the list of medicines.[120] A tour de force in this respect is Sin's "Song of the Ten Steps", *Sippo ka*; in the lines corresponding to each step, the corresponding number is used in almost every half-line. Elaboration to this degree of complexity is perhaps only possible when a literate author sits down to "improve" on a conventional theme.[121] The mask-dance dramas, too, contain examples of this kind of pun,[122] as do folk-songs.[123]

Some examples of wordplay based on similarity in sound were pointed out earlier. Here is another.[124]

> This time, what kind of time was it?
> When on the oak tree (*ttŏkkal-namu*) grew ricecakes (*ttŏk*),
> On the bushclover (*ssari-namu*) grew rice (*ssal*),
> On the heads of horses grew horns,
> On the heads of cows grew manes,
> When flying birds and crawling animals could speak
> And Man could not: that time it was.

This, as a whole, is an interesting passage which shows characteristic features of traditional Korean literature not only in its wordplay. It begins with an isolated question, while the following lines, two by two, run parallel to each other. In Korean, lines two and three and lines four, five and six rhyme. The traditional topos used in this fragment is that of "impossible things."

Redundancy as a form of wordplay
In many half-formulae, formulae and whole lines -as has been indicated before- it can be observed that part of a phrase is semantically redundant; it is used *metri causa* or for its literary effect. A particularly striking example of redundancy is the way in which numbers are often treated. The *mudang* does not say simply: "forty-nine days", but "seven [times] seven, nine-and-forty, forty-nine days" (in Korean, instead of *sasipku il*: *ch'ilch'il sasipku, mahŭn-ahŭre*; *ch'ilch'il* and *sasipku* are Sino-Korean, *mahŭn-ahŭre* is pure Korean).[125] Here redundancy is the result of two things. First the number forty-nine is presented in two ways: in the form of a multiplication and as a

simple number, and second, it is given in pure Korean and in Sino-Korean. Both procedures may be used separately. In *sawŏl ch'o-yŏdŭrennal ch'o-p'ail* redundancy is the result of the combined use of Sino-Korean and pure Korean (*sawŏl ch'o-p'ail*, or even *ch'o-p'ail* -the eighth day of the Fourth Month, the Buddha's birthday- would have been sufficient). In *sŏktal yŏrhŭl paegil* ("three months and ten days, a hundred days"), the same thing is described in two different ways.

The same thing may even be described in three different ways: "one year, twelve months, three-hundred-and-sixty days."[126]

Sometimes *mudang* enumerate the preceding numerals before they mention the one they need: "When she became one, two, three, four, five, six, seven years old....."[127] An old *mudang* whom I met in Seoul, did this even in ordinary speech. When asked her age, she replied: "Do you want to know how old I am? I'm twenty, thirty, forty, fifty, sixty, seventy years old." This can be rhetorically effective, a way to stress the passing of time, but is also used gratuitously.

Narrative style

In narrative *muga* such as the *ponp'uri* the technique of narration is characterized by repetitions and indirectness. Remarkable are also certain repeatedly used "frames."

One instance of repetition is found in the story of Pari kongju: seven times the Queen becomes pregnant and seven times her physical condition and the development of the foetus are described in the same words.[128] Incremental repetition is combined with recapitulation in the following lines:[129]

> In one year one,
> In one year one,
> In one year one,
> In three years she bore three [children].
> Then, when -each year one-
> She had born three [children]
> ....

One idea may be repeated in different words:

> If you would take the life of Tanggom-agi,
> Cut her throat and kill her,[130]
> ....

Indirectness in narration is found when basically simple information is put
in the form of a question and answer.

> Whose house is this?
> It is the house of An-ssi puin.[131]

> Where is the world of Paradise?
> The world of Paradise is outside the front gate.
> Where is the road to the Yellow Springs (= the Underworld)?
> The road to the Yellow Springs is in front of your door,
>   is it not?[132]

These lines are from a *muga*, but closely resemble lines found in the pall-
bearers' songs (*hyangdu ka*).

In the opening lines of narrative *muga*, the question is often asked where
the origin of a deity is.

> Where is the origin of the Ancestors?
> The origin of the Ancestors
> is in the Inner Suri Mountains, is it not?[133]

Commonly used interrogative phrases are: *ttae-nŭn mach'um onŭ ttae-nya*
("As for the time, what time did it happen to be?") and *i ttae-nŭn ŏnŭ ttae-nya*
("At that time, what time was it?").[134] The use of such phrases may be
regarded as typical of the "story-teller's style" in which the narrator places
himself emphatically between the audience and the protagonists of the story.
Another example of story-teller's style is the phrase: "Look what he does!"
This is common in *p'ansori*, too. For examples, see the translations in
Chapters VIII and IX.[135]

The use of rhetorical questions also may be regarded as belonging to the
category of devices for indirect narration.[136]

Several typical "frames" for sentences in the *muga* also contain elements
of indirectness.
1. If you look at ...., (you see) .....[137]
   This frame is often used as the introduction to a catalogue.
2. A is good, but what about B?[138]
3. A is good, but B is even better.[139]
4. If there is A, will there not be B, too?[140]
   "If he drinks wine, won't there be anything to eat with it?"
5. A is X, and B is X, too, (C is X, too).[141]

"The Dragon Palace of the Eastern Sea is a dragon palace, the Dragon Palace of the Western Sea is a dragon palace, too"

Concluding Remarks

In this chapter the traditional, formal patterns of the *muga* have been delineated. Not only are many formulaic patterns discernible in the *muga*, it is obvious that the songs of the *mudang* are highly "form-conscious" literature; many passages should be understood, first of all, as a play on the traditional forms of Korean poetry, as a playing with language. Attention is focussed on verbal games, rather than on the transfer of information or the expression of a wish. Form and content cannot be completely separated, but in a form of literature such as the *muga* one would be led astray if one were to assume that each verbal variation is an attempt to express an idea. More specifically, variations in the text of the *muga* do not necessarily express variations in theological conceptions. A study of the style of the *muga*, therefore, is needed to unravel what is literary variation and what expression of a (religious) concept.

A further purpose of the description of the formal patterns of the *muga* was to discover, whether on this level, links could be found between the shaman songs and other forms of vernacular literature. These links can be found in great abundance and intimate contacts between various genres are therefore likely to have existed. This is not to say that all these genres have exactly the same formal patterns. To answer the question to what extent they overlap, more detailed study is necessary of a quantitative nature. This chapter only presents a survey, without going into the distinctions between *muga* from different regions and different *mudang*, or between, for instance, *kasa* or *sijo* from different ages and different authors. It has been demonstrated, I think, that there are certain patterns which can be found in the *muga* from the whole of Korea, but this does not mean that they are everywhere used to the same degree. One impression I have formed, for instance, is that the East coast *muga* have more patterns in common with *p'ansori* than the *muga* of other parts of the country. How this should be interpreted is another matter; I incline to the opinion that it is due to the influence *p'ansori* has exerted on the East Coast *muga*, not to the influence of the *muga* on *p'ansori*.

By means of a number of examples it has been demonstrated that the parallelistic phenomena enumerated above, are not unique to the *muga*. My general impression, however, is that the *muga* make greater use of these devices and often use them in a more mechanical way than other genres. The use of parallelism could be explained as a characteristic inherited from older

Korean folk poetry, or as a practical expedient facilitating (oral) composition or memorization. There is no need to explain the use of parallelism and antithesis as due to influences from classical Chinese poetry, important as these terms may be there. From the examples of Korean parallelism given above, it will be clear that it is often more explicit than the parallelism in Chinese poems. Some influence from Chinese poetry there may well have been, but parallelism of the kind found in Korea is seen in many regions all over the world, especially in "folk poetry" (or oral poetry in the broader sense of the word). There is therefore no need to suspect Chinese influence in this matter, even though the phrases used to fill parallelistic patterns may be of clearly Chinese origin.[142]

A remarkable phenomenon, which can be observed on many different levels, is the use made of the two registers of the Korean language: the purely native forms and the Sino-Korean forms. Not only are the two used together, the juxtaposition of the two is one of the major devices whereby the peculiar diction of the traditional literary language is created. Inasmuch as the *muga* share that diction -which cannot have been the product of the *mudang* milieu alone- they cannot antedate the formation of this traditional language. The *muga* of earlier times must have been quite different in form, if not in substance.

VI   The *Muga* and Other Forms of Traditional Literature

Time and again, in studies of Korean literary history, the *muga* are mentioned as having influenced other genres; more rarely, they are said to have received influences from other forms of literature. Often the theories put forward in different works are contradictory. So has Yi Hŭisŭng suggested that the *sijo* have sprung from the *muga*, while according to others, parts of the *muga* were originally *sijo*. Many of these theories with regard to the historical development of Korean literature have in common that they regard the *muga* as a very old, if not the oldest form of Korean literature. An illustration of this tendency can be found in the work of Kim Sŏnp'ung, who has drawn up the following scheme of development. He calls the *muga*: *sin'ga*, "divine songs."[1]

> short *sin'ga* → *hyangga*, *sijo*, non-religious popular songs
>
> *sin'ga*
>
> long *sin'ga* → narrative *sin'ga*, texts for the *Ant'aek* ceremony, ritual texts (*chemun*), *kasa*, *p'ansori*

The oldest Korean literary texts still extant are the *hyangga*. Therefore these *sin'ga* that are supposed to be the source of the *hyangga*, are purely hypothetical. What then, is behind the hypothesis that the *muga* are the oldest form of Korean literature? First of all, the assumption that the oldest religion of Korea, its "native" religion, was a form of shamanism. In the oldest records (written in classical Chinese) figures called *mu* (Chinese *wu*) are repeatedly mentioned.[2] The same character has always been used for the Korean *mudang*. If there were *mudang*-like figures in ancient times, it is likely that they sang and danced to communicate with the gods, as they do today. Hence it is concluded that there must have been *muga* in those days. In the second place, "it is a generally accepted theory that primitive beliefs fulfil the role of ancestors to the arts."[3] All over the world it is seen that secular literature develops out of religious literature.

However this may be, any assumption that in the most ancient period *muga* were already in existence, is just that, an assumption. No proof is anywhere to be found; there is no way to reconstruct the songs of the shamans of the Three Kingdoms period.

Even if one assumes that shaman songs already existed in early times, one should not make the mistake of equating these songs with the *muga* we know, which -with a few exceptions- all have been recorded in the twentieth century. It would be naive to think that the present *muga*, as products of a belief which in the eyes of many is "primitive", are a kind of Stone Age relic. Not only the great religions know change; folk beliefs, too, are subject to historical development, especially when they are part of a complex society. Examples of changes in the *muga* have already been given in the chapter on their transmission. The songs of the *mudang* probably influenced other genres, in the way Kim Sŏnp'ung and others suggest, but most likely they underwent influences, too.[4] This must have been a constant process, and therefore one should not think of a straight linear development. Patterns of development will rather have resembled a zig-zag or a spiral. Perhaps the finest example of such a complicated pattern is the history of the "Tale of Sim Ch'ŏng" in all its forms, *p'ansori*, novel (Seoul version and Chŏnju version), folk-song, legend and *muga* (Chapter VII is entirely devoted to Sim Ch'ŏng *muga*).

This chapter presents some theories proposed with regard to the relationship between *muga* and other literary genres by Korean scholars, and suggests some alternatives or additions to existing theories.

Muga, myths and folk-tales

Several attempts have been made to link *muga* with the oldest recorded myths of Korea: the myths about the founders of the most ancient states on the peninsula. Sŏ Taesŏk, in his study of the narrative *muga* for the god Chesŏk, has drawn attention to similarities between these *muga* and the myth about the founder of the state of Koguryŏ, Chumong. In the *muga*, a monk visits a *yangban* house, where he only finds the daughter, whose name in many versions is Tanggŭm-aegi. With the help of magic the monk first enters the house, to which the chaste Tanggŭm-aegi has denied him access, and then, through magic again, he makes the girl pregnant. Having spent the night in the house, in the morning the monk leaves. When the other members of the family return after some time, Tanggŭm-aegi's pregnancy is discovered. Her brothers want to kill her, but in the end she is allowed to live. Having been expelled from the family, Tanggŭm-aegi gives birth to triplets, three sons. She and her sons become gods in charge of birth, life and happiness, or, in some versions, *mudang* ancestors. In the Koguryŏ myth, Chumong, too, is conceived in a supernatural way, when the rays of the sun (representing his father, the heavenly god Haemosu) impregnate Yuhwa, the daughter of the River God.[5] Sŏ Taesŏk's comparison goes into much greater detail and his conclusion that the Chesŏk *muga* go back to the Chumong myth is quite persuasive, not least because it offers an explanation for the curious role of the monk in these songs, in which he is a magical begetter, like the sun in the Chumong myth and other old myths.[6] One should be careful not to draw hasty conclusions with regard to the relationship between texts that are separated by a great span of time, but one can say that at least patterns and motifs of the old myths also are found in the *muga*.

The same motifs, however, are also found in other tales, in Korea and in other parts of the world. There is a legend about the famous Silla monk and geomancer Tosŏn (827-898), for instance, which has much in common with the myth of Chumong. Tosŏn is born in an unusual fashion: his mother becomes pregnant after she has eaten a cucumber. When a boy is born, he is abandoned in a bamboo grove. The child survives, because a bird takes care of it.[7] Chumong, too, is abandoned and protected by animals. The combined motif of the abandoned child and its animal protectors has an extremely wide distribution, the story of Romulus and Remus being one of the best known examples in Europe. It is also common in the Near East.[8] Another Asian variant is found among the Buryat.[9] It is part, moreover, of one version of the story of Tanggŭm-aegi, in which the pregnant girl is put in a stone chest by her enraged brothers, but saved from freezing and starving by a blue crane and a white crane. The fact that Tanggŭm-aegi is already of nubile age is a bit unusual; in its more orthodox form the motif is found in the *muga* of the Abandoned Princess (Pari kongju).[10]

Certain similarities exist also between the Cheju Island *muga Sinjungto p'uri*[11] and the story of the fourth King of Silla, Sŏk T'arhae.[12] The *muga* explains among other things the origin of the goddesses of the Illoedang, the "Seven-day Temple."[13] The protagonist of the *muga*, because of his lack of filial piety, is put in a stone chest, which is thrown into the sea. After three years he reaches the land of the Dragon King whose daughter he marries. T'arhae, on the other hand, comes from a country where Dragon Kings have ruled for twenty-eight generations, but he too is abandoned, this time because he enters this world in an egg, which is regarded as an ill omen. The egg is put into a chest and the chest is put aboard a ship, which lands in Silla. T'arhae, who has meanwhile emerged from the egg, is discovered by a woman, and, after a silence of seven days, he tells her his story. When he wants to select a place to live, he climbs a mountain to survey the land and stays there for another seven days. Although he obtains the house which he has selected by pure fraud, his intelligence is admired by the King, who gives him his daughter in marriage. In spite of similar elements, in its entirety, the *muga* is quite different from the story of T'arhae. The hero of the *muga*, for instance, after some time repudiates his wife and remarries, but the second wife persuades him to call his first wife back and henceforth live with them both. Such marital complications are a unique feature of Cheju Island *muga*.

Chang Chugŭn has also compared old myths and modern *muga* and noted similarities, but he explains these resemblances in a different way. He has suggested that the myth about the divine ancestors of the Yang, Ko and Pu families of Cheju Island, which is found in written sources such as the *Koryŏ sa* (History of Koryŏ), was a *mudang* song about the origin of gods (*ponp'uri*) that was put into writing. This process, he assumes, was not uncommon.[14] Striking resemblances between this myth and some Cheju Island *muga* can, indeed, be found. The advent of the brides of the ancestors of the Yang, Ko and Pu families (the women are not from the island itself, but arrive by sea, floating in a wooden box) and the opposition between the husbands, who are hunters and meat-eaters, and the women, who bring seeds and represent agriculture, are motifs frequently found in modern Cheju *muga*. It is understandable that an explanation is sought to account for these similarities, but it should be pointed out that the theory put forward by Chang Chugŭn cannot be verified, unless a Koryŏ source is uncovered which unequivocally states that the source of the story is a *muga* - which is something one can hardly hope for. The danger of this kind of theorizing becomes apparent when the same author goes on to state that the story in the *Koryŏ sa* "definitely" proves that *ponp'uri muga* already existed during the Koryŏ dynasty. First the existence of a *muga* as the source of a myth is assumed, then the existence of the recorded myth is said to be "proof" of the existence of a particular type of *muga*!

According to Kim Chongu, one of the stories which accompany the *hyangga* entitled "Sŏdong yo" in the *Samguk yusa* (Remnants of the Three Kingdoms) is an elaboration of a folk-tale or a Cheju Island *muga*.[15] This theory is based on similarities between the *Samguk yusa* story and the *muga* called *Samgong ponp'uri*. A certain resemblance cannot be denied, but again one should be aware of the fact that stories with similar content have a very wide distribution, both in space and in time. It is not necessary to assume a close relationship on the basis of a few shared motifs.[16]

Unfortunately, because we have no texts of older *muga*, it is impossible to find evidence to prove that a prototype of one of the *muga* we know, was the model for a myth or legend in the old records. For the reverse process, however, there is some evidence. Sŏ Taesŏk has pointed out that the *Kunung ponp'uri* is a retelling of a legend about the grandfather of Wang Kŏn (877-

943), the founder of the Koryŏ dynasty.[17] Although the names in the *muga* are a little garbled, they are easily recognizable. In this legend, the grandfather (in the *muga*, the father) of Wang Kŏn marries a daughter of a Dragon King. She bears him several children, but continues to make occasional visits to her father, a well near her house giving access to the Dragon King's realm. Although she has warned her husband not to look when she enters the well, one time he does not heed her words and for this reason she is unable to return to the human world. This is a mixture of Type 205 (The Heavenly Maiden and the Woodcutter, a version of the well-known Swan Maiden Tale) and Type 207 (The Dragon Woman) in Choi In-hak's *Type Index of Korean Folktales*.[18] It is unlikely that the legend would be based on a *muga*, with the names of the members of the Wang family substituted, and that the *mudang* then would have adopted this changed version of their own song. In all probability, the legend was created out of existing folk-tale motifs and only later entered the repertoire of the *mudang*, for whom the fact that the story is about members of a royal house will have been of great importance; many of the deities they venerate are, as we have seen in Chapter I, of royal blood. It is not necessary to assume that the *mudang* borrowed the legend from a written source such as the *Koryŏ sa*; more probably, the *muga* goes back to an orally transmitted version of the story.

Chang Tŏksun, who has compared narrative *muga* and folk-tales, is of the opinion that the *mudang* frequently borrowed folk-tales to enrich their performances.[19] An indication of this can be found in the plot of certain narrative *muga*, which have very little to do with shamanism. An example is the *muga* that tells the story of the Emille Bell, a well-known folk-tale about a temple bell in Silla, which would not emit a sound until a child was sacrificed.[20]

Clearly, the dividing line between folk-tales and narrative *muga* is thin. In a comprehensive scheme drawn up by Chang Chugŭn, he acknowledges both the possibility of folk-tales influencing the *muga* (in ancient times) and that of *muga* influencing (or even changing into) folk-tales (in modern times).[21] In fact, it is reasonable to assume that as long as there have been *muga*, there has been a constant exchange of motifs and plots with the folk-tale. Certainly many elements, motifs as well as types, found in folk-tales, appear also in *muga*. An example of a type represented in the *muga* is "The Magic Gem, the Cat and the Dog",[22] part of the *muga* called *Kungsangi kut*.[23] An example of a motif shared by different genres is the one called "Kind and Unkind",[24] which is found in the same *Kungsangi kut* as well as in a Buddhist tale, *Sŏnu t'aeja chŏn*,[25] and the famous story of the brothers Hŭngbu and Nolbu which is told in folk-song, *p'ansori*, *ko-sosŏl* and folk-tale.[26] Anyone familiar with the type- and motif classification will discover other examples in the plots of *muga* described elsewhere in the present study.

Muga and Buddhist tales

Buddhist tales form a category which is closely related to that of the folk-tale and, if one may assume frequent contacts between folk-tales and *muga*, the contacts between Buddhist tales and folk-tales seem to have been no less frequent.

Chang Chugŭn has argued that Buddhist tales also have exercised a considerable influence on the *muga*.[27] To account for the numerous Buddhist elements in the *muga*, Chang goes back to the early period of Buddhism in Korea, when Buddhist priests may have used various kinds of tales to expound their doctrines to the people in an easy and attractive way. In Korea there is no clear documentation, but in China there undeniably existed a literature of this kind. It is usually referred to as *pien-wen* (Transformation Texts).[28] Japan, too, knew a form of oral Buddhist literature that flourished in the Heian period. It is not unlikely, therefore, that Korean monks employed such methods to spread the faith, even though the evidence is weak.[29] The most problematic aspect of the theory is the assumption that the older oral Buddhist literature directly influenced the *muga*. Again this is a thesis which is difficult to prove because of the impermanence of oral literature. A reconstruction of oral Buddhist stories would be, to some degree, possible, if a study were made of all Buddhist tales in ancient sources, not only of those in the more well-known records such as the *Samguk yusa*, but also of the stories directly related to the origins of temples and images. But this has not yet been done and therefore proof of Chang Chugŭn's thesis is difficult to obtain.

Chang gives the following examples of narrative *muga*, which were possibly influenced by Buddhist propagandist literature. In order to convey an impression of the nature of the plot of narrative *muga*, the contents of each are described briefly.

- *Ch'ogong ponp'uri*. E.g., *AA* I, 388-415.
  This is a *muga* of the so-called *Chesŏk ponp'uri* type (or Tanggŭm-aegi type), which has been extensively treated by Sŏ Taesŏk and was mentioned earlier in this chapter. Even if Chesŏk is a god of Buddhist origin, it is difficult to regard this kind of *muga* as an example of proselytizing literature; the only message to be derived from it would be that young girls should beware of mendicant monks if they do not wish to end up as the unwed mothers of triplets. Kim Sŏnp'ung[30] connects a *muga* of this type with the legend of the historical monk Pŏmil (9th century), which is found in the Kangnŭng area. Sŏ Taesŏk, however, rightly rejects the suggestion that the *muga* would be derived

from this legend, because *muga* of this type have a nation-wide distribution and are unlikely to have sprung from one local legend.[31]

- *Igong ponp'uri.* E.g. *AA* I, 415-429.

This song describes the origin of a god who is the guardian of a bed of magic flowers and may grant his worshippers a long life or the blessing of children. When he is still a child, he has to to overcome many difficulties: he is separated from his father and his mother becomes a slave to a rich man, who maltreats her and her son. Earlier researchers have found that this *muga* has much in common with a story in the 15th century *Wŏrin sŏkpo*, the tale of Crown-Prince Allakkuk, for which no foreign source has been discovered. Besides the *Igong ponp'uri*, a *muga* from the other extreme of the country, North P'yŏngan Province, *Sinsŏn Set'yŏnnim ch'ŏngbae,*[32] too, has some elements in common with the story of Allakkuk. The names of the protagonists are similar and some of the basic motifs the same; the resemblance is less striking than in the case of *Igong ponp'uri.* This would appear to be ideal material to prove that there is a link between the *muga* and early Buddhist propagandist literature. But there are complications. There is a story regarded as a *ko-sosŏl* with the same plot: *Allakkuk chŏn.*[33] A comparison of *Igong ponp'uri* with this *ko-sosŏl* and the story in the *Wŏrin sŏkpo* shows several motifs in the *muga* (*AA* version) which are found in the *ko-sosŏl*, but that are lacking in the *Wŏrin sŏkpo*: Wŏnang puin, the mother of Prince Allakkuk, hears a cock crow when, heavy with child, she is unable to continue her journey, and so discovers the house of a rich man, to whom she persuades her husband to sell her[34]; the rich man wants to make her his concubine, but Wŏnang puin begs him to wait until she is delivered[35]; once the child is born, the rich man assigns an impossibly heavy task to him[36]; the son revives his mother (who has been killed by the rich man) with magic flowers[37]; the rich man is punished in this world.[38] This, of course, pleads against the supposition that the *muga* is a "direct lineal descendant" of the *Wŏrin sŏkpo* story and argues for a closer relationship to the *ko-sosŏl*, which is of a much more recent date, presumably the 19th century and certainly not earlier than the 18th century.[39]

- *Paep'o toŭp.* See *MSr*, 260.

In *MSs*, 310-315, this is called *Ch'ŏnji toŭp* (Capitals of Heaven and Earth). This is a *muga* about the creation of heaven and earth, similar to *Siru mal* (*AA* I, 128, 132) and *Ch'angse ka* (Son Chint'ae, *Shinka ihen*, 1-15). Apart from the fact that in the latter *muga*, Maitreya and Sākyamuni are the protagonists, the narrative is not at all Buddhist in nature. It is difficult to imagine why Chang Chugŭn has included it in his list.

- *Samgong ponp'uri*. E.g., *AA* I, 429-436.

Above it has already been pointed out that this *muga* resembles the story of Sŏdong in the *Samguk yusa*, which may be regarded as a tale explaining the origin of the Mirŭk Temple. To that extent it may be considered a Buddhist tale. The plot of the Sŏdong story is reminiscent of certain folk-tales. The *muga* belongs to Type 419 of Choi In-hak's classification; there the boy protagonist is a charcoal maker and the oven turns out to be made of gold. A similar tale exists in Japan: H. Ikeda, *A Type and Motif Index of Japanese Folk-Literature*, No. 930 B. In Eberhard's classification of Chinese tales it is Type 193, "Das Mädchen, das den Bettler heiratet."[40] Neither this story nor the narrative of *Samgong ponp'uri* is inherently Buddhist, but in the *AA* version the story is clearly placed within a Buddhist framework (not in the other *muga* versions). The plot of this version is as follows. A couple has three daughters. The youngest daughter gives an insolent answer to the question whom she owes her birth to and is therefore sent away by her parents. Her sisters try to frighten her, but in punishment for this are turned into a centipede and a toadstool. The parents loose all their property and become blind. The third daughter asks three bachelors for shelter. Only the third one kindly shows her the way to his home. An old woman gives the girl a place to sleep; then, when the three bachelors come home (they are brothers), the older two misbehave, the youngest is friendly again. The girl marries him and in the field where he digs for yams gold is found (this is the motif which is also found in the story of Sŏdong, "Yam-boy"; most of the story is quite different). The young couple, suddenly become rich, are able to live without cares, but the girl keeps thinking of her parents (this last detail is also found in the Sŏdong story and -for that matter- in the story of Sim Ch'ŏng). To find her parents (who have become beggars), she organizes a big banquet to which all beggars are invited. Her parents come too, she is reunited with them and the parents regain their eyesight. This is again strongly reminiscent of the story of Sim Ch'ŏng (see Chapter VII). Finally it is explained why everything has happened as it did; why, for instance, the parents first were rich, then poor. It is all because of what they have done in previous lives, it is all because of karma.

This *muga* is emphatically presented as a Buddhist tale, although the plot is that of a folk-tale. There is no clear division between folk-tales and Buddhist tales.

- *Ch'asa ponp'uri.* E.g., *AA* I, 507-519.
  This is a *muga* about Kangnim, a local magistrate's underling who becomes a messenger of Yama, the King of the Underworld. First, before Kangnim appears on the scene, a complicated story is told about three brothers who are killed by an evil woman. Through a curious process of changes (they turn into flowers, the flowers are burnt and turn into pearls, the woman eats the pearls) they are reborn as the sons of the evil woman. They grow up, succeed in the government examinations and then suddenly die again. This part of the story has a separate existence as a folk-tale (cf. Choi, *Type Index*, No. 324). The mother demands of the local magistrate that he send a messenger to King Yama to complain. It is Kangnim who undertakes this dangerous task. In the end, he returns with King Yama, the woman's crimes are exposed and she is punished. The boys are revived and sent back to their original parents. This story has, in fact, many Buddhist elements. It also contains a number of folk-tale motifs, for instance that of the change of corpses into flowers: a variation of the so-called "Machandelbaum Motiv"; cf. Eberhard, *Typen Chinesischer Volksmärchen*, No. 31. Almost all episodes of the *muga* are also found in the *Kin Kajang kut* from Hamhŭng.[41] There the slain boys change into fish which are eaten by the evil woman, again with a triple pregnancy as the result. The final message of this *muga* is that people who perpetrate evil will be caught by ghosts and turned into scarecrows and *changsŭng* ("devil-posts").[42] Apart from the cautionary ending the *muga* is entirely like a folk-tale, as opposed to the Cheju *muga* which, being a song of the *ponp'uri* type, explains the origin of a member of the pantheon, the messenger of King Yama: Kangnim. *Ch'asa ponp'uri* also explains the origin of certain customs related to mourning.

- *Chijang ponp'uri.* E.g., *MSs*, 368-369.
  Chijang is Ksitigarbha, the Bodhisattva associated with death and the Underworld because he enters Hell to rescue the wicked, in order to fulfil his vow to save all mankind. The fact that this *muga* is sung for the dead is consonant with this, although its protagonist is a girl called Chijangi agissi, not the Bodhisattva. All her relatives die, one after the other.[43] She obtains merit by holding rituals for them. The *muga*

contains Buddhist elements, but it would be going too far to call it a Buddhist story.

- *Munjŏn ponp'uri.* E.g., *AA* I, 529-535.

This is a *muga* about the house gods. Chang Chugŭn is unable to find marked Buddhist elements, but points out that it often happens that Buddhist elements are lacking in Chinese and Japanese literature of Buddhist origin![44]

The story contains a motif, however, which is frequently found in Buddhist stories. An evil step-mother feigns illness and claims that she will only get better if she eats the livers of her seven stepsons.[45] The liver of a hare can save the life of the Dragon King in *Sugung ka*, a *p'ansori* story which borrows its plot from an Indian *jātaka* (a story about past lives of the Buddha) about a monkey and a crocodile.[46] In *Kŭmu t'aeja chŏn*, "The Story of Crown Prince Golden Calf", another Buddhist story,[47] jealous women recommend the liver of a specific calf (a transformation of the Crown Prince) as medicine, while in the *Wŏrin sŏkpo* story of Crown Prince Inyok[48] evil ministers advise the King that he will recover from his illness only when he eats the eyes and marrow of someone who has never been angry, that is, of the Crown Prince.

A variation of this motif is presented in a *muga* (*Ch'ilsŏng kut*): a step-mother feigns illness, her seven stepsons go to look for medicine and meet a golden deer, which is a transformation of their own deceased mother. The deer offers her liver, the boys accept it, and when the step-mother eats the liver, she is struck by lightning, whereupon she turns into a mole. Fear of lightning supposedly is why the mole avoids the open air.[49]

- *Maenggam ponp'uri.* E.g., *MSs*, 381-387.

This *muga* tells a complicated story, with two, more or less independent episodes, which have in common that in both there is something related to death. First, Samani, the protagonist of the story, offers up a ritual for the ghost of a hunter who has accidentally killed himself. The grateful ghost makes him rich. This is the folk-tale motif of the "Grateful Dead."[50] Because Samani neglects the cult of his ancestors, messengers come from the Underworld to carry him off. Through cunning and bribes he escapes death and lives for 40 000 years. The Jade Emperor is disturbed by this and once again sends messengers to catch Samani. It is difficult to find Samani, because he constantly changes his shape, but the messengers think of a trick. They dress as ordinary people, go to a pond and start washing charcoal. "Why for heaven's sake are you washing charcoal?", asks Samani, who happens to pass by. "To make it white." Exclaiming: "In all the 40 000 years of my life I've never seen a thing like this!", Samani betrays himself. This last part of the story is identical to a Chinese folk-tale about P'eng-tsu, a legendary figure and symbol of longevity, who is said to have lived a thousand years.[51]

- *Wŏn Ch'ŏn'gang ponp'uri*. E.g., *AA* I, 467-479.
A literal translation of the title of this *muga* would be "Explanation of the Origin of Yüan T'ien-kang." Yüan is a famous master of divination from the T'ang period. In the *muga* the name stands for a book of divination. The story is about a girl who does not know her name or her age and whom people call Onari, "Today." As a child she is taken care of by cranes, as abandoned children often are in *muga*. One day, she sets out to look for her parents and meets a boy and a girl called "Always" and "Everyday", who must spend all their time in one place, engaged in study. She also meets a snake that is frustrated because even after many years of trying it has not been able to evolve into a dragon, a lotus plant that is dissatisfied because it has only one flower, and a group of ladies who have been banished from the court of the Jade Emperor and condemned to a Labour of Sisyphus: scooping water with a calabash full of holes. "Today" fixes the calabash and promises the others that she will consult her parents -who apparently have access to special knowledge- about their misfortunes. When "Today" is reunited with her parents, who had been obliged to abandon her because the Jade Emperor had suddenly entrusted them with the task of guarding the book *Wŏn Ch'ŏn'gang*, she learns what is wrong with her "friends" and goes back to help them. Finally, she travels from temple to temple to have copies of *Wŏn Ch'ŏn'gang* made. Because of this last detail, it is possible that this was originally a story told by Buddhist monks (who, in fact, often acted as diviners) to advertise their talents as fortunetellers.

- *Semin Hwangje ponp'uri*. E.g., *AA* I, 480-496.
This is, literally translated, "The Story of the Origin of Emperor Shih-min" (Shih-min is Li Shih-min, the founder of the T'ang dynasty). The *muga* relates how Li Shih-min descends to Hell, becomes aware of his sins and, upon receiving a last chance to better his life, returns to the living and mends his ways. As an act of piety he has the Buddhist canon brought to China from India. The same incidents are found in a *ko-sosŏl*: *Tang T'aejong chŏn*. Sŏ Taesŏk has compared the novel with the *muga* and drawn the conclusion that most likely the *muga* was derived from the *ko-sosŏl*.[52] Chang Chugŭn, however, suggests that both

muga and *ko-sosŏl* stem directly from a *pien-wen*.[53] Among the Tun-huang manuscripts there is, indeed, a "Transformation Text" about T'ai-tsung's (= Li Shih-min's) journey to Hell,[54] but it is a fragment only, which, except for the basic fact of T'ai-tsung's journey to Hell, bears little resemblance to either *ko-sosŏl* or *muga*. The *ko-sosŏl*, in all important aspects, follows the version of T'ai-tsung's journey given in the hundred-chapter edition of the famous traditional Chinese novel *Hsi-yu chi* (The Journey to the West), which was without doubt one of the most widely read books in Korea during the later Chosŏn period.[55] *Semin Hwangje ponp'uri*, the *muga*, bears the character of a Buddhist moralistic tale throughout, but it is not at all similar to the Tun-huang *pien-wen*. It may stem from an old oral tradition, or from a written version of the *Hsi-yu chi* antedating the hundred-chapter version, but this is mere speculation.[56] The most remarkable thing about the *muga* is that it is so completely a Buddhist propagandist tale; there is no trace of shamanistic elements. Considering that it seems to have had a very limited distribution -except for the *AA* text, there is only one other recorded version[57], and nowadays it is not sung at all- it seems likely that the story of T'ai-tsung, whatever its antecedents as a Buddhist tale, was only recently, and that for a short period, used as a *muga*. For the discussion of the origins of narrative *muga* in general it is of little value.

-    *Kunung ponp'uri*. E.g., *AA* I, 525-529.
     This *muga* contains the story of an ancestor of the founder of the Koryŏ dynasty and has already been discussed above. Apart from the reference to a Dragon King, it contains no clearly Buddhist elements.

-    *Segyŏng ponp'uri*. E.g., *AA* I, 436-460.
     This *muga* explains the origin of a deity in charge of the Five Cereals, called Chesŏk ("Sakro devānām Indra"). The name of the deity may be of Buddhist origin, the plot of the story is not Buddhist. The story seems to be related to a Chinese story, which in Korea was known -inter alia- in the form of a *ko-sosŏl*. The connection between *Segyŏng ponp'uri* and similar *muga* on the one hand and the *ko-sosŏl* on the other, will be discussed in another section of this chapter.

The only conclusion that can be drawn from our survey is that the evidence of the influences from the Chinese or the native *pien-wen* tradition on the *muga* is meagre. This is not to say that the *muga* do not contain many Buddhist elements -they most certainly do- but it is difficult to prove that the origin of narrative *muga* is in Buddhist literature and that the modern *muga* go back in a straight line to the older forms of Buddhist tales - the theory advocated by Chang Chugŭn.

A *muga* not mentioned above, in which Buddhist influences are undeniable, is the *Changja p'uri*.[58] This kind of *muga* relates how a rich man (a *changja*, a term that can also mean "householder" and is often used in Buddhist tales: for the villain in the story of Allakkuk, for instance), who does not take proper care of his ancestors, has a dream in which he is warned of the fate that awaits him in Hell. He takes this warning to heart and with the help of his daughter-in-law finds a way to bribe the Messengers of King Yama, who have come to take him away. In its basic pattern, this cautionary tale is, of course, similar to the story of T'ang T'ai-tsung.

Similarity in pattern is also discovered if one compares the story outline of the *muga* about Pari kongju, "the Abandoned Princess" with two Buddhist tales, the tale about Crown-Prince Sŏnu and the one about Prince Golden Calf.[59] The basic pattern which these stories have in common is as follows:
-       The protagonist leaves home (of his own free will or forcedly);
-       after tribulations and ordeals he/she marries a noble personage;
-       and finally he/she returns and saves or cures his/her parents.
This pattern can be applied without change to the story of Sim Ch'ŏng, which will be discussed in detail in Chapter VII.

Buddhist influences on the *muga* are not limited to narrative elements. Apart from pieces of Buddhist liturgy -in Sino-Korean or even Sanskrit-Buddhist *kasa*, too, furnished material for the songs of the *mudang* (cf. the section on *muga* and *kasa*).

Muga, p'ansori and the kwangdae

The relation between *muga* and *p'ansori* ("one-man opera", dramatic narratives sung by one singer, accompanied by a drummer) cannot be described without referring to the work of Kim Tonguk, who has written several important articles about the formative stage of *p'ansori*.[60] He has posited the following development as regards the narrative elements of *p'ansori*: basic (oral) tale → *p'ansori* → *ko-sosŏl*. Influence from the *mudang* on *p'ansori*, according to Kim Tonguk, is found in the music (the rhythms, *karak*) and in certain textual elements (some of the "interlude songs").[61] Leaving aside the problem of the relation between *p'ansori* and the *ko-sosŏl* - about which there is no agreement among scholars- attention will be concentrated here on the statements that directly concern the *mudang*.

Of fundamental importance in the theories of Kim Tonguk is the social relationship between the *mudang* and the *kwangdae*, "actors", who were -

among other things- performers of *p'ansori* (singers and drummers). At least during the later Chosŏn period the ties between the (predominantly female) *mudang* and the all-male *kwangdae* seem to have been very close. Both groups belonged to the social class of the "base people", the *ch'ŏnin*, and they could cooperate professionally. In a well-known picture by Sin Yunbok (1758-?) a *mudang* dances to the accompaniment provided by a male drummer and an oboe player. Although individuals might specialize, *kwangdae* as a group devoted themselves to all the performing arts, and also were active as musicians. Sharing outcaste status and professional interests, *mudang* and *kwangdae* were ideal marriage partners and indeed such unions were so frequent (especially in the South where *mudang* were mostly of the hereditary type), that the terms *mubu*, "*mudang*'s husband", and *kwangdae* became inter-changeable.[62]

Two examples of marital ties between *mudang* and *kwangdae* are recorded in recent reports. The male shaman (*hwaraengi*) Yi Yongu was born in the last decade of the 19th century in Kyŏnggi Province.[63] His father, Yi Chongha, his grandfather and his great grandfather all were heads of an organization that supervised the activities of the *kwangdae*.[64] Yi Chongman, whose name appears in *AA* II as assistant-director of an organization of *chaein* (artists/acrobats) in 1908, was Yi Yongu's paternal uncle.[65] This Yi Chongman sang *muga* himself, which were recorded by Akiba and Akamatsu.[66] The forefathers of Yi Chongman had been shamans for ten generations.[67] Yi Yongu's wife as well as his mother were *mudang*. When he was nine years old, he started to learn *p'ansori*-style singing (*ch'ang*). His father ran a travelling theatre company, which presented *p'ansori* plays in theatrical form (*ch'anggŭk*), with several singers each taking a role instead of one singer performing all the parts as in the original *p'ansori*. Afterwards Yi Yongu himself joined such a company for a few years. He also played the transverse flute (*taegŭm*). All this furnishes interesting information about the milieu from which the *muga* of Yi Chongman sprang.

Close ties between *mudang* and performers of various kinds are also seen in the family of Sŏng Hwasu, a *mudang* from Chŏnju in North Chŏlla Province,[68] who was born in 1891. Her grandfather played the *kŏmun'go* (a six-string zither) well, her father won renown as a player of the two-stringed fiddle, the *haegŭm*. A younger brother of her mother (who herself was a *mudang*) was a *p'ansori* singer. Her husband played the *p'iri* (Korean oboe), *kayagŭm* (twelve-string zither) and *haegŭm*, and assisted her in her ceremonies. Her husband's father was an acrobat and tight-rope dancer, who during the reign of King Kojong was enrolled in an army unit recruited from the *mubu*.[69]

A little more should be said about the organizations which supervised the activities of the *kwangdae*. During the second half of the Chosŏn dynasty the government gave orders to set up a nation-wide organization of *kwangdae* to expedite matters when mask-dance performances had to be given for Ch'ing envoys who regularly came to the capital.[70] The organization to which Yi Chongman belonged had, according to documents in his possession, functioned from 1784 to 1920 and from the description of its functions that he gave to Akiba and Akamatsu, it transpires that this organization (called Chaein ch'ŏng) also exercised control over *mudang*. It punished, for instance, *mudang* who held ceremonies for another *mudang*'s clientèle.[71] Akiba and Akamatsu also describe organizations of *mudang*'s husbands in Chŏlla Province.[72] These *mubu* were attached to the local magistrature as musicians and it seems most likely that their associations were equivalent or identical to the organization of *kwangdae* to which Yi Chongman belonged. In both cases the membership consisted of artists of various descriptions, mainly musicians, and the organizations were set up under government auspices.[73] After 1894, when modernizations took place, the government did not need the services of the *kwangdae* as before. The state examinations, for which the *kwangdae* formerly flocked to the capital,[74] were abolished and Korea no longer recognized China as suzerain, which put an end to the need to entertain Chinese envoys. After this time, or after Korea's loss of independence the old *kwangdae* organizations in some places apparently shifted the focus of their activities to the accompanying of shamanistic rituals.

If one considers the evidence given above there is no reason to doubt the existence of frequent contacts between *mudang* and *kwangdae* in the time when *p'ansori* was created.[75] Marshall Pihl's comment: "Although we lack sufficient explicit facts to state unequivocally that *kwangdae* of the nineteenth century were typically husbands of shamans, the circumstantial evidence points unmistakably in that direction"[76] seems to be correct, if a little cautious.

As mentioned above, Kim Tonguk does not claim that *p'ansori* in its entirety developed out of the ceremonies of the *mudang*; he singles out two elements: the rhythms (*karak*) and the textual elements that he calls *sasŏl*. What elements are exactly referred to as *sasŏl* (which in ordinary speech means "words/narration/description/chattering")? In relation to *p'ansori* the term *sasŏl* can refer to the text of a play, as in the case of Sin Chaehyo's libretti which are called *p'ansori sasŏl*. The East Coast *mudang* also use *sasŏl* (or rather *sasil*) to refer to the text of their songs. Kim Tonguk uses the term a little differently, however. He says that the *sasŏl* of the *muga* often rely heavily on repetitions and bear little relation to the narrative; they are more or less varied elaborations on a certain theme and concrete examples are descriptions of persons, costume and apparel, or descriptions of the interior and exterior of houses as listed in Chapter V. In the chapter about the *muga* for the god Sŏngju some of these *sasŏl* and their possible relation to *p'ansori* will be further discussed. In general one can say that *p'ansori* and *muga* have indeed similar *sasŏl*, but that it is difficult to prove that the development was exactly as Kim Tonguk has stated.[77] Whatever the contribution of the *muga* to the texts may have been, Kim has pointed out that many other genres, *kasa*, *chapka*, Chinese poems, folk-songs, folk-tales, anecdotes and *ko-sosŏl*, too, have exerted influence on *p'ansori*.[78]

So far, the ties between the *kwangdae* and the *mudang* have been discussed in the framework of an attempt to clarify the origins of *p'ansori*. It was the purpose of Kim Tonguk's thesis to explain the emergence of *p'ansori* out of other, older genres. But why would all the influences in the relationship between *kwangdae* and *mudang* go one way? Is it not likely that the *kwangdae* in their turn exercised influence on the *muga*? Because similarities between *p'ansori* and *muga*, as seen in the formulae, are better explained as due to the influence of the former on the latter than vice versa, it is worthwile to consider the proposition that the *kwangdae* contributed to the text of the *muga*.

The *kwangdae* had a wider spectrum of acquaintance than the *mudang* and were more mobile. Whenever large-scale examinations were held in the capital, *kwangdae* from all over the country would go there, to take part in the ceremonies for the successful candidates, whom they might follow on their journey home.[79] In a narrative *muga* from Ch'ungch'ŏng Province, there is a description of such successful candidates (the nine brothers of the heroine) on their way home, accompanied by dancing boys, *kwangdae* (i.e. singers, in this case), musicians and servants.[80] When *kwangdae* of different regions met in the capital, this was a fine occasion for the exchange of various forms of folk art.[81] The *kwangdae* would also go up to the capital for other great events. Because of this Kim Tonguk has suggested that the fact that the words of folk-songs of different regions are similar -even if there are differences in rhythm- can be explained by assuming that the texts were exchanged when the *kwangdae* met in the capital.[82] There may have been a parallel development with regard to the *muga*. Many *muga*, from the Northern Provinces to Cheju Island, show striking similarities in the use of language, while the rhythms differ according to the region. Could not the *kwangdae*, who lived in close contact with the *mudang*, be responsible for the propagation of the texts of *muga* as well as of folk-songs? It is not unlikely that the *kwangdae* were also interested in *muga* as elements that could be used in their own performances. According to an early 19th century poem, *Kwanuhŭi*, "Watching Theatricals", by Song Manjae, a *mudang* song about Chesŏk was sung by *kisaeng* for entertainment.[83] If *muga* were regularly sung for entertainment, this would, of course, increase the interest of the *kwangdae* in this genre.

Another way to explain similarities between *muga* of different regions is to assume that the *mudang* freely borrowed out of the repertoire of their husbands the formulae and themes which made up the poetic language of the *kwangdae*. This explanation -with the ties between the *kwangdae* and the *mudang* essential, but no necessity to assume that the *kwangdae* exchanged *muga* texts- I regard as not less plausible than the other explanation.

If one allows the supposition that the *mudang* were influenced by the *kwangdae*, it becomes possible to account for the presence in the *muga* of "learned elements", of elaborate Sino-Korean phrases and classical allusions. The *kwangdae* were in contact with people in the magistrature who had received a certain degree of education. It is a generally recognized fact that lower officials with an interest in the arts contributed much to the development of *p'ansori*.[84] Through government clerks (*ajŏn*) or local gentry (*hyangban*) the *kwangdae* received, according to Kim Tonguk, the following elements of *p'ansori*: fragments of Chinese poetry, folk-tales and literary anecdotes, and the narrative structure of the *ko-sosŏl*. Some of this the *kwangdae* will have passed on to the *mudang*. How else can one explain, for instance, that a *muga* from Kyŏngsang Province contains a four-line poem by Wang Wei (699-761), the famous T'ang poet?[85] In many places in the *muga* one finds traces of what one may call "popular Sino-Korean culture", those elements of Chinese culture which were known to the average Korean of some education.

There is good reason to believe that the rather long passage about the creation of the universe and Chinese and Korean history -found as an introductory part in many *muga* (cf. Chapter V, Other Themes)- also reached the *mudang* through the *kwangdae*, who themselves had learned much from their more educated acquaintances in the magistrature. The *kwangdae* who performed the rites in honour of a successful candidate in the state examinations, chanted a "... recitation of history, since the creation of the Three Kingdoms and of the Koryŏ and Yi dynasties.[86] This was part of the so-called *tŏktam*, "chant of fortune."[87] Recitations of Chinese and Korean history are also met with in the shorter songs (*tan'ga* or *hŏduga*), which *p'ansori* singers sing to loosen the voice before they begin with the songs of the regular repertoire.[88] Similar recitations abound in the *muga*.[89] A mere glance at the contents of such passages shows that it is inconceivable that they could have been created in the milieu of the *mudang* without outside influence. Therefore some explanation is needed as to how the *mudang* became acquainted with such recitations; the route outlined above: *ajŏn/hyangban* → *kwangdae* → *mudang*, fits known facts and provides an answer. Then it must have been by way of this route, too, that many of the formulae and themes mentioned in the preceding chapter were disseminated among the *mudang*.

There is a tradition about the origin of *Ch'unhyang ka* (The Song of Ch'unhyang), that usually is cited as an indication that this *p'ansori* story was derived from a shamanistic ritual. In his book about the history of *p'ansori*,

Chŏng Nosik quotes one of his teachers, who had told him that a local clerk had composed this story to console the spirit of a girl who -like Ch'unhyang- had had a love affair with a young man of the *yangban* class, but -unlike Ch'unhyang- had died without being reunited with her lover.[90] The text composed by the clerk was used by *mudang* in a ritual for the dead girl. For three years prior to this the County of Namwŏn had been visited by all kinds of disasters which had been ascribed to the grudge of the ghost of the deserted woman. After the ritual had been performed, however, prosperity returned. This may be hard to believe, but even if it is nothing but a tale, it shows that it was not inconceivable that a clerk should write a text for performance in a *kut*. Instead of indicating a shamanistic origin for the tale of Ch'unhyang, the story reinforces the theory that the *mudang* were open to influences from the *ajŏn* class, whether by way of the *kwangdae* or not.

The discussion of the relationship between *p'ansori* and *muga* began with the theory that the *muga* have contributed to the origin of *p'ansori*. Now that the likelihood of influences in the reverse direction has been demonstrated, a few remarks should be added about influence from *p'ansori* on the *muga*.

At least in one case, that of the *Sim Ch'ŏng kut*, the influence of *p'ansori* on the songs sung by the *mudang* is evident, as will be shown in Chapter VII. This cannot, however, be an influence dating from the time when the ties between *ajŏn*, *kwangdae* and *mudang* still existed, as the *Sim Chŏng kut* in all probability was not performed in the 19th century. But other *muga*, too, seem to have been influenced by *p'ansori*. Particularly the *muga* of the East Coast (of which the *muga* about Sim Ch'ŏng is one) have a "strong *p'ansori* smell", in the words of Yi Tuhyŏn.[91] The high percentage of formulae shared by *p'ansori* and the *muga* of this region is a good indication of *p'ansori* influence. The nature of many of these formulae is such that an ultimate origin in the *muga* is impossible. Although Sim Usŏng, in his introduction to an East Coast version of the *Sonnim kut* has suggested that the *muga* have influenced *p'ansori*,[92] I am unable to regard the features which this *muga* has in common with *p'ansori* as evidence for an influence as hinted by Sim Usŏng. The elements which this *muga* has in common with *p'ansori* are much better explained by the assumption that *p'ansori* influenced the *muga*. For this there is not only the internal evidence of the text: one of the informants for the *Sonnim kut*, the *hwaraengi* Kim Sŏkch'ul, claims that both his father and his grandfather were good *p'ansori* singers.[93] It is quite likely that they employed elements of *p'ansori* for shamanistic activities. Present-day East Coast *mudang*, moreover, make superficial attempts to imitate the singing style of *p'ansori* singers.[94]

A link with *p'ansori* or the singers of *p'ansori*, the *kwangdae*, explains resemblances between *muga* and *p'ansori*, but equally resemblances between *muga* and other genres. If *p'ansori* is studied on the level of the formulae, it has much in common with *sijo* and *kasa*. When the *muga* borrowed from the poetic language of *p'ansori*, it was, by the same token, inevitable that they should borrow from the language of *sijo* and *kasa* as well. It is also possible that *sijo* and *kasa* elements entered the repertoire of the *mudang* more directly, although still by way of the *kwangdae*, as the *kwangdae* also sang such poems.

Resemblances between the *muga* and the mask-dance drama texts, too, can also be explained by referring to the *mudang-kwangdae* connection, as it were the *kwangdae* who performed the mask plays.[95]

Apart from the *kwangdae*, the *mudang* may also have learned from *kisaeng*. Of course the *kisaeng* had not the same opportunities for travelling as the *kwangdae* did, but they learned to sing many different kinds of texts. Socially, the *mudang* and the *kisaeng* belonged to the same group, the despised *ch'ŏnin*. Akiba found that early in this century many daughters of *mudang* became *kisaeng*.[96] In a *kisaeng* school in Pyongyang many gods were venerated and often *mudang* were invited to perform rituals, while the *kisaeng* of Seoul liked to sing *muga*. It is not clear, however, whether in older periods *mudang* daughters were as numerous among the *kisaeng*, and concrete information about a contribution to the *muga* by *kisaeng* is not available.

Muga and ko-sosŏl

At first sight it is not very likely that *ko-sosŏl* could influence the *muga*, as the *mudang* for the most part must have been illiterate. Nevertheless, in a few cases there seems to have been such influence, and the question remains how this might have occurred. Once again one could think of the link between *ajŏn* and *kwangdae*. Through the *ajŏn* the *kwangdae* may have come into contact with written literature. Another possible channel of dissemination is the public reciter of novels. There is some evidence of story-tellers who narrated well-known novels to an audience.[97] Probably, however, such story-tellers only operated in the capital and other urban centres. It may have happened that *mudang* picked up the plot of a story or a story motif from them. A third possibility is that some *mudang* did read or had people around them who could read. In the chapter on the transmission of the *muga* it has already been shown that, at least in the last one-hundred years, this could have happened.

A complicating factor in the discussion of the relationship between *muga* and *ko-sosŏl* is the existence of the same story in several genres. There is the case, mentioned above, of the *Igong ponp'uri muga*, which is similar to a Buddhist tale, and to a text that is regarded as a *ko-sosŏl* (the story of Prince Allakkuk). With the tale of Sim Ch'ŏng, which is treated separately in Chapter VII, things get even more complicated.

One of the most popular novels during the Yi dynasty was the *Samguk chi*, "Romance of the Three Kingdoms" (i.e. the Chinese *San-kuo chih yen-i*), read either in the original language or in Korean translation. Part of this novel was used for a *p'ansori* libretto called *Chŏkpyŏk ka*, "The Song of the Red Cliff",[98] while an even smaller fragment of the story is dealt with in a song, a *chapka*.[99] *Mudang* in North Kyŏngsang Province in the 1920's used parts of the *Samguk chi* during their *kut*.[100] At present, the *Nottoo kut* from that region (from Ulchin, for instance), a ceremony dedicated to the *kunung* (warrior spirits), contains many references to heroes of the *Samguk chi*: Chu-ko Liang, Kuan Yü, Ts'ao Ts'ao, Chao Tzu-lung etc.[101] In other regions, too, heroes from the *Samguk chi* are revered as *kunung*[102]; they have become part and parcel of popular Korean culture and it is difficult to judge whether on the East Coast it really was the novel which influenced the *muga*. It certainly cannot be ruled out, considering the evidence of Son Chint'ae that the East Coast *mudang* did use the novel, and the fact that they also were familiar with *ko-sosŏl* versions of the story of Sim Ch'ŏng (cf. Chapter VII).

Two *muga*, one each from two of the most excentric parts of the country, Hamgyŏng Province and Cheju Island, have plots which are reminiscent of the *ko-sosŏl* known as *Yang Sanbaek chŏn*, "The Story of Liang Shan-po." The story is set in China and -not the same thing- is also of Chinese origin. It is often given the name of the female protagonist, Chu Ying-t'ai, and, in China, is encountered in several genres, folk-tale, theatre and novel. In Korea the novel enjoyed great popularity unto the first decades of this century, when it was available in several paperback editions.[103]

The Hamgyŏng Province *muga* is the *Mun kut*.[104] The *Mun kut* is more like the Chinese folk-tale than the Korean novel. The last can be divided into two parts: 1. Liang Shan-po and Chu Ying-t'ai study together in a temple, the girl disguised as a boy. In the end her true identity is discovered and the two become aware of their love for each other. They want to marry, but she has already been promised to another. He dies and when -on the way to her new husband's house- she passes by Liang's grave, it opens to admit her and so the two are united. 2. They are brought back to life by the Heavenly Emperor so that they may realize their predestined affinity. When the barbarians invade the country, Liang Shan-po saves the Empire. The folk-tale consists of only the first part and one way it ends is that two butterflies appear when Chu Ying-t'ai's husband has the grave opened. This is also the way the story ends in the *muga*. Eberhard says about this tale:

"Die Sage ist schon seit dem 11. Jahrhundert deutlich nach-weisbar, schon damals auch als Theaterstück bearbeitet, also wohl noch älter. Jedoch das Motiv der Verwandlung in einen Schmetterling ...... erscheint erst später, wird erst vom 17. Jahrh. häufig."

There is another version of the same tale in a *muga* from Hamhŭng (also in Hamgyŏng Province). The *muga* is called after the corrupted names of the hero and the heroine: *Ch'i Wŏndae Yang Sanbok.*[105] Here the lovers in the end change into a double rainbow. This motif, too, is found in China. According to Eberhard it is of quite recent origin. This version, like the preceding one, seems to have no connection with the *ko-sosŏl*. Instead it is a good example of a folk-tale of non-shamanistic origin adopted by the *mudang*.[106]

The Cheju *muga* with a similar content is *Segyŏng ponp'uri.*[107] Chang Chugŭn has examined this *muga* in detail and come to the conclusion that an oral story is at the basis of both *muga* and *ko-sosŏl*, and that the *muga* also was influenced by the novel.[108] It is especially the version collected by Akiba and Akamatsu which resembles the novel *Yang Sanbaek chŏn*, with which it has in common the episode of the boy and the disguised girl studying together, and the account of military exploits against a barbarian king. The passages about the early death of the boy, and about the girl entering the grave are lacking. One might also object that the content of the second part of the story -although the theme is the same- is quite different. In the *muga* it is the girl who, disguised as her husband, foils the evil plans of the barbarians. Nevertheless, this episode clearly has the smell of the so-called *kundam sosŏl*, novels about heroic military deeds, which were popular during the later Chosŏn dynasty. The motif of the wife who fights instead of, or for the sake of her husband was not unknown in these *kundam sosŏl* (cf. *Pak-ssi chŏn*, The story of Lady Pak"[109]).

Confirmation of Chang's opinion that the *ko-sosŏl* also contributed to the *AA* version of *Segyŏng ponp'uri*, perhaps can be found in the style. The Cheju *muga* collected by Akiba and Akamatsu are not in their original form, i.e. in pure Cheju dialect. The people who collected them apparently at once made a translation into standard Korean and therefore one should be careful in judging the stylistic aspects of these *muga*. Nevertheless it is striking that the text of *Segyŏng ponp'uri* contains a rather large number of literary expressions, more it seems, than other Cheju *muga* in the same volume.[110]

Segyŏng ponp'uri also contains an episode which is reminiscent of *Sukhyang chŏn* (The Story of Sukhyang), a novel, very popular during the Yi dynasty, of comparatively early date; there is a reference to this story in a 1754 version of *Ch'unhyang chŏn* in Chinese verse.[111] The girl Sukhyang has to endure many ordeals. When she is all alone and without support, Grand-mother Mago (a transformation of the Immortal Mago - in Chinese: Ma-ku; see Chapter VIII, annotation to line 732), who keeps a tavern, offers to let Sukhyang live with her. A piece of embroidery made by Sukhyang draws the attention of the man predestined to be her lover. He goes to the tavern to meet the girl but cannot get to see her. Only later, after many wanderings, does he meet Sukhyang. In *Segyŏng ponp'uri*, the heroine is sent away from home by her parents because of her unconventional behaviour. This in itself is a typical Cheju Island *muga* motif, but the result is a situation that is the same as the one in *Sukhyang chŏn*: a lonely girl without support. The heroine of the *muga* is adopted by an old woman, who in one version has a name which might be rendered as "keeper of a tavern."[112] The old woman's task is to weave silk for the girl's lover-to-be, who has become an attendant to the Heavenly Emperor. He notices the extremely fine quality of the silk sent to him (which has been woven by the young girl) and goes to enquire who made it. The girl, busy at needle-work, accidentally pricks her own finger, or, in another version, that of her lover, who flees because he cannot stand the smell of fresh blood. Therefore the meeting of the lovers, again, cannot take place until later. A further similarity in *Sukhyang chŏn* and *Segyŏng ponp'uri* is the fact that the male protagonist has already been pledged to another girl, and this girl commits suicide. The details concerning the suicide are a little different, however.

The old woman in the *muga* must weave silk because of a mistake she made when she was at the court of the Heavenly Emperor. This motif of the immortal who is exiled to an earthly existence is extremely common in the literature of the ChosӨn dynasty (whether written in Chinese or in Korean). In *Sukhyang chŏn* as good as all the important figures are exiled immortals. Together with the similar episode described above, the appearance of this motif in *Segyŏng ponp'uri* reinforces our impression that the *muga* underwent literary influences.[113]

A curious example of a *ko-sosŏl* influencing a *muga* is the *Ch'ungyŏl kut*, recorded from the lips of the same *mudang* from Hamhŭng who also had *Ch'i Wŏndae Yang Sanbok* on her repertoire.[114] Although this is not noted in secondary sources, the *muga* clearly has taken its hero, Yu Ch'ungyŏl, from a well-known *ko-sosŏl*: *Yu Ch'ungnyŏl chŏn*, "The Story of Liu Chung-lieh."[115] Apart from the similarity in name, the outline of the story is the same: the hero's father is a loyal and competent general who, slandered by evil conspirators at court, is banished (in the novel) or put in gaol (in the *muga*). His son, in spite of his youth, defeats the enemies of the ruler with the combi-nation of magical powers and military prowess so familiar from Chinese novels and is reunited with his parents, from whom circumstances had separated him. The *ko-sosŏl* is much and much longer than the *muga*, but these basic similarities make it more than likely that the plot of the *muga* is based on the novel. In details the *muga* and the novel are often different. In the latter the hero is separated from his mother during an attack by pirates, in the former he is parted from his parents almost at birth. While his father is in gaol, his mother mysteriously becomes pregnant (in the best tradition of *muga* heroines such as Tanggŭm-aegi). The child is born and put on a kind of raft, which is set afloat on the river. A turtle brings it to a patch of reeds. The baby cries as babies will, and the crying is heard by the king, who has the child brought to the palace, where it grows up. This will remind the Western reader of the story of Moses, but the motif of the abandoned child that is put into a box and thrown into the water, is -as has been said before- common in Korean *muga*. There would be no reason to think of the Old Testament, even though the reed patch and the fact that the child is brought up at court are suspiciously like the story of Moses, if, half-way through the *muga*, Ch'ungyŏl did not adress himself to an adversary called Joseph (Yosep)! It will be recalled that the stories of Joseph and Moses are closely connected. Joseph dies at the end of the Book of Genesis, Moses is born on the first page of the following Book of Exodus. Details about strife at court from the life of Joseph, when he served Pharaoh, are reminiscent of the story of Ch'ungyŏl. Joseph at one moment found himself in gaol, just like the father of Ch'ungyŏl in the *muga*, unlike the father in the *ko-sosŏl*, who was banished, which is more appropriate punishment for a high official who has fallen into disgrace. The use of the name "Joseph", which is quite unlike Korean names, is the strongest indication that this *muga* really contains "Christian" influences, confused as they may be. In conclusion, this shaman song has a plot derived from a traditional novel, as well as motifs borrowed from the Old Testament, which presumably were adopted because they were very similar to motifs which are current in the *muga*.

Muga and sijo

Against the opinion of Yi Hŭisŭng that the *sijo* developed from the *mudang* songs[116] there are statements from traditional musicians that *mudang* first began to sing *sijo* in the time of King Kojong (reign: 1863-1907). According to one of them, who had the story from one of the participants, during the reign of Kojong a *mudang* held a ritual at a shamanist shrine, the Kuksadang. There were many spectators and when the *mudang* handed out wine to them, to the delight of the audience, she sang a *sijo*, fitting the words to an existing *muga* tune.[117] Another musician, a singer, tells a similar story. In the time of Kojong the *mudang* who frequented the palace started to polish up their songs by using lofty *sijo* texts.[118] These two statements are not necessarily in disagreement with the thesis of Yi Hŭisŭng. It is possible that the *sijo* developed from Koryŏ dynasty *muga* and at the end of the Chosŏn dynasty "returned" to the *mudang*, but as there are no Koryŏ dynasty *muga* left, the thesis cannot be verified and, all in all, there is little to be said in favour of it.[119]

There is a music book called *Samjuk kŭmbo* (Samjuk's Music for the Zither) -in its present form estimated to date from the 19th century- which has a section on *munyŏ sijo*, that is *sijo* as sung by the *mudang*. Chang Sahun has made a musical analysis of this section and drawn the conclusion that the *mudang* not only used the words of existing *sijo*, but also followed the musical example of *sijo* singers. The last point contradicts the observations of musicians about the origin of the *sijo* sung by the *mudang*. These claimed that the *mudang* fitted the words to their own tunes and rhythms.[120]

The evidence of the *muga* we know corroborates the statements of musicians that the introduction of the *sijo* took place in a not too distant past. Although in *muga* of other regions there may be an occasional *sijo* fragment, only in the Seoul *muga*, and especially in the songs sung for the entertainment of the gods called *noraekkarak*, are *sijo* texts used in any quantity. Sometimes complete *sijo* are inserted in the song, sometimes *sijo* lines or half-lines are used. A *muga* with a remarkable number of *sijo* is *Sanmanura noraekkarak* (*AA* I, 78-86). It contains no less than six complete *sijo*.[121] Then there are several lines which incorporate parts of *sijo*.[122] All these *sijo* are of well-known types, with such subjects as the task of a real man, life in seclusion, the joys of wine etc., subjects which have not much to do with shamanism. There are quite a few lines which celebrate the king and wish for his longevity and health (such as are often found in *sijo*), which makes it plausible that this kind of *noraekkarak* developed among the *mudang* of the capital who frequented the royal palace.

A complete *sijo* by the celebrated 16th century *kisaeng* Hwang Chini[123] is presented in the theatrical *Kŏri kut* of the East Coast as a composition written during an examination![124] Another example of the use of *sijo* outside the Seoul area is seen in two *muga* from Andong, where the greater part of a *sasŏl sijo* ("narrative *sijo*") is inserted in descriptions of the soul's journey to the Underworld.[125] This *sijo* is a love poem, expressing the determination of the lover to join his beloved as soon as possible in spite of the high mountains separating them.[126] Because this poem has been integrated into the narrative of the *muga* -where, in a different context, it has a different purpose- it is used in a manner that contrasts with the way in which *sijo* are used in the *noraekkarak* of the Seoul area, where one sees an accumulation of unrelated *sijo* texts.

In addition to whole *sijo*, or whole lines of *sijo*, the *muga* may contain formulae and motifs which also are found in the *sijo*. Examples of shared formulae were given in the preceding chapter, an example of a shared motif is that of the apostate monk who starts a family and "recycles" his monk's paraphernalia as household items. In one *muga* such a monk breaks his wooden hand-bell in two, to use one half as a chamber-pot, one half as bowl for soy-sauce. A *sasŏl sijo* with the same motif is *Sijo sajŏn*, No. 1793.[127]

Muga and kasa

Many of the formulae and themes in longer traditional poems, the *kasa*, are also found in *muga* (Chapter V) and, although it is difficult to make a generalized statement, in many cases it is clear from the nature of the language used that the *muga* received these elements from the *kasa*. Compare the following two fragments. The first is from a *kasa* known as *Hanyang ka* (Song of the Capital) and describes a composition written during one of the government examinations.[128]

> The handwriting betrays a master's brush,
> What is written is the work of a great writer.
> Is it the work of Li Po or Tu Fu?
> Is it the handwriting of Wang Hsi-chih?

The second fragment is from the the *Sanmanura noraekkarak* and stands on its own. It has nothing to do with the preceding and following lines.[129]

> The writing that is hung on the wall
> Whose writing is it? Well-written it is!
> Is it the manner of Tu Mu?
> Is it the hand of Wang Hsi-chih?

One should not assume that the text of the *muga* was directly inspired by *Hanyang ka* (similar passages are found in other works, too), but it is obvious in view of the content that this is an instance of *gesunkenes Kulturgut*. The *mudang* may have learned to handle such passages well, to integrate them creatively into their rituals, but they cannot have been the originators of such lines.

In most cases, relatively small elements of the *kasa* were adopted for use in the *muga*, but in some instances *kasa* as a whole acquired the status of *muga*. This has happened especially with Buddhist *kasa*. The *kasa* called *Sŏwang ka* (Song of Going to the Western Paradise), ascribed to the monk Naong of the end of the Koryŏ dynasty, but probably not written down until 1704,[130] is found in the repertoire of an East Coast *mudang*.[131] The *Saja kut* for the messengers of the King of the Underworld,[132] from Pyongyang, shows a marked resemblance to the *kasa* with the title *In'gwa mun*, "Text on Causality."[133] Son Chint'ae included in his first collection a version of *Hoesim kok* (Song of Repentance), without realizing, apparently, that he was dealing with a Buddhist *kasa* text, or he would not have translated *sijo* (= *siju*) as "ancestors" instead of "believers."[134] The anonymous collection of *muga* circulating among *mudang* in the Seoul area (cf. Ch. III) also has a *Hoesim kok*. It is interesting to note that this song contains lines in which the power of the *mudang* is deprecated. If one becomes seriously ill neither the scripture readings of the exorcist nor the *kut* of the *mudang* will do any good, the *kasa* says.

These Buddhist *kasa* are always sung by the *mudang* in rituals for the dead; exactly in this kind of ritual the influence of Buddhism on Korean shamanism has been enormous, even if, in some ways, superficial. For the *mudang* it is much easier to integrate a Buddhist *kasa* about the transience of life into a ceremony, even in its entirety, than *kasa* about the joys of a hermit's life or the woes of a daughter-in-law, to name but two popular subjects, and so it becomes clear why the mudang so much favour Buddhist *kasa*.

Muga and mask-dance drama (t'alch'um)

The poetic language of mask-dance drama to a certain extent coincides with that of the *muga*, as has been shown in the preceding chapter. Not only on the level of the formula, but also on that of the theme *muga* and *t'alch'um* share certain elements. In the *Yangju pyŏlsandae nori*, for instance, one finds: the geomantic description, the crossing of a river (not a theme listed in Chapter V, but repeatedly seen in the *muga*, especially in the *Sonnim kut*, when the Sonnim, the gods of small-pox, on their journey from China to Korea have to cross the Yalu River), the list of books, the apparel of a young man, the clothing of a baby, and an examination scene. What explanation can there be for this?

Korea has known masked dancing since early times.[135] The poem "The Mask" by the Silla scholar Ch'oe Ch'iwŏn (857-?) not only testifies to the existence of mask-dances, but also shows that this dancing had a magic, ritual function.[136]

> What man is this with the golden colored whip?
> In his hand he holds the pearl whip
> > to exorcise the ghostly spirit.
> Walking quickly, then running slowly
> > he performs an elegant dance,
> Which faintly resembles the Phoenix Dance and the spring
> > [of the golden age] of [Emperor] Yao.

This tradition of mask-dances, however, in spite of its function, was not kept up by the *mudang*, at least in the period for which we have reliable information. During the Koryŏ and Chosŏn period male actors performed all major existing forms of drama. In contrast to the mask-dances performed at court, about which there is a fair amount of information, nothing is known about dramatic elements in the *mudang* ceremonies of the past. One can only go by the present state of affairs. Today there are a number of *mudang* ceremonies with a dramatic character[137] and in one of these, the Cheju Island *Yŏnggam nori*,[138] masks are used (by the two *mudang* who impersonate the possessing spirits to be chased away). However this may be, and whether such shamanistic dramatic scenes existed long ago or not, the *mudang* were not directly connected to the mainstream of mask-dance drama. To explain the overlapping of the diction of the mask-plays and the *muga* one should, again, think of the link between *kwangdae* and *mudang*. It is possible that the *mudang* were directly influenced by the actors of mask-plays (the *kwangdae*), but as the mask-plays themselves incorporated many and diverse elements from vernacular literature, it is equally possible that both mask-plays and *muga* underwent the influence of the "general poetic diction" of the second half of the Chosŏn dynasty. If the *muga* resemble the mask-plays, one need not therefore assume that the influences were mediated only by *kwangdae* who were the actors in these plays. Any *kwangdae* who handled texts in his performances could have been the source of this influence.

VII   The Song of a Dutiful Daughter

The tale of Sim Ch'ŏng is told in *ko-sosŏl*, *p'ansori*, folk-song and *muga*. In this chapter several *muga* texts will be examined to clarify the place of the Sim Ch'ŏng *muga* within the Sim Ch'ŏng traditions as a whole.

Outline of the story

A poor, blind *yangban*, Sim Hakkyu, and his wife Kwak-ssi, after many prayers, at an advanced age become the parents of a daughter, Sim Ch'ŏng. The mother dies soon after giving birth and it is not without great trouble that Sim Hakkyu manages to raise the child. Fortunately, she turns out to be an extremely dutiful daughter, who as soon as she is able to do so, goes begging for her father and herself. She attracts the attention of a rich lady who wants to adopt her, but Sim Ch'ŏng refuses to leave her father. In the meantime her father meets a monk, who tells him that he will regain his eyesight if he makes a vast donation to the Buddha of his temple. Destitute though he may be, Sim Hakkyu makes a promise to donate three hundred sacks of rice. Belatedly he realizes that he will never manage to collect this amount. He is thrown into despair and fears the wrath of the Buddha because of his lighthearted promise. Merchants come to Sim's village and offer a large sum for a virgin to be sacrificed at a dangerous stretch of sea they will have to pass. Without telling her father Sim Ch'ŏng sells herself to them for exactly three hundred sacks of rice. After a heart-rending farewell she accompanies the sailors and jumps into the water, but instead of drowning she finds herself led to the palace of the Dragon King, where she meets her mother and for some time lives happily. Eventually, however, she has to return to the world.

Hidden in a lotus, she is picked up by the same merchants who had sacrificed her. They offer the flower to the Emperor, a recent widower. When the Emperor discovers the girl in the lotus he weds her. Sim Ch'ŏng now lives in great splendour, but she is unable to forget her father. For reasons which are not made clear in every version of the tale, she cannot simply send someone to the village where he lives, but has to resort to an indirect method: she invites all blind men to a banquet, which lasts for many days. At the last moment, her father -still blind- arrives. Only when he is reunited with his daughter he regains his sight. Everybody is happy now and in some versions Sim Hakkyu, who earlier has had an unfortunate liaison with a shrew called Ppaengdŏg-ŏmi, marries a lady called An-ssi. This is the story in its most popular version. Other versions may differ in details and even in the names of the personages.

The origins of the tale of Sim Ch'ŏng

Several conflicting theories have been put forward as to the origin of the story of Sim Ch'ŏng. One school, represented by Kim Tonguk, has claimed that the *p'ansori* version came first and thus preceded the novel.[1] There exist several versions of *SC* in *p'ansori*, which all resemble the so-called "popular version" of the novel more than the story which is told in certain woodblock editions published in Seoul in the 1880's. Recently a number of scholars have propounded the view that these editions belong to an earlier stage of development than the popular version, of which the edition published in Chŏnju (*Wanp'anbon*, hereafter: *WSC*) is best known.[2] If this is correct, it will be difficult to insist that the novel developed out of *p'ansori*, as the style of the Seoul edition is quite unlike that of *p'ansori*. This is of some importance for the purposes of this discussion since the theory of *p'ansori* origin for *SC* implies a link with shamanism; the supposed creators of *p'ansori*, the *kwangdae* -as has been noted in Chapter V- often were husbands of *mudang* and acted as assistants charged with the musical accompaniment of the *kut*.

 SC has been linked to shamanism in other ways as well. According to Kim T'aegon the origin of *SC* is to be found in a ceremony for the recently deceased, the *Ogu kut*. He posits the following development: *Ogu kut* → *SC p'ansori* → *SC* novel → *SC kut*.[3] Another scholar, Sin Tongik, also accepts the fact that the present day *SC kut* is similar to the novel, but suggests that the original story can be traced to the Kangnŭng area and assumes that a primitive form of the *SC kut* preceded all versions in other genres.[4] The evidence for this is thin. Sin refers to a story in a Chinese historical source, the *Wei chih*, about an island "in the East" where young girls were sacrificed to the sea. In the same section of the book -about the Eastern Okchŏ- one finds stories about a country of Amazons and people with two faces.[5]

Similarity between *SC* novel and *kut* is also noted by Kim Sŏnp'ung, who proposes the following scheme of development: *SC* legend → *SC* novel → *SC kut* → *SC p'ansori*.[6] A comparison of the *muga* texts yields no internal evidence pointing in this direction. On the contrary, there is some external evidence against this theory. One of the *mudang* performing the *SC kut*, Yi Kŭmok, who started her career around 1935, has stated that this *kut* was introduced about fifty years ago, which would be in the twenties or thirties, when all important texts of both novel and *p'ansori* were already well established.[7] Son Chint'ae was told by a Kyŏngsang Province *mudang* in 1922 that the *mudang* of this region would use a song about Sim Ch'ŏng when they held rites to cure diseases of the eye. In the same passage he also mentions the fact that the *mudang* of Kyŏngsang Province integrated parts of the novel *Samguk chi* into their songs and he suggests that for the tale of Sim Ch'ŏng, too, the *mudang* borrowed from the novel.[8] Finally the fact reported by Yi Tuhyŏn, that the story of Sim Ch'ŏng was first sung in its totality by the *mudang* in the 1950's, argues against an origin of the story in *muga* (before that time, the *mudang* ended their performance when Sim Ch'ŏng had been sacrificed).[9]

Mudang who perform the Sim Ch'ŏng kut and their texts

In contrast to many other *muga* the Sim Ch'ŏng *muga* are found only in a limited area, usually referred to as the East Coast. The *mudang* who perform the *Sim Ch'ŏng kut* form a close-knit group, linked by family ties as well as professional relationships.[10]

There are altogether eight texts of Sim Ch'ŏng *muga* available, four of which have been examined in detail. The remaining four will be used as additional material. The basic texts were sung by Pak Yongnyŏ (born in 1912), Yi Kŭmok (1923), Pyŏn Yŏnho (1927) and Kim Yŏnghŭi (1941), the other texts by Kim Sŏkch'ul (the only male performer in this company, born in 1922), Yi Kŭmok again (two more texts) and Sin Sŏngnam (1925?).[11]

In view of the close relationship between these *mudang*, the texts of their Sim Ch'ŏng *muga* are surprisingly different from each other, but in spite of the differences the basic outline of the story is the same in all texts. In order to compare the Chŏnju edition (*Wanp'anbon*) of *Sim Ch'ŏng chŏn* (*WSC*) with the *p'ansori* libretto of Sin Chaehyo and the Seoul edition of the novel, Kim Hŭnggyu has divided the story into thirty episodes.[12] All the episodes in *WSC* are found in the *muga*, except for two: the conversation of Sim Hakkyu with women pounding rice (no. 26) and the final episode, which describes how the descendants of Sim Ch'ŏng prosper. Instead of this last, the *muga* have an epilogue explaining the purpose of the *kut* or extolling the virtue of filial piety. A comic scene about a blind man talking to a woman who is pounding rice is part of the so-called *Kŏri kut*, which is included in the repertoire of the East Coast *mudang*.[13] One episode, the invocation of Sim Ch'ŏng's spirit by the wife of Prime Minister Chang (no. 17) is found in two versions only. Episode no. 29 (Sim Hakkyu receives the title of Puwŏngun and the shrew Ppaengdŏg-ŏmi is punished) is slightly different or partly absent in the *muga*. If the contents of this episode were to be phrased in a more general way, however, all *muga* can be said to include this scene as well.

It would be a mistake to judge the relations between *kut*, *p'ansori* and novel from Kim Hŭnggyu's table of episodes -supplemented with the data for the *muga*- alone. *WSC* and the *p'ansori* libretto by Sin Chaehyo (*SSC*) are not representative of the genres of novel and *p'ansori* as a whole. As will be shown below, there are forms of the novel that are more relevant for an understanding of the *muga* than *WSC*, while *p'ansori* texts recorded from performances are quite different from *SSC*; in fact, compared with the list of thirty episodes, some are closer to *WSC* than to *SSC*. In this list *WSC* is different from *SSC* on eight points (8, 17, 18, 19, 25, 27, 29, 30). Out of these eight points, one *p'ansori* version is similar to *WSC* on five and to *SSC* only on three.[14]

The danger of drawing conclusions from a limited number of texts can also be illustrated with examples drawn from an article in which Yi Kyŏngbok has compared novel, *p'ansori* and *muga*. He used a *SC kut* by Yi Kŭmok for the *muga*, two Seoul block prints, one Ansŏng block print and *WSC* for the novel, and *SSC* for *p'ansori*.[15] This is a respectable number of texts; nevertheless, conclusions from this material can be misleading. E.g. in *SSC*, Sim Ch'ŏng before she leaves home, pays a visit to her mother's grave. This scene is also found in Yi Kŭmok's text, but not in the other texts used by Yi Kyŏngbok. On the strength of this comparison one might conclude that the *muga* are closer to *p'ansori* than to any version of the novel. A wider comparison, however, reveals that this scene is also found in the text of Kim Sŏkch'ul, but not in any of the other *muga*.[16]

In the same article the impression is created that Yi Kŭmok's text has a unique description of an immortal descending from heaven, ordering the sailors to present the lotus flower in which Sim Ch'ŏng is hidden to the Emperor. This detail, however, is also found in a version of the novel.

Of course a limitation of the number of texts cannot be avoided. Even the number of different versions of the novel alone is much too large to be used for detailed comparisons. I have concentrated my attention in the first place on an annotated edition of the novel, edited by Chang Chiyŏng (*NSC*).[17] If one uses the check-list of Kim Hŭnggyu this turns out to be even closer to the *muga* than *WSC*. Episode 26 (Sim Hakkyu talks to women pounding rice) is lacking in *NSC* and all four of the *muga*, while the order of the episodes (integration of 19 and 24) is the same in *NSC* and three of the *muga*.[18] Fieldwork among the East-Coast *mudang* undertaken after the first comparison of the basic four *muga* texts brought to light the fact that these *mudang* kept a copy of an edition of *Sim Ch'ŏng chŏn* published in 1972 in Taegu. This edition in the traditional "paperback"-style in which *ko-sosŏl* were published from about 1911 on (with a cover that originally belonged to the Sech'ang sŏgwan edition of 1925!), is virtually identical to *NSC*. Both this edition (*HSC*) and *NSC* are within a tradition which goes back to a rewriting of the story of Sim Ch'ŏng by Yi Haejo. This rewriting was entitled *Kangsangnyŏn* (The Lotus on the River) and appeared in 1912.[19] In principle, it would not seem unreasonable to use editions like *NSC* or that published in Taegu for the purposes of our investigation, because they go back to editions of the period in which the story of Sim Ch'ŏng -according to Yi Kŭmok- was first sung by the *mudang*. The comparison with the *muga* shows that the use of editions from the same tradition as *NSC* is indeed more fruitful than going to the older block prints.

For *p'ansori* four texts have been consulted.[20] Comparisons with other texts may yield information on details, but it would seem that the origins of the *muga* can be sufficiently explored with the aid of these four.

The examination of the texts was complemented by observation of the *Sim Ch'ŏng kut* in 1975, 1977 (both times by Sin Sŏngnam) and 1982. The last time the performer was a rather young *mudang*, Kim Yŏngsuk, who sang this song for the first time. Below a little more will be said about her performance, which was recorded on tape.[21]

The Sim Ch'ŏng kut of Pyŏn Yŏnho (PYM)

It will be convenient to start with an examination of the text of Pyŏn Yŏnho, as it is for the greater part very close to *NSC* and most clearly betrays its origins.

PYM opens with a scene in late spring, described in highly formulaic terms,[22] just as in *NSC*. *WSC* and *p'ansori* start with a simple indication of place and time. The introduction of *PYM* and *NSC* is similar to that of *Kangsangnyŏn* and may be typical of rewritings produced under the influence of the "new novel", *sin-sosŏl*.[23] For twelve lines (as spaced in the published text) *PYM* follows *NSC* closely. Discrepancies are due to misunderstanding on the part of the performer, the result of variations in spelling or of modernization of verb endings. E.g. the line *ch'unp'ung torihwagaeya* "a night when the blossoms of peach and plum open in the spring wind" (originally from the "Song of Everlasting Sorrow" by the T'ang poet Po Chü-i) becomes *ch'unp'ung hageya hago*.[24] Interestingly, these twelve lines are followed by the line with which *p'ansori* versions open: "In the last years of the era Hŏngp'ung of the Sung in Tohwadong in Hwangju there was a blind man; his family name was Sim, his personal name Hakkyu."

After this *PYM* again reverts to the novel for the next twenty lines. Halfway through the enumeration of the jobs which Kwak-ssi took on to support her husband, five lines are found which do not occur in *NSC*, but are similar to lines in *p'ansori* texts.[25] Then *PYM* follows the novel again for several pages, more or less accurately. Occasionally words or lines from *NSC* are omitted, but lines not found in *NSC* or not easily identifiable as corruptions of *NSC* are very rare and of little importance.

The way in which Pyŏn Yŏnho treats the scene where Kwak-ssi prays to the gods for the blessing of a child deserves special attention. Here the *mudang* is on familiar ground, and she might be expected to change this passage or add to it. Instead, she continues to reproduce words of which the meaning apparently is not completely clear to her.[26] She is not always so passive, however. After the safe delivery of the baby Sim Hakkyu prays to Samsin, the god who protects the fortunes of babies and children. Having repeated four lines from *NSC*, Pyŏn Yŏnho adds four lines which are not found in novel or *p'ansori*. The same phrases are recorded elsewhere in her repertoire and belong to her regular stock of prayer formulae.[27]

A little earlier she describes how the blind father establishes the sex of the baby, by letting his fingers run down its body. Nothing obstructs the downward movement of his hand. This scene is not found in *NSC*, but occurs in *SSC* and *WSC*, where it is said that his hand moves "smoothly, like a ferry crossing a river."[28] *PYM* (like the other *muga*) omits this image, just repeating Sim's next remark that "an old clam has given birth to a young clam." Most of the *mudang* here add a pleasantry of their own; in the words of Pyŏn Yŏnho: "People of the lower and upper village! A drought was predicted, so our family has dug a water hole."

Apart from a few variations like these, for more than twenty pages from the beginning *PYM* continually relies on *NSC*. When the story reaches the point where Sim Hakkyu goes out to look for his daughter and stumbles into a ditch, this changes. The tale is told more freely and more simply. Lines from *NSC* are still used, but they do not dominate any longer, although a somewhat extended piece of description, the painting of Sim Ch'ŏng's portrait, is again taken word for word from *NSC*.[29] In view of the tendency to stick less closely to the novel as the story progresses, it is surprising that the episode of Sim Ch'ŏng's voyage to the place where she will be sacrificed is again literally copied from the novel. This is all the more remarkable in that the passage is difficult to memorize because of the high proportion of Sino-

Korean. This fragment, of which the "Song of the Eight Landscapes of the Hsiao and Hsiang Rivers" is an important part, apparently is regarded as a highlight, well worth special effort.[30]

The attention paid to this fragment contrasts with the treatment given to the scenes following the presentation of the lotus to the Emperor. That Sim Ch'ŏng marries the Emperor and decides to organize a banquet to meet her father is taken for granted. Not a single word is spent on these events. When Sim Hakkyu meets a servant of the magistrate, the subject of the banquet is mentioned for the first time. This and a simpler style allow Pyŏn Yŏnho to finish what remains of the story after the "Song of the Hsiao and Hsiang Rivers" in only eleven pages.

In the last part one can discern influences from *p'ansori*, especially from the text we will refer to as *PH*. It is most unlikely that the *muga* would have influenced *p'ansori*; in fact, the fragmentary and corrupt nature of the similar passages in *PYM* makes it obvious that the *muga* is dependent on another text.[31]

In the end, *all the blind* gathered for the feast regain their eyesight, as in all *p'ansori* versions.[32] *NSC* does not have this detail, which is a feature common to all *SC muga*. The reason for this is easily understood if one keeps in mind that the aim of the *SC kut* is to prevent and cure blindness.

The last eleven lines are a prayer and an explanation as to why this *kut* is held. The prayer consists of formulae which are also used elsewhere in the repertoire of this *mudang*.[33]

Summing up, it can be said that the first and largest part of this *muga* closely follows *NSC*, or one of the editions published from the twenties onwards which are very similar to *NSC*. The remainder of the *muga* does not follow one original, but contains several details which strongly suggest reliance on a *p'ansori* text like *PH*. Although Pyŏn Yŏnho, especially in the last part, here and there uses phrases which are also found in her other narrative *muga*,[34] her *SC kut* as a whole has but little in common with the other texts from her repertoire.

The Sim Ch'ŏng kut by Yi Kŭmok (YIM I, II, III)[35]

PYM is to a large extent dependent on the novel and to a lesser degree on *p'ansori*. Yi Kŭmok does not follow her models so closely, but still *YIM* I betrays in many places the influences of novel and *p'ansori*. That she made use of a text similar to *NSC* is most evident in that part of the story in which Sim Ch'ŏng and the sailors are on their way to the spot where the girl is to be sacrificed. For three pages the transcribed text of the *muga* is an almost exact copy of *NSC*.[36] A very similar passage is found in *p'ansori*[37];

nevertheless it is clear that Yi Kŭmok's text here is closer to the novel (as was that of Pyŏn Yŏnho). The outline of the story as a whole is very close to *NSC*, too.

Several lines suggest reliance on a written text. E.g., in the novel one reads: *tat-to kkŭnch'yŏ, no-do ilk'o* (the anchor cable snapped, the oars were lost), which in the *muga* appears as: *tat-to kŭnch'yŏ ro-do ilk'o*.[38] Apparently Yi Kŭmok used a written text which -contrary to normal pronunciation- used the letter *r* as an initial, as does the Hyangminsa text (*HSC*) which circulates among the East Coast *mudang*. (When I obtained a copy of this text, it was in the house of Kim Yongt'aek, a son of Yi Kŭmok, where it had been used by his wife, Kim Yŏngsuk). Yi Kŭmok herself told Sin Tongik that she learned the text from a manuscript. Sin is in doubt whether this was a manuscript version of the novel, but in view of the similarities between her text and the novel this seems likely.[39]

A complicating factor is that the *mudang* do not learn a text once and for all; they remain open to new influences. Any other version of the tale which Yi Kŭmok came into contact with later, may have influenced her, too. In spite of many points of resemblance with the novel, there are also details which betray influences from *p'ansori*: e.g., Sim Hakkyu's distress when he finds that he has left his wife, Kwak-ssi, to die alone while he went out to buy medicine,[40] and the description of the monk when he comes near the place where Sim Hakkyu has fallen into the water. He hears strange noises and wonders what these might be. In *YIM* I: "Is it the crying of a fox that has changed [into a human shape] and tries to lure me? Or is it the crying of the immortal Magu at dusk in Ch'ŏnt'aesŏng?"[41] This is easy to identify as part of *PC*.[42] although the second line is garbled and does not make much sense. Originally it was the famous T'ang beauty Yang Kuei-fei crying at dusk in Ma-wei-i. Apparently Yi Kŭmok did not understand the reference or forgot the exact text and she handled this problem in a characteristic way by substituting the name of a figure who often appears in *muga*.[43] Probably also due to the influence of *p'ansori* is the speech -directly addressed to the audience- with which Yi Kŭmok concludes her performance: an exhortation to show filial piety to one's parents when they are still alive. Such epilogues one finds also in *SSC* and in *Ong Kojip chŏn*, a *ko-sosŏl* in *p'ansori* style.[44]

Occasionally Yi Kŭmok adds details of her own, as when she makes fun of the blind father holding his new-born daughter upside down.[45]

Like *PYM* this text reflects various influences. For *p'ansori*, *PC* seems to have been the dominant source. Apart from a few scenes (the "Song of the Hsiao and Hsiang Rivers", etc.) Yi Kŭmok adapts rather than copy literally.

When *YIM* II and *YIM* III are compared with *YIM* I, it becomes clear that Yi Kŭmok is not the type of *mudang* who learns a text once and then repeats it exactly. This is not to say that she recreates the song completely every time she sings it. In some cases at least, differences result from the fact that she follows different models. In *YIM* I, for example, she begins in a manner that is similar to that of *PC*, while in *YIM* II she begins in the same manner as Pyŏn Yŏnho, that is with the opening lines of *NSC*. In *YIM* III, she starts abruptly, without introducing Sim Hakkyu and his wife, by telling that they grieved about their childlessness. When no clear source in novel or *p'ansori* can be found it is, of course, possible that this is due to the creative efforts of the performer, but also that the example of another *mudang* is being followed. It is remarkable that *YIM* I in some ways is more like the text of Kim Sŏkch'ul (a younger brother of her husband) than like *YIM* II. There is no doubt that the East Coast *mudang* copy parts of the *SC kut* of their colleagues that never belonged to the original Sim Ch'ŏng story. Yi Kŭmok, for instance, when she begins to sing *YIM* II -before the tale proper begins- explains why she wears a traditional man's hat, a *kat*. The Chinese character written with at the top the part nicknamed a "hat", and below the character for "woman", means "peacefulness"; it is to express the wish for peace that the female shaman wears the *kat*. In 1982, the debutante Kim Yŏngsuk repeated this exactly.

YIM III is an interesting text, inasmuch as it fully records audience reactions and shows how a *mudang* struggles to keep the attention of the public while people quarrel, or start to dance rapturously in the performing area, and all kinds of hawkers try to sell their wares as the *kut* goes on. It would be interesting to study the way in which such things influence the text by comparing several recordings of this kind.

The Sim Ch'ŏng kut by Pak Yongnyŏ (PAM)

Pak Yongnyŏ, even more than Yi Kŭmok, retells the story in her own way. She almost never quotes a complete sentence from beginning to end. *PAM* follows *NSC* completely as far as the broad outline of the story is concerned, but *p'ansori* also seems to have been an important model. The problem is that "novel" and "*p'ansori*" are not clearly demarcated. It has already been pointed out that three *muga* (*YIM* I, *PAM* and *KIM*) combine episodes 19 and 24 of the list drawn up by Kim Hŭnggyu. Sin Chaehyo also combined those points. Does this mean that the *muga* are modelled on *p'ansori*? No, because *NSC* has the same order, while the *p'ansori* text *PH* has the same order as *WSC*.[46]

In this case, a comparison of the contents of these episodes can reveal more specific information. In all three of the *muga* Ppaengdŏg-ŏmi confesses to having consumed enormous quantities of sour apricots ("I must be pregnant"). This detail is only found in *PC* and PY, not in *NSC* or *SSC*. The conclusion therefore is -as far as the present texts are concerned- that this scene was borrowed from one of the two first *p'ansori* texts.

Other details too, indicate *p'ansori* origin. Kwak-ssi becomes ill because she has to start working too soon after childbirth. This is sometimes regarded as characteristic for the *muga* -it is also found in *YIM* and *KIM*- but can be traced to *PC*.[47]

In *PAM* Sim Hakkyu's invocation at the funeral of his wife is omitted. This is characteristic; in this version there are only a limited number of Sino-Korean phrases, while extended passages built up from lines of Chinese poetry, such as are found in novels, *p'ansori*, *PYM* and *YIM*, are completely absent.[48]

Like Yi Kŭmok, Pak Yongnyŏ sometimes adds touches of her own. After the funeral of his wife Sim Hakkyu is alone with the baby, who cries and cries. In an attempt to soothe the child Sim puts his finger and, when this does not work, his tongue in the baby's mouth. Still the little girl does not find this an acceptable substitute for her mother's breast and Sim in exasperation throws the baby on the floor. When Sim Hakkyu is looking for women who are willing to nurse Sim Ch'ŏng, she relates that not all women were kind, employing the style characterized by parallelism and antithesis which is typical for *muga*:[49]

> The kind women came to him, throwing down their hoes,
> Took the baby in their arms and nursed it,
> But the unkind women went to this end of the field,
> If Blindman Sim came to the other end,
> And they went to the other end of the field,
> If Blindman Sim came to this end,
> And they did not nurse the baby!

Although it is difficult to be certain about the origins of this version, it is my impression that *p'ansori* has been of more importance than the novel. Examples have been given of details which were reminiscent of *PC*, but influence from other *p'ansori* versions, too, is not unlikely.[50] Influence from the novel seems to be present in the scene in which the sailors take the lotus flower aboard. A voice from Heaven orders them to handle it with care and deliver it to the Emperor, threatening heavenly punishment if they fail. None of the *p'ansori* versions has anything similar.[51]

The final part of this *muga* explains why the ghosts of Sim Hakkyu and Sim Ch'ŏng are invoked: this ensures good eyesight for everybody; neither soldier, nor policeman, government clerk or office worker could do his work without this blessing.[52]

Stylistically, it is clear that Pak Yongnyŏ often falls back on proven techniques of *muga* composition. One of these is, for instance, to take two opposing terms -e.g. high and low or left and right- or a short list -e.g. a row of numbers or the points of the compass- and to elaborate on the framework these terms afford. A combination of this technique with material from the novel results in: *mŏri-wi-e-nŭn hagwan-iyo, mŏri-arae-e-nŭn kajŭn norigae, kajŭn pidan-ŭl kamŭsigo* (on her head she wore a flower crown, under her head she wore all kinds of trinkets and all kinds of silks). *NSC* has in the same passage: *mŏri-uh-ae hwagwan-io, mom-e-nŭn haŭi-roda* (on her head she wore a flower crown, on her body a robe of mist).[53] In *muga*, the application of such antithetical patterns tends to be more mechanical than in other genres. Repetition and recapitulation are also frequently used in *PAM*. E.g., when Sim Hakkyu and his wife have had a dream about the conception of Sim Ch'ŏng: *Kŭnal pam-e ch'unjŏng-ŭl puch'injira. Ch'unjŏng-ŭl puch'igo, kŭnal put'ŏm t'aegi innŭnde* (The night of that day they made love! When they had made love, from that day on, there were signs of pregnancy).[54]

The Sim Ch'ŏng kut of Kim Yŏnghŭi (KIM)

Kim Yŏnghŭi's *SC kut* is the most heterogeneous text and, in my opinion, the most interesting. She uses fragments of novel and *p'ansori*, details from the *SC kut* of the older *mudang* around her and elements of other *muga*, adding her own contributions. She also interrupts the flow of the story to talk about subjects that are only tangentially related to *SC*. *KIM* is roughly twice as long as *PYM*, *YIM* I and *PAM*.

In some places it is evident that Kim Yŏnghŭi makes use of the novel. Her *kut* starts with a lengthy explanation of its aims (not unlike the conclusion of *PAM*), after which the story proper begins with the familiar indication of place and time. This is followed by the description of late spring which is characteristic for the novel[55]; the text is sometimes misunderstood and corrupt, but it is still easily identifiable.[56]

Influences from the novel are also found in the conception dream of Kwak-ssi,[57] Sim Hakkyu's speech to comfort his wife,[58] Kwak-ssi's last words,[59] and the verse which Sim Ch'ŏng writes for the wife of Prime Minister Chang.[60]

P'ansori influence shows in smaller details,[61] in Sim's farewell to the village he leaves,[62] in the story of Sim's taking a bath,[63] and at the end, when all the blind regain their sight.[64] It is impossible to tell in most of these cases whether the influences are direct or received by way of another *SC kut*.

Direct influence from other *mudang* is found in a scene in which Sim Hakkyu, after being robbed of his clothes, is misled into thinking, by a drop in temperature caused by a cloud obscuring the sun, that night has fallen, so

that he can move around without being seen; jeering children bring him back
to reality. This comic scene does not occur in *NSC* or the *p'ansori* versions
under review here, but is found in *PAM* and *YIM* I, as well as in the text of
her father Kim Sŏkch'ul.[65]

Kim Yŏnghŭi uses numerous elements from other *muga*. When Sim
Ch'ŏng goes to the residence of Prime Minister Chang, the house is described
in a traditional manner; part of the description is the same as that used for for
the house of Tanggŭm-aegi in a *kut* by the second wife of Kim Yŏnghŭi's
father: both houses have twelve walls and twelve gates.[66] The food offered to
Sim Ch'ŏng is described with a traditional *namul t'aryŏng*, a "Vegetable
Song".[67] At the end of her *kut* there is a piece about the importance of filial
piety, which she also uses at the end of her *Paridegi muga*.[68] This, by and
large, is the same as the epilogue of the *Sim Ch'ŏng kut* of her aunt and
mentor Yi Kŭmok.[69]

Some songs which are found in all *SC* versions, such as the song which
Sim Hakkyu sings for his daughter (*sarang ka*), or the song of the pall-bearers
(*hyangdu ka*), are stretched to great lengths by Kim Yŏnghŭi. The first takes
more than two pages, as compared to seven lines in *PAM*.[70] As mentioned
above, she borrows the conception dream from the novel, but this does not
keep her from adding to it another conception dream of a type which is
current in *muga*.[71]

Personal variations are, among others, a description of the difficulties of
childbirth after the age of forty,[72] an explanation of why Kwak-ssi cannot take
her ease after the delivery of the baby,[73] realistic details concerning the way
the blind Sim Hakkyu feeds his daughter, dividing the food equally over eyes,
nose and mouth[74], and a jocular reference to the sexual activities of Sim
Hakkyu.[75]

Kim Yŏnghŭi's use of parallelism shows the difference in the usage of this
structural principle in *muga* on the one hand and novel or *p'ansori* on the
other. When Sim Hakkyu goes out to find Sim Ch'ŏng who has not come
home although it is already evening, he falls into a river:[76]

> *Palmog-e onŭn mur-i kub-wi-e olla ogo*
> *Kub-wi-e onŭn mur-i kasŭm-e ch'ullŏng ch'ullŏng*
> *Kasŭm-e onŭn mur-i mog-e-kkaji olla oni*
> The water which came to his ankles rose to above his heels,
> The water which came to above his heels, rippled against
>   his breast,
> The water which came to his breast, came up as far as his
>   neck and then ....

Superficially this is very much like other *SC* versions (novel or *p'ansori*), but a comparison reveals that in this case the parallelism is much more systematic. These lines may also be regarded as an example of a form of *Kettenbau*.

Redundancy, caused by the glossing of a difficult term borrowed from written literature or by the need to fill out a line, is also a common feature of *KIM*.

> *Kŭrŏnŭnde punyŏ-gan-e ibyŏl hallani*
> *ŏtchihayŏ kkumi ŏpkennŭnya*
> *Mongjung-i [= mongjo] ŏpkennŭnya?*
> Then, when father and daughter were about to part,
> How would there not be a dream,
> How would there not be a dream omen?[77]

The Sim Ch'ŏng kut of Kim Sŏkch'ul

The *hwaraengi* (male shaman) Kim Sŏkch'ul is a leading figure among the *mudang* of the East Coast. The fourth volume of Kim T'aegon's *muga* collection is exclusively devoted to his songs. According to him, the *Sim Ch'ŏng kut* has been part of the *kut* of the East Coast for a long time, perhaps not in its present form, as a separate performance, but as part of the so-called *Maengin kŏri*, a ceremony to heal or prevent diseases of the eye.[78] It is hard to decide whether one should believe this. The evidence of the texts of the present-day Sim Ch'ŏng *muga* unmistakably points to a recent origin, but it is of course imaginable that in the past other *muga* were sung. In that case the question remains why the *SC muga* have such a limited distribution. One would expect the *SC muga* to have spread over a wider area if they were of ancient origin, the more so because in other regions, too, rituals against blindness are found. Akiba mentions a ritual in the capital to treat eye diseases, but there is no reference to Sim Ch'ŏng at all. Part of this ritual is a ribald skit about a blind man, presumably of the same type as that in the collection of *muga* of a *mudang* from Yangju. This is followed by a "Blind Man's *T'aryŏng*" (like the one that can be found in *AA* I).[79] Perhaps such elements from the *muga* have contributed to some of the comic scenes of the "Tale of Sim Ch'ŏng" in its more popular form in *p'ansori* and novel. Conversely, Kim Sŏkch'ul has integrated something like the "Blind Man's *T'aryŏng*" into his *SC kut*. When the story of Sim Ch'ŏng itself is finished, Ppaengdŏg-ŏmi, the shrew who had a brief affair with Sim Hakkyu, has a slanging match with the man she eloped with, Blindman Hwang. The way she abuses Hwang is a variation of the Seoul "Blind Man's *T'aryŏng*."[80] It seems likely that on the East Coast, too, such texts were originally the accompaniment of the *Maengin kŏri*, not songs relating the tale of Sim Ch'ŏng.

Kim Sŏkch'ul declares that he has learned the Sim Ch'ŏng *kut* from a book (without giving any specific details about what kind of book) and from his parents. After an introductory part in which he explains the purpose of the *kut* (the ghost of Sim Ch'ŏng has to be "called" to ensure good eyesight for everybody, the precondition for prosperity and happiness), he begins with the description of the spring scene as found in *NSC*. Nevertheless, he does not follow any example as closely as, for instance, Pyŏn Yŏnho followed the novel for the first part of her *SC kut*. He frequently employs formulaic Sino-Korean expressions, most likely influenced by *p'ansori*.

Many elements of his *SC kut* are also put to good use in his other *muga*. A parallelistically repeated question pattern ("Why don't you come? Is it because of this, because of that, etc.") he also uses in a song for the dead.[81] This pattern, which has already been referred to in the chapter on style, reappears in a *sijo* and contains phrases from a Chinese poem by T'ao Ch'ien.

The Sim Ch'ŏng kut of Sin Sŏngnam

In an interview in 1982, Sin Sŏngnam told me that for older *mudang* like herself it was difficult to learn *muga* from a book. Nevertheless, her text is heavily influenced by *NSC*. Presumably one of her difficulties in learning a text from a book is that, like other East Coast *mudang*, she cannot completely understand what it all means. Often her text is close to *NSC*, but it does not always make sense.

In her *SC kut* there are also quite a few passages which have little or nothing to do with the novel. The lullaby which Sim Hakkyu sings for her new-born daughter is *de rigueur* in all popular versions of the tale, but Sin Sŏngnam's version is different from the one in *NSC*. A traditional question in such lullabies asks whether the parent would exchange the child for silver, for gold or for other treasures. Sin Sŏngnam's version also proposes the exchange against all kinds of food, tasty noodles, for instance! Her lullaby, moreover, contains a reference to the festival which is the occasion for this particular *SC kut*, and the remark that Sim Ch'ŏng will grant that no one will have an accident and that everyone's wishes will be fulfilled.[82]

When the monk appears on the scene there is a kind of guessing game with Chinese characters. The characters of his name are broken down in their constituent parts; so the family name Song is described as: "the character 'wood' under the hat-radical: the character for the Song dynasty [Chinese: Sung]." This game is also found in another East Coast *muga*, the *Sejon kut*, which tells the story of Tanggŭm-aegi.[83] When this is over, Sin Sŏngnam again follows *NSC* (or *HSC*) by describing the monk in negative terms: he is not like the hero of the *ko-sosŏl Kuunmong*, not like the historical monk Samyŏngdang.

Like some other East Coast *mudang*, Sin Sŏngnam begins her *SC kut* with an explanation of the (religious) purpose of the *kut* and she concludes it with a kind of prayer, which shows that the *SC kut*, however much it may be appreciated as entertainment, is more than that. Among the audience there are certainly some who expect some benefit from it. When I witnessed the *SC kut* in 1975, an old blind woman asked special permission to sit within the enclosure where the *mudang* performed, which permission was granted with the remark that it might do her good.

The Sim Ch'ŏng kut of Kim Yŏngsuk

During the Tano Festival in Kangnŭng of 1982, Kim Yŏngsuk, the wife of Kim Yongt'aek, made her debut as performer of the *SC kut*. She had been coached by Sin Sŏngnam and made use of *HSC* to learn the text. Some of the spectators thought that she was a bit young (being in her thirties) to do the *Sim Ch'ŏng kut*, although according to their own statements Pak Yongnyŏ and Sin Sŏngnam started to sing it at the age of twenty-three and twenty-nine (or twenty-seven?).

Kim Yŏngsuk had clearly memorized the text, not only of the story itself (for which she faithfully followed *HSC*), but also of the introductory and concluding parts. Those who sat near her, as I did, could see her straining now and then to remember the text and could note small hesitations before the words came back to memory. Half-way through, one of the *hwaraengi* commented: "She does very well, doesn't she? *Doesn't leave out a word*!" (Emphasis added, B.W.)

I have not seen Pak Yongnyŏ or Yi Kŭmok perform, but judging from their texts, their performances have a much more spontaneous character, as have those of Kim Sŏkch'ul and his wife Kim Yusŏn, which I have observed several times.

The Sim Ch'ŏng kut and other muga

Sŏ Taesŏk has pointed out that in the *Pari kongju* version of Kim Yŏnghŭi the dream that announces the birth of the seventh princess has been taken from *SC*.[84] In several other places Kim Yŏnghŭi uses odds and ends from *SC* to embellish her Pari kongju *muga*. The queen "gives birth [to the princesses] in a daze" (*honmijung-e t' ansaeng-ŭl hani*)[85]; the seventh princess is born after her mother has offered 300 sacks of white rice to the Buddha; the same phrases are used for the birth of Sim Ch'ŏng and that of the seventh princess.[86] When the princess wants to go on a quest for the elixir of life that will save her parents, these try to detain her; the daughter answers with references to famous paragons of filial piety. The whole scene is obviously modelled on the episode in which Sim Ch'ŏng offers to go begging instead of her father; in places the wording is the same.[87] The King declares that he is satisfied with his daughter and does not want a son anymore: ancestral worship can be taken care of by descendants in the female line. This is the argument which Sim Hakkyu uses to comfort his wife when she has given birth to a daughter.[88] Kim Yŏnghŭi's father, Kim Sŏkch'ul, uses the conception dream of Kwak-ssi for his *Peridegi kut* (= *Pari kongju kut*).[89]

Fragments of the Sim Ch'ŏng story are also found in the *muga* of *mudang* who do not perform the *Sim Ch'ŏng kut* themselves. In the *Kŏri kut* of Song Tongsuk a very distinctive part of the description of the monk has been borrowed from *NSC*, i.e. the description in negative terms: he is not like Sŏngjini (the hero of the novel *Kuunmong*) or Samyŏngdang.[90]

Related tales

Although the story of Sim Ch'ŏng has been part of the repertoire of the *mudang* for a relatively short time, it has influenced (in a rather superficial way) longer established *muga*. It has been suggested that there also exists a much deeper relationship between this story and *muga*. Is it possible that the tale of Sim Ch'ŏng developed out of a *muga*? Kim T'aegon has claimed that the story of Pari kongju served as the model for this tale.[91] According to his hypothesis, the *kwangdae*, regarded as the creators of *p'ansori*, took the basic plot of the Pari kongju story -which was well known to them, as it belonged to the repertoire of the *mudang* whom they used to assist as musicians- and, when they created the *p'ansori* "Song of Sim Ch'ŏng", emphasized the element of filial piety as a concession to the orthodox Confucianist morality of their day. This theory has a certain plausibility, because of a number of parallels between the two stories: in both the heroine is a young woman who exerts herself on behalf of her parents and is married to an elevated personage. There are a few objections to be made, however.

As has been said before, it is far from certain that *p'ansori* is the oldest form of the tale of Sim Ch'ŏng. If it is not, then the *kwangdae* lose their essential role in the creation of the story and the hypothesis is robbed of an important piece of "circumstantial evidence." For direct evidence Kim T'aegon refers to the prayer to Samsin, said to give thanks for the birth of Sim Ch'ŏng and to beg for future protection. This is found in the *p'ansori* versions of *SC* as well as in the Pari kongju *muga*. It contains a description of the successive stages of pregnancy, month by month. The actual wording of this description in *p'ansori* and *muga* is quite different. In *p'ansori* one finds an example of a kind of wordplay with numbers, which is rather common, not only in *p'ansori*, but also in other genres. For instance, in the seventh month the "seven apertures" of the body of the foetus open, in the ninth month the "nine apertures." In the Pari kongju *muga* this wordplay is only used with the sixth month.[92] The wording of the *muga* is on the whole less technical than that of *p'ansori*. If Kim T'aegon's hypothesis is correct, the *p'ansori* description would be a more playful, artistic variation of the description in the Pari kongju *muga*. There seems to be no convincing evidence for this possibility, nor for its oppposite. However this may be, in the chapter about the formal characteristics of the *muga* it has been pointed out that the description of pregnancy is a traditional theme in vernacular literature, and for that reason alone it is impossible to say that its occurrence in two different works is an indication that these are related.

In the same prayer to Samsin, Sim Hakkyu asks to grant the child the longevity of Tung-fang Shuo. Kim T'aegon regards this as another piece of evidence for the derivation of *SC* from *muga*, where Tung-fang Shuo's name is often mentioned. It is also used, however, in *kasa*, mask plays, puppet plays and folk-songs.[93] As in the case of the pregnancy description, this phrase is used on so wide a scale, in so many different genres that it is impossible to conclude that any two works are related just because it occurs in both. Even if the whole of this prayer were word for word the same in *p'ansori* and *muga*, this would not constitute a legitimate reason to regard the former as derived from the latter. If one could draw conclusions from such small fragments, the presence in *muga* of Buddhist prayer formulae would prove that the *muga* were of Buddhist origin.

A common element, which according to Kim T'aegon also corroborates his theory, is the dream announcing the birth of Sim Ch'ŏng and Pari kongju. This is again too widely distributed to be proof of a linear relationship between two tales. A prototypical example is the dream which Maya, the mother of the Buddha Sākyamuni, had when she conceived.

I do not want to deny that the story of Pari kongju or an earlier form of this story and the tale of Sim Ch'ŏng are somehow related. One should be careful, nevertheless, not to be led astray by genealogical metaphors. A work of written literature has an author, a father, but the paternity of works like the Story of Sim Ch'ŏng and the *muga* can never be conclusively established, as they are produced through many influences and have no fixed identity. They may change at any time as the result of the addition of new elements. If one is to use metaphors of kinship it is safer to use such a notion as "clan" to denote a group with common characteristics and similar origins. The clan into which the stories of both Sim Ch'ŏng and Pari kongju were born one might call the clan of Buddhist tales (the likelihood that some *muga* were derived from Buddhist stories has already been suggested in the chapter about the relationship between *muga* and other genres).

Perhaps because he assumes *a priori* that the *muga* are the oldest form of Korean literature, Kim T'aegon regards just that version of *Pari kongju* as closest to the original, which contains the smallest number of Buddhist elements. In view of the possible relationship between Buddhist tales and *muga* discussed earlier, the grounds for this opinion are disputable. Here I will not discuss *Pari kongju*, but only list some Buddhist elements in the story of Sim Ch'ŏng.[94]

These elements are not all of the same level; some are of a very general nature and are found also in many non-Buddhist tales, while others are more specific and limited in distribution, and therefore more useful in tracing developments of a story through the ages. An example of the first is the beginning of a story with the description of an elderly couple without children resorting to prayer to obtain offspring. This theme is already found in the Buddhist canon,[95] and in the early twentieth century -when moveable-type editions of *ko-sosŏl* started to appear- this was almost a standard introduction. A conception dream such as that of Maya is another example of a theme that came to be used so widely that it lost its usefulness as a distinguishing mark.

The legend of the origin of the Kwanŭm Temple is one of the main pieces of evidence that can be used to show the Buddhist origins of the tale of Sim Ch'ŏng.[96] The story is supposed to unfold around 300 A.D., but was recorded in 1729. It is in many ways strikingly similar to *SC*; important differences are 1. that the girl does not volunteer to sacrifice herself -so that the element of filial piety is lost-, 2. that she is not sacrificed, and 3. that she does not organize a banquet in the hope of meeting her father. Although filial piety is absent from this story, it is not necessary to assume, as Kim Tonguk does,[97] that this element was added by *yangban* who polished the rough story created by the *kwangdae*. Filial piety is a prominent theme in Buddhist tales that circulated in *han'gŭl* editions and possibly also in oral form.[98] Examples are the tale of Mongnyŏn (Maudgalyāyana) and *Sŏngnyŏ kumo tam* (A Saintly Daughter Rescues Her Mother), and -maybe even more important in this connection- the tale of Crown-Prince Inyok who sacrifices his eyes and the marrow of his bones to cure his father's illness.[99]

As said above, the sacrifice of the girl is not included in the legend of the Kwanŭm Temple but, as in the story of Sim Ch'ŏng, there is a journey by sea before the girl marries the Emperor.[100]

The motif of rebirth in a lotus occurs in the *Sŏkpo sangjŏl* and is reminiscent of the prayer of Wŏnang puin in the tale of prince Allakkuk: "I wish to be reborn in a lotus and I wish that I, together with [all] others, may realize the teachings of the Buddha."[101]

Blindness and the curing of blindness are also recurrent motifs in Buddhist literature. In *Kŭmu t'aeja chŏn* (The Story of Crown-Prince Golden Calf) the hero, after many ordeals, cures the blindness of his mother, while in *Sŏnu t'aeja tam* (The Tale of Crown-Prince Sŏnu) the prince returns home after a long quest with the medicine to cure his parents.[102] The last two stories have another element in common with that of Sim Ch'ŏng: during their long travels both heroes marry a girl of royal blood (cf. Sim Ch'ŏng's marriage to the Emperor). In another respect their marriages resemble that of Pari kongju. One cannot say that they marry above their station, but in both cases their true origin is unknown when they court the princesses: one hero has the shape of a golden calf, the other appears as a beggar. Their courtship therefore, has the character of a test, which reminds one of Pari kongju's ordeals.

Finally, in the Seoul version of *SC* the birth of Sim Ch'ŏng is explained as the result of the workings of karma.[103]

There is another story, this time from the repertoire of the *mudang*, which seems to belong to the same clan as *SC* and *Pari kongju*, and certainly deserves to be mentioned in this context. It is the story of an only son, Kamch'ŏngi, whose grandfather becomes seriously ill. It is foretold that the only medicine to cure him is his grandson. The parents of Kamch'ŏngi reluctantly decide to sacrifice their son. The Jade Emperor is moved by their filial piety and, when Kamch'ŏngi is to be put in the pot, substitutes a ginseng root in the shape of Kamch'ŏngi. Grandfather is cured of his illness, but the parents, who do not know that their son is still alive, become blind of grief when Grandfather innocently keeps asking why he never sees his grandson anymore. In the end Kamch'ŏngi comes home and at the reunion his parents are cured of their blindness. This story which is told during the *Ant'aek kut* in Hamgyŏng Province (where Buddhist elements in the *muga* are numerous) has obvious links with early Buddhist tales and the story of Sim Ch'ŏng.[104] Although it seems unlikely that the tale of Sim Ch'ŏng existed as a *muga* before the 20th century (or at the earliest the late 19th century), its addition to the stock of *muga* was a natural event, because of the kinship between this story and *muga* like the *Ant'aek kut* and the *Ogu kut* (during which the story of Pari kongju is told).

The development of the SC muga

Roughly, the story of Sim Ch'ŏng will have passed the following stages to become a *muga*: oral tale → *ko-sosŏl* (Seoul version) → *p'ansori* → *ko-sosŏl* ("popular" version: *Wanp'anbon* etc.) → *muga*. (It is also possible that *p'ansori* developed directly from the oral tale.) There are plausible arguments for believing that the antecedent of the novel was a Buddhist tale. We may add to this that the Buddhist tale most likely incorporated elements that belong to the general storehouse of Korean oral narratives. An example of a tale that is not Buddhist in character, but still has some relevance for the tale of Sim Ch'ŏng, is that of Kŏt'aji in the *Samguk yusa*.[105] A ship on its way from Korea to China cannot proceed because of a heavy storm caused by an angry Dragon King. The Dragon King will make the storm cease, if the sailors leave one bowman behind on an island. This lot falls to Kŏt'aji. Marooned on the island, with his bow and arrow he kills an old monk, who turns out to be a fox in disguise. This fox has eaten the livers of all the sons and grandsons of the Dragon King and is the source of the latter's anger. The Dragon King is greatly relieved (his own liver was the next course on the fox's menu) and gives his daughter to Kŏt'aji in marriage. For transportation back home the girl is changed into a branch of blossoms, to assume her original shape upon arrival. This is, of course, reminiscent of the tale of Sim Ch'ŏng.

As has been said earlier, Buddhist tales shared motifs with other tales or myths. The example of the story of the Buddhist monk Tosŏn, who as a child was abandoned and protected by animals, like Chumong, the founder of Koguryŏ, has been cited in Chapter VI. When Buddhist tales and other stories shared certain elements, we may assume that narrative *muga*, if they existed at the time, also made use of these or similar elements, but this is pure speculation.

Be this as it may, from the oral story there developed Sim Ch'ŏng *ko-sosŏl* and *p'ansori*. In the latter one finds many formulae, themes and patterns that are also seen in *muga* other than that of Sim Ch'ŏng. Then, in the next stage of development, the *mudang*, who at least in certain cases had adopted Buddhist tales directly (cf. Chapter VI), began to make use of the tale of Sim Ch'ŏng -with its Buddhist background- in its secularized form as *ko-sosŏl* or *p'ansori*. The pattern of the story was already familiar to them because it is the same as that of Pari kongju; they also knew well many of its formulae and themes, because the *muga* in general shared these with other genres of vernacular literature. This, of course, facilitated its acceptance.

Finally, the text of the Sim Ch'ŏng *muga*, as learned from novel and *p'ansori*, influenced the text of other *muga* sung by the performers of the *Sim Ch'ŏng kut* and other *mudang* from the same region.

Conclusions

In the case of the tale of Sim Ch'ŏng an oral narrative furnished material for a literary form, the *ko-sosŏl*, as well as for the half-literary performing art of *p'ansori*, to end up again in the repertoire of the *mudang*, who may be called oral performers if the term is not too strictly applied. Thus the history of the *Sim Ch'ŏng kut* shows that the demarcation between oral and written literature is not clearly defined.

Moreover, the *Sim Ch'ŏng kut* demonstrates that the *mudang* change the content of their songs, or even introduce completely new songs. This case may not be typical for all *muga*, but still it is good to keep it in mind when one studies the history of the *muga*. It serves as a warning not to regard the *muga* as relics of antiquity, handed down in oral tradition from generation to generation. Many *muga* may have changed radically when the flourishing of popular literature in the last part of the Chosŏn dynasty provided a fresh supply of suitable material. More evidence which points in this direction can be found in other chapters of this study.

VIII   A Song for the House God

Whereas the songs about Sim Ch'ŏng are sung in a very limited area, songs
for Sŏngju are as widely distributed as the veneration of this god, who is
worshipped throughout the country, from Hamgyŏng Province to Cheju
Island.[1] In a discussion of the relation between *muga* and other forms of
vernacular literature, the songs for Sŏngju deserve a special place; on the one
hand because songs for Sŏngju were often sung by others than the *mudang*,
by such entertainers as the *sadang* (dancing girls) and *p'ansori*-singers, and
by workers building a house (as a kind of worksong), and on the other hand
because the Sŏngju *muga* show unmistakable traces of literary influences.
Sŏngju songs are also sung by bands of farmer-musicians, who on certain
dates perform a magico-religious rite generally known under the curious name
of *Chisin palpki*, "Earth-Deity Treading" and are part of some mask dances,
which -at least originally- combined a religious purpose with one of
entertainment.

The nature of the god Sŏngju

A *muga* from North Kyŏngsang Province assigns spheres of influence to
certain deities.[2] The village is protected by Sŏnang, the household (*chiban*) by
Sŏngju, agriculture by Sijun (= Sejon = Chesŏk), the farm animals by Kunung
Changsu, fishing by the Dragon Kings. Another *muga* lists the deities who
protect the house in greater detail.[3]

In the inner men's quarters: the ancestors of the left
                        and the right,
In the women's room: Sambul-sejon,
In the upperroom: Chesŏk of the ten-thousand blessings,
In the kitchen: the eighty-thousand kitchen gods,
In the main hall: the Magistrate Sŏngju,
In the stables: the Great God of the six kinds of domestic animals,
....

Sŏngju, who is venerated in the room with wooden flooring (*maru pang*, or more grandly, *taech'ŏng*, "main-hall") is in fact one of the most important deities of this category, if not the most important. He is at the same time the tutelary god of the house as a building, of the male head of the household, and of the household as a whole.[4] Buildings other than houses in which people live may also have a Sŏngju (village offices, buildings of cooperative organisations, for instance), but basically Sŏngju is a protector of the family.[5]

The place dedicated to him is usually a cross-beam in the *maru pang* which is called the *tae-dŭlpo*, to which -in some regions- a paper envelope is attached as a concrete manifestation of his presence. Although architecturally the *tae-dŭlpo* is a girder, a cross-beam, figuratively or symbolically speaking it is a "pillar"; *tae-dŭlpo* is used as a metaphor for persons who support a household or are the mainstay of an organisation. Within the family the master of the house is the "roofbeam", the mistress the "foundation" and the children are the "pillars."[6] Sŏngju is symbolically equated with the *tae-dŭlpo*, the *tae-dŭlpo* with the house, the house with the household (Korean *chip* means both house and family) and the household with its master.

Sŏngju as a symbol of the household is encountered in a *muga* for the dead, in which spirits of the recently deceased, before they follow the Three Messengers of the Underworld, say goodbye to Sŏngju and the ancestral spirits.[7] In the same way that the head of the household is the master of all and everything in the house and represents the whole household towards the outer world, Sŏngju is the god of the whole house and of the whole family. Other deities have more specific tasks with regard to other members of the household, Chesŏk, for instance, protecting the children.

The intimate, particularistic relationship between Sŏngju and those whom he protects is often stressed in the *muga*.[8]

The age of the master of household X is fifty
And the age of Sŏngju is fifty as well.
The master of the house and Sŏngju
Are exactly the same age,

Their hour of birth the same day, the same hour.

This is in agreement with a well-known passage in the *muga*, which connects men of different ages with different Sŏngju.[9]

> Sŏngju of the first years: seventeen,
> Sŏngju of the second period: twenty-seven,
> Sŏngju of the middle years: thirty-seven,
> Old Master's Sŏngju: fifty-seven,
> Sixty-one: Sŏngju of the new sixty-year cycle.[10]

The purpose of this passage, too, seems to be to emphasize the closeness of the relationship between the god and the master of the house. In the same *muga* the virtual identity of Sŏngju and the master of the house (and that of other members of the household with other gods) is explicitly formulated.

> If Sŏngju is distracted,
> The master of the house is distracted.
> If the Earth Deity is distracted,
> The mistress of the house is distracted.
> If Antang (= Chesŏk, B.W.) is distracted,
> The children and grandchildren are distracted.

Every master of a house has his own Sŏngju and therefore one should not think of Sŏngju as the name of one deity, but rather as the appellation of a category of deities. Akiba reports that *mudang* say that there is a Nara-Sŏngju (National Sŏngju, which perhaps should be interpreted as Sŏngju of the royal palace) and that there are Chip-Sŏngju, Sŏngju of houses.[11] In the *muga* one finds different names: Sŏngju Wangsin (King-deity Sŏngju), Sŏngju Kunung and Sŏngju Taedogam; the latter seems to be Sŏngju in his capacity of protector of the building, while Sŏngju Wangsin seems to be the protector of the master of the house. Also there are Sŏngju Taejikchang and Sŏngju Taebyŏlgam, who both are underlings of Sŏngju Taedogam.[12] In practice, however, such distinctions are seldom made and usually one just speaks of "Sŏngju, the god of the house."

A brief song sung during a Cheju Island ritual for Sŏngju touches several important aspects of this deity.[13]

> It's Sŏngju, Sŏngju it is!
> From where is it
> That this Sŏngju sprang forth?
> From Andong in Kyŏngsang Province!

If a son is born,
Three years after building this house,
He will be Top of the List of the Eight Provinces.[14]
If a daughter is born,
She will be a virtuous wife.
If a calf is born,
It will be a bull.
If a horse is born,
It will be a dragon-horse.[15]
This house has been built
And a thousand-year Sŏngju, a ten-thousand-year Sŏngju
Has been installed.
In this village the family of this house is richest of all!
A sumptuous table has been laid,
There is nothing to be anxious about, to worry about,
The Sŏngju of this house is supreme!

Several facets of the cult of Sŏngju find expression in this song. His origin -as in many other *muga*- is given as Andong. It is made clear that Sŏngju is connected with the house and that his blessings extend to all members of the household. It is also obvious that Sŏngju has an individual relationship with one particular house and one family. If the Sŏngju of this house is supreme, this family will be the richest household in the village. The individuality of the relationship is also illustrated by some lines in a song for Sŏngju recorded by Sin Chaehyo, the 19th-century patron of *p'ansori*.[16]

The Sŏngju of this house
Is the Sŏngju of a house with a tiled roof,
The Sŏngju of that house
Is a Sŏngju of a house with a thatched roof.

This is not so much a statement of fact as a wish; a tiled roof is a symbol of wealth, a thatched roof of poverty.

Befitting the nature of his functions, Sŏngju is almost always thought of as a male deity.[17] Sometimes the Earth Deity (Chisin) is presented as his spouse, sometimes his wife is called Ana Puin.[18] In one *muga*, Sŏngju has three wives: the goddess of birth (Samsin Puin), the kitchen goddess (Chowang Puin) and a lady called Kongje Sŏje Puin.[19] In other *muga*, however, mention is made of a yŏ-Sŏngju, a female Sŏngju, together with a nam-Sŏngju, a male Sŏngju.[20] Presumably, yŏ-Sŏngju in this case is just another designation for the wife of Sŏngju. Something similar is seen in a *muga* recorded by Son Chint'ae, in which Sŏngju and his wife become Ipchu Sŏngju and Momju Sŏngju, which by Son is explained as male and female house-god.

The supposed origin of Sŏngju

Many *muga* tell us that Sŏngju came from the Chebi-wŏn, the "Hall of the Swallow", in Andong. Other *muga*, however, suggest that Sŏngju originally was a heavenly being. Kim T'aegon regards the latter version as more authentic.[21] He has divided a corpus of twenty-one Sŏngju *muga* into two categories: narrative *muga* which assign a heavenly origin to Sŏngju, and *muga* which mainly describe the building of a house and trace Sŏngju's origin to the Chebi-wŏn. Seven *muga* of this corpus belong to the first category, the remainder to the second, while two of the first group also incorporate a description such as one finds in the second group. Kim's argument for regarding the heavenly-origin type as the more authentic is not based on the evidence of the texts, but on a general hypothesis regarding the origin of Sŏngju.[22] This problem will not be discussed here, although it may be noted that according to Kim's own field-work *mudang* do not classify Sŏngju among the heavenly gods. Even one of the *mudang* whose heavenly-origin type *muga* he recorded, places Sŏngju in a different category.[23] Here it will only be noted that the manner in which the heavenly origin is described in the *muga*, deserves to be studied in comparison with certain episodes in other genres of narrative literature. In a *muga* from Ulchin, which, according to Kim T'aegon, is closest to the original form of the Sŏngju *muga*, it is said that Sŏngju was the eldest disciple of the Heavenly Jade Emperor, but was banished to earth, because he had made an error in writing.[24] The motif of a heavenly being who is banished to earth because of some fault or misdemeanour, is common in traditional fiction -the "Tale of Sim Ch'ŏng" providing one of the best examples- and it is possible that in the *muga* this motif is nothing but a literary embellishment and does not reflect an early belief in Sŏngju as a heavenly god.[25] There can be no doubt that the specific form in which the "heavenly-origin motif" is presented in the *muga* was influenced by literary fiction, including *p'ansori*. The oldest recorded version of a Sŏngju *muga* is also reminiscent of the "Tale of Sim Ch'ŏng" because the parents of Sŏngju are childless until they are almost forty and have a son only after many prayers and sacrifices.[26] This still leaves the question whether the literary motif is a mere addition or rather a "translation" of a motif which already was present in older *muga*. The evidence of the *muga* is inconclusive on this point and a definite answer cannot be given. In the meantime the existence of the literary motif of the banished heavenly being justifies some scepticism with regard to the passages in the *muga* that describe the god as of heavenly origin.

Rituals for Sŏngju

Sŏngju is worshipped when a new house is built, which might lead one to think that he is attached first of all to the house as a building. But he is also venerated when a family moves to another house -even if it is an old house-, which again shows that Sŏngju is attached as much -or more- to the people living inside the house. The ceremony performed during the building of the house is called *Naksŏng kut*, "Ritual for the Completion of the Building", and may be compared with the Japanese *muneage* ritual and the Chinese *shang-liang* ceremony.[27] Ceremonies are also performed when unexpected misfortune befalls a family. For Sŏngju, if neglected, may show his anger by sending catastrophes or by refusing to fulfil his task as protector of the family.[28] To avoid the wrath of Sŏngju, it is advisable to hold a ritual for him now and then, even if there is no specific occasion for it. When Sŏngju has not been worshipped for three years he will leave a house, it is said.[29] Sŏngju will also leave the house when there is a death, a birth or a wedding, unless he receives his share of ritual attention on these occasions.[30]

In many families there is a constant "presence" of Sŏngju in symbolic form. The representation of the deity ranges from a paper envelope attached to the cross-beam to a jar filled with rice, which sometimes is also placed on the *tae-dŭlpo*.[31]

Traditionally, some time after the autumn harvest in the tenth month of the lunar calendar (*sangtal*) there is a ritual for all the housegods, which sometimes is called *Sŏngju p'uri* and sometimes *Ant'aek*.[32] It may be rather simple, but Sŏngju always occupies a prominent place in it. Moreover, whenever there is a special occasion within a family, whether it be a festival day, a birthday or an ancestral service (*chesa*), Sŏngju generally receives a share of the food.[33]

Of course, there are regional and personal variations. In a village on the East Coast, Sŏngju is venerated on his birthday, on the first day of the year, after the autumn harvest, and when all the housegods are worshipped, usually in the tenth or eleventh month of the lunar calendar.[34]

Sŏngju is also worshipped as the most prominent god when bands of farmers tour the village to pray for the welfare of each family and to collect money for communal enterprises, in a ritual which is often called *Chisin palpki*, "Earth-Deity Treading."[35] This ritual takes place in the first half of the first month according to the lunar calendar. The members of these bands sing songs for the gods similar to *muga*.

Sŏngju muga

Among the *muga* for Sŏngju, three main groups may be distinguished:
1. short prayers, such as the one from Cheju Island translated above,
2. narrative songs which relate the origin of Sŏngju,[36]
3. descriptive songs, which describe the building and interior of a house.
The *Hwangje p'uri* that will be translated in full below, belongs to the third category.

Sometimes type 2 and type 3 are combined in one *muga*.[37] An example of a Sŏngju *muga* of this type is a *Sŏngju p'uri* which Son Chint'ae received from a blind male shaman in Tongnae in South Kyŏngsang Province in 1925. The text was not recorded by Son himself, but written down by an acquaintance of the performer.[38] Apart from the plot, the form of the narrative is of some interest. It is in many ways reminiscent of *p'ansori*. Sino-Korean expressions -quite complicated ones sometimes- are frequently used and obviously this song, like *p'ansori*, is a mixture of elements from upper-class culture, with a strong Chinese influence, and popular, "folk" elements. The prominence of the elements related to upper-class culture makes it difficult to argue that the similarity between this *muga* and *p'ansori* is a consequence of the borrowing of *muga* elements by *p'ansori*, whatever may have been the influence which *p'ansori* underwent from folk literature (including *muga*) in the early stage of its development. The process which led to the creation of this *Sŏngju p'uri* could be described as a zig-zag: first, folk literature and folk music provided elements for the creation of *p'ansori*; *p'ansori* then was enriched by upper-class culture and, finally, it remoulded existing forms of folk literature such as this *muga*.

The contents of this *Sŏngju p'uri* are as follows. First, the creation of Heaven and Earth is described, followed by a resumé of the emergence of ancient Chinese culture. This is a standard introductory part of *muga*, but also very much like the song which the *kwangdae* used to sing when they held a ceremony for scholars who had passed the government examinations.[39]

When this *Sŏngju p'uri* comes to the times of Confucius and his contributions to Chinese culture, it continues:

> At that time, in those days,
> Where was Sŏngju?
> He was not in China,
> Not in Korea either,
> His true origin is the Western Paradise.

The "negative description" is a stylistic device used in *p'ansori* (cf. Chapter V).

> Sŏngju's father was the Great King of the Heavenly Palace,
> Sŏngju's mother was Lady Okchin,
> Sŏngju's grandfather was King Kukpan,
> Sŏngju's grandmother was Lady Wŏlmyŏng.
> Was not Sŏngju's maternal grandfather King Chŏngban,
> Sŏngju's maternal grandmother Lady Maya,
> And Sŏngju's consort Lady Kyehwa?

In several respects this song resembles -besides *p'ansori*- tales of Buddhist origin, such as that of Prince Allakkuk in the *Wŏrin sŏkpo*. Here Sŏngju is given a Buddhist ancestry. King Chŏngban (Suddhodana) and Maya are, of course, the parents of the Buddha Sākyamuni. In this context it is permissible to interpret Kukpan as Kokpan, that is Dronodana, a younger brother of Suddhodana.

Sŏngju's parents remain childless until the father is thirty-seven and the mother thirty-nine. A fortune-teller advises them to attempt prayers and acts of piety (of a Buddhist nature!) as the means to have a child. They follow this advice. The whole passage strongly resembles that in the "Tale of Sim Ch'ŏng", sometimes even the wording is the same. The prayers are successful: Lady Okchin becomes pregnant. Her pregnancy is described in traditional manner, from month to month (cf. Chapter V). In a dream the King of the Tusita Heaven appears to Lady Okchin and he instructs her to call the son Ansimguk (cf. Allakkuk!), with Sŏngju as a second name.

When a handsome son is born, a physiognomist is called to foretell the future of the child. Everything will be fine, except that he will be banished to an uninhabited island at the age of eighteen. Sŏngju grows up and, before we know it, has turned fifteen. The formula used to indicate the passing of time: "Time flows fast as water", is the same as that used in the "Tale of Sim Ch'ŏng."[40] Sŏngju now wants to win fame. On earth, at that time, the animals could speak, trees and rocks could walk, and clothes, rice, noodles and other foodstuffs grew on trees. The people, therefore, wanted only one thing: shelter. Sŏngju decides to descend to earth and build houses for the people, but when he looks for a tree that is suitable to cut down for timber, he cannot find one. This tree cannot be cut because it is the abode of the Mountain God, that tree cannot be cut because birds are nesting in it, et cetera. A similar sequence, about the impossibility of finding a tree that may be cut down, is seen in a *p'ansori* libretto by Sin Chaehyo, *Pyŏn Kangsoe ka*.[41]

Sŏngju appeals to the Jade Emperor for help and receives pine seeds, which he sows. Three years pass and Sŏngju becomes eighteen. His parents seek a bride for him and he marries, but he misbehaves towards his wife and spends all his time indulging in sensual pleasures, completely neglecting the affairs of state. This enrages his father who sends him into exile. He is left on an uninhabited island, with sufficient food and clothes for three years. "Time flows fast as water", the three years pass, but no one comes to rescue the prince. He has eaten all his food and has to live on what he can find in nature. His appearance becomes more and more like that of an animal, hairs sprouting all over his body. One day he sees a bluebird (a traditional messenger), which he entrusts with a letter for his wife written in blood on what is left of his waistband. The letter is duly delivered and read by the wife and the mother of Sŏngju, who are moved to tears and loudly cry, three-thousand ladies-in-waiting following suit. The sound reaches the ears of the King, who is in council with his ministers. Hearing the news, the King feels pity for Sŏngju and orders him brought back.

When the prince sees a ship approaching a traditional sequence begins, in which he asks a series of alternative questions: "Is it a ship that passes by, is it a trading vessel, a ship for the transport of military supplies?" Many of these questions contain allusions to Chinese culture and lines of Chinese poetry are embedded in the text. The whole passage is reminiscent of the "Tale of Sim Ch'ŏng."[42] When the sailors have found the prince and serve him with proper food, Sŏngju reassumes his human shape. Before they set sail for home there is a ritual for a safe crossing (*pae kosa*), a theme in traditional literature we will meet again in the translation of *Hwangje p'uri*, where it is fitted into a different context. The prince says farewell to the island where he has spent four years, in a manner resembling that of Sim Ch'ŏng or her father saying farewell to their village.

In the account of the journey home, there are again many references to China and Chinese literature, to Po Chü-i and his *P'i-p'a hsing* (The Lute Girl's Song) and to Su Tung-p'o. Parts of a well-known poem by Chang Chi (*c.* 765-830), "A Night-mooring near Maple Bridge" are also incorporated in the text.[43] It should be noted that such references already were part of many works in Korean: *kasa*, *chapka* and *sijo*. There is no need to assume that in this *muga* the Chinese lines were borrowed directly from the Chinese poem. The sequence as a whole has many of the verses also used to ornament Sim Ch'ŏng's journey to the spot where she is to be sacrificed.

Sŏngju now is reunited with his parents and his wife and becomes the father of five sons and five daughters. When he has reached the age of seventy, he wonders what may have happened to the pine seeds he sowed so long ago. Accompanied by his children, he goes to take a look. They find many, many trees (theme of the catalogue of trees), but there are no tools to cut them. Together with his children, Sŏngju collects iron ore from a river, smelts it and fashions all kinds of tools needed for carpentry. Sŏngju chooses a foreman and thirty-three carpenters, who cut wood, select a site for a house, level the ground, build a house and finally, as a finishing touch, attach auspicious phrases in Chinese to the pillars of the house. It is this last part, the building of a house, which receives elaborate treatment in *Hwangje p'uri*. Sŏngju himself becomes the male Sŏngju of the house, his wife the female Sŏngju (resp. Ipchu Sŏngju and Momju Sŏngju), his five sons become the Five Gods of the Soil, his five daughters the Ladies of the Five Directions (East, South, West, North and Centre). The foreman of the carpenters becomes a guardian who, wearing "dragon-scale" armour and a helmet and brandishing a long spear, keeps out the "Thousand Disasters, Ten-thousand Evils, the Hundred Nefarious Influences and the Baleful Spirits of the Five Directions." Many *ponp'uri* have such an ending, but so have Buddhist tales such as *Allakkuk t'aeja chŏn*, wherein it is related what the protagonists will be in future existences.

Sŏngju songs other than the muga

Long ago, all Sŏngju songs may have been *muga*, but in the 19th century, if not earlier, other groups besides the *mudang* sang songs for this deity, which in content were the same as, or similar to, the *muga*. The *kŏllip-p'ae*, bands of itinerant entertainers, connected to some temple for which they collected funds, for instance, held rituals for the gods of the houses they visited. A Sŏngju kut was part of their performances.[44] The *sadang* (dancing-girls) who sold their art as well as their charms, also had a *Sŏngju p'uri* in their repertoire, according to the testimony of a famous *p'ansori* drummer.[45] Sŏngju songs were also sung by *p'ansori* singers: Kim Ch'anghwan (1854-1927) was famous for his *Sŏngju p'uri*, while Sin Chaehyo has left us a text of a *Syŏngjyo ka*, in all probability the text that he composed for his protégée Chin Ch'aesŏn (the first female *p'ansori* singer) to sing at the banquet held in the Seventh Month of 1869 in celebration of the reconstruction of Kyŏngbok Palace, which had been destroyed in the Hideyoshi invasions and lay in ruins for two centuries and a half.[46]

Sŏngju songs are also used as worksongs for the construction of a house. Kim Sŏngbae has collected no less than seventy-four of these folk-songs.[47] Almost all, though rather short, use the same kind of language as the *muga*, while some seem to be about the rebuilding of the Kyŏngbok Palace, an undertaking for which not only special taxes were levied, but also labourers were called up from the provinces, along with farmers' bands, dancing boys and *nam-sadang* (male itinerant artists) to spur on the workers. Although the reconstruction of the palace was a heavy burden for the common people, it must have been a splendid opportunity for entertainers from different parts of the country to meet each other and show off their talents.

When the Sŏngju songs were sung by others than the *mudang*, it may in many cases have been for entertainment only, or for the encouragement of labourers, but it is remarkable that even when sung by "laymen" they often have kept a magico-religious function. This is the case with the *Chisin palpki* of the farmers' bands as well as with the performances of the *kŏllip-p'ae*.[48] Kim Sŏngbae, moreover, tells us about an old, blind woman who, although she was not a *mudang*, was often asked to sing her Sŏngju song when a house was built, because people believed this would ensure smooth progress in the building activities.[49]

Hwangje p'uri: the ritual context of the song

The text which is translated in full in this chapter, *Hwangje p'uri* (Ritual for the Yellow Emperor), is part of a large-scale ceremony called *Sŏngju paji* (Receiving Sŏngju), held in the 10th month of the lunar calendar. It is from the repertoire of the *mudang* Pae Kyŏngjae. As this ceremony has not been described in a western language before, a summary will be given of the account provided by Akiba Takashi.[50]

In preparation, small tables with offerings are arranged in all the sacred places within the house: in the *anpang* (women's room) tables for Chesŏk (*Pulsa-sang*) and the ancestors; on the adjoining *maru* one table for Sŏngju Wangsin, one for Sŏngju Chikchang, and one for Sŏngju Taedogam, as well as a ricecake-steamer and the Sŏngju-rod (*Sŏngju-ttae*); in the kitchen tables for the House-Site God and the Kitchen God are arranged; in the yard a table called *Ch'ŏn'gung Pulsa-sang*; on the *changtoktae* (soy-jar terrace) a table for Taegam and one for the guardian deity of the *changtoktae*; in the main gate and in the middle gate tables for the Gate-Guarding General; in the stables and privy tables for the deities who are in charge of these places.

Special care is taken in arranging the tables for Sŏngju. The ricecake-steamer is a large vessel filled with cooked rice. Upon this ricecakes are placed and the whole is covered with a white cotton cloth. On top of this the rice bowls of the master and the mistress of the house are placed, filled with rice and covered with a few magic coins to promote long life.[51] The spoons of all the members of the family are stuck into the rice. In front of this arrangement, three bowls of white rice are placed.

The ritual starts as an ordinary *kut* for good fortune (*chaesu kut*), with *Chudang mullim* (chasing away of noxious spirits), *Pujŏng* (removing uncleanliness), *Chinjak* (offering of wine to the gods), and the usual *kŏri* for Kamang, Sangsan (Divine General) and Pyŏlsang. Then the leading *mudang*, wearing a red military tunic and a coloured hat, takes the *Sŏngju-ttae* in her hands. One of the assistant-*mudang* sings an invitation to Sŏngju Kunung. The rod then begins to move and the leading *mudang* starts to walk around, following the rod. The mistress of the house in her turn follows the *mudang*, accompanied by other members of the family, all carrying little tables with offerings. During this tour of the house, in certain places the rod stops: these are the places where Sŏngju is present. The god is welcomed and offered sacrifices. This happens three times: for the male Sŏngju, for the female Sŏngju and for the servant-Sŏngju.

Then the *mudang* returns to the *maru* with the rod, in which the Sŏngju have descended. On the *maru*, she "dresses" the rod in a garment of the master of the house. The rod is now placed in front of the table in the *anpang* with offerings for Chesŏk; the master of the house bows three times to it, whereafter all the members of the family follow his example. Next, the leading *mudang* puts on the coat and hat of the master of the house over her other garments and for a second time tours the house holding the rod, making Sŏngju descend again. She dances and finally speaks the "divine words" (*kongsu*). When this is over, the leading *mudang* and an assistant together sing the song of Sŏngju Kunung and replace the *Sŏngju-ttae* on the *maru*.

The next stage of the ceremony is the new "enshrinement" of Sŏngju. Three pieces of paper are put on top of each other; in one three coins are folded for the male Sŏngju; in another three coloured threads (red, yellow and blue) for the female Sŏngju. Akiba does not say whether anything is folded into the third piece of paper, which presumably is for the servant-Sŏngju. The pieces of paper are moistened with wine mixed with water and pasted to the roofbeam. Then cooked rice (which in Korea is always rather sticky) is thrown at the envelopes three times; the first time one says "This is a thousand bales of rice", the second time, "This is two-thousand bales of rice", and the third time, "This is three-thousand bales of rice." Three different pieces of paper are burned, both as an offering and for the purpose of divination. It is a lucky sign if the paper burns up completely and the ashes float up high in the air.[52] Three cups of wine are offered and three bowls of rice. Finally, a sacrificial vessel is dedicated in front of one of the offering tables and prayers are said. With this the "enshrinement" of Sŏngju ends.

Now the *mudang* sits down, and striking the drum she sings *Hwangje p'uri*. When this song is finished, *kŏri* for Chesŏk, Ch'ŏnwang, Hogu, Malmyŏng, Ch'angbu, Taegam and the *Twitchŏn kŏri* follow. Part of the *Ch'ŏnwang kŏri* is a narrative *muga* about the girl Tanggŭm-aegi. The *Twitchŏn kŏri* is enlivened by humorous interludes, such as a dialogue between the Male Site-God and the Female Site-God (T'ŏju).

Hwangje

Hwangje p'uri is used in Seoul and vicinity as an equivalent of *Sŏngju p'uri*.[53]
Why is Sŏngju called *Hwangje*, "Yellow Emperor", in this region? According
to E.T.C. Werner the Yellow Emperor (Huang-ti) was worshipped in China
as the God of Architecture.[54] Doré tells us that the Yellow Emperor received
the title of God of the Hearth, because he was the first to build one.[55] The
God of the Hearth is also, more generally, the God of the House.

HWANGJE P'URI: translation and commentary

The numbering of the lines in the translation does not follow that in the original text. The lines in *AA* are irregular in length; most of them are approximately as long as two half-lines in a *kasa*, but some are longer, others shorter. The lines in the translation conform roughly to units of the length of a *kasa* half-line. It has not always been possible to avoid changing the order of the lines.

The first twenty-nine lines are very difficult to understand. Generally, the opening lines of a *muga* contain standard phrases; these are often too garbled to allow interpretation. A comparison of the opening lines of this *Hwangje p'uri* with other versions suggests that some passages are, in fact, corrupt: the words in the different versions are often similar, but not the same. If the translation of the first twenty-nine lines does not make sense, this is at least to some degree due to the original.

1. Blue *vaidūrya* and yellow *vaidūrya*!
    Standing in the Flower-Treasury Hall
    Please, Mujin Kaksi
4. Enjoy yourself to your heart's content!

1-2. The translation follows the interpretation of the Japanese version in *AA*, although the Korean text on which this is based seems to be corrupt. These phrases were undoubtedly borrowed from Buddhist liturgy. *Vaidūrya*, a semi-precious stone (*lapis lazuli*), is one of the Seven Treasures (*sapta-ratna*) of Buddhism. In Buddhist texts such as the *Obang pŏn* (Banners of the Five Directions), "a world of blue *vaidūrya*" (*ch'ŏng-yuri segye*) is mentioned -the world of the Buddha of Medicine, Bhaisajyaguru-vaidūrya-, as well as the "Flower-Treasury World" (*Hwajang segye*) of Vairocana, which is a "world of yellow *vaidūrya*" (*hwang-yuri segye*).[56] The combination "Blue *vaidūrya* Flower-Treasury World" (*ch'ŏng-yuri hwajang segye*) is also found in (strongly Buddhist-influenced) *muga*.[57] The text of *Hwangje p'uri* is in Korean: *Ch'ŏng-yuri-ra, hwang-yuri-ra/ hwajang ch'ŏngnae sŏ kyesinde*. "*Sŏ kyesinde*" apparently is a corruption of *segye* (with a verb-ending added). In his *Syŏngjyo ka*, Sin Chaehyo renders the second half of the line as *hwajang ch'ŏngyang segye-ondŭi*, and a *muga* quoted in the novel *Hŭngbu chŏn* contains the phrase *hwajang ch'ŏngch'ŏng segye-nŭn*.[58] Nevertheless, *sŏ kyesinde* must be translated as "standing"; because of its position and the honorific nature of the verb *kyesida* the subject can only be Mujin Kaksi.[59]

3. In combination with a name, *kaksi*, "young woman, girl" is used to refer to female deities of a lower order. In this song several of these *kaksi* are mentioned, but only rarely are they figures about whom more is known than the name. In *KTG* I, 88, it is Taemuji Kaksi, in *Munhwajae* IV, 131, Mujin Kaksi, in Sin Chaehyo's *Syŏngjyo ka* her name is Pujin Kaksi and in *Hŭngbu chŏn* it is Taebujin Kaksi. These variations seem to support the assumption that this deity is of little or no importance. Perhaps "Mujin Kaksi" is a corruption of the misunderstood phrase *mujin kaksin* (gods infinite in number), which would fit in very well at the beginning of an invocation.[60]

5.   The Red Emperor is the Hwangje-within-the-house,
       The Blue Emperor is the Hwangje-within-the-house.

5. *AA* write *chyŏkchye-wŏlsŏng-kajyung-hwangje* and interpret *wŏlsŏng* as "moon-castle." It is difficult to understand why "moon-castle" would be inserted here. Sin Chaehyo's *Syŏngjyo ka* has instead of *wŏlsŏng* a nominalized form of the copula: *olson*. Literally translated his version runs: "What the Blue Emperor is, is the Hwangje-within-the-house/What the Red Emperor is, is the Hwangje-within-the-house." The pattern of these lines: "A is X, B is X", is typical of *muga*. I have followed Sin Chaehyo for the translation. It would be strange to translate Hwangje in these lines as "Yellow Emperor." As the *mudang* probably were not aware of the literal meaning of Hwangje, it is permissible and desirable to leave the name untranslated. The text of the *Sŏngju p'uri* in *Munhwajae* IV mentions a great many Hwangje, among them "Mountain-God Hwangje" and "Star-Hwangje." It would be absurd to insist here that Hwangje be translated as "Yellow Emperor." The enumeration of gods with one element of their name in common, as found in *Munhwajae* IV, may have been inspired by the example of Budddhist texts in which many Buddhas, Bodhisattvas and guardian deities are hailed in the opening lines.[61]

"Hwangje-within-the-house" is the translation of kajyung-Hwangje. *Munhwajae* IV, however, has *kajin* Hwangje: "all kinds of Hwangje", which makes good sense. Both *KTG* I and Sin Chaehyo are the same as *AA*.

7.   Blue Emperor! Red Emperor!
      Brass and silver five, *vaidūrya* six.
      Sasil Dragon-King, eight-hundred-thousand Hwangje,
10.   Please enjoy yourselves to your hearts' content!

    8. *KTG* I is exactly like *AA*, *Munhwajae* IV offers nothing comparable. Sin Chaehyo's text has something which makes sense: "The night [has] five [double] hours, the day [has] seven [double] hours." Perhaps this is a rationalisation.
    9. *AA* translate *sasil* as "Four Seas" (*sahae*). *KTG* I also has *sasil*. *Munhwajae* IV has *sahae*. In *Hŭngbu chŏn*, it says: *sasip yongwang*, "forty Dragon-Kings."[62]

11.   Entering the hall,
      Hwangje who grants hopes for the hall.
      Entering long life,
14.   Hwangje who grants hopes for long life.

    11-14. *Munhwajae* IV has instead of *su* (long life): *so* (meaning obscure). Sin Chaehyo's version of this passage is easier to understand[63]:
          Hwangje who, going up into the hall,
          Fills the hall.
          Hwangje who, entering the store-room,
          Fills the store-room.
          Hwangje who, going down into the yard,
          Fills the yard.

In all versions it is clear that Hwangje is praised for bestowing blessings on his believers.

15.   In the household of Family X
      The meal for breakfast [is] a meal of raw rice,
      The meal for supper [is] a meal of hulled millet.
      The two meals, both of them,
19.   On the Day of the Snake and the Day of the Boar.

16-17. The original has no copula. Such sentences are one of the characteristics of *muga* style.[64] The repetition of "meal" (*kŭnji*, an unusual word, which according to *KTG* I, p. 102, note 3, means "stuff/material") adds a certain rhythmic effect to the sentence, but also makes clear that -in spite of the lack of the copula- the nouns in the sentence are subject and complement.

18. In Korean: *Kŭnji tunji yang kŭnji. Tunji* is probably a variation of *kŭnji*, with the same meaning. Cf. Chapter V ("Variations through rhyme"). *KTG* I, 89 has *Kŭnji kŭnji yang tu kŭnji*, which confirms this supposition.

19. The Snake and the Boar occupy diametrically opposed points in the circle of the Zodiac. These lines seem to imply that these days were suitable for offerings to Hwangje. Confirmation has not been found, however.

20.   Please Hwangje, who increases long life,
        Enjoy yourself to your heart's content!
        For Family X
        Wealth of old iron is wealth, too!
        Wealth of brass is wealth, too!
25.   Polished black iron, polished brass,
        Wealth of old iron and a treasure of silver coins.
        Please Hwangje, who amasses cash and coins, pennies and taels,
        Who grants the increase of iron,
        Please enjoy yourself to you heart's content!

23-24. A common pattern: A, too, is X / B, too, is X. Cf. *Han'guk siga*, 324; *AA* I, 222 and lines 301-304 of this song.

25. *AA* translate: "black-ironware and brassware." *Taktal* in the original text, however, is a word that describes the act of rubbing or polishing.

27. This is a highly problematic line. I have assumed that *su, mun, ch'ŏn* and *yang* refer to coins of different values. For the interpretation of *son-ŭl mowa*, I follow *AA*. Considering the context, and other Sŏngju *muga*, there can be no doubt that here Sŏngju is addressed in his capacity of benefactor of the family.

        [Please grant that]
30.   Even if in the house of the Family X
        Wooden platters and serving trays with sacrificial food,
        Food from *kosa* and food from *chesa*
        Go in and go out,
        There will be no mishap,

35.   And enjoy yourself to your heart's content!

30-34. Offerings to gods and spirits are called *kosa*, sacrifices to the ancestors *chesa*. The translation of *AA* ignores the *-ki* (in their orthography: -*kŭi*) attached to *mokp'an* (wooden platter) and *chaengban* (serving tray). *Mokpan'gi* and *chaengban'gi* are not listed in the dictionary, but there is the word *pan'gi*, which refers to the food from a banquet or a ritual that is distributed to the neighbours on small wooden platters. In view of line 33 (the going in and out of dishes) and the fact that folk belief holds that such gifts of food might be a vehicle for evil influences -to avoid this it is customary to take a bit of this food and throw it away in front of the gate, before one goes in, in order to satisfy hungry ghosts that might have followed one[65]- it makes sense to translate these lines as referring to the custom of distributing *pan'gi*.

36.   In the house of Family X
       Who are supreme?
38.   ŏp-Sŏngju and Tŏk-Sŏngju!

38. *ŏp*, "karma", is used in the sense of "luck." An *ŏp-kurŏngi*, for instance, is a snake that brings good luck to the family of the house in which it lives. Cf. line 724. ŏp-Sŏngju might be translated as "Sŏngju who brings good luck." *Tŏk* means "virtue" and refers especially to the geomantic virtue of a house-site, to the favourable influence which a good house-site has on the people who live there. Tŏk-Sŏngju might be interpreted as "Sŏngju who provides a favourable house-site." For the relation betweens Sŏngju and geomancy, see below.

       If we explain the origin of the Leopard-Bones General,
40.   Of the Evil-Influences-Shooting Kunung and of Sŏngju Taedogam,
       The Sŏngju of the first period [is] seventeen,
       The Sŏngju of the second period [is] twenty-seven,
       The Sŏngju of the lower stage [is] forty-seven
       The Sŏngju of the middle stage [is] fifty-seven,
45.   Kŭlmak Sŏngju [is] sixty-seven,
       Sŏngju, the Old Master, [is] seventy-seven.

40. Evil-Influences-Shooting Kunung: Sasal Kunung. *Sin Chaehyo*, 665 has *sach'ŏn kunung*: "Four-thousand *Kunung*."

41. There seems to be no direct link between lines 39 and 40 and lines 41-45. For the list of different Sŏngju associated with different ages, see above. Perhaps the list begins with the age of seventeen, because this was the common age for marriage and hence for advancing to the status of an adult. In a briefer song for Sŏngju by the same *mudang* (*AA* I, 194) five Sŏngju are enumerated, the last being Hwan'gap Sŏngju ("Sŏngju of the return of the first term of the sixty-year cycle", i.e. Sŏngju of the age of sixty-one). This shows that the numbers in this passage refer to age.

45. Kŭlmak Sŏngju is difficult to understand. *AA* interpret it as "Sŏngju of the end", reading *kŭlmak* as a compound (a curious one) of *kkŭt* and *mak*. *Sin Chaehyo*, 665 has *kŏlmak* Sŏngju in a context which suggests that *kŏlmak* refers to a kind of house (a shack?).

46. The term for "Old Master" is Noja (Lao-tzu).

47. If we explain the origin of Sŏngju Taedogam,
     Then what is his origin?
     The Chebi-wŏn in Andong in Kyŏngsang Province
50. Is his origin!

47-48. This sort of indirect narration, here in the form of a question about the origins of a god, is very common in *muga*. Cf. *KTG* III, 364 (origins of Chesŏk) and 365 (origins of Sŏngju). It is, however, also found in *p'ansori*: Chŏng Pyŏnguk, *Han'gug-ŭi p'ansori*, 427: "Where is the Peach Garden? It is in Cho Prefecture in the Country of Han."

49. Chebi-wŏn refers to a small temple near Andong, next to which there is a huge stone Maitreya image. According to tradition, seeds from a pine-tree growing on one of the shoulders of this statue were distributed all over the country, to grow into sturdy pine-trees fit to serve as cross-beams.[66]

51. Let's take a look at the master of the house!
     Entering the Chebi-wŏn,
     Receiving five *mal* of pine seeds,
     Putting them in a jade bottle,
55. He lifts it on his shoulders,
     And when he looks for the best *myŏngdang*
     Swaying his hips [as he walks]
     With bulging eyes [as he looks for a good spot]

He goes to Yangp'yŏng, Kap'yŏng, Yanggŭn and Chip'yŏng
60.   And enters the Yongmun Mountains.

51. This is one of the so-called "story-teller's phrases": "See what So-and-so does!"

53. One *mal* is 0.055435 litre.

56. A *myŏngdang* (Chinese: *ming-t'ang*) is a geomantically auspicious site for a house (or for a grave). As becomes clear from this *muga*, there is a relation between Sŏngju and geomancy (*p'ungsu*, "wind and water"; in Chinese: *feng-shui*). In origin, geomancy has nothing to do with shamanism. How then, has this association of Sŏngju and *p'ungsu* come about? It is, of course, the fact that both have to do with the house which is responsible for this association. No one in Korea seems to see anything outré in linking Sŏngju and the concept of geomancy; certainly not the *mudang*. "During the ceremony when the roof-beam of a new house is placed, the *mudang* sing a song about the location [of the house] to praise its geomantic virtue", wrote Yi Nŭnghwa in his "Musok ko" (p. 55). Still, one might think of Sŏngju and *p'ungsu* as being in competition. When a family thrives, what is the cause? Is it the favourable influence emanating from the place where the house was built, or is it the protection of Sŏngju? Moreover, one should remember that during the Chosŏn dynasty geomancy was respectable and might well have attracted the interest of the literati, while Sŏngju was part of the popular religion, which the ruling class held in contempt. Nothing in the *muga*, however, points to an awareness of tension between Sŏngju and geomancy. Partly, no doubt, because geomancy had for a long time been inseparably linked with house-building and was not a disturbing novelty -it dates back at least to the early Koryŏ period[67]- and partly because references to geomancy during the Chosŏn dynasty were a literary convention which other genres, too, made use of. *P'ungsu* descriptions might be used in narratives to stress, in an indirect way, the characteristics of the protagonists in a story, as we see in the *ko-sosŏl Pae pijang chŏn* and Sin Chaehyo's *p'ansori* libretto *Ch'unhyang ka* (in the version for male voice: *namch'ang*), where Aerang's cunning and Ch'unhyang's virtue are highlighted in this manner. In a celebration of the splendours of the capital such as the *kasa Hanyang ka*, the geomantic description emphasizes the excellent location of Seoul. In the chapter on the formal characteristics of the *muga* geomancy was listed as one of the themes of traditional literature.

Some of the geomantic descriptions in *Hwangje p'uri* are also found in other genres and it is likely that the *muga* merely employs the conventions and themes of other forms of vernacular literature. This is only one of the ways in which the *muga* and other forms of vernacular literature show resemblance; we will come across others in *Hwangje p'uri*. For the interpretation of the *muga* as religious texts this is of importance. A text that has borrowed a substantial number of non-religious elements, cannot be approached in the same way as a text a religious specialist has composed to express his beliefs. The *mudang* may attach religious significance to the "extraneous" elements borrowed from other genres, but it is also possible that the only purpose of borrowing was embellishment of the song. In the present case, there is little reason to assume the first. Usually no attempt is made in Sŏngju *muga* to reconcile the concept of *p'ungsu* and the protection of Sŏngju. In practice, the *mudang* operate completely independently from the masters of geomancy. Whereas in *Hwangje p'uri* geomancy and Sŏngju are found side by side, in reality the two are separate and may function as alternatives. If you are vexed by unexpected reverses, you may think it is because you have chosen the wrong location for your house (or for the graves of your ancestors), or you may take counsel with a *mudang* who may tell you that your mishaps are caused by the wrath of a god or spirit. Sometimes *mudang* are invited to improve the fortune of families who have to live in a house which has bad *p'ungsu*. Here the *mudang* obviously has the task of providing an alternative to geomancy.

Only occasionally *mudang* exert their powers of imagination to reconcile - at least on the surface- the two alternatives. In one *muga* it is the *p'ungsu* expert (in the shape of the historical monk Muhak!) who selects the wood for the cross-beam.[68]

Because in the *muga* the benign or evil influences of rivers and mountains are not always explicitly mentioned, one might think that some geographic descriptions have nothing to do with geomancy. If the context is studied, however, it appears that the geomantic properties of the landscape are the focus of interest.[69]

57-58. This is similar to the descriptions of workmen in several versions of the folk-song *Kyŏngbokkung t'aryŏng*, which describes the rebuilding of the Kyŏngbok Palace in the second half of the 19th century. Here is a first indication that there is a link between this *muga* and the reconstruction of this palace. More will be said about the subject below.[70]

59. *AA* have Yŏngp'yŏng, instead of Yangp'yŏng. All the places mentioned are situated along the upper reaches of the Han River or its tributary, the Pukhan River; only Yŏngp'yŏng lies more to the North in the same province. Yangp'yŏng fits in better with the other place-names.

61. To the God of the Mountain he prays for [the use of] the mountain,
     To the God of the Soil he prays for earth,
63. To the Dragon-Kings of the Four Seas he prays for water.

62. The God of the Soil is called T'osin. According to the dictionary *Kugŏ tae-sajŏn* of Yi Hŭisŭng, T'osin is a term used by *p'ungsu* specialists. To the *mudang*, T'osin is of no importance.

On the big mountain he has sown big pine seeds!
65.   On the small mountain he has sown small pine seeds!
      After the sowing of the pine seeds
      The Dragon Kings of the Four Seas give water,
      The God of the Soil heaps up the earth!
      At night the seeds were covered with dew,
70.   During the day they were shone upon by the rays of the sun.
      Morning and evening mists descended,
      The seeds sprouted and shoots were formed.
      And when they grew
      -"Transformation without action"-
75.   They grew for one year, they grew for two years,
      And became small saplings!
      When they grew for two, three years,
      They became big saplings!
      When they grew for five, six years,
80.   A thousand branches developed,
      Three-thousand leaves appeared.
      When they grew for seven, eight, nearly ten years,
      They became towering pines with low-hanging branches,
      Weighing ten loads!
85.   When thirty, forty, nearly a hundred years passed,
      They became small giant timber!
      They became big giant timber!
      Ch'ŏngjang wood they became,
      Hwangjang wood they became,
90.   They became wood for the purlins!

64-65. This pattern: the repetition of a modifier within a half-line, is characteristic of *muga* style.

69-71. Cf. *Nongga wŏllyŏng ka*, 44-45: "In the morning mist formed, at night dew descended", and *AA* I, 575: "As if the mist lifted from the Yongmun Mountains, as if the dew lifted from the Paegok Mountains." Mist and dew are habitually associated in traditional Korean poetry.

74. This is the famous Taoist phrase: *wu-wei erh i*, (cited in *hanmun*, Chinese in Korean pronunciation).

83. "Towering pines with low-hanging branches" is a collocation which is often used in traditional literature and goes back to a poem by the Chinese poet Sun Ch'o (4th c.).

88-89. *Hwangjang* wood is a high-quality wood used for making coffins (sic!). According to *AA*, *ch'ŏngjang* wood is young *hwangjang* wood. *Hwangjang* wood (literally "yellow innards wood") is wood from the innermost part of a tree. *Ch'ŏngjang* wood seems to me a gratuitous variation (blue innards wood) on the *hwang/ch'ŏng* pattern of the first line of this *muga*.

91.   When for Family X
       They wanted to cut timber for the house,
       They went to the Board of Revenue for official papers,
       They went to the Provincial Office to obtain permission.
95.   When thirty-three workers
       With jade axes over their shoulders,
       Went into the Yongmun Mountains,
       South Gate was opened, a cymbal was struck.
       It was the Hour of Cockcrow!
100.   How would they go, having eaten [nothing but] plain rice?
       With silver axes and golden axes
       Put in straw bags,
       They went into the Yongmun Mountains.

98-99. These lines are found in a mask-play, but also in the folk-song *Kyŏngbokkung t'aryŏng*.[71]

100. This is a rhetorical question of a common type, and can be classed as one form of indirect narration. There is no "follow-up" (specifying what the workmen had for breakfast) as there is after line 105.

       When they wanted to cut wood,
105.   Would there not be a sacrifice?
       Three *mal* and three *toe* of ricecake
       Three *toe* and three *hop* of sacrificial rice [they sacrificed].
       They slaughtered a whole ox and cut it in pieces.
       [This they offered and also rice wine]
       Was it clear? [Then it was] clear rice wine.

110.   Was it cloudy? [Then it was] cloudy rice wine.
       [Also they offered]
       Dried pollack complete with the head,
       And they lit two pairs of yellow wax candles.
       Three sheets of paper they burned.

    106-108. One *toe* is 1/10 of a *mal,* and one *hop* is 1/10 of a *toe. Muga*
frequently contain descriptions of rituals.[72] Cf. lines 391-406 of this song.
    113. It is customary in Korean popular religion to burn sheets of white
paper (*soji*), partly as an offering to the gods, and partly as a form of
divination.

       The thirty-three workmen
115.   Washed their hands and feet in the lower pool.
       They washed their bodies in the middle pool
       And they washed their hair in the upper pool.
       [And they prayed]
       "We pray, we pray
       To the sun- and moon-gods of far-away mountains
                            and nearby mountains,
120.   We pray to the Mountain God and to the Spirit of the Earth
       That, even though we enter these mountains,
       And cut trees,
       You will annoy nor harm us,
       That you will help us [to ensure]
125.   That the thirty-three workmen
       Will have no diseases of the body or the feet."

    114-117. The description of the lustrations which precede the ritual for the
Mountain God, follows the triple parallelism of the high-middle-low pattern,
but it also seems to be in conformity with what really happens.[73] Similar
passages can be found not only in *muga,* but also in other genres, in *kasa* and
mask-dance drama.[74]
    120. The Spirit of the Earth is Hut'o (Chinese: Hou-t'u), who, in contrast
to Chisin, in the beliefs of the *mudang* does not occupy a prominent place.

       On the grinding stone shaped like a lotus leaf
       The silver axes and the golden axes

Slowly, little by little, sharpen!
130. Then in high spirits fling them over your shoulder!
Go up into the Yongsan Mountains
Cut on the highest mountains the highest trees!
Cut on the middle mountains the middle trees!
On the round mountain cut round timber,
135. *Ujikkŭn ttangttang,*
And when there are wood-chips
Make a bonfire
On this mountain and on that mountain!
Strip the bark off,
140. Bore holes in the wood!
Go to the outer mountains to cut wattles!
Go to the nearby mountains to cut arrowroot!
Irons to pull [the logs] have been attached!
Roll the logs over the hills,
145. Pull them where the ground is level!

135. Onomatopoeia.
141. The wattles are used for the construction of the walls of the house, or perhaps in this context sticks are meant, to roll the heavy logs along. They are cut in the outer (*oe*) mountains for purely verbal reasons; wattles, too, are called *oe*. The next line has a wordplay on "nearby mountains" (*kŭnsan*) and "to cut" (*kkŭnt'a*). In this passage the preparations for the transport of the logs are described.
142. Arrowroot vines are used to make ropes.

146. In the flowing water where two rivers come together
Let the raft float, gently!

146-147. The logs are bound together and made into rafts for transport by river to the capital. *AA* translate line 146: "The flowing water of the Yang River at Yanggu." There is a place called Yangch'ŏn-ni (Two-river Village) where the Pukhan River and the Han River meet. If "Yanggu" is not the name of a place -there is such a place, but it is not on this stretch of the river- a possible translation would be: the mouth of the two rivers ("mouth" to be understood as the spot where the rivers merge into one large stream).

A blue flag is put up in the East[-ern corner of the raft]
A white flag is put up in the West,
150.   A red flag is put up in the South,
A black flag is put up in the North.
In the middle, Sŏngju's spouse
Has put up, high and bold, a yellow star flag!

148-153. The pattern which links colours with points of the compass is of Chinese origin. It is often cited as an example of Taoist influence, but it also occurs in Buddhist texts.[75]

153. Another Sŏngju *muga* has : "They placed the Sŏngju *momtae* in the middle."[76] *Momtae*, "body pole", is the pole into which Sŏngju descends during rituals for him. Sin Chaehyo does not write "yellow star flag" (*hwang-sŏnggi*), but "yellow divine flag" (*hwang-sin'gi*), which sounds more likely, as these coloured flags are often called *sin'gi*.[77]

Boatman here on the bow!
155.   Boatman there on the stern!
Cook's mate in the middle!
The tide is running out,
Set the raft afloat,
Set the raft afloat!
160.   White rice is cooked
And the thirty-three workmen have a meal.
Millet is cooked
And an *ŏbusim* ritual is performed.
Look what the boatman on the bow does!
165.   A drum is hung [on the mast],
High he hoists the cotton sail.
Tungdung he beats the drum.
Boatman on the bow,
Set the raft afloat!
170.   It is getting late!

158-159. For similar lines in a *sijo* see *Sijo sajŏn*, No. 801.

161. The word translated as "meal" is *hŏch'am*, a banquet offered by a newly appointed official to his predecessor; hence a feast.

163. According to Cho Hung-youn, *ŏbusim* is the custom of buying water creatures on the market and setting them free.[78] Yi Nŭnghwa regards *ŏbusim*

as a corruption of *ŏbosi* (fish alms-giving).[79] In this *muga*, the latter meaning is appropriate; the fish receive cooked millet by way of alms. The dictionary *Kugŏ tae-sajŏn* of Yi Hŭisŭng gives *ŏbusim* as a variant form of *ŏbusŭm*, which is explained as feeding fish on the fifteenth day of the First Month (lunar calendar) to ward off evil during the coming year.

166. *AA* have *sangsŭng tot* (high-hoisted sail). I prefer to read it as *samsŭng tot*. *Samsŭng* is Mongolian cotton.

171.   They handed over the water tax.
       When they had gone downstream for half a day,
       They passed rapids once,
       They passed rapids twice!
175.   In deep rapids they put in the oars shallowly,
       In shallow rapids they put in the oars deeply.

171. A difficult line. *AA* translate: "They prayed for a safe passage", but how they arrived at this translation I cannot say. The translation as given by me ignores the syllables *tap i*, which I do not understand.

175-176. The Japanese text translates: "they rowed softly" and "they rowed strongly." This is perhaps a correct interpretation, but it obscures the typical chiastic structure of the Korean text.

177.   Dangerous are the Mongdu Rapids and the Aktu Rapids!
       They have passed the Monk's-hat Rapids!
       They have passed the Magpie Rapids
180.   In the sea near Ch'ilsan Island,
       They have passed the Winnow Rapids and the Pounding-board Rapids!

177-181. These lines may be regarded as an example of the theme of the itinerary. I am unable to locate most of the rapids, but, obviously, as a whole, this itinerary is not meant to be realistic. In the *muga* about the Abandoned Princess as sung by the same *mudang*, the Magpie Rapids are located in the Sea of Blood in the Nether World.[80] Ch'ilsan Island lies off the coast of Chŏlla Province and the sea around it was notoriously dangerous.[81] The sea near Ch'ilsan Island is mentioned in a *sasŏl sijo* by Yi Chŏngbo (1693-1766), where the route of a ship which follows the coastline to bring tax grain from the Southern Provinces to the capital is described.[82]

Look what Sŏngju Taedogam does!
At night they go on land to sleep,
By day they board the raft,
185.   And when they go downstream like this,
Sacrificing every time there are rapids,
[They pray]
"Hwangje who guards the Five Directions,
So that [everything is placid] as a flat bowl filled with water,
Please enjoy yourself to your heart's content!"
190.   They have passed the Chestnut Pass Rapids!
They have reached Lepers' Islands in the Simch'ŏng River!
They sacrificed in the inner shrine,
And they looked at the outer shrine.
When they reached the dry riverbed behind Ttuksŏm,
195.   They paid [tax], a hundred [coins] if [the value of the logs]
                                   was a thousand [coins],
Ten [coins] if [the value] was a hundred [coins]
One [coin] if [the value] was ten [coins].
Please Hwangje who grants this,
Enjoy yourself to your heart's content!

182. There is no description of what Hwangje does in the lines immediately following, but perhaps his activities as a guardian -mentioned in line 187- are referred to.

187-189. The prayer and ritual for a safe passage by ship can be considered a theme of traditional literature; it is found in *muga, sasŏl sijo, kososŏl* and *p'ansori*.[83] The image of the bowl with water is often used in such prayers, as well as in other prayers when tranquility is desired.[84]

190. The itinerary continues. Other examples of this theme are *AA* I, 556-557; *THM*, 246; *HMCCP Kyŏnggi*, 125; *KTG* I, 287-288; *Namwŏn kosa*, 348-349; *Pae pijang chŏn*, 11; *Sin Chaehyo*, 534-535. It is also seen in a modern poem in traditional style, *Sori naeryŏk* (The Story of a Sound), written by Kim Chiha.[85]

191. Different stretches of the Han River had different names. Simch'ŏng River may be one of those, although I have not been able to identify it as such.

192-193. The shrines mentioned may have been temples of the Dragon Gods. There was one at Kwangnaru, which is about the place the raft would have reached by then, if one considers the placenames that follow.[86]

194. Ttuksŏm was outside the walls of the old capital. Today it lies within the city of Seoul. From this point on place names are easily recognizable.

195-198. Literally this should be translated: "Hwangje who pays a hundred if it is a thousand, who pays ten if it is a hundred", etc. My translation is an interpretation based on a comparison with the text of Sin Chaehyo, which reads: "When they moored at Ttuksŏm and wanted to pay the Water Tax to the Board of Revenue, they gave one if it was ten, and they gave ten if it was a hundred."[87]

200.   Quickly they passed Sŏbinggo
      And they passed Malmudŏm.
      They passed the Daughter-in-law Rapids,
      The Pogye Rapids and Sojang-gol.
      They rowed past Tongjak-so
205.   And they went past Paduk Island.
      Quickly they passed Hŭksŏk, Nodol and Saep'uri.
      Where is this wood to go?
      They moored the raft at Yongsan, at Samgae.
      The wagon square is at Tturin-gol, in Samgae near Yongsan.
210.   It is fine, too, as the site for a palace,
      But even better is the scenery of mountains and rivers!
      Let's have a roll-call of the wagoners!
      Wagoner Kim and Wagoner Yi,
      Old wagoners and young wagoners,
215.   Respectable wagoners employed by the Court!
      Having had a roll-call for the wagoners,
      Will there not be a roll-call for the oxen?
      Oxen with horns turned to the right,
      Oxen with horns turned to the left,
220.   Oxen with two horns turned inwardly, one high, one low,
      Oxen with a blaze, spotted oxen
      Oxen with white feet, sturdy oxen
      And ŭna-horned oxen!
      After the roll-call of the oxen
225.   See what the wagoners do!
      "When you inspect the wheels,
      Select [carts with] high wheels and low wheels!"
      On the [carts with] high wheels
      They load the big trees.
230.   On the [carts with] low wheels
      They load small trees.

See what the wagoners do!
They have cut both ends [of a branch] of an ash tree of Mt.Suyang
And attached whip-crackers to it.
235.   The oxen in front they whip on the back,
The oxen in the back they whip in front.
When they drive them forwards: *ira kkilkkil!*
They quickly pass the wagon square.

207. The word *chyujyŏm* in this line is unclear.

208. Samgae is modern Map'o, one of the wards of Seoul (the first is a purely Korean reading of the Chinese characters for Map'o).

212. "Roll-call" in standard language is *chŏmko*; Sin Chaehyo has a variant of this in the old orthography: *chyŏmko* in a corresponding passage.[88] The *AA* text has *chyŏngku* which can, without difficulty, be taken to read *chŏmko*, *u/o* alternation being very common, and the change from *m* to *ng* also occurring in this text in Samgae, which is spelt Sanggae. For the roll-call theme (in *ko-sosŏl* and *p'ansori* applied in the first place to *kisaeng*), see Chapter V, Catalogues 15.

222. The text in *AA* has *waktae-so*, the *Sŏngju p'uri* in *Munhwajae* IV: *ŏktae* (p.137). The North-Korean dictionary *Chosŏn munhwa-ŏ sajŏn*, p. 963, has the entry *ŏktae-u katt'a*, "to look strong, having a big body and heavy bones"; hence the translation: "sturdy oxen."

223. *Ŭna*-oxen is unclear.

They have passed the China Pass!
240.   They come to Minari Fields, Ch'ŏngp'a, the Ship-Bridge,
Imun-dong, Pansŏng Road, the Cross-Roads!
They have passed in front of Namdaemun!
Now they have entered Ch'ilgant'ong.
Quickly they pass Ch'ang-gol and Hoe-dong,
245.   Chang-dong, Mi-dong and the Copper Pass.
They crossed Little Kwangch'ung Bridge
And Big Kwangch'ung Bridge,
Turned at the crossing of Bell Street
And passed in front of the Court of Inquisition.
250.   Be careful not to hurt the errand boys of the Six Markets!
Ascending Hwangt'o Ridge [they looked down].

239. Here begins the description of another itinerary, which will bring the carts with timber within the walls of old Seoul. It is worthwhile to trace the route on an old map, such as the one attached to J.S. Gale's article "Han-Yang (Seoul)."[89] Unlike some itineraries which, as traditional themes, incorporate place-names which do not fit the context -Sim Ch'ŏng, for instance, passes the Hsiang and Hsiao Rivers in China, as does Sŏngju in the *Sŏngju p'uri* recorded by Son Chint'ae (summary in the introductory part of this chapter)- this one is realistic. One must be sure, for this passage to look at an old map of Seoul; to compare it with a modern one will be very confusing. Present-day Imun-dong, for example, is quite different from old Imun-dong. From the South-West the wagons approach the Great South Gate (Namdaemun). Once inside the gates, they first head in a north-easterly direction, turning to the North at Mi-dong, crossing a few bridges and passing the Government Court of Inquisition (Kŭmbu) to the North of the intersection with Bell Street (Chongno). North of Chongno, the catalogue of place-names ends with the "Yellow-earth Ridge" (Hwangt'o-*maru*), which I have not been able to locate with certainty, although the name is found in Gale's article (p. 33). Near the end of the route the map shows "Pine Pass" (Song-hyŏn), a ridge which was famed as offering a fine view of the city.[90] If with Hwangt'o-maru this Song-hyŏn is meant or a ridge close to it, this would fit the context very well, because there follows a description of the site of the capital as it might be seen from a high spot. In any case, the itinerary has led the wagons close to the Kyŏngbok Palace. Basically it is the same route which the carts follow in Sin Chaehyo's *Syŏngjyo ka* which, it may be remembered, was written for the reconstruction of the Kyŏngbok Palace. There is no doubt that in the latter text the building materials are in fact for the reconstruction of this palace. The *Sŏngju p'uri* text from P'och'ŏn in the magazine *Munhwajae* (vol. IV) has the same itinerary and states explicitly that the timber is meant for the royal palace, adding that part of the material is transported to the village in P'och'ŏn County where the officiating *mudang* lives. In *KTG* I, 93 the materials are unloaded at "Yellow-earth Pass" (Hwangt'o-hyŏn).

The conclusion is warranted that in all these texts the journeys described are connected with the reconstruction of the Kyŏngbok Palace. The *mudang* apparently base their *muga* on this event. Sin Chaehyo's text was, as far as we know, only published in book form in this century, but the celebrations for the rebuilding of the palace -which had been a focus of attention for the whole country- offered ample opportunity for oral transmission. Thus we may safely state that, even if the itinerary-theme was an element of the *muga* or of the folk-literature of an earlier period, the *mudang* of the late 19th century borrowed for their songs elements of a work that was composed by a literate author, who for his part, had written a new text for an existing ritual of shamanistic origin. This is fresh evidence of the complexity of the development of Korean vernacular literature. Genres do not grow one out of the other in a simple linear development, but continue to interact and influence each other.

The *mudang* did not necessarily directly copy Sin Chaehyo's *Syŏngjyo ka*. My argument is that they followed a tradition that began with the reconstruction of the Kyŏngbok Palace, the first and foremost example of which was Sin Chaehyo's text.

250. The Six Markets were the most prominent markets of the capital. They were abolished in 1894.

252.   The ancestor of mountains is the K'un-lun,
        The ancestor of rivers is the Yellow River.

252-253. These lines are in fact the introduction to the geomantic description of Seoul, which continues at line 264. It is most common to start a description of the geomantic aspects of a place by referring to a mountain and river in China, namely the K'un-lun and the Yellow River, before the place in question is described. Lines 254-263 are an insertion which is not exactly consistent with the preceding and the following lines. In Sin Chaehyo's text there is no such inconsistency.

        They unloaded at the wood market!
255.   Boss Kim and Boss Yi,
        With their hats on the back of their heads,
        Briskly entered the wood market.
        When they wanted to buy wood,
        A modest price was agreed,
260.   Taking the good [quality wood] with the bad.
        The wagoners of each of the [Five] Barracks
        Noisily loaded the wagons.
        They have unloaded at the building site!
        When the building site was chosen,
265.   They took a look at the famous mountains of the Eight Provinces.
        The T'aebaek Mountains in Kyŏngsang Province
        Are encircled by the Naktong River,
        The Kyeryong Mountains in Ch'ungch'ŏng Province
        Are encircled by the Kŭm River of Kongju.
270.   The Chiri Mountains in Chŏlla Province
        Are encircled by the Seryu River.

The Kŭmgang Mountains in Kangwŏn Province
Are encircled by the Soyang River.
The Myohyang Mountains in P'yŏngan Province
275. Are encircled by the Taedong River.
The Samgak Mountains in Kyŏnggi Province
Are encircled by the Imjin River.
Unsurpassed in myriads of ages,
In former and present worlds!
280. Steeply fall the snowy ridges of Mt. Paektu,
High rise the peaks of the Samgak Mountains!

261. The Five Barracks (O-yŏngmun) were the barracks of the Five
Military Units (O-wi), whose main task in the later Chosŏn period was the
defense of the capital. The fact that government employees are used,
reinforces the impression that the house to be built is not that of a private
person.

265-277. These lines, the continuation of the geomantic description begun
in line 252, form a more or less self-contained unit which is found in almost
the same form in various other works.[91]

Kim Tonguk supposes that the descriptions of the landscapes of the Eight
Provinces found in *Ch'unhyang chŏn*, is derived from *muga*.[92] Considering the
fact that such descriptions occur in many different genres, that they do not
contain elements which inevitably link them to shamanism, and that they do
not infrequently contain phrases which point to a literary derivation, this is
questionable.

281. I give another interpretation to *kibong*, "high-rising peaks", than *AA*,
because only then do lines 280 and 281 form an antithetic parallel couplet. Cf.
also *Hanyang ka*, 79.

North Peak is the Main Mountain,
South Mountain is the Bench Mountain,
Wangsimni becomes the Blue Dragon,
285. The Thousand-miles Pass is the White Tiger.
The Han River is the Facing River
And pierces a Water Opening at Tongjak-so.
The site of the house is excellent,
At the left the Blue Dragon, at the right the White Tiger.
290. The descending slope of the Blue Dragon at the left
Turns into Mt. Inwang.
The Main Mountain in front hesitatingly slopes down,

Becoming South Mountain, then Parasol Peak pushes itself forward.
The Main Mountain behind hesitatingly slopes down,
295.   Becoming Mt. Inwang, then Rice-stack Peak pushes itself forward.
The site of the house has been found!
It is a Butterfly-*myŏngdang*!
It is a Bee-*myŏngdang*!
A *myŏngdang*-site has been found!
300.   Let's distinguish the configuration (*sagak*) of
                                the surrounding mountains!
A fish[-shaped] configuration is a configuration
And a silkworm[-shaped] configuration is a configuration, too!
A mother-configuration is a configuration
304.   And a spouse-configuration is a configuration, too!

282. Here begins the more technically geomantic description of Seoul. The oldest description of the location of the capital in verse form is a poem by Chŏng Tojŏn (?-1398), *Sindo ka*, "Song of the New Capital", in the *Akchang kasa*. Much closer to the *muga* is the description in *Hanyang ka*, which is quite similar, although more complicated. *Hanyang ka* is a text which has a special importance for the study of this *Hwangje p'uri* and will be repeatedly referred to hereafter. This *kasa* describes the site of the capital, the royal palaces, courtiers and officials, streets and markets, famous spots and fashionable amusements, as well as important events, such as the palace examinations. The poem was apparently quite popular in 19th century Korea. This may be inferred from the publication of a commercial wood-block edition in 1880 (quite unusual for a *kasa*). In this edition it is said that the *kasa* was composed by "Hansan kŏsa", i.e. a "scholar without office from the capital", in the year *kapchin*, which confidently may be assumed to refer to 1844. Apart from the wood-block edition, there are several manuscript versions. The *kasa* with the contents as described should not be confused with a group of works which sometimes bear the same name, but relate the history of the Chosŏn dynasty and its capital.[93]

North Peak (Pugak-san) is to the North of Kyŏngbok Palace and so has the character of the Main Mountain, i.e. the mountain which lies to the North of a geomantically favourable spot.[94]

283. The Bench Mountain (Ansan) is the mountain which lies to the South of a *myŏngdang*, an auspicious site (sometimes another character is used for An, justifying the translation of "Peace Mountain").

284. The Blue Dragon is the mountain ridge to the East of a *myŏngdang*.

285. The White Tiger is the mountain ridge to the West of a *myŏngdang*.

286. The Facing River is the river that flows to the South of a *myŏngdang*.[95]

287. Some lines in the geomantic description are difficult to understand. Although my knowledge of geomancy is too superficial to express a definite opinion, I suspect that Pae Kyŏngjae, the singer of this *Hwangje p'uri*, made a number of mistakes. In lines 290-295, especially, it is hard to discover any logic. In line 287, *sugŭi*, which by *AA* is translated as "the energy of water", is a mistake for *sugu*, "water opening", i.e. the place where a stream leaves ("breaks") the "enclosure" of mountains around a *myŏngdang*.[96] Sin Chaehyo, in fact, writes "Tongjak syugu."[97] I assume that *tullŏtkuna* is a form of *ttult'a*: "to pierce."

The description of Seoul's geomantic location in *Hanyang ka* is much more convincing.[98]

297-298. The shapes of *myŏngdang* and their surrounding mountains have all sorts of fanciful names. Cf. also lines 300-304.

300. The *sa* in *sagak* refers to the mountains which encircle the *myŏngdang*. The *kak* (-*gak* in the compound) most likely means "angle" and the combination *sagak* refers to the configuration of the mountains around the building site.[99] Lines 301-304 follow a characteristic pattern of *muga* style.

305. After distinguishing the configurations
      Let's have a roll-call of the carpenters!
      Foreman Kim and Foreman Yi,
      Respectable foremen employed by the Court they are.
      Young carpenters plane the wood,
310. Old carpenters draw markings.
      The supervisor takes measurements.
      Big trees they saw with big saws,
      Small trees they saw with small saws,
      Silgŭn-silgŭn they draw the saw.
315. After having made the beams,
      They made the rafters, all different kinds!
      As for the little sticks that were left over,
      They were painted in brilliant colours
      And made into a chicken coop!
320. Now that we build a house,
      Let's level the ground!
      Thirty-three workmen!
      When you level the ground,
      Tie silver ropes to a silver shovel,
325. Tie golden ropes to a golden shovel,

Tie hempen ropes to an iron shovel,
And when, pulling quietly, stealthily,
You level the East-side,
Be careful not to startle the Blue Lion!

330. This is a site where male descendants will be abundant,
Therefore gently, gently level the ground!
Eyŏra, we are levelling the ground!
If you level the ground on the West-side,
Be careful not to startle the White Lion!

335. This is a site where female descendants will be abundant,
Therefore gently, gently, level the ground!
Eyŏra, this is the levelling of the ground!
If you level the ground on the South-side,
Be careful not to startle the Red Lion!

340. This is a site where [the people who live here] will be
                          rich, prominent, meritorious and famous,
Therefore gently, gently level the ground!
Eyŏra, we are levelling the ground!
If you level the ground on the North-side,
Be careful not to startle the Black Lion!

345. This is a site where [the people who live here] will get along
                          without trouble, live in peace,
Therefore gently, gently level the ground!   '
Eyŏra, We are levelling the ground!
When you level the ground in the centre,
Be careful not to start the Golden Turtle!

350. Gently, gently level the ground!
Eyŏra, we are levelling the ground!
Level the ground in such a way,
That it is good to hear for people who are far away,
Good to see for people who are near!

355. *Eyŏra*, this is the levelling of the ground!
Level a site that will last a thousand years!
Level a site that will last ten-thousand years!

318. I have assumed that the *osaek ch'aedan*, "silks in the five colours",
of the text is a mistake for *osaek ch'allan*, "brilliance of the five colours."

324. A Korean shovel is worked by three men; one holds the shaft, two
others assist him by pulling ropes which are attached to the blade.

327-357. This part of the *muga* (actually including the preceding lines 322-
326), with the refrain characteristic of work-songs, is a replica of a folk-song

sung when this kind of work was done. It is typical of these songs that the
Five Colours are linked to the Five Directions, but the animals which might
be hurt or startled if the work is done carelessly, are not always lions.
Sometimes they are cranes. The borderline between the *muga* and the folk-
song is vague. In this *Hwangje p'uri* the "levelling song" has the formal
characteristics of a work-song, but in a number of folk-songs which are sung
as worksongs to accompany building activities, lines from the Sŏngju *muga*
have found a place, for instance those about the origin of Sŏngju.[100]

<blockquote>

Thirty-three workmen! [If you work so hard that]
When two or three men pull [the shovel]
360. It is as if ten or twenty men are levelling the ground.
When you bend and stretch your rump and waist,
Your little topknots bob up and down.
After the levelling of the ground,
Will there be no stones to rest the pillars on?
365. Quickly they go outside the Little East Gate
And ascend to the Upper Nowŏn Beck.
With ink they draw lines and they cut out
Big stones and small stones.
Blue tuff they cut as if into a square,
370. Lengthwise and crosswise.
They cut out eight-cornered stones for the upper structure,
They cut out six-cornered stones for the foundation.
They have made the pillar-stones of the four corners!
The stones for the floor of the *ondol*
375. They have nicely hewn out of large flat stones from Haeju.
With some stones that were left over
They made a capstone for the fire-place and a laundering stone.
The corner-stones for the lotus pavillion [are] stones shaped
              like squashes.
Better still are the stones for the foundation!
380. The wagoners of the Barracks of the Right and of the Left
              flocked together
And unloaded everything at the building site!
When the Supervisor had the framework erected,
Over here and over there they placed
Eight-cornered stones for the framework,
385. Six-cornered stones for the base!
On the day *muo*, on the hour *muo*
The placing of the pillars and the raising of the beam

</blockquote>

are all the better!
After placing the corner-stones,
They have put up the pillars!
390. When the great roof-beam is raised
Could they do so without a ritual?
Rice-cake of glutinous rice and a whole cow's head
[they offer].
In a bowl of rice they place a ladle,
Money in horse-loads, money in bundles they add,
395. White cotton and fine cotton they add,
Offering jackets of husband and wife X.
Look what the Supervisor does!
He lifts his outstretched hands [and prays]
"Please assist us,
400. That before two years, a good three years
Have passed after the building of this house
[the people who live in this house]
Will become wealthy, become millionnaires,
Will become the richest in the land,
Have an abundance of descendants, wealth, reputation,
merit and fame.
405. Please assist us,
So that the carpenters will not hurt themselves
with their tools."

363-364. A typical pattern: a résumé followed by a rhetorical question.

366. I have been unable to find an Upper Nowŏn Beck, but follow the interpretation of *AA*.

386. *Muo* is the fifty-fifth term in the cycle of sixty used to count years, months, days and hours.

387. In the construction of a Korean house the building of the walls, which most westerners would think to be of great importance, is not one of the first concerns. First a wooden framework is erected to bear the roof. The pillars of this framework are placed on stones. Only when this structure is finished (including the roof), the walls are made with wattles, straw and mud.

391-406. This is one of the descriptions of *kosa*, small-scale rituals for the gods performed on certain occasions. Another example of a *kosa* is the *pae kosa*, "Boat Ritual", for safe passage. Descriptions of offerings are a theme in the *muga*; see, for instance, *KTG* III, 291.

After [some of the offerings] had been scattered,
They attached the upper lintels,
They attached the base-boards and they attached the rafters.
410. After nailing down the bar along the edge of the eaves,
After plaiting lattice-work and covering it with mud,
When they had to lay the rooftiles,
They went to the Tile Bureau outside the Great South Gate.
They bought tiles and gently, gently,
415. They unloaded them at the building site!
Japanese tiles and blue tiles!
The slaters are called,
"Lay the female tiles on their back,
Lay the male tiles on their belly."
420. They have covered the roof so that it nicely slants.
When they put the capping tiles at the end of the male tiles
And put the crest on the roof,
Please enjoy yourself, Dragonhead General!
After the covering of the roof,
425. They put in an *anpang* of three *kan*!
They put in a storeroom of two *kan*, a hall of six *kan*,
A room opposite the *anpang* of three *kan*,
A room attached to the kitchen and a room to store food!

413. The Tile Bureau was a government institution during the Chosŏn dynasty, charged with the fabrication of tiles. It was abolished in 1883. The text says "Waesae", but this is obviously a corruption of "Wasŏ." The Wasŏ is also mentioned in *Hanyang ka*.[101]

418-420. The wider "female" roof-tiles are laid first with the convex side, the "back", downwards, then the joints between the rows of female tiles are covered by the narrower "male" tiles, which are placed with the convex side upwards over the edges of two rows of female tiles. These two lines are a good example of antithetical parallelism.

423. The "Dragonhead" is the crest of the roof.

425. One *kan* is 36 square feet.

When we look at the yard in front and at the back
430. The adornments of the galleries are even better.
They have built loft closets!
Closets between the panelling and the ceiling and kitchen closets,

Closets with shelves and Kitchen-God closets they have made!
When you look left and right, [you see that]
435. They have made inner and outer sliding doors
For the hall of six *kan*,
And a porch, most magnificently!
They have made a kitchen of three *kan*!
Inner reception rooms and outer reception rooms,
440. A room for the steward, and servants' quarters they have put in!
Granaries there are in great number.
Even better are the rooms on both sides of the high-towering gate.
Steps and flowerbeds have been nicely made.
In the back garden they have built a mountain pavillion,
445. In front of the mountain pavillion they have built a thatched hut,
In front of the thatched hut they have built a six-cornered pavillion.
In a shady spot they placed a mill,
In a sunny spot they dug a well
And in the middle of the grounds they made a rock garden!
450. High-towering walls and fine walls they built!
They constructed a gate frame!
The female part of the hinges they affixed with an upward movement,
The male part of the hinges they affixed with a downward movement.
With a hammer they affixed the hinges!
455. Pushed aside they were, the sliding doors!
Fine straw mattings and swastika-patterned lattice-work
[there were]
Masons were engaged!
They laid the flues of the *ondol* heating!
They covered them with flat stones!
460. "Put up the partition walls!"
Please Great General of the Walls, enjoy yourself!
They put plaster between the rafters,
They put plaster on the walls!
Paper-hangers were engaged!
465. When they did the papering,
They pasted on the first coat of paper
And matching the notches pasted on the second coat.
When the hanging of the second coat is finished
Will there be no adornment by pictures?

429-430. This is an example of a typical "frame": "when you look at X, it is even better". Cf. Chapter V and Kim Sŏngbae, *Han'gug-ŭi minsok*, 303.

447-448. *Namwŏn kosa*, 129 has exactly the opposite arrangement in the description of Ch'unhyang's house: "A mill was placed in a sunny spot, a well was dug in a shady spot." The *Sŏngju p'uri* in *Munhwajae* IV (p.137) is the same as *Namwŏn kosa*. Probably Pae Kyŏngjae made a mistake.

450. These walls are not the walls of the house, but the walls which surround the buildings and the gardens. "Fine walls", *se tam*, perhaps should be understood as *saeu tam*, "mud walls."

469. From this point on, the description of the building of the house in this *muga* is difficult to distinguish from the more general theme of the description of an existing house. Kim Tonguk has pointed out that many themes of *Ch'unhyang chŏn* (several among them which are related to the description of a house) are also found in this *Hwangje p'uri*.[102] This seems to be the basis for the claim that such passages in *p'ansori* (from which the *ko-sosŏl* about Ch'unhyang sprang) were borrowed by the *kwangdae* from the *muga*. It is certainly a fact that there are remarkable resemblances between various versions of the tale of Ch'unhyang and this *Hwangje p'uri*, but it is questionable whether this should be interpreted as the result of borrowing from the *muga* by the singers of *p'ansori*. It seems to me that the text of *Hwangje p'uri* is so full of elements from the sinicized upper-class culture that it is inconceivable that this *muga* was not influenced by the literature of the *yangban* and the *ajŏn*. It has already been argued that Sin Chaehyo -or a tradition which relied on Sin Chaehyo- changed the form of the Sŏngju *muga*. Positive evidence for the influence of upper-class literature on the *muga*, through the *kwangdae*, is much stronger than that for the reverse. It is possible that simpler descriptions of houses and house interiors were part of the older *muga*, but for this there is no immediate proof. There is only circumstantial evidence, such as the fact that catalogues are found in the folk-literature of many countries and periods, to corroborate the claim put forward by Kim Tonguk.

Whatever the direction of borrowing may have been, it is remarkable that nearly all of the sub-species of the theme of the description of the exterior (including the garden) and the interior of a house can be found in both *Hwangje p'uri* and in one of the versions of the tale of Ch'unhyang, *Namwŏn kosa*. The *p'ansori* libretto about the two brothers Hŭngbu and Nolbu, *Pak t'aryŏng*, too, employs almost all the variations on this theme, whereas elements of it, one by one, occur countless times in vernacular literature. Many of these are also found in *Hanyang ka*, not in the description of a house, but in a description of the markets of the capital, where furniture, paintings, screens, pots and pans, et cetera are sold.

470. On the door of the wall-closet is a picture of a brushholder
                                with the character *pok*: (happiness),
      On the door of the loft a picture of flowers in a vase.
      If you look at the hall,
                                [calligraphy which reads:]
      "Longevity of a thousand years for the parents,
      Ten-thousand generations prosperity for the descendants"
475. Hangs there in a prominent place.
      If you take a look at the *anpang*,
      There, for the parents, shines Mt. Suyang,
      A mountain for a hundred years!
      If you take a look at the room across the *anpang*,
480. [There is written] "Longevity of ten-thousand years for the
                                descendants."
      Turtles and phoenixes have made it their lair!

473-474. The auspicious phrases in these lines are in pure Chinese. The
same goes for lines 488-491.
    477. The reference, presumably, is to a mountain where hermits live who
know the secret of longevity. The picture of this mountain expresses the wish
for a long life, "a hundred years", for the parents. There are several mountains
in China and Korea with the same name and there is no way to identify this
particular Mt. Suyang. Its name is mentioned here, it seems, as a typical abode
for those who seek immortality.
    481. Turtles and phoenixes are symbols of longevity.

      When you look at the Southern wall,
      Three old men on the Three Sacred Mountains
      Play *paduk*, white and black stones in their hands.
485. When you take a look at the Northern wall,
      There is no doubt: these are the ten symbols of longevity!
      On the pillars of the four corners there are auspicious phrases:
      "Heaven increases the years,
      Man increases his longevity",
490. "Spring fills Heaven and Earth,
      Happiness fills the home."
      When you look at the kitchen door,
      Unmistakably, [you discern] a rooster and a dog,
      A lion and a tiger, a couple of unicorns.

495. If you look at the doors of the storehouses [you read]:
"The country prospers, the people are at peace,
The family provides, man is satisfied."
On the middle gate [you see] three scholars,
On the front gate, unmistakably, Ŭlchi Mundŏk and Ch'in Shu-pao.

482-486. Here begins the theme of the paintings adorning the four walls (which may be regarded as a sub-theme of the theme of the interior of the house). In this place, the theme is not complete; in a fuller form it is found in lines 502-522. This is an example of a theme which, with its allusions to literature and Chinese and Korean history, cannot have been created by the *mudang*. Once it becomes clear that there are themes which must have been borrowed by the *mudang*, it is necessary to consider whether themes which might have been created by the *mudang*, really do stem from the shamanistic tradition.

The enumeration of paintings is arranged according to a formulaic pattern: that of the cardinal points of the compass. In *Namwŏn kosa*, 140-141, this theme is examined comparing several versions of *Ch'unhyang chŏn*. The subjects of the four paintings as mentioned in lines 502-522 of this *muga*, turn out to be exactly the same as those described in the 30 and 16 leaf Seoul block-print editions of *Ch'unhyang chŏn*. The four subjects -minus the four-directions frame- are also mentioned in *Hanyang ka*, 118-121.

The Three Sacred Mountains in line 483 are P'eng-lai, Fang-chang and Ying-chou, the islands of the immortals in the Eastern Sea. The ten symbols of longevity are the sun, the mountains, water, rocks, clouds, pine-trees, the herb of perennial youth, the turtle, the crane and the deer.

487. The auspicious phrases are pasted on the pillars when spring begins according to the lunar calendar (that is in the First Month) and are called *ipch'unsŏ*. The *ipch'unsŏ* are also a sub-theme of the house descriptions.[103]

493-494. The language used for the animals, *chyegyŏn saho ssang kirin*, is Sino-Korean and difficult to understand for the uneducated. Akiba and Akamatsu translate *chyegyŏn saho* as "pig, dog, lion and tiger", but *che* in *chyegyŏn* most likely is a dialect variant of *kye*, "rooster." *Hanyang ka*, 118-119 has, in fact, *kyegyŏn saho*. To interpret chye as "rooster" is also more in accordance with actual practice. Pictures of roosters were often used to protect the house against evil, while I have never seen an example of a picture of a pig used in this manner.[104]

499. Two historical figures are here mentioned as door-gods. The first is Ŭlchi Mundŏk, a famous general from Koguryŏ, who defeated the armies of the Sui Emperor Yang-ti. He also appears in the *muga* as a deified warrior (*kunung*).[105] The second figure is not Ch'en Shu-pao (553-604) -whose name

in Sino-Korean is homophonous with that of Ch'in Shu-pao- the last Emperor
of Chen, as *AA* suggests and *Namwŏn kosa*, p. 128, note 2, repeats. As Ch'en
Shu-pao was known as a "wretched poltroon",[106] he would have made a
curious door-guardian! Ch'in Shu-pao was a military official at the court of
the first T'ang Emperor who, as we may read in the Chinese novel *Hsi-yu chi*
(The Journey to the West), stood guard at a time when the Emperor was being
disturbed by the ghost of a dragon. Ch'in was assisted in this task by Yü-ch'ih
Ching-te (whose name in Korean pronunciation becomes: Ulchi Kyŏngdŏk).
Because the Emperor felt pity for these ministers who had to stay awake all
night, he decreed that their pictures be painted to keep ghosts away, so the
Hsi-yu chi adds. Both in China and Korea Ch'in Shu-pao and Yü-ch'ih Ching-
te, in pictorial representation, guarded the gates of many houses.[107] The similarity of the names of Ŭlchi Mundŏk and Ulchi Kyŏngdŏk no doubt is
responsible for the fact that, in this *muga*, the Korean general keeps Ch'in
Shu-pao company.

500.   After the adornment with pictures
       Will there not be wall-paintings on the four sides?
       On the Eastern side is vividly depicted
       How T'ao Yüan-ming, the recluse of Chin,
       After giving up his position in P'eng-che,
505.   Has set afloat a boat on the autumnal river
       And goes to Hsin-yang.
       If you take a look at the Western side,
       It is vividly depicted
       How among the tribulations and turmoil of the Three Kingdoms
510.   Liu Hsüan-te, scion of the Imperial House of Han,
       Astride his horse Red Rabbit
       In snow and cold at the cottage in Nan-yang
       Waits for Master Wo-lung.
       If you take a look at the Southern Wall,
515.   Sŏngjini, Grand Preceptor Sŏsan,
       On a stone bridge dallies with eight heavenly nymphs,
       Respectfully greeting them with folded hands.
       If you look at the Northern wall,
       It is vividly depicted
520.   How Chiang T'ai-kung, in the poverty of his first eighty years,
       Fishes in the River Wei with a straight piece of iron for a hook,
       While King Wen waits for him.

503. T'ao Yüan-ming or T'ao Ch'ien (376-427), the famous poet.

510. The adventures of Liu Hsüan-te (=Liu Pei,162-223), his two blood brothers Kuan Yü (?-219) and Chang Fei (?-220), and his advisor Chu-ko Liang (= Master Wo-lung, 181-234) were well-known and popular in Korea because of the novel *San-kuo chih yen-i*, which circulated both in the original Chinese and in Korean translations and adaptations. Red Rabbit was, in fact, Kuan Yü's horse.

515. Sŏngjini, the hero of the *ko-sosŏl Kuunmong* (Cloud Dream of the Nine) by Kim Manjung (1637-1692), is here confused with the historical Sŏsan Taesa (1520-1604), a monk famous both for his teachings and for his leadership in the resistance to the Japanese troops during the Hideyoshi invasions.[108]

520. According to tradition, Chiang T'ai-kung (= Chiang Tzu-ya, 1210-1120 B.C.) was already eighty years old when King Wen of Chou sought his advice. The first time King Wen came upon him, he was fishing in the River Wei with a straight piece of metal instead of a curved hook. Nevertheless, the fish, sensible of his virtue, of their own accord came to him to be caught.

       If we let the adornment of the wall paintings be,
       Will there not be adornment of the rooms?
525. If you enter the *anpang* and look up,
       [You will see] a coffered ceiling,
       If you look down, the varnished paper of the *ondol* floor.
       Even better are the dragon-chests and the phoenix-chests,
       Three-tiered chests and wardrobes,
530. Chests inlaid with mother-of-pearl and chests which open in front,
       Chests with drawers and chests of red sandalwood decorated
                     with butterfly-shaped brass ornaments.
       When you look what is on top of the chests,
       Boxes of mother-of-pearl and Japanese mirror-boxes,
       Leather boxes and wooden boxes
535. Have been placed in pairs on top of them!
       If you want to look at the adornments of the room
       [You see that] cushions and blankets have been spread out!
       Tiered chests, square étagères
       And back-rests from Chinju have been placed there!
540. Document chests of red sandalwood have been placed there!
       Big screens and small screens,
       A screen with filial children, a picture with the bliss of Kuo Tzu-i
       And a screen with a hundred playing children have been placed there!

A rack to hold comb-cases, on which a pair of phoenixes is drawn,
545.   Is prettily hanging from a decorative knot
       Made of scarlet silk in the form of a bee!
       A chamber-pot brilliant as the Morning Star,
       Ash-trays and cuspidors
       Are scattered, over here and over there.
550.   Hwangje, who gives
       Wash-basins with a wide rim, wash-basins with a cover
       Small basins and big basins, complete sets of ten,
       Please enjoy yourself to your heart's content!

525. Here begins the catalogue of furniture.[109]

542. Kuo Tzu-i or Kuo Fen-yang (697-781) is a figure from Chinese history. He quelled the rebellion of An Lu-shan, but is especially famous for having enjoyed the bliss of living to a ripe old age under one roof with eighty grandchildren. The translation given here in all probability runs counter to the *mudang*'s understanding of the text. She seems to have understood Kwak Punyang (the Sino-Korean pronunciation of Kuo Fen-yang) as the name of an object. Accordingly it is translated in *AA*: "incense in a box." This and the following words become: "Incense in a box and a picture of bliss." When we consider the context and note that in a similar passage in *Hanyang ka* (pp. 118-119) the phrase *Kwak Punyang haengnak to* (a picture of the bliss of Kuo Fen-yang) is found, while the Hundred-Children Painting of line 543 is also mentioned, there can be no doubt that the *mudang* corrupted a passage which she did not fully understand. This mistake -once again- suggests that the *mudang* borrowed from other genres.

544. For a "rack to hold comb-cases", *pitchŏp kobi*, *AA* read *pitchŏp kori*; *Namwŏn kosa*, 135, however, has *pitchŏp kobi* with a similar attributive phrase: "on which a pair of dragons is drawn."

547. The same phrase is found in *Namwŏn kosa*, 136 and elsewhere in vernacular literature.[110]

       Bronze braziers with a fire of the best charcoal,
555.   Tobacco pipes from Kimhae, pipes from Pusan,
       Specially made pipes,
       Pipes with a silver band to join the head and the stem
       Have been placed over here and over there.
       A tobacco pot of red marble
560.   Is filled with tobacco from Sŏngch'ŏn moistened with honey-water!

Look what Mrs. So-and-so does!
She has put on garments of satin and silk!
Go up to the lofts,
The adornments of the lofts are even better!
565. They have been locked up with a slanting lock
In the form of a golden turtle!
When you open the doors of the lofts,
They are crammed with all kinds of silk!
The moon has risen: moonbeams silk
570. The sun has risen: sunbeams silk
Sleeping Dragon silk of Chao Tzu-lung.
Stepping clippity-clop: the rhythm of horses' feet.
The tide comes in: silk with a pattern of sea shells,
Mouth wide-open: Chinese silk,
575. Good to wear: *toribulso.*
Woven in the night: midnight gauze,
Woven in the daytime: sunrise silk,
Fine hemp cloth and thick hemp cloth,
Cotton from Kyŏngju in Kyŏngsang Province,
580. Cotton from Haeju in Hwanghae Province,
Cotton from Naju in Chŏlla Province.
With full rolls of all this
[the lofts] were filled to overflowing!

554-560. *Namwŏn kosa* has in the description of the interior of Ch'unhyang's house many items which are the same or similar. The half-line 554 is exactly the same as the phrase in *Namwŏn kosa* (p. 136), where it is preceded by an enumeration of pipes and different kinds of tobacco, similar to the lines which follow 554.

568. Here begins the *pidan t'aryŏng* (silk song), an enumeration of several kinds of silk, brocade, cotton and other fabrics, in which each item is preceded by a phrase which in one way or another -through meaning, through sound or some other association- is linked to it (see Chapter V). Songs in which nouns are modified by such loosely connected phrases were often sung by itinerant artists. A good example of such a *t'aryŏng* is the *chang t'aryŏng* (also called *kaksŏri t'aryŏng*), of which many specimens are to be found in various folk-song collections. In a *chang-t'aryŏng* recorded by Sin Chaehyo, a representative half-line is the following: *i sul chapsu, Chinju chang*, "Drink this wine: the market of Chinju." Here Chinju is associated with the wine because its homophone *chinju* means "to offer wine."[111]

The *pidan t'aryŏng* is found in other Sŏngju *muga*[112] in a similar context, but also in other *muga* (for instance, a *Sŏnwang kut* from Osan and a *ponp'uri* from Cheju Island[113]), as well as in *p'ansori* (*Pak t'aryŏng*),[114] *ko-sosŏl*[115] and the *kasa Hanyang ka.*[116]

A comparison of the *pidan t'aryŏng* in *Hanyang ka* and this *Hwangje p'uri* shows that they have many elements in common, although *Hanyang ka* uses more Sino-Korean and adds complete half-lines in Sino-Korean to introduce certain kinds of silk. Where *Hwangje p'uri*, for example, has: "the sun has risen: sunbeams silk", in easily understandable language, the *kasa* has a phrase which entirely consists of Chinese characters.[117] Nevertheless this *Hwangje p'uri* and other *muga* do not lack Chinese phrases which allude to Chinese history and Chinese literature, as the description of the paintings on the four walls shows. Another example is found in the *Sŏnwang kut* of Yi Chongman, which has references to the Tung-t'ing Lake in China, to the episode of Liu Pei solliciting the help of Chu-ko Liang, and to the T'ang poet Li Po.[118] Moreover, the *pidan t'aryŏng* in this muga also has longer introductory phrases like those in *Hanyang ka*, one whole phrase comprising two half-lines. The actual contents of the *pidan t'aryŏng* of the *Sŏnwang kut* and *Hanyang ka* are quite different. There is a great deal of resemblance, on the other hand, between the *pidan t'aryŏng* in Sin Chaehyo's *Pak t'aryŏng* and a *muga* text from Kyŏngsang pukto.[119] Out of twelve varieties of silk in *Pak t'aryŏng*, nine are also found in the *muga*, which lists fifteen. Except for one line, the wording of these nine lines is quite similar. Both versions have references to Confucius and to the First Emperor, of the Chinese Ch'in Dynasty. A *pidan t'aryŏng* in another *muga* contains phrases like *T'aebaeg-i kigyŏng sangch'ŏn-hani*, "When Li Po, riding a whale, ascended to Heaven" - all Sino-Korean, except for the final verb.[120] This strongly suggests an origin outside the circles of the *mudang*, while there is no positive evidence that the enumeration of silks was originally created by the *mudang*. If the *pidan t'aryŏng* really was part of a *muga* first, one must assume that an earlier, simpler form of *pidan t'aryŏng* was given new wording by people who were in touch with the culture of the upper-class (as the *kwangdae* were) and that the refurbished version then was reabsorbed into the repertoire of the *mudang*. It is also possible that the proto-type of the *pidan t'aryŏng* was a simple song that existed independent of the *muga*, a folk-song, for instance, which in the 17th and 18th century, when folk-literature and upper-class literature began to interact on an unprecedented scale, was transformed by the *kwangdae* and then, in a third stage, reached the repertoire of the *mudang*. There would seem to be no evidence to justify a preference for the one theory above the other.

571. In this line "Chao Tzu-lung" (one of the comrades of Liu Pei) is a mistake for Chu-ko Liang, whose sobriquet was Sleeping Dragon, Wo-lung.[121] The names of the silks are sometimes fanciful.

572. The wordplay in this line is not translatable. The noun which ends it is *changdan*, which fits the enumeration only because it ends in *dan*, like the names of the silks. I, at least, have not been able to find any reference to a kind of silk called *changdan*. *Changdan* means rhythm and from this comes the association with the sound of horse's feet.

574. Perhaps the mouth falls open in admiration?

575. *Toribulsu* (not *toribulso*) is mentioned in *Hanyang ka* (pp. 114-115 and 128-129), where it is explained, erroneously I think, as a combination of two words: *tori* (a kind of hemp) and *pulsu* (a kind of silk). Actually it seems to have been one word referring to a certain kind of silk, not a combination of two independent words.[122]

579-580. Note the alliteration. In line 581, the Na of Naju (=*ra*) is repeated in Chŏlla (Chŏn + ra).

        If you want to have a look
585.   At the trinkets of Mrs. So-and-so,
            [You will see that]
        She has hairpins carved like dragons,
        Hairpins carved like phoenixes, and bride's hairpins.
        Hwangje, who gives sets of ten
        Of hairpins made of amber, coral and gold,
590.   Please enjoy yourself to your heart's content!
        A set of dishes on delicate feet from Tongnae,
        All kinds of tableware, branches of coral,
        Citrus fruits made of amber, jewels of silver and gold.
        Treasure Kaksi, please enjoy yourself
595.   To your heart's content!
        When you go out to the *maru*
        And want to have a look at the adornments of the *maru*,
            [You will see that]
        Food-cupboards and shelved cupboards
        Have been placed there in pairs!
600.   When you take a look at what is in the cupboards,
            [You will see that]
        Round wooden bowls and wooden platters
        Have been placed there in pairs!
        If you open the door of the storage closet,
        It is crammed with all kinds of dishes
605.   And all kinds of platters!
        If you go down to the kitchen,
        Small pots and big pots,

Copper kettles from Chŏnju and pots of brass there are!
Alabaster rice-pots are lined up there!
610. A large water kettle is supported on a trivet.
Blue *vaidūrya* and yellow *vaidūrya*,
Dragon-King Kaksi, please enjoy yourself
To your heart's content!
On the kitchen shelves Taegŏng Kaksi dances.
615. Hwangje, who gives pure honey on the platform where the
soy-crocks are placed,
Please enjoy yourself to your heart's content!
Please enjoy yourself in the *kimch'i* storage room,
With the smell of raw onions in your nose.
In the outhouse, Ch'ilmok Kaksi
620. During the day lets down her fifty-five feet long hair
And enjoys herself on the squatting boards.
Please enjoy yourself to your heart's content,
[Grant that] male and female children and grandchildren
Will not have in their stomachs and their bowels
625. Dysentery, bloody faeces and colics!
The chimney is erected
And the Great General of the Chimney enjoys himself.
The front gate is erected
And the Gate-Guarding General enjoys himself.

585. Here begins the catalogue of *norigae*, trinkets worn by ladies. Cf.
Hanyang ka, 116-119.

612. The Dragon-King Kaksi, like the Dragon King, apparently is
connected with water.

614. For "kitchen shelves", *AA* have *sarŭngjang*, which they translate as
"blue lantern." *Sarong* is Kyŏnggi Province dialect for *salgang*, a kind of
kitchen shelf for food and crockery. I am assuming that something like that
was meant. *KTG* I, 99 has *sallangjang*. The meaning of Taegŏng is uncertain.

619. Ch'ilmok could mean "seven eyes." Other names for the goddess of
the outhouse are Puch'ul Kaksi, "Miss Squatting-board" and Ch'iksil puin,
"Lady Latrine." "Puch'ul Kaksi" is also used by Pae Kyŏngjae, the *mudang*
who sang this *Hwangje p'uri*.[123]

629. There is a short separate prayer for the Gate-Guarding General in the
Kosa ch'ugwŏn prayers belonging to the ritual held for the house-gods in the
Tenth Month by the same *mudang*.[124]

630. Roosters and dogs in the frontyard,
      Doves in the backyard.
      A wild falcon is caught and trained,
      Sent to hunt pheasants in a village deep in the mountains.
      The hooves of a white horse are washed
635. And it is tied to a pine tree in the park behind the house.

   630-631. Cf. *Namwŏn kosa*, 129: "Keeping dogs in the frontyard, raising
chickens in the backyard."
   632-635. There is a remarkable similarity between these lines and the
opening lines of two *sijo* (*Sijo sajŏn*, Nos. 1108 and 1110). Influence from the
sijo on the *muga* is most likely.

      If you go down to the reception rooms,
      The adornments of these rooms are even better.
      They have thick oiled paper on the floor, coffered ceilings,
      Big screens and small screens
640. And screens with calligraphy, all around!
      All kinds of scrolls hang there,
      Cushions and blankets have been spread out!
      Document boxes and inkstone cases [you find there].
      There hangs a cuckoo-clock!
645. A pair of chamber-pots, brilliant as the Morning Star,
      A pair of cuspidors and a pair of ashtrays
      Have been placed over here and over there!
      Hwangje, who gives a complete set of ten
      Pipes of spotted bamboo from the Hsiang and Hsiao Rivers,
                              twelve joints long,
650. Please enjoy yourself to your heart's content.
      On one side a *yanggŭm* and a *kŏmungo* have been placed!
      On another side *paduk* and chess sets have been placed!
      On another side [again] smooth talking parrots
      And dancing cranes have been painted.
655. If you look at the [yard] in front of the reception rooms,
      [You will see that] curiously shaped rocks have been placed there.
      A lotus pond has been dug, squarely shaped.
      In it floats a dragon boat,
      In the middle a six-cornered pavillion has been built.
660. Goldfish [as big] as soup bowls
      From time to time will swill some water.

More than thirty budding lotus flowers
Float on the water.
Is this not a wonderful spectacle?

636. The reception rooms are the rooms in which the master of the house receives his friends (*sarangbang*).

651. The *yanggŭm* is a Western-style steelwire zither, the *kŏmun'go* a six-stringed zither.

656. *AA* translate *kosŏk* as "old stones", but it is also used as a variant of *koesŏk*, curiously shaped stones such as were often found in elegant gardens.

661. The English translation is based on the Japanese translation of *AA*. I suspect that the Korean text of *AA* is corrupt. *KTG* I, 101 has in a corresponding passage: "Goldfish as big as soup bowls/following the waves, go to and fro, time and again."

665. The flower adornments are even better!
        Pine trees have been planted and made into a bower,
        Cypresses have been planted to form a hedge,
        Blue grapes and red plum blossoms there are!
        Gardenias, camellias, Japanese pomegranate, tree-peonies
670. White-flowered peonies, spotted bamboo, azaleas,
      , Cockscomb, touch-me-not, royal azaleas
        And rhododendron indicum, in the wide and spacious garden,
        Have been planted over here and over there!
        In the front garden cranes are kept,
675. In the back garden storks are kept.
        The crane from the blue mountains, stretching its short neck,
        With a flutter spreads its wings.
        It calls *ttururuk* going here,
        It calls *ttururuk* going there.
680. Look what So-and-so, the master of the house, does!
        Wearing a crane's coat with wide sleeves
        And on his head, over a skull-cap with meshes fine as crab's eggs,
        At a slant, a silken hat from T'ongyŏng,
        Spectacles with crane's legs high on his nose.
685. He strolls [up and down], in front and in back.
        "The fellow who built this house
        Surely had a fine eye!"

665. Here begins the catalogue of flowers and plants, part of the description of gardens.

676. A crane with a short neck, how could that be? The explanation is that the *mudang* was influenced by descriptions, found in some *sijo*, of roosters stretching their necks and flapping their wings before they start to crow.[125] Cf. line 698 of this *muga*, which also contains an echo of these *sijo*.

681-684. An example of the theme of dress. A crane's coat is the name of a kind of coat worn by scholars. Its colours, white with black (or blue) trimmings, resemble the plumage of the crane. Crane's legs are the ear-frames of spectacles. T'ongyŏng (modern name: Ch'ungmu) was famous for the manufacture of the traditional Korean hat, the *kat*.

686. This line contains a word, *tangdoragi*, which *AA* translate as "architect." It is not found in any dictionary at my disposal. On the basis of the context I have translated it as "fellow."

       Male servants like horses and falcons,
       Female servants [pretty] like parrots,
690. Child servants [trustworty] like a lock.
       In the frontyard Boss Kim,
       In the backyard Boss Yi.
       When they sweep the frontyard and the backyard,
       Gold is raised, silver is raised.
695. When they keep chickens
       They will be speckled chickens.
       When the fourth or the fifth watch approaches,
       The cocks crow, spreading their wings with a flutter.
       Is this not a wonderful spectacle?
700. When they raise dogs,
       The shaggy dogs, the short-tailed dogs
       Go to the far mountains for the pheasant hunt.
       When they raise horses
       These become thousand-mile horses,
705. Ten-thousand-mile horses, dragon-horses!
       When they raise cows
       These become sturdy cows, black-and-white cows!
       When the share is attached
       To the half-moon-shaped plough
710. They pull it *hwangdŏk p'ungdŏk*.
       High places are used as dry fields,
       Low places are used as rice fields.

690. Literally, this line is "Child servants like keys", with uncertain connotations. I assume that "trustworthy/safe" was meant, which fits better with "lock" than with "key."

691-692. One of the many examples of the front/back opposition.

695-710. Such passages are very common in texts about a geomantically auspicious location, which ensures that children born there will be full of piety towards their elders, women chaste, et cetera.[126]

711-712. High/low opposition in a parallelistic construction, Cf. lines 717-718.

The amount of seed [needed to plant them] is ten-thousand bales.
The acreage of the dry fields is such that it takes one man three
                                months to plough them.
715. Load [the harvest] on the carts, so that [they] sway and creak,
      Pile up the grain in stacks, in front and in back.
      On top of the stacks sprouts spring up,
      Under the stacks new shoots are formed.
      An owl settles on the stacks:
720. When it flutters one wing,
      Ten million bales [of grain] gush forth,
      When it flutters the other wing,
      A hundred-million bales [of grain] gush forth.
      The luck-bringing snake twists and turns,
725. The luck-bringing weasel shows its face.
      Please Siksin Kaksi,
      Enjoy yourself to your heart's content!

724-725. Yi Nŭnghwa ("Musok ko", 56) lists three kinds of ŏp: (luck-bringing divinities): human ŏp, snake ŏp and weasel ŏp.

726. "Siksin" is defined by the *Kugŏ tae-sajŏn* of Yi Hŭisŭng as: "the god in charge of food", which fits this passage better than the definition of Gale in his *Korean-English Dictionary*: "one's luck in eating as found by magic."

      Look what So-and-so, the master of the house, does!
      When friends are to be received,
730. *Kisaeng* to the left and to the right,
      Play the *yanggŭm* and the *kŏmungo*.
      Thousand-Day Wine of Mago sŏnnyŏ
      And Three-Times-Five Wine,

734.   Fallen with a thud: Fallen-Flower Wine.

732-734. This is a brief version of the *sul t'aryŏng*, the enumeration of various kinds of alcoholic drinks, a common theme, with possibly a long history. In a more elaborate form, the *sul t'aryŏng* is also part of the *Taegam t'aryŏng* of the same *mudang*, where the description of the food eaten with the alcohol, too, is similar.[127]

The oldest instance of an enumeration of different kinds of liquor is found in a song from the Koryŏ dynasty, *Hallim pyŏlgok* (Song of the Literati), which was recorded in the *Akhak kwebŏm*, a musical compendium published in 1493. This song consists almost exclusively of catalogues.[128] The catalogue has been called one of the marks of the oral style,[129] but *Hallim pyŏlgok* has a distinctly literary flavour. All the catalogues in this poem have something to do with the life of the scholar and clearly belong to written literature. First there are lists of outstanding writers and literary works, then there is an enumeration of styles of calligraphy. This is followed by catalogues of wines, of flowers, musical instruments and of places famous for their scenery. According to the section on music in the *Koryŏ sa* (History of Koryŏ), *Hallim pyŏlgok* was composed by Confucian literati at the court of King Kojong (1192-1213-1259).[130] A major part of the song is in Sino-Korean. It is noteworthy that a number of the catalogues in *Hallim pyŏlgok* also occur in later vernacular literature. In this *Hwangje p'uri*, one finds, besides the *sul t'aryŏng*, a catalogue of flowers, while the catalogue of famous landscapes in *Hallim pyŏlgok* approximates the geomantic descriptions in the *muga*. Musical instruments are only mentioned briefly, but the theme appears in other *muga* (e.g., *AA* I, 156) and *ko-sosŏl* (e.g., *Namwŏn kosa*, 136). It has proved impossible, so far, to trace the relationship between *Hallim pyŏlgok* and later forms of vernacular literature, but this use of similar themes is striking. One thing is obvious: many of the themes of the "new vernacular literature" of the 18th and 19th century were not merely themes which had been handed down in oral tradition from time immemorial, but if, indeed, of oral origin, they were given a new content by literate authors, in the same way that *Hallim pyŏlgok* perhaps was a new song on an old pattern. The content of many of the themes and of the allusions they contain clearly betrays the interference of members of the literate classes.

In order to strengthen this claim one more example of a theme will be examined, that of the enumeration of books, which is also found in *Hallim pyŏlgok*. It is not part of the present *Hwangje p'uri*, but could easily have been slipped in, as, indeed, it is in several Sŏngju *muga* of this type (e.g., *KTG* IV, 83 and *THM*, 153). Even though this is a theme in vernacular literature, the books mentioned are books written in Chinese.[131]   In this respect, the lists are very similar to the one in *Hallim pyŏlgok*. Also similar is the little flourish near the end of the lists. In *Hallim pyŏlgok* these books have to be studied "including the commentaries"; in *Ong Kojip chŏn*, Ong declares that he has many books "including the tables of contents." Whatever the relationship between *Hallim pyŏlgok* and later works, no further argumentation will be needed to convince the reader that these lists cannot originally, in this form, have been part of the *muga*. The same goes for the theme of the enumeration of government offices (cf. the list of catalogues in Chapter V).

732. "Mago sŏnnyŏ" could be rendered as "the Immortal Ma-ku." According to Werner, *A Dictionary of Chinese Mythology*, this is the name of no fewer than three immortals, the second of whom (an avatar of the first) restored her father's sight by giving him a special wine, which she had made while she was living in the mountains as a hermit.[132] The name Mago appears quite often in the *muga*, frequently in the combination Mago halmŏni, "Grandmother Mago."[133] Grandmother Mago is also the name of a poor and kindhearted old woman (again a transformation of the Immortal Ma-ku), who sells wine in a *ko-sosŏl*, *Sukhyang chŏn* (cf. Ch. VI). When Mago figures in narrative *muga*, it is usually as such a kindly old grandmother, rather than as the immortal depicted in Chinese paintings.

733. The interpretation of the name of this wine is difficult. The translation is arbitrary. Perhaps one should think of the Sino-Korean phrase *sam-sam-o-o*: "in small groups of three or five persons"; then *sam-o chu* might be "wine drunk in company."

734. "Fallen with a thud" is pure Korean, "Fallen Flower Wine" is Sino-Korean, a typical pattern.

735.   In a large brass bowl steamed spare-ribs,
       In a small brass bowl tender steamed chicken and pheasant legs.
       What is folded, are the dried persimmons,
       What is shelled, are the chestnuts.

735-738. A description of the food presented to the guests with the wine is one form of the theme of food, of which the *namul t'aryŏng*, the enumeration of vegetables is a sub-theme. The theme of food overlaps that of offerings to the gods.

       Respected Sunbeam Wangsin,
740.   Respected Moonbeam Wangsin,
       Respected Wangsin of the Deep Palace,

Respected Wangsin of the Undeep Palace,
Respected Wangsin of Kŭmsŏng near Naju in Chŏlla,
Respected Wangsin of the Crown Prince, the Son of the Nation,
745.   Respected Wangsin of the Hwaju-dang across the water,
Respected Purple Mist Wangsin
Of the Kullebang Bridge near the Purple Mist Gate,
Respected hereditary Wangsin of Family So-and-so,
Respected Sŏngju Wangsin!

739. Wangsin is literally "King-Deity"; this is awkward, even more so when combined with epithets. Therefore it has been left untranslated. In modern speech, *wangsin* may be used as a nickname for a cantankerous person, an indication of the capricious, demanding character attributed to (some of) the gods by the Koreans.

"Respected" is used in the translation to render *manura*, which in old Korean was used to address a woman respectfully and in modern Korean refers to one's own wife. In the *muga*, however, it is a suffix to the names of gods, irrespective of sex. San-manura, "Mountain-manura", for instance, refers to the deified General Ch'oe Yŏng.[134]

Nothing, apparently, is known about Ilgwang Wangsin and Wŏlgwang wangsin, "Sunbeam Wangsin" and "Moonbeam Wangsin." There are the Sunbeam Bodhisattva and the Moonbeam Bodhisattva, however, attendants of the Buddha of Medicine.

741. The Deep Palace suggests the Inner Palace, where the court ladies reside. The Undeep Palace may be nothing but antithetic fancy.

743. Historical records show that at least as early as the Koryŏ period a deity was worshipped at Kŭmsŏng Mountain near Naju in Chŏlla Province. This god is often called Kŭmsŏng Taewang, "Great King of Kŭmsŏng."[135]

744. This may refer to Crown Prince Changhŏn, who was nick-named the "King-in-the-rice-chest" (cf. Ch. I).

745. During the construction of the fortress Namhan sansŏng, a certain Hong was falsely accused of fraud. When he was decapitated, a falcon flew up out of his head. People believed this falcon to be his soul and took the occurrence as proof of his innocence. They called him the Wangsin of the Falcon Hall and built a temple for him. This is the Hwaju-dang in Namhan sansŏng, which is "across the river", as seen from Seoul. Hong's wife committed suicide on Cheja Island in the Han River. For her the Ch'ungnyŏl Hwaju-dang was erected. This tradition has been recorded by Akiba and Akamatsu.[136]

747. The Purple Mist Gate is the Chaha-mun, or Little North Gate. Within this gate there seems to have been a place were a Sŏnang was worshipped.[137]

In present-day Seoul Kullebang Bridge (Kullebang tari) remains as a place name only.

748. "Hereditary" here is a translation of *puri* (a noun), which refers to ancestor spirits or to deities who have been venerated in a family for successive generations. *Puri* also seems to be used in the meaning "ancestry/heredity" in *oe-buri* and *chinju-buri*, "ancestry on the maternal side" and "ancestry on the paternal side."[138]   Another *muga* of Pae Kyŏngjae contains the phrase: "*Puri yŏngsan* [are] ancestor *yŏngsan*."[139]

Concluding remarks

One of the reasons for choosing this *muga* for translation and annotation has been the fact that in Kim Tonguk's discussion of the relationship between the *muga* and other genres of vernacular literature it is repeatedly referred to as a source for elements in other genres. While agreeing that there are many elements which this *Hwangje p'uri* and, for instance, *Namwŏn kosa*, have in common, I cannot agree with Kim's conclusion that the *ko-sosŏl* borrowed from the *muga*. As far as the evidence of this *Hwangje p'uri* is concerned, it seems, rather, that the *muga* have absorbed many influences from other genres.

If one accepts the latter conclusion, it means that this *Hwangje p'uri* is of value for the study of Korean shamanism because it indicates that the *mudang* were not merely a despised out-caste group who maintained their primitive beliefs in complete isolation from the culture of the higher social strata, but that, to some extent, they were in contact with the culture of the *yangban*. This song does tell us something of the beliefs of the *mudang*, but it tells us even more about their social position. The references to the building of the Kyŏngbok Palace and the elements borrowed from the literature of the ruling class evoke a picture of late 19th century *mudang* who were not the despised representatives of a coarse peasant creed, but who -in spite of all social discrimination- "went in and out of the royal palace", as the Korean phrase goes, to minister to the needs of such august persons as the formidable Queen Min and her entourage.

IX A *Mudang* Sings of Herself

In marked contrast to the shamans of Northern Asia, the Korean *mudang* in her songs does not describe her own exploits. The Evenki shaman for instance, appears in his own songs in a way that is never found in Korea.[1] The songs of the *mudang* are, therefore, in certain respects less personal than those of the Evenki shaman. This is also reflected in the fact that generally she does not in her songs invoke her personal guardian spirits, as do Siberian shamans.[2]

There is a *muga*, however, which -in variation on the titles of the mythological songs of the Ainu- one might call: "A *Mudang* Sings of Herself." This is the *Kyemyŏn kut muga*, which deals with some of the most important aspects of a *mudang*'s life.[3] This song is about a proto-typical *mudang* who is called Kyemyŏn halmŏni, "Grandmother" Kyemyŏn.

The meaning of kyemyŏn

In this chapter the term *kyemyŏn* is used following the standard set by Yi Hŭi-sŭng's authoritative dictionary *Kugŏ tae-sajŏn*.[4] In practice, however, the form *kyemyŏn* occurs less frequently than its variants: *kemyŏn, kimyŏn, chemyŏn, chemin, chimin,* or *chimyŏn*. The semantics of the word are a little confusing. It is used to refer to a certain kind of rice cake and as such occurs in the combination *kyemyŏn ttŏk*. At other times, however, it seems to refer to a *mudang* who is regarded as a "*mudang* ancestor": a woman who originated the practice of shamanism. In such cases the combination Kyemyŏn halmŏni is used (Chemyŏn halmŏni in the *muga* translated below). Kyemyŏn halmŏni is similar to Kyemyŏn malmyŏng, the spirit of a deceased *mudang* who lends a hand when *kyemyŏn ttŏk* (rice cake) is offered to the guardian deity of a new *mudang*.[5] Kyemyŏn halmŏni and Kyemyŏn malmyŏng, too, may be regarded as guardian deities of the *mudang*. Another female figure is Kyemyŏn Kaksi, about whom a little more will be said later.

It has also been suggested that *kyemyŏn* is the area in which the *mudang* has her regular clients (*tan'gol*).[6] The expression *kyemyŏn tolda* (to go around in the *kyemyŏn*) which denotes a *mudang*'s visiting the houses of her clients to collect grain, seems to lend credence to this suggestion. In a *muga* from the Osan area, for instance, one finds the lines: "The *kyemyŏn* in which the elder sister went around, will not the younger sister go around in it too?"[7] Then there is a *muga* from Seoul which says: "After going around the *kyemyŏn* of the Circuit of the Right, and the *kyemyŏn* of the Circuit of the Left ..."[8]

All the meanings of *kyemyŏn* have a common element: in one way or another they have something to do with the relation between the *mudang* and her regular clients. It is this relationship which is the subject matter of the story of Kyemyŏn halmŏni as told in the *muga*. It may not be clear at once how the meaning "rice cake" comes into this, but in the context of Korean popular religion the link is a very natural one. A person who is about to become a *mudang* often first falls into a "divine illness" (*sinbyŏng*), an illness which is interpreted as an instrument which gods or ghosts use to force someone to become a *mudang*.[9] In a crucial stage of this illness the patient, in a kind of ecstacy, leaves her house and wanders around, dropping in at people's homes at random. At the houses where the future *mudang* calls, she receives, in exchange for prayers and oracles, some rice to make rice cake to offer to the gods.[10] The families on whom she calls will form the basis of her regular clientèle, her *tan'gol*. Going around in this way is also called *kyemyŏn tolda*. It is sometimes said that, as she goes around the village, the new *mudang* is led by a deity called Kyemyŏn Kaksi.[11]

After her initiation a *mudang* will continue to visit her *tan'gol* from time to time in order to receive rice (or other grains) to make cakes, *ttŏk*. *Ttŏk* is an important element in the communication between the *mudang* and her clients. At the end of every *kut* the clients receive, to take home, some of the rice cakes which are arranged on the sacrificial tables. This symbolizes the transfer of good luck to the clients. In one *muga* Kyemyŏn Kaksi sells rice cakes:[12]

> If you receive this cake
> You will live a thousand, ten thousand years.
> If you receive *kyemyŏn ttŏk*
> It is *ttŏk* which makes that grandsons you did not have
>   are born to you,
> That grandsons you already have live long.
> When Kyemyŏn Kaksi goes around with *kyemyŏn ttŏk*

It is *ttŏk* which brings happiness.

In the ceremonies of the *mudang*, *ttŏk* is the Bread of Communion. This sym-
bolism is not limited to ceremonies which have a separate part called *Kyemyŏn kut*; a well-known proverb says: "If you want to watch a *kut*, you must
stay until the *kyemyŏn ttŏk* is given" (*kut kugyŏng haryŏmyŏn, kyemyŏn ttŏk
naol ttae kkaji hayŏra*, which means that once you have started something,
you should see it through to the end).

In the *muga* of Cheju Island one finds the word *chemin*, in the combina-
tions *chemin tan'gwŏl* and *chemin kungyŏn*. According to Hyŏn Yongjun this
chemin is Sino-Korean, meaning "all the people."[13] If one takes into con-
sideration the context -there are references to *tan'gol* (= *tan'gwŏl*) and, in
several cases, to *ttŏk*- there can be no doubt but that this *chemin* is a variant
form of *kyemyŏn*.

The meaning of *kyemyŏn*, as sketched above, possibly has some relevance
to an entry in the *Dictionnaire Coréen-francais* of 1880: "*chyemyŏn changsă*,
Faire des instances pour vendre sa marchandise. Marchand qui sacrifie une
partie de ses marchandises en les vendant à très-bon marché pour gagner des
pratiques et se rattraper sur les autres."[14] A translation into modern English
might be "dumping", but one could also regard the practice here described as
the attempt of a merchant to gain a circle of regular customers, a *tan'gol*.

Texts of Kyemyŏn kut muga

For the writing of this chapter nine texts were available.

Text A. Source: a male hereditary shaman from Kyŏnggi Province, called Yi
Chongman. Recorded in the 1930's.[15]

Text B. Source: a possessed *mudang*, Sŏ Chŏmsun, from Inch'ŏn. Recorded
in 1966.[16]

Text C. Source: Pyŏn Yŏnho, a hereditary *mudang* from Kyŏngsang Province. Recorded in 1968.[17]

Text D. Source: Sŏng Hwasu, a hereditary *mudang* from Chŏnju. Recorded
in 1971.[18]

Text E. Source: Sa Hwasŏn, a hereditary *mudang* from the East Coast.
Recorded in 1972.[19]

Text F. Source: a possessed *mudang*, Kim Suhŭi, from Kyŏnggi Province.
Recorded in 1973.[20]

Text G. Source: a hereditary *mudang* from Kyŏnggi Province, Sim Poksun.
Recorded in 1973.[21]

Text H. Source: the possessed *mudang* Pak Yongnyŏ from Kangnŭng. Recorded in 1974.[22]

Text J.   Another text of Sa Hwasŏn (cf. E.). Recorded in 1980.[23]

Among those who perform the *Kyemyŏn kut* (which invariably is part of a much larger ceremony) the two main types of *mudang*, the hereditary and the possessed, are both represented.[24] Some of the texts are very brief and have no narrative content. Texts C, D, E, H and J -which, except for D, are all from the East Coast area- tell something like a story. Text D is quite short and suddenly breaks off. E and J are by far the longest texts, elaborating on the basic story by adding several scenes. Text E seems rather fragmentary and, unlike C, does not include the brief account of the career of a *mudang*. Pyŏn Yŏnho's text (C) has been chosen for translation and analysis as being most suitable.

The text of the muga

1.   Chemyŏn, oh Chemyŏn, oh Chemyŏn!

Pyŏn Yŏnho often starts a *muga* by invoking the name of the god for whom the *kut* is held.[25] It is safe, therefore, to assume that in this line Chemyŏn refers to Chemyŏn halmŏni.

2.   Long long ago, in times past [it was]

This is a common introductory formula, which is also used by other *mudang*; e.g., *KTG* IV, p. 105: *yennal yetchŏg-e, kannal chŏ katchŏg-e.*
Note the alliteration and the form *katchŏg-e*, which seems to be ungrammatical and apparently was created to complete the alliterative parallelism. As indicated in Chapter V, creation of new words on the basis of some phonetic pattern (alliteration, rhyme) is not uncommon in *muga*.[26]

3.   As for the origin of Chemyŏn halmŏni,
       Chemyŏn halmŏni sprang forth
5.   From the Chiri Mountains in Chŏlla Province.

Even when they are mainly about other subjects, *muga* often start with the matter of a god's place of origin. There is a famous goddess associated with the Chiri Mountains: Sŏngmo, the "Holy Mother", whose cult already existed in the time of the Koryŏ dynasty (935-1392). She was a mountain goddess who was traditionally also regarded as a *mudang* ancestor; the eight daughters born out of her union with a Buddhist priest spread the faith over the Eight Provinces of old Korea.[27] The information given in this *muga* about the origin of Chemyŏn halmŏni cannot, however, be accepted as necessarily correct. In text E Chemyŏn halmŏni is represented as an ordinary child, although it is hinted that she was born into a prominent family (texts H and J are similar in this respect). This fits the story, even as given in C, better than some form of supernatural birth. In text E, the words *sin* (god, spirit) and *sosanada* (to spring forth) are used, but, there, only to signify that the gods take possession of the who is to be a *mudang*. The name of a mountain, "Drum Mountain", in the same passage in E has nothing to do with the origin of Chemyŏn halmŏni, but serves to explain why she has to become a *mudang*: if one buries one's ancestors on this mountain, for generation after generation the family will produce *mudang* because of the geomantic influence of this mountain as a grave site.[28] Lines 3-5 in the present text have only a limited "theological value."

6.   What about the house of Chemyŏn halmŏni?
       Her house is in the capital.
       When she received the gods,
9.   It was at the age of seven that she received them.

Lines 6 and 7 are an example of indirect narration, e.g., not a simple statement, but a question followed by an answer. In text E it is told how Chemyŏn halmŏni finds it impossible to stay in the countryside, because she feels ashamed of her activities as a *mudang*. Her feelings are, of course, a consequence of the contempt in which *mudang* are held in Korean society. "Receiving the gods" means that Chemyŏn halmŏni is possessed by the gods, who use the "divine illness" to force her to become a *mudang*. It is worthy of notice that this *muga* is about a *mudang* of the possessed type, while the *mudang* who sings the song is of the hereditary type.

10.   When she was fifteen, sixteen the gods began
        to speak through her mouth, to write by her hand.

In line l0, in the Korean text, the phrases "gate of words" (*malmun*) and "gate of writing" (*kŭlmun*) are used. If the gods begin to speak through the mouth of a *mudang*, it is said that "the gate of words has been opened".[29] *Kŭlmun* is not used frequently, but it does occur in at least one other *muga*.[30]

11.   With a divining table in front of her
       She practised all kinds of divination.
       In this way and that way Chemyŏn halmŏni earned money,
14.   Plenty to live on.

Divination is an important activity of almost all *mudang*. Special powers are, in this respect, ascribed to the recently initiated *mudang*.[31] Text E tells how Chemyŏn halmŏni's powers are discovered when she divines the whereabouts of lost property.

15.   She bore a son,
       Obtained a daughter-in-law,
       Raised a daughter, too,
       And gave her away in marriage.
       But although in this way
20.   She had plenty to eat and to live on,
       She could not withstand the gods:
       She went to the gate of each and every house
       To beg without minding the season.

Line 17 does not have *ttal*, "daughter", but *tam*. None of the meanings of *tam* fits, whereas the substitution of *ttal* in its place makes lines 17 and 18 a perfect parallel to lines 15 and 16.

   With line 22 begins the description of the collecting of rice from the regular clients.[32] It is stressed that Chemyŏn halmŏni is not forced to go begging because of poverty; the gods want her to go. The same point is strongly emphasized in text E, where it is said that Chemyŏn halmŏni's body starts to ache in every joint if she does not go out to collect rice.

   The line "To beg without minding the season" is probably taken from the story of Sim Ch'ŏng as sung by the same *mudang*.[33] As shown in Chapter VII, Pyŏn Yŏnho borrowed most of her Sim Ch'ŏng *muga* from a version of the novel *Sim Ch'ŏng chŏn*. Derivation from *Sim Ch'ŏng chŏn* is likely, because this line does not really fit the *Kyemyŏn kut*. The *mudang* does not collect rice or other grains all the year round, as this line would suggest, but usually twice a year: in late spring after the barley harvest, and in autumn after the harvesting of the rice.[34] Text H explicitly mentions that Chemyŏn halmŏni visits her *tan'gol* twice a year.[35] Similarly, one should not take too literally the text of E at the point where it says that Chemyŏn halmŏni goes around to collect rice in "the month of the winter solstice and the last month, on snowy days in deepest winter" (*ŏmdong sŏrhan tongjisŏttal*): this is just a formula.

> Great is the greed of Chemyŏn halmŏni,
> 25.   Astonishing is her temper.
> One day she said to her daughter-in-law:
> "My daughter-in-law, my child,
> I will obtain hemp seeds
> And give them to you.
> 30.   You must grow hemp,
> Weave hemp cloth
> And make a piece of Seven-stars cloth.

In this text lines 26-32 do not seem to follow lines 24 and 25 naturally. In text H, both the greediness and the ill-naturedness of Chemyŏn halmŏni are mentioned as a logical part of the story. There Chemyŏn halmŏni gives seeds both to her daughter and to her daughter-in-law. Anxious to make her daughter-in-law fail, she roasts the seeds which she intends to give to her. Here the classical antagonism between mother and daughter-in-law in traditional Korean society is expressed. Unfortunately she forgets which seeds were roasted (and are therefore useless for sowing) and which were not; it is her own daughter who receives the spoiled seeds. In H, Chemyŏn halmŏni's greediness shows when she wants to have all the cloth that has been woven for her own use, even though she does not need it.

The translation of lines 30-32 presents some problems. Line 30 reads: *chilssam-ŭl karasŏ. Chilssam* (standard Korean: *kilssam*) means "weaving", the verb *kalda* to "cultivate, to sow". I assume, partly on the basis of a comparison with H, that *chilssam* is a mistake for *sam*, "hemp." I do not know what "Seven-stars cloth" is. The Seven Stars (the constellation of the Big Dipper) are associated with funeral rites; *ch'ilsŏng p'an*, "Seven-stars board", is the board on which a corpse is laid. This would seem to be completely unrelated to the *Kyemyŏn kut*. There is an indirect link, however. The term *ch'ilsŏng p'an* is used in a folk-song called *Pet'ŭl yo*, "The Song of the Loom."[36] As will be shown below, the description of weaving in the present *muga* contains several elements from this folk-song. In the "Song of the

Loom", of which there are many versions, the story is told of a young woman, whose husband has gone to the capital to win fame through the state examinations.[37] During his absence his wife makes for him a garment called *chigyŏn* (or *chingnyŏng*) *top'o*.[38] When the news arrives that he is on his way home, she goes out to meet him, only to discover that he is returning "on a *ch'ilsŏng p'an*", i.e. as a corpse. It is possible that Pyŏn Yŏnho has confused the words *chigyŏng top'o* and *ch'ilsŏng p'an*.

33.   "Make a shoulder bag with two ends
34.   Make a sack with four corners!

The shoulder bag is a long sack which can be opened on two sides and has a partition in the middle.

35.   "The homes of my clients out there
       The homes of my 10 000 clients I will visit.
       I can live without behaving like this,
       But I cannot withstand the gods.
       Once in every season
40.   I have to go around like this."

As argued above, it is unlikely that "in every season" here means "four times a year."

       So she spoke
       And her daughter-in-law made cloth
       In the way she had said.
       She sowed the hemp
45.   Then after a while cut it
       And [started] weaving.
       She put the loom by the Jewelled Balustrade.
       Four legs has the loom,
       Three brothers are the heddle shafts.
50.   The naturally curved *sinnamu*,
       Is it the fishing rod of Chiang T'ai-kung
       Cast in the River O?
       The way the shuttle goes back and forth

Is like red cranes, hatching eggs,
55.   Going in and out [of the nest].

Lines 47-55 are all from the folk-song *Pet'ŭl yo*. The "Jewelled Balustrade" (or "beautifully adorned balustrade") occurs in most versions of this song.[39] In some versions, however, one finds not *ongnan'gan*, but *ongnanggang*, which in a *kasa* version of this song -because of the context- cannot be understood as other than the name of a river: "the River of the Beautiful Maiden".[40] In anonymous literature of this kind it is impossible to say which of the two readings is correct, although one can, of course, make judgements about the appropriateness of the phrase in the context, or about its literary effect.

The "legs" of line 48 are in this text called *pet'ŭl-tari*, but it is clear, from their number and from several folk-songs about weaving, that what is meant is not what the dictionary *Kugŏ tae-sajŏn* calls *pet'ŭl-tari*. According to the dictionary these are the two horizontal shafts of the loom. In the *muga* the four vertical posts of the loom (called *pet'ŭl-kidung* in the *Kugŏ tae-sajŏn*) must be meant. The folk songs use the word *pet'ŭl-tari* in the same way as the *muga*. "Making high the front legs, making low the hind legs", one folk song says, obviously referring to the vertical posts.[41] Another folk song says: "Four legs has the loom, two legs has the maiden."[42]

The heddle shafts are not just called "three brothers" because there are three of them; "three brothers" refers to three figures out of Chinese history: Liu Pei (162-223), the founder of the Shu-Han dynasty, and his comrades Kuan Yü (?-219) and Chang Fei (?-220), who in Korea were very well known through the romanticized account of their adventures in the *San-kuo chih yen-i* (Romance of the Three Kingdoms).[43] The three became blood brothers through their famous vow in the Peach Garden.

Sinnamu (in line 50) is a part of the loom that is made of bamboo. The text of the *muga* has *sinnan'gan*, suggesting a parallel with *ongnan'gan*. This is a false analogy, as *nan'gan* here undoubtedly is a mistake for *nanggŭnŭn* or *nanggŭn*, dialect forms of *namu*, "wood", followed by the topic marker. Such dialect forms occur also in the other *muga* by Pyŏn Yŏnho[44], and in text H, which in the corresponding passage has *sinnanggŭnŭn* (= *sinnamu-nŭn*).

Chiang T'ai-kung (line 51) is another figure out of Chinese history who often appears in Korean folklore and *muga* (cf. the annotations to line 520 of *Hwangje p'uri*).[45] In line 52, O is a mistake for Wi, the Korean pronunciation of Wei, as the river is called in Chinese.[46] In line 54, "red cranes" (*honghak*) is rather uncommon. Other texts have, more plausibly, "blue cranes"[47], "yellow cranes"[48] or "blue birds and jade birds."[49] One may also think of a phrase which occurs quite often in *muga* and is used to symbolize auspiciousness:

ponghag-i nŏmnonŭn tŭt, "as if phoenixes and cranes flew up and down."[50] In line 54, too, the verb *nŏmnolda* is used.

Lines 47-55 are not only found in various versions of the *Kyemyŏn kut*, but also in a *Sŏngju kut*[51] and an *Ogu kut*.[52] In the latter this passage seems to be linked up with a *muga* for Sŏngju, which here is a part of the much larger ceremony called *Ogu kut* (similar to the ceremony that elsewhere is called *chinogi kut*). It should be noted that in the *Sŏngju kut* this passage fits in as naturally as in the *Kyemyŏn kut*. In the whole of Korea *muga* about Sŏngju contain passages describing all kinds of material riches to be found in a prosperous house. An enumeration of countless varieties of silks and other fabrics is usually part of this. The *Pet'ŭl yo* passage is an apt introduction to this enumeration. It is typical of *muga* that elements like this folk-song fragment serve more than one purpose and are deftly fitted into different contexts, sometimes with slight adaptations.

56.   She wove *yŏngp'o*, she wove *ch'ilp'o*,
       She wove hemp and produced a piece of *ch'ilsŏngp'o*.

I have not been able to find a reference to a fabric called *yŏngp'o*. *Ch'ilp'o* may mean "lacquered cloth" and is also used to refer to the kind of cloth that is put over a coffin. None of the meanings seems particularly appropriate (cf., however, the comments about line 32). Line 57 has *chinsŏngp'o* instead of *ch'ilsŏngp'o*, which must be a mistake.

       She made a shoulder bag with two ends,
       Made a sack with four corners.
60.   Grandmother Chemyŏn with the sack over her shoulder
       Went to the house of one of her clients.

In texts D, E, H and J she first goes to houses where she is not well received. In D she is violently kicked out of the house by a servant, after which she cruelly curses the family. In E, H and J people hide or think of all kinds of excuses to refuse what is due to her; e.g., "We believe in Jesus."[53]

62.   See how her clients act!

This kind of phrase (... *kŏdong poso*) is extremely common in narrative *muga* as well as in other traditional genres, such as *p'ansori*.

"We cut off the cuff of a sleeve of [the jacket of]
                    our child Ch'ŏndegi
And when Chemyŏn halmŏni put the child's name on it,
65.   Thanks to Chemyŏn halmŏni
       It thrived, never being ill!"

Mudang often "adopt" or "buy" the children of their clients. Although the children are taken care of by their own parents, they enter into a special religious relationship with the *mudang* in order to ensure health and long life. Through the adoption by the *mudang* the children obtain the protection of the gods; indirectly, they are adopted by the gods themselves. This is made explicit, in one case, by a written "contract", in which the child is called the "grandson of General Ch'oe Yŏng."[54] (Ch'oe Yŏng, 1317-1389, a general of the late Koryŏ period, is -as has been said before- widely venerated by the *mudang*). This adoption of children may be regarded as the core of the *tan'gol*-relationship.[55] Often the adoption is symbolized by writing the name of the child on a long piece of cloth called *myŏngdari* (life-bridge). I have not been able to trace in literature a reference to the writing of a name on the sleeve of a jacket. Nevertheless, lines 63-66 clearly allude to such an adoption procedure.

When Chemyŏn halmŏni entered this house
They were picking straw in the yard.
Seeing that Chemyŏn halmŏni had come,
[They said]
70.   "Why! Ch'ŏndegi's Grandma has come!
       Please come in, come in here!"
       They escorted her to a room,
       Filled with tobacco a pipe with a big bowl and a long stem
       And, offering this to Chemyŏn halmŏni,
75.   At once made her sit down where the floor was warm,
       Feeling with their hands if the temperature was right.
       There she stayed for the night,
       Taking a good, long rest.

Chemyŏn halmŏni is given the place of honour, the *araemmok*, the place where the *ondol* floor is the hottest. Line 73 has *hajuk sŏltae chin tambŏttae*, which probably should be *hojuk sŏltae chin tambaettae*, and has been translated as such.

> Enormous was the greed of Chemyŏn halmŏni!
> 80.   They say that even when she went to the house of her daughter
>   She took nine sacks with her.

In other words, she would even take from her nearest and dearest.

> The next day, the people of that house,
> While Ch'ŏndegi's Grandma, Grandmother Chemyŏn
>   was not aware of it,
> Filled the two-ended bag with rice they had grown,
>   tilling the land,
> 85.   Filled the sack with rice
>   so that the four corners stood out
> [And said]
> "Take this rice with you,
> Pound it in the mortar
> And make *chemyŏn ttŏk* of it.
> Pray well before the gods,
> 90.   Pray that our Ch'ŏndegi will grow up well!"
> When they spoke like this,
> See what Chemyŏn halmŏni does!
> She could not take the rice with her [herself] and went home.
> [The people of the house] called a middle servant.
> 95.   The middle servant had work to do in the house.
> They called an upper servant
> And said: "Carry this,
> Bring it to the house of Chemyŏn halmŏni!"
> He carried the rice on his back to the house of Chemyŏn halmŏni.
> 100.   She pounded the rice
> And made *chemyŏn ttŏk*.
> *Chemyŏn* on the near side of the pounding board!
> It is the *chemyŏn ttŏk* of Chemyŏn halmŏni.
> *Chemyŏn* on the far side of the pounding board!
> 105.   It is the *chemyŏn ttŏk* of the daughter-in-law.

In lines 102 and 103 we have the verb form *kinŭn*, which -if it is regarded as standard language- would be the participium praesentis of *kida*, "to crawl." It might be a form of *ki:da* (with a long vowel), *koeda* in standard Korean, one of the meanings of which is "to be piled up", which seems appropriate.[56] Because of the uncertainty regarding this point, the translation avoids the use of a verb.

106.   The daughter-in-law takes care of the gods
       And the mother-in-law takes care of the gods as well.

The verb used in lines 106 and 107 is a little strange: it is *kŏnarida* (standard: *kŏnŭrida*) which means "to lead/take care of an inferior." Nevertheless, the substance of the statement made in these lines is clear: both mother and daughter-in-law are *mudang*. This is a common pattern in Korean shamanism.

       "**Whó** has less rice cake?!"
       "Do you think **I** have more?!"
110.   So mother and daughter-in-law quarreled.
       See what the daughter-in-law does!
       Fuming with rage
       Raging with anger,
       [She strode out]
       And while she was away to fetch water
115.   The shaggy dog of the house in front came
       And completely gobbled up her *chemyŏn ttŏk*!
       The daughter-in-law became angry,
       Took up a three-year old iron poker
       And went after him.

In line 118, "three-year old" (*samnyŏn mugŭn*) is a set phrase, which is used in a number of proverbs and in other *muga*. It has the connotation of "well-used" or "worn."

120.   She lifted the poker once and struck.
       She cleft *tchugŭlt'ŏk* the front part of the front paws.

> She lifted the poker a second time and struck,
> Cleaving *tchultt'ŏk* the back of the back paws.
> She lifted the poker for the third time and struck
> 125.   And then [the dog] breathed his last!

What has been translated as "front part of the front paws" and "back part of the back paws" are phrases which are found in many *muga* in descriptions of meat that is offered to the gods.[57] *Tchugŭlt'ŏk* and *tchultt'ŏk* are onomatopoeia.

> She stripped off the skin
> And buried it in a barrel of dung.
> Then she removed the fat
> In the water of the river in front
> 130.   And she removed the hairs
> In the water of the river at the back.

The skin is buried in dung to facilitate the curing of the leather. Lines 128-131 offer an example of antithetical parallelism based on a simple opposition that is used for its own sake only.[58]

> 132.   She fixed [the skin] to the barrel of a drum
> Made of the wood of the Paulownia tree.

The drum mentioned here is the *changgo*, which is shaped like an hourglass. The *mudang* of the East Coast actually use dog-skin for their *changgo*, although for other *changgo* horse-skin is used.[59] The wood reputed to be best for the body of the drum is that of the Paulownia Coreana (*odong-namu*). In text A a *changgo* is made along with a smaller drum, the *puk*. Text A also has an account of the making of other instruments used for the musical accompaniment of the *kut*: the *p'iri* (the Korean oboe), the *chŏttae* (a cross flute) and the *haegŭm* (a two-stringed fiddle). A *changgo*, a *puk*, a *haegŭm*, a *chŏttae* and two *p'iri* together form the ensemble called *yukkak*, which is depicted in eighteenth- and nineteenth-century genre paintings by Kim Hongdo and Kisan Kim Chun'gŭn.

When it is struck once,
135. The *mudang* of this world dance.
      When it is struck twice,
      The *mudang* of the nether world dance.
      When it is struck thrice,
      In the palace the royal *mudang* dance,
140. In the villages the village *mudang* dance.

The "royal *mudang*" (*mudang* who conducted ceremonies in the palace) were, called *nara-mudang*. The "village *mudang*" (*an-mudang*) were chosen by the local authorities to assist in village festivals, to perform when a new magistrate was welcomed, and to take part in the celebrations when someone from the region returned home after passing the government examinations.[60]

      As for the way to strike the *changgo*,
      The way we *mudang* strike the *changgo*
      Is not striking it at random;
      We strike the *changgo*
145. For the Great God of Heavenly Thunder.
      As for striking the gong,
      We strike the gong
      For the Great God of Earthquakes.
      As for striking the *kkwaenggwari*,
150. We strike the *kkwaenggwari*
      For Kwangmok Ch'ŏnwang.
      As for striking the cymbals
      We strike the cymbals
      For Pibi Pisang Ch'ŏnwang.

It would be wrong to draw from these lines the conclusion that the gods mentioned are of great importance to the *mudang*. The Great God of Heavenly Thunder (Ch'ŏndung-taesin) and the Great God of Earthquakes (Chidung-taesin) rarely figure in other *muga* and apparently were chosen for the relevance of their names to the sound of drum and gong. Line 151 actually has Kwangmu Ch'ŏnwang instead of Kwangmok Ch'ŏnwang. Kwangmok Ch'ŏnwang is one of the Four Heavenly Kings of Buddhism (Virūpāksa). The instrument that is played for him, the *kkwaenggwari*, is a small gong. There is no Pibi Pisang Ch'ŏnwang in the Buddhist pantheon, but there is a term which has a similar sound: *pisang pibisangch'ŏn*, that is the "heaven where there is neither thinking nor not-thinking." Furthermore, another of the Heavenly Kings is called Pisa Ch'ŏnwang. This Pisa Ch'ŏnwang (or Pisamun Ch'ŏnwang: Vaisravana) is mentioned together with Kwangmok Ch'ŏnwang in a *muga* that probably dates back to the 16th century, namely the song "Sŏnghwang pan" in the *Siyong hyangak po*. It is likely that Pyŏn Yŏnho has created a new god, Pibi Pisang Ch'ŏnwang, by mixing up two terms.

If the gods named are of little consequence to the actual practices of the East Coast *mudang*, the musical instruments are those which are in fact used to accompany their rituals. These instruments are basic; sometimes the *nallari* (conical oboe) is used.

155.   As for holding the fan,
       We hold the fan for the immortals (*sŏnja*).

Here a pun may be intended: *sŏnja*, "immortals" has the same pronunciation as *sŏnja*, "fan". The word for fan used in line 155, however, is the more usual *puch'ae*.

       As for holding the Divine Sword,
       When Master Kang Kamch'ŏl was alive
       He caught ghosts and struck the (brass) drum
160.   On the first and the fifteenth day of the month.

Swords, just as fans, are common attributes of the *mudang*. Kang Kamch'ŏl would seem to be Kang Kamch'an (949-1032), the famous general of the Koryŏ period who defeated the Liao. A nearly identical passage in another *muga* from the East Coast, the *Kŏri kut*[61] actually has "Kang Kamch'an." During the Choson dynasty, Kang Kamch'an lived on in the popular imagination; it was said that he had not really died, but had become a Taoist immortal.[62] He also figures in folk-tales.[63] The fact that Kang is referred to as "Master" suggests that the *mudang* thinks of him as a famous exorcist of olden days; in *muga* the names of such exorcists are usually followed by the title *sŏnsaeng*, "Master." Examples from other *muga* are Kwigok sŏnsaeng, Son Pin sŏnsaeng and Kwakkak (= Kwakkwak) sŏnsaeng. These are all figures out of Chinese history. In Chinese their names read Master Kuei-ku (real name: Wang Hsü), Sun Pin and Kuo P'u (Kwakkak is a corruption of Kwak Pak; cf. Ch. I).[64] They were famous for their knowledge of divination. As fortune-telling is one of the most important activities of the *p'ansu*, the

Korean exorcist, it is a natural development that these figures, too, came to be regarded as exorcists.[65] It is possible that *ch'ŏl* in Kang Kamch'ŏl, as Pyŏn Yŏnho calls Kang Kamch'an in line 158, is used because a similar figure, So Kangjŏl, appears in several *muga* as a fortune-teller.[66] So Kangjŏl was a Chinese (Shao Chiang-chieh, 1011-1077), and the author of a work on divination which was known in Korea.

Line 159 has chŏnggu where the corresponding passage in the *Kŏri kut*[67] has *kŏmgu*. *Chŏnggu* can be interpreted as *changgo* (or *changgu*): hour-glass drum. *Kŏmgu* probably is the same as *kŭmgu* or *kŭmgo* in standard Korean. A *kŭmgu* is a brass drum such as is used in Buddhist temples and by exorcists when they recite scriptures.[68]

161. The Heavenly King Bodhisattva shook the fallen flowers
And the ghosts were all scattered to the worlds of the
eight directions.

The combination "Heavenly King Bodhisattva" is not found in the large dictionary of Buddhist terms I consulted,[69] although the Heavenly Kings, of course, are well-known (cf. line 151). In a Cheju *muga*, the Heavenly King Bodhisattva is mentioned as the grandfather of the deity who watches over child-birth.[70] The fallen flowers are apparently used to chase away evil spirits. I have not been able to trace the exact origin of this line. It may be that "fallen flowers" stands for "hand-bells." According to Hyŏn Yongjun,[71] *ch'ŏnan nakhwa* or *ch'ŏnang nakhwa* refers to the hand-bells that are an important attribute of *mudang* all over the country. Unfortunately, he offers no further explanation, but as this part of the *Kyemyŏn kut* deals with the paraphernalia of the *mudang*, it is tempting to interpret the fallen flowers as hand-bells, the more so because of the phonetic resemblance between the phrase in the Cheju *muga* and this *muga*, which has: *ch'ŏnwang posal nakhwa*. One of the uses of these hand-bells is the chasing away of evil; one *muga* has the line: "If these bells sound three times, the Three Disasters and the Eight Misfortunes disappear."[72]

In this way it is
That we hold the Divine Sword.
165. Through the Gate of Words
Made by the Saints of the past

> We too, we *mudang*, hear and see,
> Visiting each and every place,
> If there is a house where a *kut* is held.
> 170. The people there, [themselves] having tried medicine,
>   Tried whatever they could,
>   When [the condition of the patient is so desperate
>   that] even dying is no cause for regret,
>   Fetch a *mudang*:
>   "Please hold a *kut*",
> 175. And when they ask in this way,
>   We *mudang* of Kyŏngsang Province
>   Go to that house
>   And hold a *kut*.

The term Gate of Words (*malmun*) occurred earlier in the text, in line 10 (not, however, so translated there). Here it seems to have a rather more comprehensive meaning, referring to the whole of the "mechanism" through which the *mudang* are able to communicate with the supernatural.

The final lines are about the medical activities of the *mudang*. The calling of the *mudang* here is represented as a last resort. *Mudang* often express resentment over the fact that people do not appeal to them earlier. On the other hand, at least these days, they accept the fact that sometimes it is better to use medicine -either Chinese medicine or Western medicine- and they declare themselves especially suited to treat complaints against which medical doctors are powerless, diseases which cannot be explained completely by medical science, in other words diseases "caused by the spirits."

Related muga.

The distribution of the *Kyemyŏn kut* -especially in its narrative form- is rather limited. Certain elements of the *Kyemyŏn kut*, however, reappear in other *muga*. Very similar is a *muga* from Cheju Island, which tells the story of "Lady Yi", the goddess of a local shrine, who at the age of seven became possessed, left home at fifteen and, carrying bags and sacks, called at every house in every village to beg for rice.[73] This goddess is, of course, a deified *mudang*.

Another Cheju *muga* which in some respects resembles the *Kyemyŏn kut* is *Ch'ogong ponp'uri*. This *muga*, which belongs to the Chesŏk or Tanggŭm-aegi *muga* type,[74] explains the origins of three male *mudang*-ancestors. Near the end of the story the making of the first drum and of other paraphernalia is related. This again is followed by the story of a female *mudang*-ancestor, "the daughter of Prime Minister Yu", who as a child accepts a coin from a monk called Yukkwan Taesa (the name of a figure from the traditional novel *Kuunmong!*), and then falls ill. Her illness is the initiatory illness of the shaman (*sinbyŏng*), and only cured when after long years of suffering she becomes a *mudang*.[75]

A *muga* from Kanggye in the far North, called *Sŏnsaengnim ch'ŏngbae*, tells of the predecessors of the male *mudang* who sang this *muga*. They apparently act as guardian spirits, opening the "Gate of Words" (*malmun*) and the "Gate of Writing" (*kŭlmun*), but also the "Gate of Cymbals" and the "Gate of the Drum."[76] This *muga*, too, has an account of the origin of musical instruments (beginning with the drum), and of the sword and the fan, and of the custom of giving rice to the shaman when he holds a *kut* for his clients. The rice is here said to come from Chemi Mountain. *Chemi* is probably the same as *chaemi*, "sacrificial rice/rice offered to the Buddha." It is tempting to assume a relationship with *chemyŏn*, but I can offer no convincing explanation for the shift from *chemi* to *chemyŏn*. *Sŏnsaengnim ch'ŏngbae* also lists the origin of offerings such as wine and *ttŏk*.

Final remarks

The version of the *Kyemyŏn kut muga* translated above has a limited geographical distribution as far as the plot is concerned, but it contains various themes and elements which are found more widely, in other *muga* as well as in other genres. The story the *muga* tells is about a *mudang*, but is in the third person, not the first as some of the songs of Siberian shamans that have the shaman himself as the protagonist, and it is also different from the latter because it describes episodes from the normal daily life of the *mudang*, rather than heroic exploits such as ascents to heaven, descents to the underworld or fierce battles with ghosts. Both form and content of this song are the product of the conditions of Korean society, which in many respects is different from that of Siberian shamans. Traditional Korea was a nation of farmers, and only an agricultural community will produce songs in which rice cakes feature so prominently as they do in this *muga*.

This is a much simpler *muga* than *Hwangje p'uri*, and it is less influenced by other genres of literature, but even here one may note a variety of elements from different sources. Some lines have a *p'ansori* flavour, others use folk-song material; there are Buddhist elements and frequent references to figures from Chinese and Korean history or fiction. Herein, too, the song reflects the nature of Korean culture. Irrespective of whether this *muga* can be said to belong to oral literature, it is clearly the product of a culture that knows the use of writing.

X   Summary of Conclusions

Cho Hŭng-youn, in his study of the life of Yi Chisan, has pointed out that Korean shamanism is not just a primitive religion, but has known a long and complicated historical development. This is well illustrated by the *muga*.

Our examination of the songs of the *mudang* has shown that the *muga* have undergone great changes in the course of time and absorbed influences from many quarters. It is absolutely impossible to maintain that the *muga* as we know them, are the products of a far distant past, handed down without change century after century, untouched by history. Not much can be said with certainty about the *muga* of the past, but the *muga* collected in the present century are sufficiently marked by the process of history to allow this conclusion.

Among religious systems that can be said to have exerted great influence on the *muga*, Buddhism easily takes first place. As to the literary form of the *muga*, it seems that their present form cannot be understood without reference to the emergence of popular literature in the second half of the Chosŏn period. Influence from the vernacular literature that began to flourish in the 18th century is especially prominent in the stylistic characteristics of the *muga*, which share formulae, formulaic systems and themes with that literature. In many cases it is most unlikely that this sharing of common elements is the result of borrowing by other genres from the *muga*. The examination of the formal features of the *muga* in Chapter V, therefore, has led to the conclusion that the songs of the shamans must have changed a great deal under the impetus of the emergence of the new vernacular literature.

Some narrative motifs in the *muga*, and even some concatenations of these motifs, may be of great antiquity, but from the survey of the relationship between the *muga* and various forms of narrative literature in Chapter VI, it becomes obvious that the stories as well as the style of the *muga* have changed with the times.

In Chapter IV a survey of the modern *muga* had already led to the conclusion that today the *muga* are open to outside influences, that there are no strong forces working to preserve the original forms of the songs. The material of the subsequent chapters has given a more concrete content to this conclusion and suggests that at least during the later Chosŏn period a similar state of affairs existed. In Chapter VII it has been shown that most likely the *Sim Ch'ŏng kut* is a twentieth century development, and in Chapter VIII substantial changes in the song for the Ritual for the Yellow Emperor (*Hwangje p'uri*), prompted *inter alia* by an important event in the late nineteenth century (the rebuilding of the Kyŏngbok Palace), have been suggested. The *muga* translated in Chapter IX is a relatively simple, "unliterary specimen", but there too, a variety of influences has been found in its constituent parts.

In view of all this, the researcher who wants to use the *muga* as a source for the study of Korean shamanism cannot but take into account the historical development of the *muga*. The naïve assumption that the *muga* are a direct expression of the beliefs of the *mudang* and nothing more, is untenable. Sometimes the *muga* provide straightforward information; they tell us, for instance, what kind of death makes someone a *yŏngsan* (drowning, being hit by a car or a train, and other kinds of violent death), what is the cause of *pujŏng*, "defilement" (slaughtering of animals, death, sex), or what kind of things the gods of smallpox detest (chicken droppings, mugwort, night soil, red peppers). More often, however, the texts cannot be understood without an awareness of the complexity of their composition.

The attempt to shed light on the historical development of the *muga* inevitably involves clarification of the relationship between the songs of the shamans and other forms of literature. Many questions still remain in this respect. Progress can only be expected when individual works are closely compared with each other. The analysis in terms of formulae, formulaic systems and themes can be a suitable tool to that end, together with the analysis of narrative elements.

The study of the history of the *muga* also has implications for the history of the *mudang* and their relations with the rest of Korean society. The fact that the *mudang* absorbed, on a substantial scale, elements of the vernacular literature of the eighteenth century and after -which was not the product of simple, illiterate farmers and fishermen, but of intermediate layers of society- suggests the existence of channels through which the culture of the lower government officials and government clerks could filter down to the *mudang*. Most likely, members of the class of actors and performers, the *kwangdae*, fulfilled the function of intermediaries in this. Thus, the *kwangdae* not only contributed to the creation of *p'ansori* by an upward transmission of shamanistic elements to higher layers of society, as has been suggested in earlier theories, they also transmitted elements in the reverse direction. The *mudang*, in their turn, having borrowed elements from upper-class culture from the *kwangdae*, contributed to the diffusion of this culture among the common people.

Another conclusion drawn in the present study is that the (modern) *muga*, which are generally regarded as part of Korea's oral literature, in their entirety are not oral literature in the sense given to the term by Parry and Lord. The discussion of the transmission of the *muga* in Chapter III has shown that *muga* -at least in the twentieth century- have been transmitted in various ways and in most cases are not oral poetry as defined by the oral-formulaic school: "poetry composed *in* oral performance by people who cannot read and write." Even where something resembling oral composition can be observed, on closer inspection there often are factors which are in conflict with the definition of oral poetry, as in the case of the *hwaraengi* Kim Sŏkch'ul, who is able to compose instantaneously with the help of standard elements, but who is not illiterate.

One aspect of the *muga* has not been considered: their literary value. There is no doubt that many *muga* are interesting and amusing to read, but it would be unjust to subject texts that never were meant to be read in print to a purely aesthetic appraisal. Those who have seen the *muga* performed will realize that only in performance the *mudang* display the full range of their talents: as inspired mediums, as counsellors on spiritual and worldly matters, as healers, as priests, as actors, as clowns, as dancers, as musicians, as singers and, finally, as creators and transmitters of *muga*.

Appendices

Appendix I: Formulae
Note: minor variations are disregarded, more important variations noted between brackets.

A. *kodae kwangsil nop'ŭn chip*
    MSs, 384; *CCM*, 260, 281; *THM*, 187, *KTG* I, 292; *Cheju sajŏn*, 463.
    Usually a particle is added to *chip*, completing a regular 4-4 rhythmical pattern.

B. *ne kwi-e p'unggyŏng tara*
    AA I, 359; *MSs*, 298; *Cheju sajŏn*, 194; *Ong Kojip chŏn*, 94 (*ne kwi-e p'unggyŏng-ira*); *THM*, 270 (*ne kidung-e p'unggyŏng tara*).

C. *yŏngsan hongnok pom param-e*
    Han'guk siga, 118 (cf. 117); *Maehwa chŏn*, 286.

D. *illak sŏsan-e hae-nŭn chigo*
    CCM, 276; Sim Usŏng, *Han'gug-ŭi minsokkŭk*, 111. Cf. *KTG* IV, 45:
    (*tong-e tongsan todŭn hae-ga*) *illak sŏsan kiurŏjinŭnguna*.

E. *simya samgyŏng kip'ŭn pam-e*
    THM, 132, 362; *KTG* III, 370 (*ch'irya samgyŏng kŭmŭm pam-e*);
    Maehwa chŏn, 273 (*ch'irya samgyŏng kip'ŭn pam-e*).

F.   *mŏkko namke towa chugo*
      ssŭgo namke towa chugo
      (*AA* I, 101)

Two formulae, usually occurring as a pair, which consist entirely of
verb forms.
Cf. *mŏkku namke towa chusigo*
      ssŭgu namke sŏmgyŏdaga
      (*KTG* II, 263)

      mŏkko namtorok chŏmji hasigo
      ssigo namtorok chŏmji hasigo
      (*KTG* I, 276)

      mŏkko namtorok ssŭgo namtorok
      chŏmji hasigo
      (*THM*, 263, 265)

Appendix II: Formulaic Systems

A

A I
1. *tongjisŏttal kin'gin pam-e*; *KTG* IV, 85
2. *tongjittal kinagin pam-ŭl*; *Sijo sajŏn*, No. 672
3. *tongjittal ch'uun kyŏur-e*; *Han'guk siga*, 331
4. *tongjisŏttal sŏrhanp'ung-e*; Ch'oe T'aeho, *Naebang kasa*, 288;*KTG* I, 126; *CCM*, 271

A II
1. *tongjisŏttal kin'gin pam-e* (= A I, 1)
2. *ch'an sŏri kin'gin pam-e*; *Nongga wŏllyŏng ka*, 52-53
3. *odong ch'uya kin'gin pam-e*; *Kasa chŏnjip*, 439
4. *changjang ch'uya kin'gin pam-e*; *Kasa chŏnjip*, 439

B

B I
1. *ch'ŏpch'ŏp-han kip'ŭn kor-e*; *Sin Chaehyo*, 542-543
2. *manch'ŏp ch'ŏngsan kip'ŭn kor-e*; *Maehwa chŏn*, 274
3. *Syuyangsan kipp'un kol-lae*; *HMCCP Kyŏngbuk*, 210
   Cf. the phrase *Suyangsan nop'ŭn san-e* ("in the high mountains of Mt. Suyang"; *THM*, 374), in which the second part is antithetical to that in B I, 3.
4. *Suyangsan kip'ŭn kol-lo*; Sim Usŏng, *Minsokkŭk*, 115
5. *Ch'ŏngt'aesan kip'ŭn kor-e*; *HMCCP Kyŏngnam*, 220
6. *sumok nowi kip'ŭn kos-e*; *Sin Chaehyo*, 480-481
7. *ch'ŏngsallim kipp'ŭn kod-ae*; *Kasa chŏnjip*, 21
8. *osaek un kipp'ŭn kos-ŭi*; *Kasa sŏnjip*, 59, in a poem attributed to Cho Wi (1454-1503).
9. *noksu ch'ŏngsan kipp'un kor-e*; *Sijo sajŏn*, Nos. 484, 485
10. *Sot'aebaeksan kip'ŭn kor-e*; Sim Usŏng, "Sonnim kut", 189

In this system all the variable parts refer to secluded places in nature, in most cases to mountains. In 1 it is an adjectival phrase often used for mountains, in 3, 4, and 5, the names of mountains are substituted. The latter three examples make clear why one cannot define the formula as a unit of only three or four syllables. These names of mountains fill the first halves of the hemistichs by themselves and in isolation are formulaic only in so far as all language is formulaic or conventional. It is their use in a specific context that makes them formulaic in the sense employed here.

A system that is related to B I, although less closely than A I to A II, is the following:

B II
1.   *ch'irya samgyŏng kip'ŭn pam-e*; *Maehwa chŏn*, 273
2.   *yasamgyŏng kip'ŭn pam-e*; *Ong Kojip chŏn*, 103
3.   *yaban saemgyŏng chip'ŭn pam-e*; *Kwanbuk muga* I, 143
4.   *simya samgyŏng kip'ŭn pam-e*; *THM*, 362
5.   *ch'uyajang kipp'ŭn pam-e*; *Sijo sajŏn*, No. 563

B I and B II have only one word per half-line in common (*kip'ŭn*), but in the same position in the sentence, while the syntactic structure of the verses is the same: a Sino-Korean phrase is followed by a purely Korean phrase, consisting of a modifying form of a verb of description, a noun and a particle.[1] Moreover, in all these sentences, as in those of A I, II, and III, the second part to a certain degree overlaps the meaning of the first part. In A II, 4, for example, the only semantic element which is absent in the second part and present in the first is *ch'u*, "autumn." It is a characteristic of these verses that the second part serves as a gloss to the meaning of the first part. This feature can be seen in many Korean formulae and is closely linked to the mixed Sino-Korean diction of traditional Korean poetry.

One may take another step, to a still higher level of abstraction. *Han'gangsu kip'ŭn mur-e* "in the deep waters of the Han-river": *Maehwa chŏn*, 279 (cf. *Han'gangsyu kip'ŭn mur-e*; *Sijo sajŏn*, No. 565), has the same syntactic structure as B I and B II, while there also is a relation of antithesis between this verse and the verses in B I that have the name of a mountain as the first element (B I ,3,4,5). The substitution of the names of other rivers for "*Han'gangsu*", and like changes, will create a new formulaic system, B III.

B III
1.   *Han'gangsu kip'ŭn mur-e*; *Maehwa chŏn*, 272, 279
2.   *taehaesu kip'ŭn mur-e*; *AA* I, 362

B III, in its turn, is related to B IV which has little in common with B III lexically, but has the same structure: (noun phrase referring to water; for instance, the name of a river) + adjective + *mul* ("water") + particle.

B IV
1. *kuyŏn ch'isu malgŭn mur-ŭn*; *THM*, 241
    Kuyŏn ch'isu, "nine years controlling floods" is a mere ornament in this use of the formula. The phrase refers to the legendary Chinese ruler Yü, who brought under control floods that had lasted for nine years; it has nothing to do with the context of the *muga* in which this half-line is used.
2. *iltae changgang malgŭn mur-ŭn*; *Sin Chaehyo*, 458-459
3. *tohwa yusu malgŭn mur-e*; *Maehwa chŏn*, 286
4. *kuryongso malgŭn mur-e*; *Sijo sajŏn*, No. 220

C

Example A of the formulae also is part of a formulaic system:

C I
1. *kodae kwangsil nop'ŭn chip*; cf. Examples formulae: A
2. *kodae kwangsil nop'i chitko*; Kim Sŏngbae, *Han'gug-ŭi minsok*, 295
3. *kodae kwangsil nanŭn mada*; *Sijo sajŏn*, Nos. 137, 322
4. *kodae kwangsil nobi chŏndap*; *Sijo sajŏn*, No. 650
5. *kodae kwangsil Abang-gung-i*; *Pulgyo kasa*, 333

C I, 3 and 4 do not, in the second half of the phrases, have a semantic element that is shared by the other members of the system. When 3 and 4 are examined in combination with 1 and 2, the possibility suggests itself that the substitutions of 3 and 4 are based on phonetic similarity; it is probably no accident that both begin with the letter *n*.[2]

C II
1. *kodae kwangsil nop'ŭn chip*; = C I, 1
2. *kogŭm ch'ŏnha nop'ŭn chip*; *Kasa chŏnjip*, 27
3. *koru kŏgak nop'ŭn chip*; *Ong Kojip chŏn*, 99

D

D I
1. *mŏlgo mŏnŭn hwangch'ŏn kil-ŭn*; *Kubi munhak sŏnjip*, 221
2. *mŏlgo mŏn hwangch'ŏn kir-e*; *AA* II, " furoku Fukyō", p. 77
3. *mŏlgo modŏn hwangch'ŏn kir-e*; *KTG* I, 343
4. *mŏlgo mŏnŭn Indangsu*; *THM*, 215

In D I, the pattern differs from that in the previous examples. Here, a purely Korean phrase precedes a Sino-Korean phrase or a phrase in mixed diction.

D II
1. *Hwangsŏng ch'ŏlli mŏn mŏn kir-ŭl*; *Kubi munhak sŏnjip*, 255, 256
2. *Hwangsŏng ch'ŏlli ŏi kalko*; Chŏng Pyŏnguk, *P'ansori*, 347
3. *Hwangsŏng ch'ŏlli mŏn mŏn kir-e*; *THM*, 232

The following system is also, loosely, related:

D III
1. *sumalli mŏn kir-e*; *CCM*, 267
2. *subaengni chŏndo-e*; *YIM* I, 121, 123; Sim Usŏng, "*SC kut*", 218
3. *subaengni t'agwan kir-e*; Sim Usŏng, "*SC kut*", 219
4. *subaengni t'ahyang-eda*; Chŏng Pyŏnguk, *P'ansori*, 348

"*Subaengni*" and "*sumalli*" differ only in the number of miles, "several hundreds" and "several ten-thousands" respectively.

E

E I
1. *mujŏng sewŏr-i yŏryu haya*; *Pulgyo kasa*, 491
2. *mujŏng sewŏr-i tŏt ŏpkuna*; *KTG* III, 197
3. *mujŏng sewŏr-i yangnyup'a-ra*; *AA* I, 40
4. *sewŏr-i yŏryu haya*; *AA* I, 34; *THM*, 364, 366, 367; *NSC*, 120, 127; *KTG* I, 266

These formulaic sentences are often used to indicate the swiftness of the passing of time. In a narrative a formula of this type may bridge a gap of a few years in which nothing important happens, the gap, for instance, between the birth of a child and the age of fifteen or sixteen, when he or she starts to play an active role in the story.

In the formulaic systems presented earlier, the second part to some extent explained the first. This does not happen in the present system, but one may assume that the intelligibility of E I, 3 -which is completely Sino-Korean- depends at least partly on the existence of the other members of the system, which are easier to understand. Because there is this system, when one hears *mujŏng sewŏr-i*, one expects an expression to follow that means "is swift like water/ceaselessly flows like water" and even when the hearer is unable to understand the exact meaning of *yangnyup'a-ra* ("is like flowing waves"), he will get the drift of the verse. The modern reader, struggling with the vocabulary of traditional Korean literature, sometimes wonders how the public of the past, who in many cases heard these texts recited or sung and did not read them at leisure, were able to understand their meaning. The existence of formulae and formulaic systems must have been a great help; these traditional units -certainly in the specific form which they assumed in Korea- should not be seen only as building blocks for the composer of poetry, but also as an aid to understanding for the audience. A formula often contains a gloss to a part of itself, and formulaic systems make transparent verses that on their own would be obscure.

It should be noted that Sino-Korean expressions are not only explained by glosses within the formula or by the whole of the formulaic system. Sometimes a half-line in pure Korean roughly repeats the contents of a Sino-Korean half-line.[3]

The following verses may be regarded as a system related to E I.

E II
1.   *yusu sewŏl hŭllŏ hŭllŏ*; Ch'oe T'aeho, *Naebang kasa*, 274
2.   *yusu kach'i hŭrŭnŭn pam-e*; *KTG* I, 258

P'ungu kat'ŭn yusu sewŏl (Ch'oe, *Naebang kasa*, 275) is related to E II, 1. In its imagery this half-line is a bit of a hodge-podge, *p'ungu kat'ŭn* meaning "(swift) like wind and rain" (a conventional simile), and *yusu sewŏl*: "time which flows (ceaselessly/swiftly) like water." The oddity of the expression will not have been felt sharply because of the conventional, well-worn character of its parts.
Hyanggyu sewŏr-ŭn mŭl hŭrŭdŭt tinaganda (*Kasa sŏnjip*, 345) does not easily fit E I or E II, still it is useful to consider it in combination with these two systems. Where other half-lines have *mujŏng*, "heartless/cruel", this half-line has *hyanggyu*, "fragrant boudoir." Most likely the "echo" of *mujŏng* (or its synonym *musim*), the more common prefix of *sewŏl*, was perceived by those listening to this *kasa*, and this will have contributed to the impression of desolation conveyed by the poem.

F
1.   *saba segye Namsŏm Puju*; *Pulgyo kasa*, 476; *KTG* II, 296; *KTG* III, 42; *Sangyong ŭibŏm*, 28a; *Minyochip* III, 222

2.   *saba segye i ch'ŏnji-ga*; *Pulgyo kasa*, 416

These formulaic verses of Buddhist derivation are remarkable for their redundancies. *Saba* (or *sap'a*; Sanskrit: *sahā*) and *segye* both mean "World" and Namsŏm Puju (Sanskrit: Jambu-dvipa) is "the world in which we live." *Ch'ŏnji* is literally "heaven-and-earth", but can also be translated as "universe/world."

F 1 is completely filled with nouns, F 2 almost, with only a demonstrative (*i*) added.

G

In the following formulaic half-lines, attention should be paid to syntactic structure.

G I
1.   *hae-ga todasŏ ilgwangdan*; *AA* I, 243
2.   *hae-ga toda Ilgwang posal*; *KTG* I, 271

G II
1.   *tar-i todasŏ wŏlgwangdan*; *AA* I, 243
2.   *tar-i toda Wŏlgwang posal*; *KTG* I, 271

The syntactic structure of these half-lines: noun + particle + verb + inconclusive ending + noun, would be extraordinary in natural speech, but it is not unusual in *muga*.

Cf.   *malgŭna ch'ŏngju hŭrina t'akchu*; *AA* I, 227

   mal chabŏ taema pujŏng
   so chabŏ uma pujŏng; *AA* I, 63

   san-e olla ho-yŏngsan
   tŭr-e naeryŏ kaeksa-yŏngsan; *KTG* I, 49

   chŏr-ŭl chiyŏ wiin kŏngdŏk; *AA* I, 31

A similar syntax is also found in folk-songs such as the *chang t'aryŏng* - which contains lines like: *i sul chapsu* Chinju *chang*, in a *sasŏl sijo*: *puing puing tora mulle chyangsa*, and in a song from a mask-play: *mog-i kilta hwangsae pyŏng*/*mog-i tchalta chara pyŏng*.[4]

Occasionally it is possible to find a formulaic system for a unit as long as a whole line.

H
1.   *Tyesŏk sambul yŏsinŭn kir-e/ŭnhasu-ro tari nosso*; *AA* I, 93
2.   *Sŏngju wangsin yŏsinŭn kir-e/kayago-ro tari nosso*; *AA* I, 99

The formulaic system is a more abstract concept than the formula, as it refers to an intangible "formulaic matrix" from which all the members of the formulaic system can be derived. The formulaic systems presented above and in the appendix all have a word, or group of words, as a constant. It is possible to move to a higher level of abstraction by including verses which do not share lexical items, but have other elements -for instance of a semantic or syntactic nature- in common. As long as the purpose of analysis is not the counting of the frequency of formulaic expressions but an understanding of the diction of the texts, there can be no objection to this, although it remains useful to distinguish between the various levels of abstraction.

There is a limit, however, beyond which abstraction ceases to be helpful for understanding. If the analysis moves onto the level of syntax, in many cases the "formulaic patterns" to be found will be nothing but the usual syntactic rules of the language. Patterns found at this level are of importance only if they are different from the normal rules of syntax. In the examples given of formulae and formulaic systems there were, indeed, syntactic patterns which departed from those of ordinary language. Within an ordinary formula a syntactic poetic pattern of this nature is a characteristic which makes it easy to distinguish the formula in question from a habitual collocation in natural speech, the other distinguishing features being metre (which is of limited use as such in Korean, because of the closeness of verse metre to natural speech), the use of poetic (often Sino-Korean) vocabulary, and devices such as alliteration or rhyme.

An example of formulaically related phrases which are not lexically similar:

> *ha-ha taeso usŭmyŏnsŏ*; *Sin Chaehyo*, 606-607
> "laughing ha-ha, with a loud laugh",

and

> *pangsŏng t'onggok urŭm-ŭl uni*; *THM*, 369
> "when crying, weeping with abandon"

The translations do not do justice to the syntactic similarity of the two phrases. In both the first halves describe the manner of the action of the verb of the second part, and both have the peculiar poetic diction which foregoes the use of particles or verbal conjunctions that would normally clarify the relation between the constituent parts of the phrases. An important reason for classifying the two verses together is that in addition there is a semantic connection: a relation of antonymy. The use of antonyms or antithesis for the creation of parallel verses is extremely common in Korean traditional poetry; common enough, in fact, for one to be certain that this was a conscious device.[5]

The antithetic parallelism of the two verses quoted above (which are from different works) might be called paradigmatic parallelism in contrast to the parallelism between the lines of one work, which is dealt with in Chapter V.

The syntax of the formulaic half-lines sometimes is not different from that of sentences in ordinary speech, although even then the half-line may still exhibit peculiarities of another kind, such as pleonastic use of Korean and Sino-Korean. In other cases formulaic half-lines depart from the usual syntactic patterns and have a special "poetic" syntax. Examples have already been cited above. This poetic syntax allows the poet to express himself more succinctly than in natural speech, which often cannot do without the verb forms and particles that poetry does not need. Take the half line: *ŏdum ch'im-ch'im pin pang an-ŭ*, "in an empty room in gloomy darkness."[6] *ŏdum ch'im-ch'im*, "in gloomy darkness", in the original phrase acts as a modifier to the empty room, but no modifying verb form (such as *han*) is added to the *ch'im-ch'im*. Another example is *oenŭn sori ch'ŏnha-ga yodonghanŭnjira*, "the world rang with the sound of their cries."[7] Here the relationship between *oenŭn sori* and *ch'ŏnha-ga yodong-hanŭnjira* completely depends on the context. Nothing, not even a particle, indicates that it is the sound of the cries (*oenŭn sori*) which makes the world reverberate; *ch'ŏnji* is the explicit subject of *yodong-hanŭnjira*, *oenŭn sori* is not explicitly linked to the remainder of the half-line.

Where there is no explicitly indicated syntactic relation between the two parts of a half-line, the first half can usually be understood as loosely modifying the second. E.g., A II, 2: *ch'an sori kin'gin pam-e*, "in the long, long nights (with) cold frost." In an ordinary sentence with the same structure (modifying verb + noun + modifying verb + noun + particle) it would be natural to assume that the first noun is the subject of the second verb (or possibly its object, if the verb is transitive). In the verse, it is perhaps the small caesura which follows the first half of the half-line which "marks" the possibility of another interpretation.

Appendix III: Themes

A. Catalogues

1. Animals
    KTG I, 296; *KTG* III, 207-208; *Namwŏn kosa*, 60. *Namwŏn kosa*, it will be remembered, is used here to refer to Kim Tonguk a.o., *Ch'unhyang chŏn pigyo yŏn'gu*. In this book the episodes of many different editions of *Ch'unhyang chŏn* are compared. When a theme is found in the version of this story called *Namwŏn kosa*, it is easy to ascertain, by referring to *Ch'unhyang chŏn pigyo yŏn'gu*, whether it is also part of other versions.

2. Birds (*sae t'aryŏng*)
    Son Chint'ae, *Shinka ihen*, 130-131; *HMCCP Kyŏngnam*, 275; *Namwŏn kosa*, 58; *Pae pijang chŏn*, 48 (different kinds of bird-song).

3. Books
    AA I, 135, 177; *THM*, 153, 286; *KTG* IV, 83, Ch'oe Kilsŏng, "Muga Kŏri kut", 185; *HMCCP Kyŏngbuk*, 213; *HKMT* 7-2, pp. 845, 846; *HKMT* 7-7, pp. 258-259; *MSs*, 291; *Kasa chŏnjip*, 558; *Sin Chaehyo*, 116-117; *Namwŏn kosa*, 105; *Maehwa chŏn*, 284; *Ong Kojip chŏn*, 115; *T'alch'um taesa chip*, 17. Cf. Chapter VIII.

4. Fish
    Sim Usŏng, "Sonnim kut", 184; *KTG* I, 290; *KTG* IV, 80-81; *THM*, 125-126, 140, 242; *HMCCP Kyŏngbuk*, 212; *Hanyang ka*, 108-109.

5. Flowers (*kkot t'aryŏng, hwach'o t'aryŏng*)
    AA I, 138; *HMCCP Kyŏngnam*, 275; *KTG* III, 59; *Namwŏn kosa*, 56-57. *Ong Kojip chŏn*, 95; Ch'ŏng Pyŏnguk, *P'ansori*, 343.
    Cf. Sŏ Taesŏk, "P'ansori-wa sŏsa muga", p. 40.

6. Food (*ŭmsik t'aryŏng*)
    HMCCP Kyŏngnam, 275; *THM*, 242, *Namwŏn kosa*, 142, 445.

7. Fruit
    KTG I, 291; *HMCCP Kyŏngbuk* 212; *THM*, 242; *Hanyang ka*, 108-109. *Nongga wŏllyŏng ka*, 18-19.

8. Furniture
   Chang and Ch'oe, *Kyŏnggi-do musok*, 173-174; *KTG* III, 206; *Han' guk siga*, 290; *Maehwa chŏn*, 283; Sim Usŏng, *Minsokkŭk*, 344. Cf. Ch. VIII.

9. Games
   MSs, 350; *Han' guk siga*, 287; *Sin Chaehyo*, 540-543.

10. Gods and ghosts
    E.g., *AA* I, 193, 193-194.

11. Government posts
    AA I, 528; *KTG* II, 142-143; *KTG* IV, 32, 213; *Sin Chaehyo*, 130-131; *Pae pijang chŏn*, 9; Skillend, "Words from the Heart", 160-161; *Kasa chŏnjip*, 560; Yi Tuhyŏn, *Kamyŏn' gŭk*, 316.

12. Medicine
    Son Chint'ae, *Shinka ihen*, 135; *Sin Chaehyo*, 566-567; *Hanyang ka*, 122-123; Yi Tuhyŏn, *Kamyŏn' gŭk*, 323.

13. Mountains and rivers (*sanmaek p' uri, P' alto kangsan*)
    AA I, 371; *KTG* III, 368; *Sin Chaehyo*, 548-549. *Hanyang ka*, 78-81. Cf. Ch. VIII. Cf. also the theme of mountain passes (*kogae t' aryŏng*): *THM*, 378; Sŏ Taesŏk, "P'ansori-wa sŏsa muga", 40.

14. Paintings
    AA I, 240 (see the translation in Ch. VIII, lines 482-522); *Namwŏn kosa*, 130-132 (also cf. pp. 140-141, for this theme in other versions of the "Tale of Ch'unhyang"); *Hanyang ka*, 118-119; Yi Tuhyŏn, *Kamyŏn' gŭk*, 301-302; Sim Usŏng, *Minsokkŭk*, 118.

15. Roll-call
    Hanyang ka, 134-135; *Namwŏn kosa*, 471-473; *Pae pijang chŏn*, 45-46. Very similar is a passage in *Pyŏn Kangsoe ka* featuring *sadang*, "dancing girls": *Sin Chaehyo*, 606-609. For other examples of the theme of the roll-call, see Ch. VIII.

16. Ships (*pae t' aryŏng*)
    Son Chint'ae, *Shinka ihen*, 141-142; *Pae pijang chŏn*, 89-90.

17. Silks and other fabrics (*pidan t'aryŏng*)
     AA I, 176, 243, 355; Son Chint'ae, *Shinka ihen*, 42; *MSs*, 292; *KTG* I,
     36; *KTG* III, 206; *KTG* IV, 85; *THM*, 155; *HMCCP Kyŏngbuk* 183-184,
     212; *Sin Chaehyo*, 376-377 (*Pak t'aryŏng*); *Hanyang ka*, 114-115.
     According to Chang Sahun, the *pidan t'aryŏng* was one of the *chapka*
     (a poetic form similar to the *kasa*) in the fast *hwimori* rhythm and first
     sung by the singer Yi Hyŏnik from Seoul, in the beginning of this
     century. As a *chapka*, therefore, it is of more recent origin than as an
     element of *p'ansori* (Sin Chaehyo's *Pak t'aryŏng* possibly was written
     before 1873 and cannot be later than 1884, the year of Sin's death);
     Chang Sahun, *Kugak ch'ongnon*, 335.

18. Temples (*chŏl t'aryŏng*, *chŏl kwanggyŏng p'uri*)
     THM, 105-106.
     Cf. Sŏ Taesŏk, "P'ansori-wa sŏsa muga", 40.

19. Trees
     Kim Sŏnp'ung, "Ko Kim Sunhŭi-ŭi muga (1)", 152 (*Sŏngju kut*);
     Namwŏn kosa, 57; *Minyo chip* I, 614 (this is from *Pyŏn Kangsoe ka*,
     in *Sin Chaehyo*, 548-551, but according to the compiler there are also
     orally transmitted versions).

20. Vegetables (*namul t'aryŏng*)
     KTG I, 290, 345-346; *THM*, 140, 242, 380; Sim Usŏng, "Sonnim kut",
     184; *HMCCP Kyŏngnam*, 275; *Andong munhwa-kwŏn haksul chosa
     pogosŏ 1967-1969*, p. 106; *Kujŏn minyo chip*, 139-140, 135.

21. Wine (*sul t'aryŏng*)
     Kwanbuk muga I, 48-49; *AA* I, 156, 249; *KTG* I, 291; *KTG* IV, 80;
     Han'guk siga, 284; Sim Usŏng, "Sonnim kut", 184; *HMCCP
     Kyŏngnam*, 275; *HMCCP Kyŏngbuk*, 212; *Namwŏn kosa*, 142; Sim
     Usŏng, *Minsokkŭk*, 119, 344; *Kujŏn minyo chip* I, 190-193.
     See Ch. VIII.

B. Other Themes

1.   Auspicious geomantic location (*myŏngdang p'uri*)
     AA I, 211, 233, 257; *KTG* I, 108-109. In combination with Creation of
     Heaven and Earth: *KTG* I, 109-110; *KTG* II, 23; *KTG* III, 365-366; Son

Chint'ae, "Fugeki no shinka (1)", 147-150; *Sin Chaehyo*, 136-137, 354-355, 670; *Kasa chŏnjip*, 338, 557-558; *Hanyang ka*, 78-81.

2.	A beautiful woman
AA I, 363, 366, 462, 527; *KTG* I, 116; *KTG* IV, 36; *CCM*, 266; *Han'guk siga*, 287-288, 290; Sim Usŏng, "Sonnim kut", 185 (in this *muga* the traditional description of a beautiful woman is applied to one of the gods of smallpox, Kaksi-sonnim!); *Namwŏn kosa*, 63-64; *Maehwa chŏn*, 285; *Sin Chaehyo*, 106-107, 532-533; *Pae pijang chŏn*, 50-52.

3.	A child growing up
THM, 364; Son Chint'ae, *Shinka ihen*, 100; *AA* I, 32-33; *KTG* I, 142; *Kasa chŏnjip*, 558; Im Tonggwŏn, *Han'guk minyo yŏn'gu*, 268-269; *NSC*, 8 (*Hong Kiltong chŏn*); Yi Sangbo, *Han'guk kojŏn munhak* I, 230 (*Pak-ssi chŏn*).

4.	Complaint about misfortune (*sinse t'aryŏng, chat'an ka*)
THM, 297; *KTG* I, 292; *Kwanbuk muga* I, 144-145; Chŏng Pyŏnguk, *P'ansori*, 345-346, 349; *Namwŏn kosa*, 252.

5.	Creation of Heaven and Earth
AA I, 148, 257, 369-370; *KTG* I, 279, 367; *KTG* IV, 30; Son Chint'ae, *Shinka ihen*, 1; Ch'oe Kilsŏng, "Muga Kŏri kut", 183; *MSs*, 310; *THM*, 280; *Hanyang ka*, 78-79; *Nongga wŏllyŏng ka*, 2-3; *Kasa chŏnjip*, 326, 386, 556; *Pulgyo kasa*, 164; *Minyo chip* I, 86-88.
Cf. Other Themes 1.

6.	Dress
AA I, 111, 144-145; *KTG* I, 123-124; *KTG* III, 290; *THM*, 356-357; *Han'guk siga*, 324; Sim Usŏng, "Sonnim kut", 185, 191; *MSs*, 315, 317, 357, 362, 389; *Maehwa chŏn*, 282, 285; *Sin Chaehyo*, 104-105, 108-109; *Namwŏn kosa*, 52; *Pae pijang chŏn*, 40-42.
"Rags and tatters": *NSC*, 122 (Sim Ch'ŏng); *Sin Chaehyo*, 334-335 (Hŭngbu), 580-581 (an acrobat, a *ch'orani*).

7.	Examination scene
AA I, 405; *KTG* II, 250-251; *Munhwajae* IV, 137; *HKMT* 2-3, pp. 633-635; *Hanyang ka*, 166-175; *Kasa chŏnjip*, 559.
Thriumphant return home: *CCM*, 272.

8.   Explanation of Chinese characters
     AA I, 217; *KTG* I, 287; *HMCCP Kyŏngnam*, 206; *Namwŏn kosa*, 155-156 (*Ch'ŏnja p'uri*, "explanation of the Thousand Character Text"); Yi Tuhyŏn, *Kamyŏn'gŭk*, 314.
     Explanation of the Korean alphabet, *han'gŭl*: Yi Tuhyŏn, *Kamyŏngŭk*, 265.

9.   Itinerary (*nojŏnggi*)
     AA I, 556-557; *KTG* I, 287-288, 349; *THM*, 246; *HMCCP Kyŏnggi*, 125; *Namwŏn kosa*, 226-227, 348-349; *Pae pijang chŏn*, 11, 42; *Sin Chaehyo*, 540-541; *Sijo sajŏn*, No. 1849; Yi Tuhyŏn, *Kamyŏn'gŭk*, 320. Cf. Chapter VIII.

10. Landscape
     Son Chint'ae, *Shinka ihen*, 129-130; *CCM*, 261; YIM I, 115; *KTG* I, 328; *Namwŏn kosa*, 45-46; *Maehwa chŏn* 286; Chŏng Pyŏnguk, *P'ansori*, 336-337; *Minyo chip* III, 645; 658 (*Yusan ka*); Yi Tuhyŏn, *Kamyŏn'gŭk*, 302, 306; *Kasa chŏnjip*, 373.

11. Lullaby (*sarang ka*)
     CCM, 278; *THM*, 99-100, 255-259, 370, 397-398; Sim Usŏng, "Sonnim kut", 191, Yi Tuhyŏn, *Kamyŏn'gŭk*, 314.

12. Magistrate's procession
     MSs, 316, 317; *KTG*, 291; *Pae pijang chŏn*, 40-41.

13. Monk (*chung t'aryŏng*)
     AA I, 137-138, 320-321; *KTG* I, 270; *KTG* III, 367; *THM*, 72-74, 86, 106, 243; *Han'guk siga*, 285, 325; *HMCCP Chŏnnam*, 200; *MSs*, 342; *NSC*, 135; *Ong Kojip chŏn*, 98; Sim Usŏng, *Namsadang-p'ae yŏn'gu*, 124-126, 134-140.
     Sākyamuni as a mendicant monk: *Han'guk siga*, 287. A monk's special skills: *Ong Kojip chŏn*, 99; *MSs*, 357.

14. Pall-bearers' song (*hyangdu ka*, *sangyŏ sori*)
     AA I, 163, 282, 314; *THM*, 388-391; *KTG* I, 146; *KTG* IV, 72-73; *Sin Chaehyo*, 600-601; *Pae pijang chŏn*, 87; Chŏng Pyŏnguk, *P'ansori*, 319-320; Yi Tuhyŏn, *Kamyŏn'gŭk*, 380.

15. Parting (*ibyŏl ka*)
     Pae pijang chŏn, 20-21, *Namwŏn kosa*, 186-187.
     Part of song for the deceased: *KTG* IV, 65.

16. Prayers for a child
    AA I, 390, 416, 440; Son Chint'ae, *Shinka ihen*, 86-88; *KTG* I, 124;
    KTG III, 113; *KTG* IV, 77. Also: *Sin Chaehyo*, 462-465 (*Chŏkpyŏk ka*);
    Yi Sangbo (tr.), *Han'guk kojŏn munhak* I, 228 (*Pak-ssi chŏn*); Kim
    Tonguk, *Kayo-ŭi yŏn'gu*, 418 (*Paebaengi kut*).

17. Pregnancy/formation of the child in the womb
    AA I, 8, 130, 141, 205, 441-442, 510, 573; *KTG* I, 260, *KTG* III, 65,
    94; *CCM*, 268, 279, 283; *THM*, 358, 383; *Han'guk siga*, 291, 306;
    MSs, 315, 343, 360; *Pulgyo kasa*, 169; *NSC*, 94; Chŏng Pyŏnguk,
    P'ansori, 315.

18. Prognostication by dreams
    AA I, 215, 363, 521; *MSs*, 307, 343; *Han'guk siga*, 291; *CCM*, 276;
    Ch'ŏng Pyŏnguk, *P'ansori*, 333, 352.
    Cf. Yi Nŭngu, *Ko-sosŏl yŏn'gu*, 72-117.

19. Sawing song (*t'opchil norae*)
    KTG I, 292; *KTG* III, 205; *HMCCP Kyŏngnam*, 206-207.
    Sin Chaehyo, 366-367 and 374-375 (both: *Pak t'aryŏng = Hŭngbu ka*);
    Pae pijang chŏn, 85-86; *Minyo chip* I, 612-613; *Minyo chip* II, 113-
    114; *Minyo chip* III, 102-104.

Notes

For abbreviations see the list of abbreviations; for full titles of books and articles see the bibliography.

NOTES TO CHAPTER I

1. Yi Tuhyŏn a.o., *Han'guk minsokhak kaesŏl*, 139-163.
2. Eliade, *Le chamanisme*, 22.
3. In: *Religions-Ethnologie*, herausgegeben von C.A. Schmitz, 265-295.
4. Cited in Youngsook Kim Harvey, *Six Korean Women: The Socialization of Shamans*, 4.
5. A. Hultkrantz, "Ecological and Phenomenological Aspects of Shamanism", 30.
6. Cf. Harald Motzki, *Schamanismus als Problem Religionswissenschaftlicher Terminologie*.
7. These are reviewed in B.C.A. Walraven, "Korean Shamanism", which also contains a brief description of types and functions of the *mudang*. To the books mentioned in this article should be added Hung-youn Cho, *Mudang; Der Werdegang Koreanischer Schamanen am Beispiel der Lebensgeschichte des Yi Chi-san* and two works by Laurel Kendall, *Shamans, Housewives and Other Restless Spirits* and *The Life and Hard Times of A Korean Shaman*.
8. Frits Vos, *Die Religionen Koreas*, 66-67.
9. Yu Tongsik, *Han'guk mugyo-ŭi yŏksa-wa kujo*, 120.
10. Text in Yu Tongsik, *Mugyo-ŭi yŏksa-wa kujo*, 154-157.
11. Cho Hung-youn, *Werdegang*, 124-130.

12. Gari Ledyard, *The Dutch Come to Korea*, 222.
13. In North Korea the social system seems to have left no place for the *mudang*. According to Hong Kimun, *Chosŏn sinhwa yŏn'gu*, 216, they have disappeared completely. In South Korea the number of *mudang* is still quite large.
14. *Korea Newsreview*, December 3, 1983, XII, 49, p. 25.
15. Chang Chugŭn, *Han'gug-ŭi hyangt'o sinang*, 22-36, shows, rather surprisingly, that in the 1970's such local festivals still survived in considerable number in the modern metropolis of Seoul.
16. *THM*, 159.
17. Cf. Cho Hung-youn, *Werdegang*, 260-261, for a pessimistic view concerning the social position of the *mudang* as voiced by the famous shaman Yi Chisan. An example of a folklorist exhibiting a negative attitude toward shamanism is found in Kang Muhak, *Hanguk sesi p'ungsok ki*, 53-58.
18. Hans Findeisen, *Schamanentum*, 50-60. In contrast to the shamans of Siberia, the *mudang* do not know the ecstatic journey (which, according to Eliade, is the most important characteristic of the shaman).
19. This is a simplification. A much more detailed account of various forms of the *kut* -including *kut* for the welfare of the state, which are no longer held except, occasionally, as conscious reconstructions, as well as *kut* for the welfare of villages, which here and there still may be observed- is found in Cho, *Werdegang*, 226-234. Cho distinguishes twelve kinds of *kut*, held for seven different purposes. Among those twelve kinds there are several that have, or had, different forms and names according to the social status of the believers for whom they were performed. Social differentiation of *mudang* ceremonies perhaps was stronger in the area of the capital -which is the focus of Cho's study- than elsewhere.
20. Cho, *Werdegang*, 216 ff.
21. For the expense of holding a *kut* and the cost of other services of the *mudang* cf. Cho, *Werdegang*, 210-212.
22. Cho, *Werdegang*, 225.
23. Son Chint'ae, *Shinka ihen*, 207.
24. A *mudang* of this type, whom I interviewed in Seoul in 1975, used a gong (instead of the drum, an indispensable attribute of the regular *mudang*, which is, however, more difficult to play) and a few simple Buddhist prayer formulae. Her history, with a typical combination of illness and marital and economic problems, was not fundamentally different from that of the *mudang* described in Harvey, *Six Korean Women* and in other literature.

25. Sŏ Taesŏk, *Han'guk muga-ŭi yŏn'gu*, also contains a study of the *mugyŏng*, pp. 303-320.
26. Cho, *Werdegang*, 247.
27. It is not quite clear whether this part is a *kŏri*; Cho, on the basis of the ceremonies of Yi Chisan and other Seoul *mudang*, says it is not, but not far away, in Yangju, there is a *mudang* who does dance and sing during the very first part, *haengch'u mullim*; Chang Chugŭn & Ch'oe Kilsŏng, *Kyŏnggi-do chiyŏk musok*, 153.
28. Change of costume is typical for Central Korea and not found everywhere. It is impossible to treat all regional variations in this brief survey. The description here refers primarily to the ceremonies of the *mudang* of Central Korea, which includes Seoul.
29. E.g. *KTG* III, 182. This is one of the indications that in regions where both types of *mudang* are known, the differences between them tend to be blurred.
30. Cho Hung-youn, *Koreanischer Schamanismus*, 121.
31. Cho, *Werdegang*, 77-83, describes several classes of *mudang*, distinguished according to the gods which are venerated and the corresponding functions of the *mudang* during a ceremony.
32. The list is based on the text of the songs that go with this *kut* in *AA* I, 63-119. In this source the preliminary rites to chase away malicious spirits, etc., as mentioned in Cho, *Werdegang* 236, are not mentioned, as there are no songs to accompany these rites. The explanations are mainly based on *AA* II, Chapter 4.
33. *AA* I, 126.
34. Cho, *Werdegang*, 238, 317; Cho, *Koreanischer Schamanismus*, 107.
35. Laurel Kendall, "Caught Between Ancestors and Spirits: Field Report of a Korean Mansin's Healing Kut", 17.
36. *T'aejo sillok*, III:2a.15-2b.3.
37. *AA* II, 76; Cho Hung-youn, *Koreanischer Schamanismus*, 108; Kim T'aegon, *Han'guk musok yŏn'gu*, 99; Chang and Ch'oe, *Kyŏnggi-do chiyŏk musok*, 171.
38. Cf. Vos, *Religionen*, p.25, note 29.
39. Cho, *Koreanischer Schamanismus*, 83, 107-108.
40. Yi Nŭnghwa, "Chosŏn musok ko", 52-53, claims that Kunung is a corruption of *kunwang*, "Sovereign." The content of the Kunung *muga*, however, supports the interpretation "deified warriors."
41. *KTG* II, 301. A *kisaeng* is the Korean equivalent of the Japanese geisha.
42. Cho Hung-youn, *Koreanischer Schamanismus*, 108. For more information about the actual *ch'angbu* see Chapter VI.
43. Cho, *Werdegang*, 242-246.
44. *AA* II, 83.

45. Cho Hung-youn, *Werdegang*, p. 33, note 338.
46. *AA* I, 199.
47. *KTG* I, 100.
48. See, for instance, the (*Yŏnse taehakkyo chungang tosŏgwan*) *Kosŏ mongnok*, 12, 13, 14, 16, 17, 24, 38, 117, 494.
49. *KTG* I, 17.
50. Cho Hung-youn, *Werdegang*, 243. Here they appear as *maengin*, "blind exorcists."
51. C.A. Clark, *Religions of Old Korea*, 180.
52. Yu Tongsik, *Mugyo-ŭi yŏksa-wa kujo*, 267-270.
53. C.A. Clark, *Religions of Old Korea*, 203.
54. Interview, 8 August 1982, Seoul.
55. Florence Ayscough, "Cult of the Ch'êng Huang Lao Yeh", 131-155. Many terms in Korean shamanism are of Chinese origin; another example is *Hwangch'ŏn*, "Yellow Springs", an old appellation of the Underworld (cf. Eikemeier, "Wohin gehen Koreaner nach dem Tod?", 105).
56. Kim T'aegon, "Han'guk sindang yŏn'gu", 67-99.
57. Chang Chugŭn, *Han'gug-ŭi hyangt'o sinang*, 104ff. A *mudang* from Kanghwa Island suggested to me that the female pae-Sŏnang is none else than Sim Ch'ŏng, the heroine of a popular traditional novel (see Chapter VII).
58. Yi Nŭnghwa, "Musok ko", 42. This formula was, indeed, known to the *mudang*, although they may not have understood its meaning: *AA* I, 199. In a Cheju *muga* which explains the origin of Kangnim he is definitely not a bachelor: he has nine wives, who, interestingly, are living in different places and visited by their "wandering husband"; *MSs*, 361.
59. Laurence Delaby, *Chamanes toungouses*, 154-155.
60. *MSr*, 292.
61. Judging from the example of the worshipped Communards, this pattern of acceptance of new deities also exists among the Buryat. Tragic death may result in deification in Japan as well: J. Herbert, *Les Dieux Nationaux de Japon*, 285-286, cites the example of a palace lady who became a *kami* because of her suicide.

NOTES TO CHAPTER II

1. Hong, *Chosŏn sinhwa-ŭi yŏn'gu*, 207.
2. *AA*, I, 163-167.
3. G. Sandschejew, "Welt-Anschauung und Schamanismus der Alaren-Burjaten", 590-591.
4. Son Chint'ae, *Shinka ihen*, 210.
5. *AA*, I, 574-575.
6. The enumeration of all the terms from a certain row, e.g. a row of numbers or -as in this case- of directions of the compass is typical of the style of the *muga*. Cf. Chapter V. The last two lines of the second song are a variation on a formula frequently found in *muga*: *mŏkko namko ssŭgo namtorok*.
7. *KTG* I, 85: *Twit-yŏngsil*.
8. Yi Tuhyŏn a.o., *Han'guk minsokhak kaesŏl*, 84-87.
9. "Cherished child" is a translation of *kija*, which I take to be a variant of *kwija*. A linguistic peculiarity of this song -shared by other *muga* of the *kongsu* type- is the fact that the honorific infix -*si*, against the rules of normal grammar, is used for the first person. This reflects the ambiguity of the situation: it is the *mudang* who actually speaks, but the words come from a spirit.
10. Kim T'aegon, "Muga charyo mojib-ŭi hyŏnhwang kŏmt'o", 50-66.
11. Chang Chugŭn & Ch'oe Kilsŏng, *Kyŏnggi-do musok*.
12. Son Chint'ae, for instance, published more than twenty muga in magazines. I have not been able to procure the *muga* collected in *Sin kajŏng* IV, 4.5 (1936), which are not included in *Son Chint'ae sŏnsaeng chŏnjip*.
13. Sŏ Taesŏk, *Muga-ŭi yŏn'gu*, devotes a whole chapter to this song, pp. 277-302.Cf. also Ch. IV, note 21.
14. Kim Tonguk, *Han'guk kayo-ŭi yŏn'gu*, 177. This book has a long chapter about the *Siyong hyangak po*.
15. Im Tonggwŏn, *Han'guk minyo sa*, 176-177.
16. *Sin Chaehyo*, 582-583 and 612-613. It is not certain whether, or to which extent, Sin changed the words of these songs.
17. *Torang sŏnbae . Ch'ŏngjong kakssi* in *Shinka ihen*, 60-77.
18. Albert B. Lord, *The Singer of Tales*, 126-128.
19. Kim T'aegon, one of the most assiduous collectors, is of the opinion that it is all but impossible to make a complete transcription of a *muga* from only one recording made in normal circumstances. Private conversation, 2 August 1982.
20. Private conversation, 7 July 1982.
21. Hong, *Chosŏn sinhwa yŏn'gu*, 222.

22.   Hong, *Chosŏn sinhwa yŏn'gu*, 223.
23.   Could she be the *mudang* named Pae, whom Cho Hung-youn, *Werdegang*, 128, mentions as working for the Japanese Government-General?
24.   *CCM*, 61.
25.   See Kim T'aegon, "Muga charyo mojib-ŭi hyŏnhwang kŏmt'o", and In Kwŏnhwan, *Han'guk minsokhak sa*, 217-219.
26.   Byeng-sen Park, *Le récit de la "Princesse abandonnée", et les médiums à travers l'histoire de Corée.*
27.   Jung-Young Lee, *Korean Shamanistic Rituals*. Detailed criticism of this book is found in Walraven, "Korean Shamanism."
28.   Chun Shin-yong (General editor), *Folk Culture in Korea*, 71-83 (the translations are part of an article by Chang Chu-keun, "Mu-sok: the Shaman Culture of Korea").
29.   Vos, *Religionen*, 53-59.
30.   Alan C. Heyman, "The Ritual Song of the God Sonnim", 50-57.
31.   *The Folk Treasury of Korea: Sources in Myth, Legend and Fable*, ed. by Chang, Duk-soon (=Chang Tŏksun).
32.   A few Western scholars have recently published articles about the contents of *muga*: Alexandre Guillemoz, "Les aristocrates, les moines, les femmes" (about a Tanggŭm-aegi *muga*), Clark Sorensen, "The Myth of Princess Pari and the Self-Image of Korean Women" (about Pari kongju) and B.C.A. Walraven, "The Root of Evil" (about mythological explanations of the existence of evil in the *muga*) and "The Deity of the Seventh Day- and other narrative *muga* from Cheju Island." Choi Chungmoo, in an interesting article entitled "Ritual Aesthetics of Urban Shamans" describes among other things the way *muga* function to achieve the intended effect of the *kut*.

NOTES TO CHAPTER III

1.   Sŏ Taesŏk's *Muga-ŭi yŏn'gu* is an important contribution in this respect, esp. Chapter IV, pp. 111-145. An article devoted to the problem of transmission is Kim T'aegon, "Muga-ŭi chŏnsŭng pyŏnhwa ch'egye."
2.   Cho Hung-youn, *Werdegang*, 131.
3.   Kim T'aegon, *Musok yŏn'gu*, 206.
4.   Cho Hung-youn, *Werdegang*, 102-108.

5. *AA* I, 81.
6. The spelling has been slightly changed in conformity with the principles generally used in this book. For a translation of this passage, see Cho, *Werdegang*, 108.
7. The *sijo* makes clear that *sŏngju* here originally meant "Sage Ruler", not "Lord of the Castle"; cf. Cho, *Werdegang*, p. 305, note 222. At present *mudang* tend to interpret it as the name of the House God, Sŏngju, which aptly illustrates the possibility of giving new religious meanings to elements borrowed from the non-religious sphere.
8. *HKMT* 7-5, pp. 263-264.
9. Interview, 20 July 1982 in Seoul, with the Hwanghae Province *mudang*, Kim Kŭmhwa.
10. *KTG* III, 295.
11. A is a rather illogical variation of "the mountains are the mountains of the past and the waters are the waters of the past, but ... (the human beings of the past are no more)." This phrase occurs in other *muga* (*KTG* III, 163) and *Ch'unhyang chŏn* (Kim Tonguk, Kim T'aejun and Sŏl Sŏnggyŏng, *Ch'unhyang chŏn pigyo yŏn'gu*, 381; this book will henceforth be referred to as *Namwŏn kosa*, after the text of *Ch'unhyang chŏn* which it presents). B is reminiscent of phrases in Buddhist *kasa* (Yi Sangbo, *Pulgyo kasa chŏnjip*, 169, 175, 181 and 455; this book will hereafter be referred to as *Pulgyo kasa*) and also in other *kasa*, such as "Words From The Heart" (W.E. Skillend, "'Words From The Heart': An unpublished kasa", 160).
12. The stereotyped nature of these words does not diminish their efficacy: they often move the audience to tears. Carmen Blacker has noted something similar in Japan, where the words of the dead spoken by mediums are "stereotyped utterances, classifiable into different *kata* or types, which the medium in the course of her training learns by heart. That such utterances should strike the sobbing audiences as convincing communications from the dead argues a suspension of disbelief of the same order as that which sees the invisible world behind the sacred drama, the ritual mask or the recital of a myth." Carmen Blacker, *The Catalpa Bow*, 162-163.
13. Cf. Chang Chugŭn and Ch'oe Kilsŏng, *Kyŏnggi-do musok*, 122, where it is said that in the *sin-ŏmŏni/sin-ttal* relationship the inheriting of the regular clientèle is most important.
14. E.g., *KTG* I, 153.
15. Cf. Ruth Finnegan, *Oral Poetry: Its Nature, Significance and Social Context*, 135-136, 140-141.
16. *AA* I, 119.
17. *KTG* I, 24.

18. *KTG* II, 297. For deified warriors, see Chapter I.
19. *KTG* III, 62. Kim Seong Nae, in her article "Lamentations of the Dead", discusses *muga* referring to the Cheju Rebellion of April 1948.
20. E.g., *AA* I, 105.
21. In *AA* I, 151, there is an explicit reference to the "New Palace."
22. The term which Pak Yongnyŏ used for the words of the song was *sasil* (= *sasŏl*), which in the parlance of the East Coast *mudang* is regularly used for the words of the *muga*. Perhaps this is due to the influence of *p'ansori*, where *sasŏl* refers to the libretto; interview with Pak Yongnyŏ: 27 June, 1982. For the jargon of the East Coast *mudang*, cf. Ch'oe Kilsŏng, *Han'guk musok non*, 93-116, esp. 104.
23. Maurice Courant, *Supplément à la bibliographie coréenne (jusqu'en 1899)*.
24. Yi Nŭnghwa, "Musok ko", 42.
25. Kim Tonguk, "Muga 'Pari kongju'", 39-56.
26. *HMCCP Kyŏngbuk*, 202-213. Several of the *muga* in this collection are also reproduced in *KTG* IV. Kim Sŏkch'ul is also known as Kim Kyŏngnam.
27. *HMCCP Kyŏngbuk*, 173-175, 175, 175-179, 198. Some of these texts, too, can be found in *KTG* IV, which is exclusively devoted to the muga of Kim Sŏkch'ul!
28. *KTG* IV, 16-17.
29. *HMCCP Chŏnbuk*, 128-133; for the date see p. 131. If it is not 1927, it can only be earlier: 1867, for instance.
30. Reproduced in *Han'guk siga*, 338-364.
31. *HMCCP Kyŏnggi*, 121. It is possible that this is the source of the curious Kunung *muga* in *AA* I, 148-163, which -within the limits of one song!- contains a summary of all the *kŏri* of a complete *kut*.
32. Hong Kimun, *Chosŏn sinhwa yŏn'gu*, 215.
33. Son Chint'ae, "Fugeki no shinka (1)", 147-150.
34. E.g., *HMCCP Kyŏnggi*, 111 and 113; Kim T'aegon, *Musok yŏn'gu*, 63, 81; Cho Hung-youn, *Werdegang*, 143.
35. Murayama, *Chōsen no fugeki*, 92. His classification, which comprises six categories, is rather odd. The first three categories are not based on the manner of instruction, but on the *period* of instruction (one, two and three years), the last three categories are "those who learned by looking at others", "those who learned from written sources" and "those who learned by themselves." It is conceivable, of course that writing was used by the first three categories as well, while the last category is an enigma; how does someone learn who has no teacher, does not learn by studying others and does not make use of written materials?
36. Chang Chugŭn and Ch'oe Kilsŏng, *Kyŏnggi-do musok*, 129.

37. Sin Sŏngnam, interview 27 June 1982, Kangnŭng.
38. E.g., a recently initiated *paksu mudang*; 12 August 1982, Seoul.
39. *HMCCP Kangwŏn*, 217-218. This *mudang* was able to read and often, when alone, taught herself Buddhist sutras, which she presumably integrated into her performances.
40. Albert B. Lord, *The Singer of Tales*, 30.
41. A.B. Lord, "Oral Poetry", 591-593.
42. Lord, *The Singer of Tales*, 129.
43. Sŏ Taesŏk, "P'ansori-wa sŏsa muga-ŭi taebi yŏn'gu"; *Muga-ŭi yŏn'gu*, 111-145.
44. Sŏ Taesŏk, *Muga-ŭi yŏn'gu*, 140.
45. Sŏ Taesŏk, *Muga-ŭi yŏn'gu*, 144.
46. Ch'oe Kilsŏng, *Musok non*, 140-145.
47. *THM*, 266-279; *HKMT* 2-3, pp. 618-658.
48. *KTG* I, 345-357, and *THM*, 240-265.
49. The Sonnim in question is called Sijun Sonnim, that is, Bhagavat Sonnim. Bhagavat, in Korean: Sejon (corrupted to Sijun), is one of the appellations of the Buddha. In *muga*, Buddhas and Bodhisattvas are commonly described as having the appearance of Buddhist monks. Also in the *Wŏrin sŏkpo*, in the story of Mongnyŏn (Maudgalyāyana), the Buddha has the attributes of a monk: a monk's robe, an alms-bowl and a monk's staff (*Wŏrin sŏkpo*, XXIII:5b-15a).
50. *THM*, 244: the *Sinmyojanggu tae-darani*; cf. *Sangyong ŭibŏm* (*Pulgong chaesik --*), 5.
51. *THM*, 255-259.
52. Sim Usŏng, "Sonnim kut", 180-193 and *HKMT* 7-2, pp. 794-839.
53. Munsu Sonnim might be translated as Manjusri Sonnim and Munsin Sonnim as Civil Minister Sonnim. From both *muga* can be inferred that he is charged with keeping records and in both he is depicted as a government official of the civil service. Munsin therefore seems more correct, although in the 1972 version Munsu Sonnim carries with him a record of temple donations (*kwŏnsŏnmun*). Variations in names of gods are by no means uncommon in the *muga*.
54. Hwang P'aegang, *Silla pulgyo sŏrhwa yŏn'gu*, 175.
55. *Chōsen jisatsu shiryō*, 246. Cf. also the story of the Yujŏm Temple in the *Tongguk yŏji sŭngnam* (XLV:16a.5-b.12), in which the Buddha images are split up in the same way: 50 + 3. The fifty-three Buddhas of this temple are mentioned in the text of the Pongsan mask-dance drama; Yi Tuhyŏn, *Han'guk kamyŏn'gŭk*, 306. The "Fifty-three Buddhas" are mentioned in several sutras; cf. Tsukamoto Yoshitaka (comp.), *Bukkyŏ daijiten*, 1210-1212.

56. *HKMT* 7-4, pp. 575-576. This song is quite short and about the only *muga* this *mudang* knew. Adaptation, therefore, may be more of a necessity to her than to her colleagues with a wider repertoire.
57. *HKMT* 7-2, pp. 839-882 and *HKMT* 7-7, pp. 246-337.
58. *HKMT* 7-2, p. 845.
59. Ch'oe Kilsŏng, "Muga Kŏri kut", 183-221. When this version was recorded, Kim Yongt'aek acted as drummer.
60. *THM*, 280-353.
61. This assumption agrees with the observation by Sŏ Taesŏk that first the shorter non-narrative *muga* are memorized. Sŏ, *Muga-ŭi yŏn'gu*, 139.
62. Sŏ Taesŏk, *Muga-ŭi yŏn'gu*, 137-138.
63. Cho, *Werdegang*, 131.
64. Sŏ Taesŏk, *Muga-ŭi yŏn'gu*, 89-110. Hong Kimun, on the other hand, has warned against easy identification of *muga* with old myths; *Chosŏn sinhwa yŏn'gu*, 234.
65. E.g., Yi Nŭnghwa, "Musok ko", 6-7.
66. *Chungjong sillok*, LXXXIII:63a.1-2.

NOTES TO CHAPTER IV

1. *Han'guk kubi munhak taegye*, comp. by Han'guk chŏngsin munhwa yŏn'guwŏn (*HKMT*).
2. E.g., *Pulgyo kasa*, 136 and 501-503.
3. Pak Hyosun, "Honam chibang-ŭi yŏryu kasa yŏn'gu", 157-176, refers to an old woman who had made a *kasa* about her own life and presented this to the author in 1969.
4. Marshall Pihl, "Korea in the Bardic Tradition", 81-83.
5. Cf. Hans H. Frankel, *The Flowering Plum and the Palace Lady*, Chapter 6.
6. *Sijo sajŏn*, Nos. 1410, 1412, 2152.
7. Yang Chudong, *Yŏyŏ chŏnju*, 332-334. Cf. *Sijo sajŏn*, No. 475; the wording in one *muga* is similar to that in the *sijo*: *KTG* I, 114. See also Peter H. Lee, *Celebration of Continuity*, 33-36.
8. The topos is used in *Sijo sajŏn*, No. 1538. Cf. also No. 17.
9. Kim T'aegon, *Musok yŏn'gu*, 332; translation by the present author.
10. Hong Kimun, for example, has pointed out that on Cheju Island different origins are given for the same gods in different *muga*: *Chosŏn*

sinhwa yŏn'gu, 233. See Chapter IX for different theories about the origin of the deity Kyemyŏn halmŏni.

11. The popular practice of even the higher religions tolerates contradictions that the systematic theologian could not bear to live with.

12. G. Sandschejew, "Weltanschauung", 599.

13. John. F. Embree, *A Japanese Village: Suye Mura*, 180.

14. Laurence Delaby, *Chamanes toungouses*, 47.

15. Chang and Ch'oe, *Kyŏnggi-do musok*, 32 and 188-203.

16. Ch'oe Kilsŏng, *Musog-ŭi yŏn'gu*, 17.

17. The *Sonnim kut* of Sa Hwasŏn recorded in *HKMT* 2-3, pp. 600-618, for example, omits the first half of the story.

18. *CCM*, 48.

19. There is a belief that generous spending for the purpose of a *kut* increases its efficacy, but this is not bound to an absolute standard. One should not grudge money and should spend freely, but according to one's financial position. A poor man's ceremony taking only one day is therefore not less efficacious than a rich man's ceremony that lasts for three days. Cf. Ch'oe Kilsŏng, *Musog-ŭi yŏn'gu*, 189.

20. Chang Tŏksun a.o., *Kubi munhak kaesŏl*, 139.

21. There is a voluminous literature about this brief song. For the purpose of this discussion the most important works are the following. Kim Tonguk, "Ch'ŏyong ka yŏn'gu" in *Han'guk kayo-ŭi yŏn'gu*, 121-168; Sŏ Taesŏk, *Muga-ŭi yŏn'gu*, 277-302; Vos, *Religionen*, 60-63; D. Eikemeier, "Volksgodsdienstige verschijnselen in de oudste Koreaanse letterkunde", *Forum der Letteren* XIX, 284-292 (1978).

22. Translation from: Frits Vos, "Tales of the Extraordinary: An Inquiry into the Contents, Nature and Authorship of the *Sui chŏn*", 11.

23. Akiba Takashi, *Chōsen fuzoku no genchi kenkyū*, 88-89.

24. *KTG* III, p. 150, note 10.

25. This is called *kil karŭm*. See Ch'oe Kilsŏng, *Musog-ŭi yŏn'gu*, 282-285.

26. *MSr*, 325-329. For a text of this play, *Segyŏng nori*, see: *Cheju sajŏn*, 380-397.

27. Traditionally, in Korea, the cow is used as a work animal, rather than raised for its milk or meat. For the *So-nori kut* see: Ch'oe Kilsŏng, "Minsokkŭk-kwa musok sinang", 41.

28. M. Durand, *Technique et panthéon des médiums Viêtnamiens (Dông)*, 34. An important difference between the *mudang* and these mediums is that the latter do not sing themselves.

29. Cf. also *KTG* III, 217: *manhi mŏkko ssŏk mullŏsŏra*, and *AA* I, 183-184: *manhi mŏkko, kagŏra*.

30.   Hartmut O. Rotermund, *Majinai-uta: Grundlagen, Inhalte und Form-elemente japanischer magischer Gedichte des 17.-20. Jahrhunderts*, 113.

31.   Cf. Sŏ Taesŏk, *Muga-ŭi yŏn'gu*, 19-198.

32.   *KTG* I, 116-117.

33.   Yim Suk-jay (=Im Sŏkchae), "Introduction au Mouïsme", p. 11.

34.   Cho, *Werdegang*, 113.

35.   *AA* I, 113-114; *KTG* I, 45; Sŏng Kyŏngnin a.o., *Seoul chiyŏg-ŭi musok*, 64-65; Chang Chugŭn and Ch'oe Kilsŏng, *Kyŏnggi-do musok*, 165-166; also *Minyo chip* V, 110.

36.   *Sin Chaehyo*, 582-583.

37.   Halla Pai Huhm, *Kut; Korean Shamanist Rituals*, 79-80; cf. also p. 67.

38.   Yi Kyŏngbok, *Sim Ch'ŏng kut yŏn'gu*, 159; Sim Usŏng, "Sim Ch'ŏng kut", p. 197; *MSs*, p. 184, note 1.

39.   Im Sŏkchae and Chang Chugŭn, *Kwanbuk muga* I, 8.

40.   G.M. Wassiljewitsch, "Schamanengesänge der Ewenken (Tungusen)", 381.

41.   *HKMT* 7-7, p. 258.

42.   E.g., *KTG* II, p. 290 for the Pujŏng, and p. 298 for the Kamung; *HKMT* 1-2, p. 542: for the Ch'angbu, and p. 546: for the Taegam.

43.   *KTG* III, 66. In the Story of Crown Prince Allakkuk in the *Wŏrin sŏkpo* (first published in 1459; cf. A.M. Olof, "The Story of Prince Allakkuk: *Wŏrin sŏkpo* Vol. 8", pp. 13-20), Wŏnang, written with the Chinese characters for "mandarin duck", is the name of the mother of the hero, while the "*Gāthā* of Rebirth in Paradise" (*Wangsaeng kye*), which opens with the words: *wŏn wang saeng*, has a prominent place in this tale. The confusion between *wŏnangsae* and *wŏn wang saeng*, therefore, may have existed as long ago as the 15th century. The compilers of the *Wŏrin sŏkpo* possibly were the first to put the interpretation "mandarin duck" to the name of the mother, by adding Chinese characters chosen for their connotations with conjugal love, when they reproduced an oral story. A written source for this story has not yet been found, but even if the tale had its ancestor in written literature, it is not unthinkable that the compilers of the *Wŏrin sŏkpo* used an orally transmitted version of it.

44.   *KTG* I, 102.

45.   *KTG* I, 41; see Chapter VIII.

46.   *AA* I, 163. For several Chesŏk on Cheju Island, see *Cheju sajŏn*, 66-67; there Chesŏk seems to be hardly more than an honorific added to the names of deities.

47.   Alexandre Guillemoz, *Les algues, les anciens, les dieux*, 123-125; cf. also p. 259.

48. Embree, *A Japanese Village*, 186.
49. J. Cauberghe, *Vroomheid en volksgeloof in Vlaanderen*, 41, 63, 112.

NOTES TO CHAPTER V

1. Im Sŏkchae, "Kankoku no fuzoku - gaisetsu", 24.
2. R. Finnegan, *Oral Poetry*, 90.
3. Cf. Finnegan, *Oral Poetry*, Chapter 5.
4. M. Parry, "Studies in the Epic Technique of Oral Verse-making, I: Homer and Homeric Style", 80.
5. H.L. Rogers, "The Crypto-Psychological Character of the Oral Formula", 102.
6. Lord, *The Singer of Tales*, 4.
7. Parry, "Studies, I", 84.
8. A.C. Watts, *The Lyre and the Harp*, 85.
9. A.B. Lord, "Oral Poetry", 592.
10. Marshall Pihl has applied the theory in an attempt to prove that the texts of *p'ansori* originally were orally composed; Pihl, "Bardic Tradition." A similar attempt is made by Kim Pyŏngguk, "Kubi sŏsasirosŏ pon p'ansori sasŏl kusŏng pangsik", 120-149.
11. A.C. Watts, *The Lyre and the Harp*, 86-87.
12. C.H. Wang, *The Bell and the Drum*, 46-48.
13. In Old-English poetry there are the examples of the poems of Cynewulf and the Metres of Boethius; Robert E. Diamond, "The Diction of the Signed Poems of Cynewulf", 228-241 and Larry D. Benson, "The Literary Character of Anglo-Saxon Formulaic Poetry", 334-341.
14. Wang, *The Bell and the Drum*, 46.
15. E.g., F.P. Magoun, "The Oral-Formulaic Character of Anglo-Saxon Narrative Poetry", 104.
16. The situation is similar, but to put it that way for Korea would be a simplification. For instance, the statements should be qualified according to the period. It is, however, beyond the scope of this study to delve more deeply into this problem.
17. Lord, *The Singer of Tales*, 4.
18. Lord, *The Singer of Tales*, 69.
19. Lord, *The Singer of Tales*, 94.
20. A.C. Watts, *The Lyre and the Harp*, 39.

21. *Sijo sajŏn*, No. 1167. For formulaic elements in the work of Kim Ch'ŏnt'aek also see: Walraven, "Han'guk sijo munhag-ŭi p'wŏmyulla punsŏk", pp. 71-80.
22. Cf. Rogers, "Crypto-Psychological Character", 93-94.
23. In his analysis of a fragment of *Sim Ch'ŏng ka*, Marshall Pihl regards *Sim Ch'ŏng-i hanŭn mar-i* ("Sim Ch'ŏng said") as a formula. It fits the verse line, but would be the normal way to phrase the same idea in natural speech; Pihl, "Bardic Tradition", 88.
24. Chŏng Tongwha, *Han'guk minyo-ŭi sa-jŏk yŏn'gu*, 18-42.
25. Chŏng Pyŏnguk, *Han'guk kojŏn siga-ron*, 13-38; W.E. Skillend, "Words from the Heart", 177-184; David McCann, "Structural Elements of the Kasa", pp. 27-34 or *Form and Freedom in Korean Poetry*, 27-30; Kim Chinu (Chin-W. Kim), "Sijo-ŭi unnyul kujo-ŭi sae koch'al", pp. 299-325.
26. McCann, "Structural Elements", 30.
27. E.g., the manuscript of a *kasa* dating from 1828 or earlier, which is kept in the library of Leiden University; See: Boudewijn C.A. Walraven, "Ch'ŏnjamun-ŭro poa-on Han'guk kasa", *Kugŏ kungmunhak* XCIII, *purok* (1984).
28. E.g., Kim Ingyŏm, *Iltong changyu ka*, and *Hanyang ka*, wood-block edition (1880), in the possession of the National Library in Seoul.
29. McCann, "Structural Elements", 30.
30. *THM*, 71.
31. *AA* I, 473, lines 14 and 15 have a noun in line 14 and the corresponding particle in line 15! *KTG* IV, 65 prints two lines in completely regular *kasa* metre (3 4 4 4/4 4 4 4) as one line: "When the swallowtail butterfly of Mt. Suyŏng/In a deep slumber amidst the flowers/Thinks of man's life and death/Sad, all too sad it is."
32. The *Ch'angbu t'aryŏng* in *AA* I (p. 109) by re-arrangement can be made to look more regular than it looks in the printed text (p. 109, first line to p. 111, line 6).

Syllable groups according to *AA*	re-arrangement
4 3 3 3	4 3 3 3
3 4	3 4 3 3
3 3 4 4	4 4 4 4
4 4	3 4 3 4
3 4 3 4	
4 4 (p. 110)	4 4 (p. 110)
3 4 4 4	3 4 4 4
4 3 3 3	4 3 3 3
5 5 5 4	5 5 5 4

5 5	5 5 5 5
5 5	5 4 5 5
5 4 5 5	5 4 5 4
5 4	5 4 5 4
5 4 5 4	5 4 5 4
5 4 5 4	6 6
5 4	3 5 4 4
6 6	3 5 5 3
3 5 4 4	4 3 3 3
3 5 5 3	
4 3 3 3	
4 4 5 4 (p. 111)	4 4 5 4 (p. 111)
5 4 5 6	5 4 5 6
4 5 3 4	4 5 3 4
3 5	3 5
5 3	5 3 3 3
3 3	

Some half-lines stand on their own in the rearrangement. This is because, for semantic reasons, it does not make sense to combine them with the following half-line. These independent half-lines all end in the emphatic copula-form *ra*; this is no accident. There is a tendency for half-lines with special emphasis (also those ending in -*kuna*, for instance) to remain isolated.

33. Sŏ Taesŏk, *Muga-ŭi yŏn'gu*, 135. Chŏng Tonghwa, in his study of *minyo*, has pointed out that a foot of three syllables, when sung, may last as long as a foot of four syllables; *Minyo-ŭi sajŏk yŏngu*, 25-27. The most important Korean student of the music of the *mudang* is Yi Pohyŏng, who has described i.a. the music of the East Coast *mudang*: *HMCCP Kyŏngnam*, 265-280. A recent treatment of the subject is: Howard, *Bands, Songs and Shamanistic Rituals*.

34. Pihl, "Bardic Tradition", 85. One should note, that although so far the terms "line" and "half-line" have been used, this is a possible source of misunderstanding. Not every half-line has a counterpart to make up a full line, certainly not in the *muga*. When half-lines are consistently combined into lines in *kasa*, one sees that parallel half-lines often end up in different lines and that other half-lines are paired with half-lines which start a completely new train of thought. Perhaps it would have been better to call the half-line a line and the line a couplet as has been suggested by W.E. Skillend, in "Words From the Heart", 182, but this runs counter to current usage.

35. Parry, "Studies", I, 85.

36. *Kasa chŏnjip*, 353, 429.

37. *Kasa sŏnjip*, 249.
38. Lord, *The Singer of Tales*, 4.
39. Lord, *The Singer of Tales*, 68-98.
40. Sŏ Taesŏk, "P'ansori-wa sŏsa muga-ŭi taebi yŏn'gu", pp. 7-44; Kim Tonguk "P'ansori sabip kayo yŏn'gu", originally published in 1958, reissued in *Han'guk kayo-ŭi yŏn'gu*, pp. 439-551.
41. Chŏng Pyŏnguk (ed. and annot.), *Pae pijang chŏn. Ong Kojip chŏn*, 22-24 and 114. All references with regard to these two *ko-sosŏl* are to this edition.
42. That theme is a broader category than interlude song, has been recognized by Yi Hŏnhong, "P'ansori-ŭi 'p'omyulla'-e tae-hayŏ", 137-162, esp. p. 149.
43. *THM*, 242.
44. *KTG* I, 346.
45. *KTG* I, 142.
46. *Namwŏn kosa*, 51.
47. Sŏ Taesŏk, *Muga-ŭi yŏn'gu*, 19-198.
48. An English translation of a pall-bearers' song can be found in Roger L. Janelli & Dawnhee Yim Janelli, *Ancestor Worship and Korean Society*, 66-69.
49. Hans Frankel, *The Flowering Plum and the Palace Lady*, 81.
50. Wolfram Eberhard, "Pounding Songs from Peking", 170.
51. Sŏ Taesŏk, "P'ansori-wa sŏsa muga", 40.
52. This is an analytic distinction. In practice, half-lines that belong to a formulaic system or to a group of related formulaic systems, may also appear as parallel half-lines within one and the same text.
     tongji-ya kin'gin pam-gwa
     haji-il kin'gin nar-ŭi
     ttae-mada syangsae-roda (*Namwŏn kosa*, 212)
     (The long, long nights around the winter solstice/And the long, long days around the summer solstice/Always I long for my lover!)
     The first half-line can be fitted into system A II, the second into A III.
53. Yi Kyŏngbok, *Sim Ch'ŏng kut yŏn'gu*, 73.
54. M.B. Emeneau, "Style and Meaning in an Oral Literature", 329.
55. *AA* I, 163-164.
56. *KTG* I, 276-277.
57. "Nival" and "pluvial" in the translations are not in the wrong register. The original uses Sino-Korean expressions which are uncommon in ordinary speech. These lines, incidentally, have the peculiar diction described earlier in the text: noun + particle + verb + inconclusive ending + noun phrase.
58. Finnegan, *Oral Poetry*, 98.

59. *HKMT* 2-3, p. 605.
60. *THM*, 247.
61. *HKMT* 2-3, p. 636.
62. *THM*, 372.
63. *Kwanbuk muga* I, 139.
64. Cf. Finnegan, *Oral Poetry*, 98.
65. *KTG* III, 204.
66. *Minyo chip* IV, 452.
67. *Namwŏn kosa*, 55-56.
68. *MSs*, 296.
69. *MSs*, 296.
70. *Akchang kasa*, compiler and date unknown (facsimile ed., publ. by Taejegak, in the set *(Wŏnbon) Han'guk kojŏn ch'ongsŏ* II: Seoul, 1973), 50-51.
71. *Han'guk siga*, 291.
72. *MSs*, 369.
73. *MSs*, 369.
74. *AA* I, 67.
75. Hans Frankel, *The Flowering Plum and the Palace Lady*, 165-167; for Chinese parallelism in general cf. Gustave Schlegel, *La loi du parallélisme en style chinois demontrée par la préface du Si-yü ki.*
76. *KTG* III, 281.
77. Kim Tonguk, *Kayo-ŭi yŏn'gu*, 225; on p. 213 there is an example of antithetical parallelism (inside/outside) in the *Siyong hyangak po.*
78. *AA* I, 168.
79. Son Chint'ae, *Shinka ihen*, 46.
80. R. Austerlitz, *Ob-Ugric Metrics*, 65-69, 126. For an example of terrace lines in *kasa*, see *Kasa chŏnjip*, 361: *saenggak kkŭd-e hansum-io/hansum kkŭd-e nunmur-ira/nunmul-lo chiŏnaeni.*
81. *AA* I, 503.
82. *MSs*, p. 11. note 4.
83. *MSs*, 286.
84. *AA* I, 574.
85. One may regard the Five Bonds as one of the themes of traditional Korean literature. Cf. *Kasa sŏnjip*, p. 422.
86. *HKMT* 2-3, p. 649.
87. *Kwŏn* VIII: 99b.
88. *Sangyong ŭibŏm*, 48b.
89. *KTG* III, 264.
90. *KTG* III, 364-365; *AA* I, 128; *CCM*, 279.
91. *KTG* IV, 84.

92.   The points of the compass are used in a similar way in *AA* I, 263; *KTG*
      I, 91; *KTG* III, 217; *KTG* IV, 32, 95; *THM*, 136; *Hanyang ka*, 108-109;
      Pae pijang chŏn, 59-60; Yi Tuhyŏn, *Kamyŏn' gŭk*, 301-302. This list is
      far from exhaustive. Cf. the frequent use of this pattern in *Hwangje
      p'uri* (translated in Chapter VIII).
      Finnegan, *Oral Poetry*, 104, quotes a Pueblo song in which the four
      cardinal points of the compass provide the framework.
      Cf. also N. Poppe, *Mongolische Volksdichtung*, 80-83 and 264-265.
93.   Sim Usŏng, "Sonnim kut", 189. Cf. the translation of the Kyemyŏn *kut*,
      lines 120-125, in Ch.IX.
94.   *HKMT* 7-2, p. 811.
95.   *Kasa chŏnjip*, 558; cf. *THM*, 364; *CCM*, 280.
96.   *AA* I, 498.
97.   Lord, *The Singer of Tales*, 266, presents an example of expansion by
      this method in a song from Montenegro. "... the father asks his son if
      he is angry because he is lacking money, clothes, a horse, and other
      accoutrements, and the son answers that he is not angry because of this,
      nor that, since that could be corrected easily, but he is angry that...."
98.   *KTG* IV, 61-62.
99.   *Sijo sajŏn*, No. 2152.
100. Cf. also *Sijo sajŏn*, No. 1412; HMKT 7-2, p. 831; Sim Usŏng, "Sim
      Ch'ŏng kut", p. 205.
101. Son Chint'ae, *Shinka ihen*, 141.
102. Yen Tzu-ling lived in the first century A.D. Although he was a friend
      of the Han Emperor Kuang-wu, he declined to take office and preferred
      to sustain himself fishing and working the land.
103. In the same *muga* (the contents of which are summarized in Chapter
      VIII), this kind of verbal game is seen when the hero intends to cut a
      tree for timber.
104. E.g., Chŏng Pyŏnguk, *P'ansori*, 342.
105. *NSC*, 136.
106. *KTG* III, 366.
107. There is another verbal game in these lines. The monk of the first line
      is a *ttaengttaengi chung*, that of the second line a *hwaju-sŭng*. In
      substance the two terms are alike; both refer to a monk who begs for
      alms. *Ttaengttaengi chung*, however, with the onomatopoeia imitating
      the tinny sound of a small gong, is a rather folksy and irreverential
      word, while the Sino-Korean term *hwaju-sŭng* sounds more formal. The
      contrast in register of pure Korean and Sino-Korean is used deliberately
      to achieve a literary effect. Cf. a dialogue between Ch'unhyang and her
      lover, Yi Mongnyong, in a *p'ansori* libretto by Sin Chaehyo (*Sin
      Chaehyo*, 114-115):

Yi Mongnyong: *"Myŏs-sal mŏgŏnni?"* - "How old are you?"
Ch'unhyang: *"Yŏlyŏssŏs-sar-iyo."* - "I'm sixteen." (pure Kor.)
Yi Mongnyong: *"Na-nŭn simnyuk-se-da."* - "I'm sixteen." (Sino-Korean)

108. *AA* I, 142. This pattern is also found in a *sijo* by Yun Sŏndo; *Sijo sajŏn*, No. 814.

109. *KTG* III, 203; same wordplay in *AA* I, 146.

110. *AA* I, 568; also in a *minyo*: Chŏng Tonghwa, *Minyo-ŭi sajŏk yŏn'gu*, 26 and *Minyo chip* III, 223. Cf. *CCM*, 305.

111. According to Yi Nŭnghwa, "Musok ko", 56, there are three kinds of *ŏp*, "household mascots", beings that bring luck: snakes, weasels and humans.

112. *KTG* III, 296-297.

113. *Sijo sajŏn*, No. 772.

114. *HKMT* 7-2, p. 820.

115. *THM*, 363; *KTG* IV, 45.

116. *THM*, 375. Compare this with the opening words of *Ong Kojip chŏn*: *Ongjŏng Ongyŏn-ŭi Ongjin-gol Ongdang-ch'on-e hansaram issŭdoe, sŏng-ŭn Ong-iyo, myŏng-ŭn Kojip-ira* (*Ong Kojip chŏn*, 94). Also: *Tyesŏng-nim-ŭi abŏji-nŭn Hăesu-stŭl Hăesu sŏnbi, Tyesŏng-nim-ŭi ŏmnŏni-nŭn Ryonggung-stŭl Ryongnyŏ puin* (*AA* I, 133).

117. *MSs*, p. 9, note 5.

118. *Cheju sajŏn*, p. 197, note 98 and p. 192, note 13. Cf. *THM*, 384: *ŏkpau tŏkpau*; *HKMT* 7-2, p. 820: *aewŏn t'aewŏn*; *Sin Chaehyo*, 600-601: *oŭksae toŭksae*. Also see Ch. IX, note 2.

119. *Han'guk siga*, 303:
ilch'im changsa Han T'aejong-a
igwan mulsa igwan mulsa Che Wangch'o
samgu myŏngnyŏng Chegal Myŏng
sawŏlch'ŏr-e sawŏlch'ŏr-e Ch'o Paewang
ogwanch'ŏn-e ogwanch'ŏn-e Kwan Unjang
yukku munjang yukku munjang Chin Sihwang-a
ch'illyŏn-e ch'illyŏn-e Sam T'o
p'alsiwŏr-e p'alsiwŏr-e Chin Kabyu
kusi tŏngmang kusi tŏngmang Chang Puryŏng-a
sip-nyŏn chigi Sip-nyŏn chigi Ham Sŏbang

Similar passages: *KTG* IV, 89 and *KTG* I, 342. Because of corruptions and the nature of the wordplay itself these passages are difficult to translate. In *KTG* I, 342, the name of a book, the *Chŏnggamnok* (Records of Chŏng Kam), a book of prophecies, appears as the name of a general!

120. *Sin Chaehyo*, 566-567.
121. *Sin Chaehyo*, 675-677. Sin's catalogues, too, with their extreme length, could probably only have been created by someone familiar with writing.
122. Yi Tuhyŏn, *Kamyŏn'gŭk*, 320; Sim Usŏng, *Minsokkŭk*, 99, 117.
123. *Kujŏn minyo chip* I, 164-167; *HMCCP Chŏnnam*, 687-691.
124. *AA* I, 129.
125. *Han'guk siga*, 280; *KTG* I, 272.
126. *THM*, 265. Cf. Chŏng Tonghwa, *Minyo-ŭi sajŏk yŏn'gu*, 65. Various kinds of wordplay with numbers can also be found in a *sasŏl sijo*: *Sijo sajŏn*, No. 1849.
127. *MSs*, 376.
128. *AA* I, 6-24.
129. *THM*, 383.
130. *Han'guk siga*, 293.
131. Yi Kyŏngbok, *Sim Ch'ŏng kut yŏn'gu*, 153-154.
132. *KTG* III, 66.
133. *KTG* III, 292.
134. *AA* I, 109, 129; *CCM*, 248, 253; Sŏ Taesŏk, *Muga-ŭi yŏn'gu*, 412.
135. Cf. Pihl. "Korea in the Bardic Tradition", 85-86.
136. For example, Sim Usŏng, "Sonnim kut", 189: "Whose orders will a slave defy?"
137. *AA* I, 225; Sim Usŏng, "Sonnim kut", 184; *Hanyang ka*, 111-112, 118-119; *Kasa sŏnjip*, 425, 427.
138. *AA* I, 117-118, 231; *HMCCP Kyŏngbuk*, 207; *Sijo sajŏn*, No. 800.
139. *AA* I, 117-118, 231; Kim Sŏngbae, *Han'gug-ŭi minsok*, 302.
140. *AA* I, 106; also *KTG* I, 287.
141. *AA* I, 37; also *AA* I, 105; *KTG* I, 140-141, 145.
      Cf. Yi Tuhyŏn, *Kamyŏn'gŭk*, 260: "Tohwa-dong is a neighbourhood, Anam-dong is a neighbourhood, too."
142. Finnegan, *Oral Poetry*, 101: "One could list numerous instances (of conscious use of parallelism, B.W.) from different kinds of oral literature: Mongolian and Fijian poetry ...., the Rgveda ...., Old English, Malay, Christian liturgy - but the device is so widespread that it scarcely needs further exemplification."

NOTES TO CHAPTER VI

1. *Han' guk siga*, 261.
2. Vos, *Religionen*, 66.
3. Kim T'aekkyu, *Han' guk minsok munyeron*, 2; cf. Sŏ Taesŏk, "Musok-kwa kungmunhak", 183, and Kim Pyŏngguk, "Kubi sŏsasi-rosŏ pon p'ansori sasŏr-ŭi kusŏng pangsik", 125.
4. Chang Tŏksun a.o., *Kubi munhak kaesŏl*, 141.
5. Sŏ Taesŏk, *Muga-ŭi yŏn' gu*, 89-110.
6. Vos, *Religionen*, 30, 43; the story of Chumong is found on pp. 32-37, in a translation of a version from the *Sejong sillok*. *Muga* with a similar basic pattern -a heavenly being descends to earth and has an affair with a woman, whom he deserts before the children are born, to return to heaven- are *Siru mal* (*AA* I, 128-132) and *Ch' ogamje* (*AA* I, 369-387).
7. *(Sinjŭng -) Tongguk yŏji sŭngnam*, p. 631 (XXXV:33b.9-15; "Yŏng-nam: kojŏk").
8. Donald B. Redford, "The Literary Motif of the Exposed Child", 209-228.
9. Sandschejew, "Weltanschauung und Schamanismus der Alaren-Burja-ten", 946.
10. Cf. the motif of the animal nurse, in Stith Thompson, *Motif-Index of Folk-Literature*, B 535: Animal Nurse.
11. *AA* I, 503-507.
12. Translation of the *Samguk yusa* version of T'arhae's story in Vos, *Religionen*, 39-40.
13. In *AA* erroneously translated as "One-day Temple."
14. Chang Chugŭn, *Hyangt'o sinang*, 84 and *MSr*, 306; for a translation of the story of the Three Families see Vos, *Religionen*, 53.
15. Kim Chongu, "Sŏdong ka yŏn'gu", I, 67.
16. It should be remembered that for the historic-geographic method of studying the folk-tale it is essential that a large number of versions -the largest number possible- be studied. No serious scholar would attempt a study of the dissemination of a folk-tale on the basis of only two versions. Cf. Stith Thompson, *The Folktale*, 439.
17. Chang Tŏksun, *Han' guk sŏrhwa munhak yŏn' gu*, 55-69 and 339.
18. Choi In-hak, *A Type Index of Korean Folktales*. For a German translation of the *Koryŏ sa* version of the legend of the grandfather of Wang Kŏn, see Vos, *Religionen*, 45-50.
19. Chang Tŏksun, *Sŏrhwa munhak yŏn' gu*, 349.
20. English translation of this story in *The Folk Treasury of Korea*, 99-101. For the *muga*, see Son Chint'ae, "Fugeki no shinka (2)", *Seikyū gakusō*

XXII, 199-207. Cf. Eberhard, *Typen Chinesischer Volksmärchen*, Type 99, "Das Bauopfer."

21. *MSr*, 306.
22. Choi, *Type Index*, No. 265; A. Aarne and S. Thompson, *The Types of the Folktale*, No. 560, "The Magic Ring." According to Aarne, this type, which is well-known in Europe, is ultimately of Indian origin; Thompson, *The Folktale*, 70-71.
23. *KTG* III, 79-82.
24. Stith Thompson, *Motif-Index of Folk-Literature*, Q 2.
25. A tale in the *Wŏrin sŏkpo*, XXIII:26b-53b.
26. Choi, *Type Index*, No. 457.
27. Chang Chugŭn, "Sŏsa muga-ŭi siwŏn-gwa minsok yesulsa-sang-ŭi wich'i", 5-31.
28. For the *pien-wen*, cf. Eugene Chen Eoyang, *Word of Mouth: oral story-telling in the 'Pien-wen'*.
29. Perhaps some of the Buddhist stories recorded in the 15th century in the *Wŏrin sŏkpo* were based on an oral *pien-wen* tradition, but this cannot -as yet- be stated with certainty.
30. *Han'guk siga*, 42-46.
31. Sŏ, *Muga-ŭi yŏn'gu*, 94.
32. Son Chint'ae, "Fugeki no shinka (2)", 195-198.
33. Text in Kim Kidong (comp.) *Chosŏn pulgyo sosŏl sŏn*, 43-71.
34. *AA* I, 417; *Allakkuk chŏn*, 54.
35. *AA* I, 419; *Allakkuk chŏn*, 59.
36. *AA* I, 420; *Allakkuk chŏn*, 61.
37. *AA* I, 427-428; *Allakkuk chŏn*, 69.
38. *AA* I, 427; *Allakkuk chŏn*, 70.
39. Sa Chaedong, "'Allakkuk t'aeja chŏn' yŏn'gu", 105. This work is regarded as a novel, but it is significant that it was copied in one volume with two Buddhist sutras.
40. W. Eberhard, *Typen Chinesischer Volksmärchen*, 248-250. For a translation of the story of Sŏdong, see Ilyon, *Samguk Yusa*, transl. by Tae-Hung Ha and Grafton K. Mintz, 142-144.
41. *KTG* III, 92-97.
42. Cf. Vos, *Religionen*, 91-99.
43. Formally, the enumeration of their deaths is similar to that of the ill-fated husbands of the heroine of *Pyŏn Kangsoe ka* (Sin Chaehyo, 532-533).
44. Chang, "Sŏsa muga-ŭi siwŏn, 18.
45. *AA* I, 532.
46. E.B. Cowell (ed.), *The Jātaka or Stories of the Buddha's Former Births*, Vol. II, pp. 110-112 (No. 208). Cf. also "Die Geschichte von der

Schildkröte und dem Hasen", in Vos, *Religionen*, 144-145 and 145, note 61.

47. Cf. Sa Chaedong, *Pulgyo-gye kungmun sosŏr-ŭi hyŏngsŏng kwajŏng yŏn'gu*, 54-55.

48. *Wŏrin sŏkpo*, XXI:213a-223b.

49. *KTG* I, 129.

50. Cf. Choi, *Type-index*, No. 337 and Thompson, *The Folktale*, 50-53.

51. Eberhard, *Typen Chinesischer Volksmärchen*, No. 155. For P'eng-tsu, see E.T.C. Werner, *A Dictionary of Chinese Mythology*, 372 and 431-432.

52. Chang Tŏksun a.o., *Kubi munhak kaesŏl*, 134.

53. Chang Chugŭn, "Sŏsa muga-ŭi kiwŏn", 23.

54. Wang Chung-min a.o., *Tun-huang pien-wen chi*, Vol. I, 209-215; translated in Arthur Waley, *Ballads and Stories from Tun-huang*, 165-174.

55. For the contents of the *Tang T'aejong chŏn* I have relied on the summary in Kim Kidong, *Han'guk kojŏn sosŏl yŏn'gu*, 52-54.

56. Cf. Glen Dudbridge, The *Hsi-yu Chi*, Chapter 4, for evidence that *Hsi-yu chi* material was known in Korea before the hundred-chapter edition appeared.

57. Chin Sŏnggi, *Namgug-ŭi muga*, 805-808.

58. *KTG* I, 132-137; *KTG* III, 345-350. Cf. Choi, *Type-index*, No. 312, "The Man Who Extended His Life."

59. Sa Chaedong, *Pulgyo-gye kungmun sosŏl*, 48-55.

60. Kim Tonguk, "P'ansori-ŭi palsaeng ko", *Han'guk kayo-ŭi yŏn'gu*. sok, 297-327 and 329-356. Moreover, Kim's *Ch'unhyang chŏn yŏn'gu* also has a bearing on the subject.

61. Kim, *Kayo-ŭi yŏn'gu.sok*, 303.

62. Murayama, *Chōsen no fugeki*, 22-23, lists *chaein* ("acrobat"), *kongin* ("musician") and *kwangdae* as appellations for male *mudang*. Yi Nŭnghwa, "Musok ko", 23: "Actors (*paeu*) are also called *kwangdae*, i.e. *mubu*."

63. *HMCCP Kyŏnggi*, 120-123.

64. Although one character is different in the name of Yi Chongha as given in *HMCCP*, he must be the same person as the Yi Chongha mentioned in *AA* II, 286, who also lived in Pusan Village. Such variations in writing are by no means uncommon.

65. *HMCCP Kyŏnggi*, 121 and *AA* II, 285.

66. *AA* I, 125-189.

67. *AA* II, 285. Yi Chongman was the eleventh generation.

68. *HMCCP Chŏnbuk*, 134-135.

69. Yi Nŭnghwa, "Musok ko", 23.

70.   Kim Tonguk, *Kayo-ŭi yŏn'gu*, 300-304.

71.   *AA* II, 286.

72.   *AA* II, 277-283.

73.   See *AA* II, 275-292 for documentary evidence of these organizations.

74.   *AA* II, 287.

75.   Kim Tonguk suggests that such bonds between *kwangdae* and *mudang* already existed during the Koryŏ dynasty; *Kayo-ŭi yŏn'gu*, 198. This will be difficult to prove, but does not concern the present discussion, for which only the 18th century -the period when *p'ansori* emerged- is of importance.

76.   Pihl, "Bardic Tradition", 67.

77.   In *Kayo-ŭi yŏn'gu*, 541-542, Kim Tonguk suggests that *p'ansori* took over the "technique" of the *sasŏl* rather than the content. This is more plausible than a claim that the content was borrowed, but no easier to prove.

78.   Kim Tonguk, *Kayo-ŭi yŏn'gu.sok*, 303.

79.   Yi Ik, *Sŏngho saesŏl*, Vol. I, pp. 433-434.

80.   *CCM*, 272.

81.   Kim Tonguk, *Kayo-ŭi yŏn'gu*, 310.

82.   That the texts were exchanged and not the rhythms, was probably because rhythm is a more fundamental element than text and more difficult to change, just as in ordinary speech it takes effort to alter one's accent and intonation, while adopting new words is easy.

83.   Yi Hyegu, "Song Manjae-ŭi Kwanuhŭi", in his *Han'guk ŭmak yŏn'gu*, 325.

84.   Kim Tonguk, *Kayo-ŭi yŏn'gu*, 309.

85.   *HMCCP Kyŏngbuk*, 175.

86.   Yi Hyegu, *Ŭmak yŏn'gu*, 351; quoted from Pihl, "Bardic Tradition", 64.

87.   Contrary to what Pihl states, such a *tŏktam*, although the term is often used by the *mudang*, is not part of the *Ch'angbu kŏri* in *AA* I, 107-115. The Sirhak philosopher Chŏng Tasan (1762-1836) mentions the term *tŏktam* in his *Mongmin simsŏ*. He relates that in the Southern Provinces, every spring and summer actors perform farces called *tŏktam*; Chŏng Yagyŏng, *Chŏng Tasan chŏnjip*, III, 536. A literal translation of *tŏktam* would be "virtue talk." Here "virtue" should be understood as "beneficial influence"; the performance of a *tŏktam* was supposed to have a beneficial effect, hence the translation "chant of fortune." The plays mentioned by Tasan apparently had the purpose of inviting good luck and casting out misfortune, as had other forms of theatre in traditional Korea.

88.   *Sin Chaehyo*, 655-656; Chŏng Pyŏnguk, *P'ansori*, 31-32.

89. *Inter alia*: *THM*, 280-282, an account starting with the beginning of creation and ending with the rule of President Park Chung-hee; Ch'oe Kilsŏng, "Kŏri kut", 183-184; *KTG* I, 107-108; *KTG* III, 258-259.

90. Chŏng Nosik, *Chosŏn ch'anggŭk sa*, 15-16.

91. Yi Tuhyŏn, "Tonghaean pyŏlsin kut", 180.

92. Sim Usŏng, "Sonnim kut", 182.

93. Interview, Kangnŭng, 26 June 1982.

94. Personal communication from the musicologist Yi Sora, Kangnŭng, 27 June 1982.

95. *AA* II, 311.

96. Akiba, *Genchi kenkyū*, 147.

97. Im Hyŏngt'aek, "18.19 segi-ŭi 'iyagikkun'-gwa sosŏr-ŭi palsŏn", 310-332.

98. *Sin Chaehyo*, 448-529; Chŏng Pyŏnguk, *P'ansori*, 427-466.

99. The genre of the *chapka* is very similar to that of the *kasa*; as distinguishing features are mentioned a less regular syllable count, a different style of singing and a more popularized content. Nevertheless, the border line between *kasa* and *chapka* is vague. Cf. Chang Sahun, *Kugak ch'ongnon*, 332-333.

100. Son Chint'ae, *Shinka ihen*, 204.

101. *KTG* I, 341-345.

102. *AA* I, 154; Osan; *AA* I, 289: Sihŭng.

103. Skillend, *Kodae sosŏl*, 136; Eberhard, *Typen Chinesischer Volksmärchen*, 265. Cf. Chang Tŏksun a.o., *Kubi munhak kaesŏl*, 133.

104. *Kwanbuk muga* I, 137-148.

105. *KTG* III, 98-101.

106. Eberhard assumes that the origin of this tale is in Kiangsu. A similar tale is listed by Choi, Type Index, No. 311: "Butterflies." A young man engaged to a girl dies before he can marry. The girl, who regards herself as his widow, goes to his grave and prays that it may open and admit her. Her prayers are granted. The distinctive episode of the boy and girl studying together, found in the Chinese version of the tale and in the *muga*, is lacking.

107. *AA* I, 436-479; *MSs*, 341-356; Chin Sŏnggi, *Namgug-ŭi musok sŏsa-si*, is a copiously annotated edition of this very long *muga*.

108. *MSr*, 323-324.

109. Skillend, *Kodae sosŏl*, 84-85; French translation in *Histoire de Dame Pak . Histoire de Suk-hyang*.

110. A few examples:
     hago-ro narŏnnŭnya? (*AA* I, 438)
     "For what reason have you come down?"
     chung-i tap wal (*AA* I, 438)

"The monk said in reply"
kwihu hyŏnmong-i issŭl kŏs-imnida (AA I, 440)
"After your return home there will be a dream revelation"

111. Skillend, *Kodae sosŏl*, 126-127. There is also a *sijo* by the 18th c. poet Kim Sujang with an allusion to the story of Sukhyang: *Sijo sajŏn*, No. 1684.

112. *MSs*, 184.

113. *AA* I, 453-455; *MSs*, 352. A French translation of *Sukhyang chŏn* is found in *Histoire de Dame Pak . Histoire de Suk-Hyang*.

114. *KTG* III, 101-106.

115. Skillend, *Kodae sosŏl*, 163-164.

116. Yi Hŭisŭng, "Sijo kiwŏn-e tae-han ilko", *Haktŭng*, 2 (1933), cited in Chang Sahun, *Kugak non'go*, 385.

117. Chang Sahun, *Kugak non'go*, 386.

118. Chang Sahun, *Kugak non'go*, 387.

119. Much more promising are attempts to explain the origin of *sijo* through reference to older poetic genres of which we do have examples that may be studied, such as the *hyangga*, the *Koryŏ kayo* or Chinese poems, all verse forms which have been proposed as antecedents of the *sijo*; see Chang Tŏksun, *Kungmunhak t'ongnon*, 155-162.

120. Chang Sahun, *Kugak non'go*, 385-415. Chang is not quite sure about the origin of the kind of song called *noraekkarak*, which is found both as a form of *muga* and as a kind of folk-song; it may have developed out of the *munyŏ sijo*, or it may have developed out of the *sijo* and influenced the singing of the *munyŏ sijo*. The style of singing is the distinguishing characteristic of *noraekkarak*, the words are from *sijo*. Therefore in a discussion of texts -such as the present one- there is no need to deal with the *noraekkarak*.

121. *Sijo sajŏn*, Nos. 1824 (*AA* I, 83), 1851, 1314 and 770 (*AA* I, 84), 1327 and 62 (*AA* I, 85).

122. Cf. the last two lines of *AA* I, 80 with *Sijo sajŏn*, No. 2152, the fourth line of p. 81 with *Sijo sajŏn*, No. 825, and the eighth line with No. 385.

123. *Sijo sajŏn*, No. 2056.

124. *THM*, 294.

125. *KTG* III, 219, 239; *Sijo sajŏn*, No. 825.

126. An English translation of this poem can be found in Richard Rutt, *The Bamboo Grove: An Introduction to Sijo*, No. 228. There is a Dutch translation in B.C.A. Walraven, "Tien Sasŏl Sijo", p. 38: "Bergpassen zo hoog."

127. For this motif in the repertoire of the *namsadang*, see Sim Usŏng, *Namsadang-p'ae yŏn'gu*, 140.

128. *Wŏllyŏng ka . Hanyang ka*, 168-169.

129. *AA* I, 84.
130. Ch'oe Kanghyŏn, "Kasa-ŭi palsaeng sa-jŏk yŏn'gu", 192-258, esp. 257.
131. *KTG* IV, 197-199.
132. *KTG* III, 65-67.
133. *Pulgyo kasa*, 349-351.
134. Son, *Shinka ihen*, 16-25: *Hoesaeng kok*. Several versions of *Hoesim kok* are to be found in *Pulgyo kasa*, 164-189.
135. Yi Tuhyŏn, *Kamyŏn'gŭk*, 51ff.
136. For the original text and Korean translation, see Yi Tuhyŏn, *Kamyŏn'gŭk*, 75. The English translation is by William Henthorn: *A History of Korea*, 77.
137. E.g., the *Kŏri kut* of the East Coast, the *Changnim t'aryŏng* (Chang Chugŭn and Ch'oe Kilsŏng, *Kyŏnggi-do musok*, 176-182), the *So-nori kut* (Yi Tuhyŏn, "Yangju So-nori kut", 169-200).
138. Yi Tuhyŏn, *Kamyŏn'gŭk*, 28. Cf. also Seong-Nae Kim, "Dances of *Toch'aebi* and Songs of Exorcism in Cheju Shamanism", pp. 65-68.

NOTES TO CHAPTER VII

1. Kim Tonguk, *Kayo-ŭi yŏn'gu*, 378-382.
2. A survey of theories about *SC* is given in In Kwŏnhwan, "Sim Ch'ŏng chŏn yŏn'gusa-wa kŭ munjetchŏm", 189-207. For a description of the Seoul version see W.E. Skillend, "Puritas Submersa Resurgit", 126-139. A very thorough study of various editions of the novel *Sim Ch'ŏng chŏn*, which not only discusses the older manuscripts and block-prints, but also modern editions in movable type, is Ch'oe Unsik's *Sim Ch'ŏng chŏn yŏn'gu*. Ch'oe agrees with the conclusion that the Seoul version described by Skillend is older than the Chŏnju edition: p. 124.
3. Kim T'aegon, *Hwangch'ŏn muga* yŏn'gu, 140-155.
4. Sin Tongik, "Sim Ch'ŏng sŏrhwa-ŭi musok-chŏk chŏnsŭng-e kwanhan ilko", 55-70.
5. Translation in modern Korean by Yi Kawŏn in *Hyŏndae munhak*, IV.8, pp. 265-266 (1955).
6. *Han'guk siga*, 85-87.
7. This information was given by Yi Kŭmok to Alexandre Guillemoz, who kindly passed it on to the present writer in a letter dated 7 February 1981.
8. Son Chint'ae, *Shinka ihen*, 204.

9.   Yi Tuhyŏn, "Tonghaean pyŏlsin kut", 172.
10. Information about these *mudang* is found in the following works: *HMCCP Kyŏngnam*, 187-200; Choe Kilsŏng, *Musog-ŭi yŏn'gu*, 103-121; *Han'guk siga*, 85, 278; *THM*, 13-19, 65-70.
11. Resp. *Han'guk siga*, 306-321; Sin Tongik, "Muga 'Sim Ch'ŏng chŏn'", 93-125; *KTG* I, 296-341; *THM*, 175-239; and Sim Usŏng, "Sim Ch'ŏng kut", 197-221; Yi Kyŏngbok, *Sim Ch'ŏng kut yŏn'gu*; *HKMT* 7-7, pp. 126-227; *HKMT* 2-1, pp. 767-902.
     Still another performance by Yi Kŭmok was recorded by Ch'oe Kilsŏng: *Sim Ch'ŏng kut*, and published by the Munhwajae kwalliguk in 1971.
12. Kim Hŭnggyu, "Pansori no nigensei to shakai-teki haikei", 98. Original Korean version in *Ch'angjak-kwa pip'yŏng* IX, 1 (1974).
13. *THM*, 33, 35 and 331-337.
14. The text of this *p'ansori* version is found in Chŏng Pyŏnguk, *Han'gug-ŭi p'ansori*, 313-357. This version will be referred to as *PC*. Points 8, 18, 25, 27 and 29 are like the *Wanp'anbon*, points 17, 19 and 30 like Sin Chaehyo's text, which will be referred to as *SSC*.
15. Yi Kyŏngbok, "Sim Ch'ŏng ka . Sim Ch'ŏng Chŏn . Sim Ch'ŏng kus-ŭi ch'aitchŏm koch'al", 292.
16. Yi Kyŏngbok, "Ch'aitchŏm koch'al", 294.
17. Chang Chiyŏng (ed.), *Hong Kiltong chŏn . Sim Ch'ŏng chŏn*, (*NSC*).
18. The *muga* are those by Yi, Pak and Kim. Episode 19 is missing from Pyŏn's *SC kut*.
19. It is one of the merits of Ch'oe Unsik's *Sim Ch'ŏng chŏn yŏn'gu* that it devotes attention to the paperback editions (*yukchŏn sosŏl*, "Sixpenny Novels" or *ttakchi sosŏl*, "Pulp Novels") and carefully traces their relationship. Cf. pp. 67-93. The edition kept by the *mudang* is: *Sim Ch'yŏng chyŏn*, published by Hyangminsa. In 1982, I bought in Kangnŭng an identical edition, from the same publisher, dated 1978. This edition will be referred to as *HSC*.
20. Apart from *PC* and *SSC* (see note 14 and note 28), a version sung by Han Aesun, published in *Han'guk kubi munhak sŏnjip*, 238-259 (*PH*) and a text in Yi Ch'angbae (comp.), *Han'guk kach'ang taegye*, Vol. I, 492-530 (*PY*).
21. In every instance the *Sim Ch'ŏng kut* was observed during the Tano Festival in Kangnŭng, which is held annually around the fifth day of the fifth month according to the lunar calendar.
22. Examples of similar descriptions can be found in *AA* I, 43 and 212.
23. Yi Nŭngu, *Ko-sosŏl yŏn'gu*, 291.
24. *NSC*, 83; *KTG* I, 296.
25. *KTG* I, 298.

26.   *KTG* I, 300.

27.   *KTG* I, 279, 283, 286, 303.

28.   *SSC* (=Kang Hanyŏng (ed.), *Sin Chaehyo p'ansori sasŏl chip*), p. 160-161; *WSC*, *kwŏn* I:4a; also in the so-called *Songdong-bon* edition of the novel: cf. Ch'oe Unsik, *Sim Ch'ŏng chŏn yŏn'gu*, 29.

29.   *KTG* I, 326; *NSC*, 170.

30.   Speaking about a *p'ansori* version of *SC* Chŏng Pyŏnguk has called this part of the story the most essential part, the "yolk", of *SC* (*P'ansori*, 149). For the Hsiao and Hsiang Rivers, see Ch. V, Other Themes 10.

31.   E.g., the reference to Koguryŏ and Silla; *KTG*, 340. Cf. *PH*, 259.

32.   *SSC*, 247; *PC*, 355; *PH*, 259; *PY*, 529.

33.   Cf., for example, *KTG* I, 276.

34.   Other narrative *muga* by Pyŏn Yŏnho are the *Sejon kut* (*KTG* I, 251-279) and *Sonnim kut* (*KTG* I, 345-357 and *THM*, 240-265).

35.   *YIM* I in Sin Tongik, "Muga 'Sim Ch'ŏng chŏn'", *YIM* II in Yi Kyŏngbok, *Sim Ch'ŏng kut yŏn'gu*, *YIM* III in *HKMT* 7-7. Cf. note 11.

36.   Sin Tongik, "Muga '*SC* chŏn'", 115-117.

37.   *PC*, 336-338; *PH*, 249-251; *PY*, 512-513.

38.   Sin Tongik, "Muga '*SC* chŏn'", 117; *NSC*, 191.

39.   Sin, "Muga '*SC* chŏn'", 94.

40.   Sin, "Muga '*SC* chŏn'", 101; *PC*, 318.

41.   Sin, "Muga '*SC* chŏn'", 108.

42.   *PC*, 327. Cf. also *PH*, 245 and *PY*, 505.

43.   The name of Magu (Chinese: Ma Ku), an immortal in Chinese story and legend, often appears in *muga*. Vide *THM*, 375; *AA*, 106 and 109; *MSs*, 293, 326, 338, 360, 362. "Ch'ŏnt'aesŏng" should be Ch'ŏnt'ae-san, the name of the mountain which is Magu's abode. Cf. Ch. VIII, annotations to line 732 of the translation. Sin Sŏngnam in the corresponding passages of her *SC kut* mentions the fox and Magu, and Yang Kuei-fei as well: *HKMT* 2-1, p. 826. Certain "mistakes" are taken over by other *mudang* and gain a wider currency. Magu is also mentioned by Kim Sŏkch'ul: Sim Usŏng, "Sim Ch'ŏng kut", 208.

44.   Also, however, in *NSC*.

45.   Sin Tongik, "Muga '*SC* chŏn'", 98, 99. This detail is also found in the text of Sin Sŏngnam: *HKMT* 2-1, p. 785.

46.   *PC* and *PY* in this respect resemble *NSC* and *SSC*.

47.   *PC*, 317. Also in *HKMT* 2-1, p. 786.

48.   In *YIM* I it is mainly the "Song of the Hsiao and Hsiang Rivers" -with succeeding passages- which contains much Sino-Korean.

49.   *Han'guk siga*, 310.

50. Cf. details of the conversation between Ppaengdŏk-ŏmi and Sim Hakkyu; *Han'guk siga*, 317 and *PY*, 524.
51. *Han'guk siga*, 316; *NSC*, 216.
52. *Han'guk siga*, 320-321. This gives the *Sim Ch'ŏng kut* a clear religious purpose and gainsays the opinion that it is nothing but entertainment.
53. *Han'guk siga*, 306; *NSC*, 90.
54. *Han'guk siga*, 306.
55. *THM*, 176-177.
56. E.g., *NSC*, 83: *hwanggŭm kat'ŭn skoeskori-nŭn yangnyu-gan-ŭro nara tŭlgo* and *THM*, 177: *hwanggŭm kat'ŭna kkoekkori-nŭnga yangyugang-ŭro hŭllŏ kago* (sic). Such corruptions are common in all cases where material from the novel has been used, additional proof that the *mudang* borrowed from the novel and that it was not the novel which underwent the influence of the *muga*.
57. *THM*, 180; *NSC*, 90.
58. *THM*, 182; *NSC*, 95.
59. *THM*, 189; *NSC*, 102.
60. *THM*, 213; *NSC*, 171.
61. E.g., *THM*, 214 (*aengdu ttago nodŭn il*); *PH*, 249; *PC*, 335; *PY*, 510.
62. *THM*, 226-227; *PC*, 347.
63. *THM*, 228-229; *PC*, 349; *PH*, 256; *PY*, 526.
64. See note 32.
65. *Han'guk siga*, 318; Sin, "Muga '*SC* chŏn'", 121; Sim Usŏng, "*SC* kut", 218.
66. *THM*, 86 and 201.
67. *THM*, 140, 242, 380; *KTG*, I, 290.
68. *THM*, 237 and 398.
69. *THM*, 69; *YIM* I, 124-125.
70. *THM*, 184-186; she uses the same material elsewhere: *THM*, 383 (*Paridegi kut*); *PAM*, 307.
71. *THM*, 179. Cf. *THM*, 92 and 357; also *AA* I, 9.
72. *THM*, 181.
73. *THM*, 183.
74. *THM*, 196.
75. *THM*, 180; this joke is used for other occasions as well: *THM*, 231 and 259 (*Paridegi kut*). It is a variation of a joke her father, Kim Sŏkch'ul, uses.
76. *THM*, 203-204.
77. *THM*, 210.
78. *KTG*, IV, 22-23.
79. Chang Chugŭn and Ch'oe Kilsŏng, *Kyŏnggi-do musok*, 176-182 (from the Yangju *mudang*) and *AA* I, 569.

80. Sim Usŏng, "Sim Ch'ŏng kut", 221.
81. *KTG* IV, 61-62.
82. *HKMT* 2-1, pp. 781-785.
83. *THM*, 73.
84. Sŏ Taesŏk, *Muga-ŭi yŏn'gu*, 218-219. He regards this as an indication that the scene was borrowed from *p'ansori*. A close comparison of the *muga*, the *p'ansori* text to which Sŏ Taesŏk refers (Yi Hyegu, Sŏng Kyŏngnin, Yi Ch'angbae, *Kugak taejŏn*, 356) and *NSC* reveals, however, that the *muga* is closer to *NSC* than to *p'ansori*.
85. *THM*, 355; *NSC*, 94.
86. *THM*, 359, *NSC*, 94.
87. *THM*, 369-370; *NSC*, 121.
88. *THM*, 394; *NSC*, 95.
89. *KTG* IV, 109; *NSC*, 90.
90. *THM*, 315; *NSC*, 136.
91. Kim T'aegon, *Hwangch'ŏn muga*, 124-155, esp. 154-155.
92. Kim T'aegon, *Hwangch'ŏn muga*, 149-150.
93. Cf. Frits Vos, "Tung-fang Shuo, Buffoon and Immortal, in Japan and Korea."
94. It is only after this had been written that I read a long article by Sa Chaedong, "Sim Ch'ŏng chŏn yŏn'gu sŏsŏl." Sa persuasively argues that the story of Sim Ch'ŏng is indeed of Buddhist origin and that the Seoul version is its oldest written version.
95. *Koryŏ taejanggyŏng*, Vol. XIII, 193.
96. *Chōsen jisatsu shiryō*, comp. by Chōsen Sōtokufu, 244-247.
97. Kim Tonguk, *Kayo-ŭi yŏn'gu*, 381-382.
98. For a survey of early Buddhist tales see Sa Chaedong, *Pulgyo-gye kungmun sosŏr-ŭi hyŏngsŏng kwajŏng yŏn'gu*.
99. Respectively, *Wŏrin sŏkpo* XXIII:72a-91b, *Wŏrin sŏkpo* XXI:19a-29b and *Wŏrin sŏkpo* XXII:213a-223b.
100. Interestingly, there are versions of the Pari kongju *muga* in which the girl, when she is abandoned, is put into a stone chest and thrown into the sea as a sacrifice to the Dragon King. Cf. Dieter Eikemeier, "Wohin gehen Koreaner nach dem Tod?", 97, 104-106.
101. *Sŏkpo sangjŏl* XI:24a-36b and *Wŏrin sŏkpo* VIII:89b-103b.
102. *Sŏkka yŏrae sipchi suhaeng ki*, 14a-24a and *Wŏrin sŏkpo* XXII: 26b-53b.
103. Skillend, "Puritas Submersa Resurgit", 136. Skillend has pointed out, however, that the final part of the Seoul edition contains no Buddhist elements at all. If the story is indeed of Buddhist origin, the Seoul version about which Skillend has written, is already some way removed from the original tale.

104.   *Kwanbuk muga* I, 28-51. The name Kamch'ŏngi seems to be a corruption of Sino-Korean *kamch'ŏn*, "to move Heaven" (by one's sincerity, *chisŏng*); cf. Han Sangsu, *Ch'ungnam mindam*, p. 113. For a folk-tale variant of the story of Kamch'ŏngi see pp. 123-127 of this collection.

105.   *Samguk yusa*, ed. by Ch'oe Namsŏn, 89-91 (*kwŏn* II, "Chinsŏng yŏ-wang . Kŏt'aji").

NOTES TO CHAPTER VIII

1.   Several etymologies have been suggested for Sŏngju, which also occurs in the variant form of Sŏngjo, the alternation of o and u being a common phenomenon in Korean. In these pages, "Sŏngju" will be used throughout, except when the variant form is of importance for the argument. "Sŏngjo" (as opposed to Sŏngju) can be written with two characters that mean "to make" and "to construct", which is thought to be appropriate by many, because in a number of Sŏngju *muga* the construction of a house is described and in other songs Sŏngju appears as a prototypical carpenter. (Cf. Yi Nŭnghwa, "Musok ko", 54.) These characters are used to write the name of this deity in a comparatively old source, the *Tongguk sesi ki* of 1849 (text in Kang Muhak, *Han'guk sesi p'ungsok*, 303), as well as in *mugyŏng* (*AA* II, "Furoku: fukyō", p. 57, pp. 64-65). Nevertheless it is difficult to accept that this is the true etymology of the name. Sŏngju (as opposed to Sŏngjo) can be written with characters that mean "Lord of a Castle" or with characters meaning "Sage Ruler." The latter possibility has been suggested by Ch. Haguenauer ("Sorciers et sorcières de Corée", 29). It will be remembered that in a *sijo*, "Sŏngju" was used in the meaning of "Sage Ruler", although *mudang* interpreted the name in this context to be that of the god (see Ch. III). This does not amount to etymological proof, but derivation from Sŏngju: "Sage Ruler", has at least the advantage of a certain plausibility. Kim T'aegon suggests that Sŏngju is a corruption of Sangju: "Lord-on-High" (*Musok yŏn'gu*, p. 281, note 5), an interpretation inspired, it seems, by the heavenly origin of Sŏngju as assumed by some scholars. For none of the theories concerning the etymology of Sŏngju there is conclusive evidence.

2.   *KTG* I, 357.

3.   *HKMT* 2-2, p. 312.

4. Yi Nŭnghwa, "Musok ko", 54-55.
5. Guillemoz, *Les algues, les anciens, les dieux*, 171 and 258-260.
6. *AA* II, 161.
7. *KTG* I, 145.
8. Son Chint'ae, *Shinka ihen*, 208-209.
9. *AA* I, 194.
10. Perhaps the list begins with "seventeen" because this was the age to get married.
11. *AA* II, 161.
12. *AA* II, 77, 82.
13. *Cheju sajŏn*, 466.
14. A reference to the government examination system, which was abolished in 1894.
15. *Cheju sajŏn* interprets this as "spirit horse."
16. *Sin Chaehyo*, 665.
17. Ch'oe Kilsŏng, "Musog-e issŏsŏ 'chip'-kwa 'yŏsŏng'", 101.
18. *AA* I, 205.
19. *KTG* II, 244.
20. "Sŏngju p'uri", *Munhwajae* IV, performed by Kwŏn Hoyong, recorded by Ch'oe Kilsŏng, 132.
21. Kim T'aegon, "Muga-ŭi chŏnsŭng pyŏnhwa ch'egye", 1-24. For the heavenly origin of Sŏngju, see also Yu Tongsik, *Mugyo-ŭi yŏksa-wa kujo*, 302.
22. Kim T'aegon, "Sŏngju sinang ko", 204.
23. Kim T'aegon, *Musok yŏn'gu*, 288-289. The *mudang* is Sim Poksun from Wŏnan.
24. *KTG* I, 286.
25. For other examples of this motif see *KTG* III, 79-92 (*Kungsangi kut*) and *Minyo chip* I, 62.
26. Son Chint'ae, *Shinka ihen*, 87-88.
27. Vincent S.R. Brandt, *A Korean Village*, 20-21; John Embree, *A Japanese Village*, 93-95; K. Ruitenbeek, *Bouwbedrijf en bouwmagie in het traditionele China*, 26-27 or Ruitenbeek, *The Lu Ban Ching*.
28. Son Chint'ae, *Shinka ihen*, 209.
29. There seems to be a special link between Sŏngju and the number three (cf. the thirty-three workmen who build the house in *Hwangje p'uri*), for which, however, I am unable to tender an explanation.
30. *AA* II, 161.
31. Yi Nŭnghwa, "Musok ko", 54; Yi Tuhyŏn a.o., *Han'guk minsokhak kaesŏl*, 166.
32. In this ritual as performed by the *mudang* who also sang the *Hwangje p'uri* translated in the present chapter, there are songs for Chesŏk,

Sŏngju, Taegam, Chisin, T'ŏju, the Gate-Guarding General, the deity of the privy and the *kŏllip*: *AA* I, 193-201.

33. Yi Tuhyŏn a.o., *Han'guk minsokhak kaesŏl*, 167.
34. Guillemoz, *Les algues, les anciens, les dieux*, 171.
35. Yi Tuhyŏn a.o., *Han'guk minsokhak kaesŏl*, 229-232.
36. One Sŏngju *muga* of this type has been translated (in an abbreviated version) into English: *The Folk Treasury of Korea*, 74-80.
37. E.g., *KTG* III, 185 and 297. Cf. Kim T'aegon, "Chŏnsŭng pyŏnhwa", 6-7.
38. Son Chint'ae, *Shinka ihen*, 79-176.
39. Cf. *THM*, 280; Son Chint'ae, *Shinka ihen*, 1; *AA* I, 257, 271, 369, 370; *MSs*, 75; *KTG* I, 367 and *KTG* IV, 30-31 (Koreanized!); cf. Ch. V.
40. Such fixed phrases to indicate the passing of several years probably are used in the formulaic narratives from many countries. In an old Turkish work, *The Book of Dede Korkut* (translation by Geoffrey Lewis, p. 30) there is a description of a hero, who has been born to aged parents after special prayers (cf. Sim Ch'ŏng!). First it is told how good-looking he was as a baby, then the years until he becomes fifteen are bridged by the formula: "The horse's hoof is fleet as the wind,/ The minstrel's tongue is swift as a bird."
41. *Sin Chaehyo*, 548-551. Dutch translation in B.C.A. Walraven (transl.), *De redder der armen*, 161-162.
42. *NSC*, 175-188; Chŏng Pyŏnguk, *P'ansori*, 338-339.
43. Original text and English translation in *Three Hundred Poems of the T'ang Dynasty*, transl. by Witter Bynner, 4.
44. Sim Usŏng, *Minsokkŭk*, 66.
45. Chang Sahun, *Kugak ch'ongnon*, 337.
46. *Sin Chaehyo*, 32 and 665-667; Pak Hwang, *P'ansori sosa*, 87.
47. Kim Sŏngbae, *Hyangdu ka . Sŏngjo ka*.
48. It is possible that the present-day farmers' bands have taken over this function from the -now extinct- *kŏllip-p'ae*, who were, if not religiously inspired like the *mudang*, at least religiously affiliated (with Buddhist temples).
49. Kim Sŏngbae, *Han'gug-ŭi minsok*, 301. This woman, before she undertook the task, would ritually purify herself. From this it appears that, for some of the tasks usually performed by the *mudang*, the distinguishing characteristic of the *mudang*, the ability to communicate directly with the supernatural world, is not a sine-qua-non.
50. *AA* II, 162-163.
51. Such coins are described in Yu Chahu, *Han'guk pyŏlchŏn ko*. Cf. also Ramsden, *Corean Coin Charms and Amulets* and Frederick Starr, "Korean Charms and Amulets."

52. Guillemoz, *Les algues, les anciens, les dieux*, 173-174.
53. The *Hwangje p'uri* in *KTG* I, 88-102 is a version taken from a Seoul *mudang*, while Chang Chugŭn and Ch'oe Kilsŏng in their *Kyŏnggi-do musok*, 172-175, present a Hwangje *muga* from Yangju. A *muga* with almost the same contents from P'och'ŏn, also in Kyŏnggi Province, is called *Sŏngju p'uri* (in *Munhwajae* IV, 131-140 (1969); the singer was a male shaman, Kwŏn Hoyong, the text was recorded by Ch'oe Kilsŏng).
54. E.T.C. Werner, *A Dictionary of Chinese Mythology*, 186.
55. H. Doré, *Recherches sur les superstitions en Chine*, IIème Partie, Tôme XI, 902.
56. *Sangyong ŭibŏm*, 99b-100a.
57. *AA* I, 281, 300.
58. *Sin Chaehyo*, 665. The phrase from *Hŭngbu chŏn* is cited in Im Tonggwŏn, *Han'guk minyo sa*, 176.
59. For similar phrases, see *KTG* I, 88; *KTG* IV, 95; *Munhwajae* IV, 131; *Pulgyo kasa*, 476.
60. A *mugyŏng* for Sŏngju has "Sŏngju maeil kaksin": *AA* II, "Furoku: fukyō", 57.
61. *Sangyong ŭibŏm*, 7a-b.
62. Im Tonggwŏn, *Minyo sa*, 176.
63. *Sin Chaehyo*, 665.
64. Cf. *AA* I, 118: *puri-yŏngsan-ŭn chosang yŏngsan*.
65. Cf. Laurel Kendall, "Wood Imps, Ghosts and Other Noxious Influences: The Ideology of Affliction in a Korean Village", 134.
66. *KTG* I, 102; Yi Nŭnghwa, "Musok ko", 55.
67. For the history of geomancy in Korea see Vos, *Religionen*, 129.
68. *THM*, 123. While *p'ungsu* and shamanism were almost completely independent, Buddhism, in practice if not in theory, had close links with geomancy. Tosŏn (827-868), the first great geomancer of Korea, was a monk, as were many *p'ungsu* masters of later generations. Muhak, the adviser of Yi T'aejo, is an example.
69. *P'ungsu* in the *muga*: *AA* I, 172, 211, 257; *KTG* I, 107-108, 156, 279-283; *KTG* III, 50; *THM*, 159-165; *Kwanbuk muga* I, 38, 139; *Hanguk siga*, 338; *HMCCP Kyŏngnam*, 204, 207; *HMCCP Chŏnnam*, 198. For Korean geomancy also see Hong-key Yoon, *Geomantic Relationships Between Nature and Culture in Korea*.
70. For the folk-songs, see *Minyo chip* I, 242 and *Minyo chip* III, 340-342.
71. Sim Usŏng, *Minsokkŭk*, 114; *Minyo chip* I, 242; *Minyo chip* III, 340.
72. E.g., *MSs*, 364, 365, 386; Sim Usŏng, "Sonnim kut", 190.
73. Cf. Cho, *Werdegang*, 110-111, where the water of the highest pool is used to offer to the gods.

74. *Pulgyo kasa*, 498; *T'alch'um taesa chip*, 260; another example in the *muga* is *AA* I, 147.
75. E.g., *Sangyong ŭibŏm*, 99b-100a.
76. *Munhwajae* IV, 133.
77. *Sin Chaehyo*, 665.
78. Cho, *Werdegang*, 224, 331.
79. Yi Nŭnghwa, "Musok ko", 47.
80. *AA* I, 29.
81. Cf. *Pae pijang chŏn*, 16.
82. *Sijo sajŏn*, No. 801.
83. Examples of this theme in *sijo*, *ko-sosŏl* and *p'ansori*: *Sijo sajŏn* No. 801; *NSC*, 191; *Pae pijang chŏn*, 18-19; *Sin Chaehyo*, 194-195.
84. Cf. *KTG* I, 142.
85. Kim Chiha, *Kim Chiha chŏnjip*, 164.
86. Clark, *Religions of Old Korea*, 203.
87. *Sin Chaehyo*, 666.
88. *Sin Chaehyo*, 666.
89. Gale, "Han-Yang (Seoul)", 1-43.
90. Allen D. Clark and Donald N. Clark, *Seoul: Past and Present*, 156.
91. *Kasa chŏnjip*, 557. Cf. *AA* I, 150, 257; *KTG* III, 305; *KTG* IV, 30; *THM*, 164; *Han'guk siga*, 338; Kim Sŏngbae, *Hyangdu ka . Sŏngjo ka*, 45, 53, 56, 58, 191-192 (this sequence is part of both the pall-bearers' and the Sŏngju folk-songs).
92. *Namwŏn kosa*, 51.
93. Pak Sŏngŭi (ed.), *Nongga wŏllyŏng ka . Hanyang ka*, 9-18.
94. For the terminology in these lines see: Yoon, *Geomantic relationships*, 34-39.
95. Yoon, *Geomantic relationships*, 78.
96. Murayama Chijun, *Chōsen no fusui*, 17.
97. *Sin Chaehyo*, 666.
98. *Hanyang ka*, 78-81.
99. Yoon, *Geomantic relationships*, 34.
100. Kim Sŏngbae, *Han'gug-ŭi minsok*, 285-311.
101. *Hanyang ka*, 96-97.
102. Kim Tonguk, *Kayo-ŭi yŏn'gu*, 333; *Namwŏn kosa*, 132, 140.
103. Cf. *AA* I, 170; *KTG* II, 143; *CCM*, 247; *Namwŏn kosa*, 132.
104. *Han'guk minhwa*, 215.
105. *AA* I, 153; *KTG* III, 57.
106. Herbert A. Giles, *A Chinese Biographical Dictionary*, 101.
107. Yi Nŭnghwa, "Musok ko", 58; Doré, *Recherches sur les superstitions en Chine*, IIème Partie, Tôme XI, 976; Wu Ch'eng-en, *Journey to the West*, Vol. I, Chapter Ten.

108. Vos, *Religionen*, 149-150.
109. *KTG* I, 120; *KTG* III, 206; *Namwŏn kosa*, 134-137; *Pae pijang chŏn*, 23; *Maehwa chŏn*, 283; *Sin Chaehyo* (section "Pak t'aryŏng"), 378-379; Sim Usŏng, *Minsokkŭk*, 344; Yi Tuhyŏn, *Kamyŏn'gŭk*, 317.
110. *KTG* III, 307; *KTG* IV, 46; *Han'guk siga*, 290. For the place of the pot-de-chambre in Korean culture, *vide* B.C.A. Walraven, "Blinkend als de Morgenster", 51-56.
111. *Sin Chaehyo*, 598-599.
112. E.g., *KTG*, IV, 85; *THM*, 155.
113. *AA* I, 176, 355.
114. *Sin Chaehyo*, 376-377.
115. *Pae pijang chŏn . Ong Kojip chŏn*, 23, 115.
116. *Hanyang ka*, 114-115.
117. Cf. the use of a verse by Wang Wei as an introductory phrase for a willow flower in *Namwŏn kosa*, 56.
118. *AA* I, 172-180.
119. *HMCCP Kyŏngbuk*, 212.
120. *HMCCP Kyŏngbuk*, 183-184.
121. In another *muga* for Sŏngju (*Munhwajae* IV, 138) Chu-ko Liang is in fact coupled with Sleeping-Dragon silk.
122. Sŏk Chusŏn, *Han'guk poksik sa*, 146, 161.
123. *AA* I, 199; *KTG* I, 100.
124. *AA* I, 199.
125. Yu Ch'angdon, *Ko-sijo sinsŏk*, No. 618 and No. 598.
126. E.g., Kim Sŏngbae, *Hyangdu ka . Sŏngjo ka*, 138.
127. *AA* I, 105-106.
128. For an English translation, see Adrian Buzo, "Koryŏ Kayo: Songs of the Koryŏ Period", 36-37.
129. Pihl, "Bardic Tradition", 36.
130. *Koryŏ sa*, Vol. II, 468-469 (*kwŏn* 71).
131. Except for some modernistic additions such as the East Coast *mudang* frequently make to the old themes. After *Sohak* ("Learning for the Small", the *Hsiao hsüeh* by Chu Hsi) *chunghak* (Junior High-School) is added; *THM*, 153. The addition of items that are related to the preceding more by sound than by meaning is often observed in the *muga*.
132. Doré, *Superstitions*, IIème Partie, Tôme XII, 1124-1125.
133. *AA* I, 106, 509; *MSs*, 293, 326, 338, 360, 362 (here she is the same as Chowang halmŏni, the Kitchen-Goddess); *THM*, 375; Chin Sŏnggi, *Namgug-ŭi sŏsa si*, 228; *CCM*, 281.
134. *AA* I, 78, 121.
135. Yi Nŭnghwa, "Musok ko", 7, 76.

136. *AA* II, 75.
137. *KTG* I, 47.
138. *HMCCP Kyŏnggi*, 109, also pp. 111 and 117.
139. *AA* I, 118.

NOTES TO CHAPTER IX

1. Cf. G.M. Wassiljewitsch, "Schamanengesänge der Ewenken (Tungu-sen)", 381-404.
2. An exception to this is found in Son Chint'ae, "Chōsen fugeki no shin-ka (3)", 134, in a *muga* from P'yŏngan Province.
3. A form of self-description is also found in some *muga* where *mudang* describe the rituals they perform. In a ceremony from Pyongyang, for instance, there is a description of a *mudang* mounting the sharp edge of a pair of straw-cutters, one of the extraordinary feats the *mudang* are able to perform when possessed by the gods; *KTG* III, 58. In a *kut* from Kyŏnggi Province one even finds, in one *muga*, a short description of all the parts of a complete ceremony: *AA* I, 148-163. None of these *muga* tells anything about the life of a *mudang* however.
4. Yi Hŭisŭng (comp.), *Kugŏ tae-sajŏn*, 3rd. ed.
5. Akiba Takashi, "Fujin kotsuryū no uta", 92.
6. *THM*, 34.
7. *AA* I, 180. This apparently refers to the practice that a junior *mudang* takes over the *tan'gol* of a senior *mudang*.
8. Akiba, "Kotsuryū", 96. During the later Chosŏn dynasty *mudang* and entertainers were organised by province. Kyonggi Province was sub-divided in two, a Circuit of the Right and a Circuit of the Left. The same lines are also found in a more recently recorded *muga*; *KTG* II, 278.
9. *AA* II, 55-61; Youngsook Kim Harvey, *Six Korean Women*, 235-240.
10. *AA* II, 48-50.
11. The Buryat shaman, too, during initiation visits homes and receives offerings; *AA* II, 65.
12. *KTG* III, 211.
13. *Cheju sajŏn*, 288, 758, 778, and 843.
14. *Dictionnaire Coréen-francais, par les missionnaires de Corée.*
15. *AA* I, 180-182.
16. *KTG* II, 278-279.

17.   *KTG* I, 360-364.
18.   *HMCCP Chŏnbuk*, 143.
19.   *THM*, 266-279.
20.   *KTG* III, 313-314.
21.   *KTG* III, 210-211.
22.   *Han'guk siga*, 332-334.
23.   *HKMT* 2-3, pp. 618-658.
24.   Vos, *Religionen*, 68-69.
25.   E.g., *KTG* I, 250, 341 and 345.
26.   E.g., *THM*, 390: *alttŭri salttŭri* and *Cheju sajŏn*, 192 and 197: *kanan hago sŏnan hanan* and *miyŏjibengdwi manyŏjibengdwi*.
27.   Yi Nŭnghwa, "Musok ko", 44, 73. She is also called Sŏngmo Ch'ŏnwang; see Vos, *Religionen*, 82.
28.   For the importance of the drum to the *mudang* see the text of this *muga*.
29.   Kim T'aegon, *Musok yŏn'gu*, 77, 360; *AA* II, 68.
30.   Son Chint'ae, "Fugeki no shinka (3)", 134.
31.   Cho Hung-youn, *Koreanischer Schamanismus*, 27. For a concrete example see *AA* II, 55.
32.   In E, the term used for this kind of begging is *siju kŏllip hada*, in this context equivalent to *kyemyŏn tolda*. *Siju kŏllip* is a term of Buddhist derivation, meaning a house-to-house visit to ask for alms. *Siju* may mean "benefactor/almsgiver" as well as "donation/offering." It is the translation of the Sanskrit *dānapati*, "almsgiver", which is rendered phonetically in Sino-Korean as *tanwŏl*. If one keeps in mind that it is largely through alms rounds that Buddhist temples and *mudang* establish a regular "clientèle", and further remembers that on Cheju Island the regular customers of a *mudang* are called *tan'gwŏl*, it is reasonable to assume that *tan'gol* is derived from *tanwŏl*. Another example of the insertion of *g* after *n* is found in *tan'gida*, a variant form of *tanida*, "to go to and from." As the etymology of *tanida* is undisputed (*tat* + *nida*) it is evident that in *tan'gida* the *g* has been inserted and that *tan'gida* does not reflect an older form of this verb. Another possible example of *g* inserted after *n* is found in Yu Ch'angdon, *ŏhŭi-sa yŏn'gu*, 46. An alternative explanation of the *g* in *tan'gol* is that it is due to the regressive influence of the *g* in the common combination *tanwŏlga*, "a household of believers", which may be abbreviated to *tan'ga*. Less plausible etymologies have been put forward by Ch'oe Namsŏn (*Yuktang Ch'oe Namsŏn chŏnjip*, Vol. II, 336), who supposes a relation with Tan'gun and the Mongol word *tengri*, "heaven", and by Samuel E. Martin (Samuel E. Martin, Yang Ha Lee and Sung Un Chang, *A Korean-English Dictionary, 394*), who takes it as a combination of *tan*,

"single", and *kol(s)*, "channel/route." Derivation from *tan'wŏl* (without supporting evidence as given above) was proposed by Murayama Chijun, *Chōsen no fugeki*, 489-490.

33. *KTG* I, 313.
34. Murayama, *Chōsen no fugeki*, 477, 478, 480, 482; *KTG* III, 152.
35. *Han'guk siga*, 334.
36. *Minyo chip* I, 63-67.
37. Cho Tongil, *Sŏsa minyo yŏn'gu*, 218-226; Type: *uri sŏnbi*.
38. Cho Tongil, *Sŏsa minyo yŏn'gu*, 220, 221, 229.
39. *Minyo chip* I, 66; in Chinese characters, which were, no doubt, added by the editor.
40. Ch'oe T'aeho, *Naebang kasa*, e.g., p. 276: *Ongnanggang hŭrŭn mur-e*.
41. *Minyo chip* I, 62.
42. *Minyo chip* I, 80.
43. Cho Tongil, *Sŏsa minyo yŏn'gu*, 224.
44. *KTG* I, 367: *nangge = namu-e*.
45. E.g., *AA* I, 241, 568.
46. Correct in some folk-songs: *Minyo chip* II, 143; Cho Tongil, *Sŏsa minyo yŏn'gu*, 224.
47. *Minyo chip* I, 62.
48. *Han'guk siga*, 333.
49. *Minyo chip* I, 64.
50. E.g., *AA* I, 195.
51. *THM*, 155.
52. *HMCCP Kyŏngbuk*, 183.
53. *Han'guk siga*, 334.
54. *AA* II, 299.
55. *AA* II, 302.
56. Ch'oe Hakkŭn (comp.), *Han'guk pangŏn sajŏn*, 1283.
57. E.g., *KTG* III, 264.
58. Cf. *HKMT*, 2-3, 643.
59. *Han'guk akki taegwan*, 128; Howard, *Korean Musical Instruments*, 123, 125-126.
60. Chang Chugŭn and Ch'oe Kilsŏng, *Kyŏnggi-do musok*, 124.
61. *THM*, 299.
62. Yi Nŭnghwa, *Chosŏn Togyo sa*, tr. by Yi Chongha, 118-119.
63. Choi Inhak, *Type Index*, Type 730.
64. Cf. *Cheju sajŏn*, 143 and Ch. I of this book.
65. *AA* II, 76-77.
66. *KTG* II, 214; *KTG* III, 346 and *AA* I, 216, where, incidentally, the Japanese translation has the wrong character for the family name.
67. *THM*, 299.

68. See *AA* II, Plate 145.
69. Tsukamoto Yoshitaka (comp.), *Bukkyō daijiten.*
70. *AA* I, 496.
71. *Cheju sajŏn*, 72, 11O, 173.
72. Kim Yŏngil, "Musok sinhwa-ŭi hyŏngsŏng ko", 78.
73. *Cheju sajŏn*, 767-77O.
74. Cf. Sŏ Taesŏk, *Muga-ŭi yŏn'gu*, 19-198.
75. *Cheju sajŏn* has only the story about the drum etc., not the story about the girl.
76. Son Chint'ae, "Fugeki no shinka (3)", 133-137.

NOTES TO APPENDIX II

1. According to Lord, *The Singer of Tales*, 47, one word in the same position in the line with other lines or half-lines may be sufficient to make a line "formulaic", if it conforms to the basic patterns of rhythm and syntax. It is unclear whether this implies that all verses which have this one word in the same position belong to one and the same system. In my opinion, it is good to note the kinship of systems such as B I and B II, but they should not be integrated. Cf. also B III.
2. "Parry [observed] that once a singer was aware of a phrase as a type, the representative of the type could well lead him unconsciously to coin new phrases strictly upon the old models. Doubtless the singer would be guided in analogical manufacture mostly by meter, syntax and idea, but also by sound": Ann C. Watts, *The Harp and the Lyre*, 31.
3. E.g., *Shinka ihen*, 79: *irwŏl sŏngsin chorim hani/nal-gwa tar-i palga itko.*
4. Resp., *Sin Chaehyo*, 598-599; *Sijo sajŏn*, No. 817; Sim Usŏng, *Minsokkŭk*, 237.
5. Cf. the section on parallelism in Chapter V.
6. Chŏng, *P'ansori*, 356.
7. *Han'guk siga*, 314.

Bibliography

Only works cited in the text or the notes have been listed. For the purpose of alphabetization no distinction has been made between aspirated and unaspirated consonants, or between vowels with or without breve or macron.

A: Works in Korean, Japanese and Chinese

Akamatsu Chijō and Akiba Takashi: *Chōsen fuzoku no kenkyū*, 2 vols., Ōsaka yagō shoten (Keijō, 1937-1938).

Akchang kasa, Taejegak (facsimile ed. in the series Han'guk kojŏn ch'ongsŏ, Vol. II: Seoul, 1973).

Akiba Takashi: "Fujin kotsuryū no uta", *Seikyū gakusō* VI, 99-100 (1931).

---: *Chōsen fuzoku no genchi kenkyū*, Yōtokusha (Tamba-shi, 1950).

Allakkuk chŏn: see Kim Kidong, *Chosŏn pulgyo sosŏl sŏn*.

Andong munhwa-kwŏn haksul chosa pogosŏ, comp. by Sŏnggyun'gwan Taehakkyo kugŏ kungmunhakkwa (Seoul, 1971).

Chang Chiyŏng (ed.): *Hong Kiltong chŏn . Sim Ch'ŏng chŏn*, Chŏngŭmsa (Seoul, 1964).

Chang Chugŭn: "Sŏsa muga-ŭi siwŏn-gwa minsok yesulsa-sang-ŭi wich'i", *Munhwa illyuhak* V, 5-31 (1972).

---: *Kankoku no minkan shinkō*, 2 vols.: *ronkō-hen*, *shiryō-hen*, Kinkasha (Tōkyō, 1973).

---: *Han'gug-ŭi hyangt'o sinang*, Ŭryu munhwasa (Seoul, 1975).

Chang Chugŭn, Ch'oe Kilsŏng: *Kyŏnggi-do chiyŏk musok*, Munhwajae kwalliguk (Seoul, 1967).

Chang Sahun: *Kugak non'go*, Seoul Taehakkyo ch'ulp'anbu (3rd ed.: Seoul, 1974).

---: *Kugak ch'ongnon*, Chŏngŭmsa (Seoul, 1976).

Chang Tŏksun, Cho Tongil, Sŏ Taesŏk, Cho Hŭiung: *Kubi munhak kaesŏl*, Ilchogak (2nd ed.: Seoul, 1973).

Chang Tŏksun: *Kungmunhak t'ongnon*, Sin'gu munhwasa (Seoul, 1977).

---: *Han'guk sŏrhwa munhak yŏn'gu*, Seoul Taehakkyo ch'ulp'anbu (Seoul, 1978).

Chin Sŏnggi: *Namgug-ŭi muga*, Cheju-do minsok munhwa yŏn'guso (reprint: Cheju-si, 1968).

---: *Namgug-ŭi musok sŏsa-si*, Chŏngŭmsa (Seoul, 1980).

Cho Tongil: *Sŏsa minyo yŏn'gu*, Kyemyŏng Taehakkyo ch'ulp'anbu (rev. and enl. ed.: Taegu, 1979).

Ch'oe Chŏngnyŏ, Sŏ Taesŏk: *Tonghaean muga*, Hyŏngsŏl ch'ulp'ansa (Seoul/Taegu, 1971).

Ch'oe Hakkŭn (comp.): *Han'guk pangŏn sajŏn*, Hyŏnmunsa (Seoul, 1978).

Ch'oe Kanghyŏn: "Kasa-ŭi palsaeng sa-jŏk yŏn'gu", *Sae kugŏ kyoyuk* XVIII-XX, 192-258 (1974).

Ch'oe Kilsŏng (comp.): "Sŏngju p'uri", *Munhwajae* IV, 131-140 (1969).

---: "Minsokkŭk-kwa musok sinang", *Munhwajae* V, 38-43 (1971).

---: "Muga Kŏri kut", *Sŏnangdang* III, 183-122 (1972).

---: *Han'guk musog-ŭi yŏn'gu*, Asea munhwasa (Seoul, 1978).

---: *Han'guk musok non*, Hyŏngsŏl ch'ulp'ansa (Seoul/Taegu, 1981).

Ch'oe Kilsŏng: "Musog-e issŏsŏ 'chip'-kwa 'yŏsŏng'", in Kim Inhoe a.o., *Han'guk musog-ŭi chonghap-chŏk koch'al*, 91-125.

Ch'oe Namsŏn: *Yuktang Ch'oe Namsŏn chŏnjip*, 15 vols., Hyŏnamsa (Seoul, 1973).

Ch'oe T'aeho: *Naebang kasa*, Hyŏngsŏl ch'ulp'ansa (Seoul/Taegu, 1980).

Ch'oe Unsik: *Sim Ch'ŏng chŏn yŏn'gu*, Chimmundang (Seoul, 1982).

Chŏng Nosik: *Chosŏn ch'anggŭk sa*, Chosŏn Ilbosa (Seoul, 1940).

Chŏng Pyŏnguk (comp.): *Han'guk sijo charyo sajŏn*, Sin'gu munhwasa (Seoul, 1966).

---: (ed. and annot. by -): *Pae pijang chŏn . Ong Kojip chŏn*, Sin'gu munhwasa (Seoul, 1974).

---: *Han'guk kojŏn siga-ron*, Sin'gu munhwasa (Seoul, 1977).

---: *Han'gug-ŭi p'ansori*, Chimmundang (Seoul, 1981).

Chŏng Tonghwa: *Han'guk minyo-ŭi sa-jŏk yŏn'gu*, Ilchogak (Seoul, 1981).

Chŏng Yagyŏng: *Chŏng Tasan chŏnjip*, 3 vols., ed. by Munhŏn p'yŏnch'an wiwŏnhoe (Seoul, 1961).

Chōsen jisatsu shiryō, comp. by Chōsen sōtokufu (reprint Kokusho kankōkai: Tōkyō, 1971).

Chosŏn munhwaŏ sajŏn, Sahoe kwahagwŏn ŏnŏhak yŏn'guso (Pyongyang, 1973).

Chosŏn wangjo sillok, (Reprint, ed. by Kuksa p'yŏnch'an wiwŏnhoe, 48 vols.: Seoul, 1955-1958).

Chungjong sillok: see *Chosŏn wangjo sillok*.

Han Sangsu, *Ch'ungnam mindam*, Hyŏngsŏl ch'ulp'ansa (Seoul, 1982).

Han'guk akki taegwan, comp. by Munhwajae kwalliguk (Seoul, 1969).

Han'guk kubi munhak sŏnjip, comp. by Chang Tŏksun, Kang Hanyŏng, Cho Tongil, Sŏ Taesŏk and Cho Hŭiung, Ilchogak (Seoul, 1977).

Han'guk kubi munhak taegye, comp. and publ. by Han'guk chŏngsin munhwa yŏn'guwŏn (Sŏngnam, 1980-).

Han'guk minhwa, Chungang Ilbosa (4th ed.: Seoul, 1980).

Han'guk minsok chonghap chosa pogosŏ, 12 vols., comp. and published by Munhwajae kwalliguk (Seoul, 1969-1981).

Hanyang ka, wood-block edition (1880), in the collection of the National Library, Seoul.

Hanyang ka: see also *Nongga wŏllyŏng ka . Hanyang ka.*

Hŏ Chun (comp.): *Tongŭi pogam*, Namsandang (reprint of the 1814 ed. in 2 vols.: Seoul, 1974).

Hong Kimun: *Chosŏn sinhwa yŏn'gu*, Sahoe kwahagwŏn ch'ulp'ansa (Pyongyang, 1964).

Hwang P'aegang: *Silla pulgyo sŏrhwa yŏn'gu*, Ilchisa (3rd ed.: Seoul, 1980).

Hyŏn Yongjun: *Cheju-do musok charyo sajŏn*, Sin'gu munhwasa (Seoul, 1980).

Im Hyŏngt'aek: "18.19 segi-ŭi 'iyagikkun'-gwa sosŏr-ŭi palsŏn", *Kojŏn munhag-ŭl chajasŏ*, ed. by Kim Yŏlgyu, Sŏ Chaeyŏng and Hwang P'aegang, Munhak-kwa chisŏngsa (2nd ed.: Seoul, 1976).

Im Sŏkchae: "Kankoku no fuzoku - gaisetsu", *Han* VIII, 3.4, pp. 3-57 (1979).

Im Sŏkchae, Chang Chugŭn: *Kwanbuk chibang muga* I, II, Munhwajae Kwalliguk (Seoul, 1965-66).

--- and Chang Chugŭn: *Kwansŏ chibang muga*, Munhwajae kwalliguk (Seoul, 1966).

Im Tonggwŏn: *Han'guk minyo sa*, Munch'angsa (Seoul, 1964).

Im Tonggwŏn: *Han'guk minyo yŏn'gu*, Sŏnmyŏng munhwasa (Seoul, 1974).

--- (comp.): *Han'guk minyo chip* I-VI, Chimmundang (Seoul, 1980-81).

In Kwŏnhwan: "Sim Ch'ŏng chŏn yŏn'gu-sa-wa kŭ munjetchŏm", *Han'guk hakpo* III,4, pp. 189-207 (1977).

---: *Han'guk minsokhak sa*, Yŏrhwadang (2nd ed.:Seoul, 1980).

Iryŏn: *Samguk yusa*, ed. by Ch'oe Namsŏn, Minjung sŏgwan (4th ed.: Seoul, 1971).

Kang Hanyŏng (ed.): *Sin Chaehyo p'ansori sasŏl chip (chŏn)*, Minjung sŏgwan (*Han'guk kojŏn munhak taegye* 12, 2nd ed.: Seoul, 1972).

Kang Muhak: *Han'guk sesi p'ungsok ki*, Tongho sŏgwan (Seoul, 1981).

Kim Chiha: *Kim Chiha chŏnjip*, comp. by Kim Chiha chŏnjip kanhaeng wiwŏnhoe, Hanyangsa (augmented 3rd ed.: Tōkyō, 1977).

Kim Chinu (Chin-W. Kim): "Sijo-ŭi unnyul kujo-ŭi sae koch'al", *Han'gŭl* 173/174, pp. 299-325 (1981).

Kim Chongu: "Sŏdong ka yŏn'gu", in Kim Yŏlgyu and Sin Tonguk (eds.), *Samguk yusa-wa munye-jŏk haemyŏng*, Saemunsa (Seoul, 1982), I, 61-73.

Kim Hŭnggyu: "Pansori no nigensei to shakai-teki haikei", *Han* VI, 7, pp. 76-113 (1977); original Korean version in *Changjak-kwa pip'yŏng* IX, 1 (1974).

Kim Ingyŏm: *Iltong changyu ka*, Asea munhwasa (facsimile ed.:Seoul, 1974).

Kim Inhoe a.o.: *Han'guk musok-ŭi chonghap-chŏk koch'al*, Koryŏ Taehakkyo minjung munhwa yŏn'guso (Seoul, 1962).

Kim Kidong (comp.): *Chosŏn pulgyo sosŏl sŏn*, Tongguk Taehakkyo pusŏl yŏkkyŏngwŏn (Seoul, 1979).

---: *Han'guk kojŏn sosŏl yŏn'gu*, Kyohaksa (Seoul, 1981).

Kim Pyŏngguk: "Kubi sŏsa-si-ro pon p'ansori sasŏr-ŭi kusŏng pangsik", *Han'guk hakpo* VIII, 2, pp. 120-149 (1982).

Kim Sŏngbae (comp.): *Hyangdu ka . Sŏngjo ka*, Chŏngŭmsa (Seoul, 1975).

---: *Han'gug-ŭi minsok*, Chimmundang (Seoul, 1980).

Kim Sŏngbae, Pak Noch'un, Yi Sangbo and Chŏng Iksŏp (comp.): *Kasa munhak chŏnjip*, Chŏngyŏnsa (Seoul, 1961).

Kim Sŏnp'ung: *Han'guk kayo-ŭi minsokhak-chŏk yŏn'gu*, Hyŏngsŏl ch'ulp'ansa (Seoul/Taegu, 1977).

---: "Ko Kim Sunhŭi-ŭi muga (1)", *Kubi munhak* III, 147-154 (1981).

Kim T'aegon: "Han'guk sindang yŏn'gu", *Kugŏ kungmunhak* XXIX, 67-99 (1965).

---: *Hwangch'ŏn muga yŏn'gu*, Ch'angusa (Seoul, 1966).

---: "Sŏngju sinang ko", *Hujin sahoe munje yŏn'gu nonmun chip* II (1968).

---: "Muga-ŭi chŏnsŭng pyŏnhwa ch'egye", *Han'guk minsokhak* VII, 124 (1975).

---: *Han'guk musok yŏn'gu*, Chimmundang(Seoul, 1981).

---: "Muga charyo moji-bŭi hyŏnhwang kŏmt'o", *Kubi munhak* I, 50-66 (1979).

---: *Han'guk muga chip*, I, II, III, IV, Chimmundang (Seoul, 1979-1980). The first three volumes were originally published by Wŏn'gwang University Press in Iri, in 1970, 1971 and 1978.

---: *Han'gug-ŭi musok sinhwa*, Chimmundang (Seoul, 1985).

Kim T'aekkyu: *Han'guk minsok munye-ron*, Ilchogak (2nd ed.: Seoul, 1982).

Kim Tonguk: "Muga 'Pari kongju'", *Hwang Ŭidon sŏnsaeng kohŭi kinyŏm sahak nonch'ong*, comp. by Tongguk Taehakkyo sahakhoe and Hwang Ŭidon sŏnsaeng kohŭi kinyŏm nonch'ong p'yŏnch'anhoe, Tongguk Taehakkyo ch'ulp'anbu (Seoul, 1960).

---: *Han'guk kayo-ŭi yŏn'gu*, Ŭryu munhwasa (Seoul, 1961).

---: *Han'guk kayo-ŭi yŏn'gu.sok*, Sŏnmyŏng munhwasa (Seoul, 1975).

---: *Ch'unhyang chŏn yŏn'gu*, Yŏnse Taehakkyo ch'ulp'anbu (augmented ed.: Seoul, 1976).

Kim Tonguk, Kim T'aejun, Sŏl Sŏnggyŏng: *Ch'unhyang chŏn pigyo yŏn'gu*, Samyŏngsa (Seoul, 1979).

Kim Yŏngbae: *Sŏkpo sangjŏl che isipsam.sa chuhae*, Ilchogak (Seoul, 1972).

Kim Yŏngil: *Han'guk muga-ŭi sŏsa kujo yŏn'gu*, MA thesis Sŏgang Taehakkyo Taehagwŏn (Seoul, 1974).

---: "Musok sinhwa-ŭi hyŏngsŏng ko - chusul wŏlli-rŭl t'ong-haesŏ pon -", *Kyŏngnam Taehak nonmun chip* III, 69-85 (1976).

Kim Yŏngjin: *Ch'ungch'ŏng-do muga*, Hyŏngsŏl ch'ulp'ansa (Seoul/Taegu, 1976).

Koryŏ sa, Kokusho kankōkai ed. (reprint of the ed. of 1909, in 4 vols.: Tōkyō, 1977).

Koryŏ tae-janggyŏng, 48 vols., Tongguk Taehakkyo (Seoul, 1960).

Kosŏ mongnok (Yŏnse Taehakkyo chungang tosŏgwan -), Yŏnse Taehakkyo chungang tosŏgwan (Seoul, 1977).

Kubi munhak kaesŏl: see Chang Tŏksun a.o..

Kujŏn minyo chip I, comp. and ed. by Rim Hogwŏn, Kungnip munhak yesul sŏjŏk ch'ulp'ansa (Pyongyang, 1958).

Maehwa chŏn, ed. and intr. by Chŏng Pyŏnguk, in *Han'guk hakpo* II, 4, pp. 257-287 (1976).

Murayama Chijun: *Chōsen no fusui*, Chōsen sōtokufu (Keijō, 1931).

---: *Chōsen no fugeki*, Chōsen sōtokufu (Keijō, 1932).

Nongga wŏllyŏng ka . Hanyang ka, ed. and annoted by Pak Sŏngŭi, Minjung sŏgwan (*Han'guk kojŏn munhak taegye* 7: Seoul, 1974).

Ong Kojip chŏn: see Chŏng Pyŏnguk.

Pae pijang chŏn: see Chŏng Pyŏnguk.

Pak Hwang: *P'ansori sosa*, Sin'gu munhwasa (Seoul, 1974).

Pak Hyosun: "Honam chibang-ŭi yŏryu kasa yŏn'gu", *Kasa munhak yŏn'gu*, comp. by Kugŏ kungmunhakhoe, Chŏngŭmsa (Seoul, 1979).

Pakssi chŏn: see Yi Sangbo.

Pulgong chaesik sangyong ŭibŏm, comp. by Samyŏng ch'ulp'ansa p'yŏnjippu (Taegu, 1978).

Sa Chaedong: "'Allakkuk t'aeja chŏn' yŏn'gu", *Ŏmun yŏn'gu* V, 99-127 (1967).

---: *Pulgyo-gye kungmun sosŏr-ŭi hyŏngsŏng kwajŏng yŏn'gu*, Asea munhwasa (Seoul, 1977).

---: "Sim Ch'ŏng chŏn yŏn'gu sŏsŏl", in Yi Sangt'aek a.o., *Han'guk kojŏn sosŏl yŏn'gu*, pp. 170-219.

Samguk yusa: see Iryŏn.

Sim Ch'ŏng chŏn: see Chang Chiyŏng.

Sim Ch'yŏng chyŏn (Kodae sosŏl-), ed. by Hyangminsa p'yŏnjippu, Hyangminsa (Taegu, 1972).

Sim Chy'ŏng chyŏn: also see *Wanp'anbon*.

Sim Usŏng: "Sonnim kut", *Kiwŏn* I, 3, pp. 180-193 (1973).

Sim Usŏng: "Sim Ch'ŏng kut", *Kiwŏn* II, 1, pp. 197-221 (1974).

---: *Namsadang-p'ae yŏn'gu*, Tonghwa ch'ulp'an kongsa (2nd ed.: Seoul, 1980).

---: *Han'gug-ŭi minsokkŭk*, Ch'angjak-kwa pip'yŏngsa (Seoul, 1975).

Sin Chaehyo: see Kang Hanyŏng.

Sin Tongik: "Sim Ch'ŏng sŏrhwa-ŭi musok-chŏk chŏnsŭng-e kwan-han ilko", *Munhwa illyuhak* IV, 55-70 (1971).

---: "Muga 'Sim Ch'ŏng chŏn'", *Han'guk minsokhak* IV, 93-125 (1971).

Sŏ Taesŏk: "P'ansori-wa sŏsa muga-ŭi taebi yŏn'gu", *Han'guk munhwa yŏn'guwŏn nonch'ong* XXXIV, 7-44 (1979).

---: "Muga yŏn'gu-ŭi hyŏnhwang-gwa munjetchŏm", *Kubi munhak* I, 67-72 (1979).

---: "P'ansori-ŭi chŏnsŭngnon-jŏk yŏn'gu: sŏsa muga-wa-ŭi taebi-esŏ", *Hyŏnsang-gwa insik* III, 3, pp. 122-142 (1979).

---: Han'guk muga-ŭi yŏn'gu, *Munhak sasangsa* (Seoul, 1980).

---: "Musok-kwa kungmunhak", in Kim Inhoe a.o.: *Han'guk musog-ŭi chonghap-chŏk koch'al*, pp. 181-206.

Sŏk Chusŏn: *Han'guk poksik sa*, Pojinjae (Seoul, 1971).

Sŏkka yŏrae sipchi suhaeng ki: see Sosil Sanin.

Sŏkpo sangjŏl: see Kim Yŏngbae and also Yi Tongnim.

Son Chint'ae: *Chōsen shinka ihen*, Kyōdo kenkyūsha (Tōkyō, 1930).

---: "Chōsen fugeki no shinka (1)", *Seikyū gakusō* XX, 140-154 (1935).

---: "Chōsen fugeki no shinka (2)", *Seikyū gakusō* XXII, 189-208 (1935).

---: "Chōsen fugeki no shinka (3)", *Seikyū gakusō* XXIII, 125-145 (1936).

---: "Chōsen fugeki no shinka (4)", *Seikyū gakusō* XXVIII, 126-150 (1937).

---: "Mugyŏg-ŭi sin'ga", *Sin kajŏng* IV, 4, pp. 97-104 and IV, 5, pp. 69-76 (1936).

---: "Mugyŏg-ŭi sin'ga", *Munjang* II, 7, pp. 164- 187 (1940).
---: *Son Chint'ae sŏnsaeng chŏnjip*, 6 vols., Taehaksa (Seoul, 1981).
Sŏng Kyŏngnin a.o.: *Seoul chibang-ŭi musok*, Munhwajae kwalliguk (Seoul, 1971).
Sosil Sanin: *Sŏkka yŏrae sipchi suhaeng ki*, wood-block ed. publ. at the Tŏkchu Temple (Ch'ungju, 1660).
T'aejo sillok: see *Chosŏn wangjo sillok*.
T'alch'um taesa chip (Chungyo muhyŏng munhwajae -), compiled and published by Han'guk munhwajae poho hyŏphoe (Seoul, 1981).
Tongguk yŏji sŭngnam (Sinjŭng -), Tongguk munhwasa (facsimile of the 1530 ed., Kojŏn kanhaenghoe: Seoul, 1958).
Tsukamoto Yoshitaka (comp.), *Bukkyō daijiten*, 10 vols., Sekai seiten kankō kyōkai (Tōkyō, 1967-1971).
Walraven, Boudewijn C.A.: "Ch'ŏnjamun-ŭro poa-on Han'guk kasa", *Kugŏ kungmunhak* XCIII, 459-472 + *purok* (1984).
---: "Han'guk sijo munhag-ŭi p'wŏmyulla punsŏk", *(Chesamhoe) Tongyanghak kukche haksul hoeŭi nonmunjip*, Sŏnggyungwan Taehakkyo Taedong munhwa yŏn'guso (Seoul, 1985), pp. 63-80.
Wang Chung-min a.o.: *Tun-huang pien-wen chi*, 2 vols., Jen-min wen-hsüeh ch'u-pan-shê (Peking, 1957).
Wanp'anbon Sim Ch'yŏng chyŏn (reprint *Yŏnse Taehakkyo kwahak charyo ch'ongsŏ 8, panggakpon ch'ongsŏ* 2: n.y., n.p.).
Wŏrin sŏkpo, reprint in three volumes: *kwŏn* 7.8, *kwŏn* 9.10 and *kwŏn* 17.18, Yŏnse Taehakkyo tongbanghak yŏn'guso (Seoul, 1957, 1956, 1957).
Yang Chudong: *Yŏyo chŏnju*, Ŭryu munhwasa (Seoul, 1947).
Yi Ch'angbae (comp.): *Han'guk kach'ang taegye*, 2 vols, Hongin munhwasa (Seoul, 1976).
Yi Hŏnhong: "P'ansori-ŭi 'p'omyulla'-e tae-hayŏ", *Han'guk minsokhak* XV, 137-162 (1982).
Yi Hŭisŭng (comp.): *Kugŏ tae-sajŏn*, Minjung sŏgwan (3rd ed.: Seoul, 1963).
Yi Hyegu: *Han'guk ŭmak yŏn'gu*, Kungmin ŭmak yŏn'guhoe (Seoul, 1957).
Yi Hyegu, Sŏng Kyŏngnin, Yi Ch'angbae: *Kugak tae-jŏnjip*, Sinsegi rek'oodŭ chusik hoesa (Seoul, 1968).
Yi Ik: *Sŏngho sasŏl*, 30 *kwŏn*, Kyŏnghŭi ch'ulp'ansa (reprint in 2 vols.: Seoul, 1967).
Yi Kyŏngbok, *Sim Ch'ŏng kut yŏn'gu*, M.A. thesis Myŏngji Taehakkyo (Seoul, 1975).
---: "Sim Ch'ŏng ka. Sim Ch'ŏng chŏn. Sim Ch'ŏng kus-ŭi ch'aitchŏm koch'al", *Sae kugŏ kyoyuk* XVIII-XX, 291-300 (1974).
Yi Nŭnghwa: "Chosŏn musok ko", *Kyemyŏng* XIX, 1-85 (1927).
---: *Chosŏn togyo sa*, tr. by Yi Chongha, Posŏng munhwasa (Seoul, 1977).
Yi Nŭngu: *Ko-sosŏl yŏn'gu*, Sŏnmyŏng munhwasa (Seoul, 1974).
Yi Sangbo: *Pulgyo kasa chŏnjip (Han'guk -)*, Chimmundang (Seoul, 1980).
---: *Han'guk kasa sŏnjip*, Chimmundang (Seoul, 1979).
Yi Sangbo (ed.): *Han'guk kojŏn munhak* I, Myŏngji Taehak ch'ulp'anbu (Seoul, 1982).
Yi Sangt'aek, Sŏ Taesŏk and Sŏng Hyŏngyŏng (eds.): *Han'guk kojŏn sosŏl*, Kyemyŏng Taehak ch'ulp'anbu (Taegu, 1974).

Yi Tongnim: *Sŏkpo sangjŏl (Chuhae -)*, Tongguk munhwasa (Seoul, 1959).
Yi Tuhyŏn: "Yangju So-nori kut", *Kugŏ kungmunhak* XXXIX-XL, 169-200 (1968).
---: *Han' guk kamyŏn' gŭk*, Munhwa kongbobu, Munhwajae kwalliguk (Seoul, 1969).
---: "Tonghaean pyŏlsin kut", *Han' guk munhwa illyuhak* XIII, 159-182 (1981).
Yi Tuhyŏn, Chang Chugŭn, Yi Kwanggyu: *Han' guk minsokhak kaesŏl*, Minjung sŏgwan (Seoul, 1974).
Yu Ch'angdon: *Ko-sijo sinsŏk*, Tongguk munhwasa (Seoul, 1959).
---: *Ŏhŭi-sa yŏn' gu*, SŏnmyƟng munhwasa (Seoul, 1974).
Yu Tongsik: *Han' guk mugyo-ŭi yŏksa-wa kujo*, Yŏnse Taehakkyo ch'ulp'anbu (Seoul, 1975).

B: Works in European Languages

Aarne, A. and S. Thompson: *The Types of the Folktale*, FF Communications 74, Academia Scientiarum Fennica (Helsinki, 1928).
Austerlitz, Robert: *Ob-Ugric metrics: The Metrical Structure of Ostyak and Vogul Folk Poetry*, FF Communications 174, Academia Scientiarum Fennica (Helsinki, 1958).
Ayscough, Florence: "Cult of the Ch'êng Huang Lao Yeh", *Journal of the North China Branch of the Royal Asiatic Society* LV, 131-155 (1924).
Benson, Larry D.: "The Literary Character of Anglo-Saxon Formulaic Poetry", *Publications of the Modern Language Association* LXXXI, 334-341 (1966).
Blacker, Carmen: *The Catalpa Bow*, George Allen and Unwin (London, 1975).
Brandt, Vincent S.R.: *A Korean Village*, Harvard University Press (Cambridge, Mass., 1971).
Buzo, Adrian: "Koryŏ Kayo: Songs of the Koryŏ Period", *Korea Journal* XIX, 10, pp. 32-41 (1979).
Bynner, Witter: *Three Hundred Poems of the T'ang Dynasty*, transl. by- , Wen-hsing shu-tien (Taipei, 1952).
Cauberghe, J.: *Vroomheid en volksgeloof in Vlaanderen*, Uitgeverij Heideland (Hasselt, 1967).
Chang Chu-keun (= Chang Chugŭn): "Mu-sok - the Shaman Culture of Korea", in Chun Shin-yong (general ed.), *Folk Culture in Korea*, International Cultural Foundation (Korean Culture Series 4: Seoul, 1974), 59-88; contains *muga* translations by Alan Heyman.
Cho, Hung-youn: *Koreanischer Schamanismus*, Wegweiser zur Völkerkunde, Heft 27, Hamburgisches Museum für Völkerkunde (Hamburg, 1982).
---: *Mudang: der Werdegang koreanischer Schamanen am Beispiel der Lebensgeschichte des Yi Chi-san*, Gesellschaft für Natur- und Völkerkunde Ostasiens e.V. Hamburg, Mitteilungen Band 93 (Hamburg, 1983).
Choi, Chungmoo: "The Artistry and Ritual Aesthetics of Urban Korean Shamans", *Journal of Ritual Studies* III,2, pp.235-249 (1989).

Choi, In-hak: *A Type Index of Korean Folktales*, Myong Ji University Publishing (Seoul, 1979).

Chun Shin-yong (General ed.): *Folk Culture in Korea*, Korean Culture Series 4, International Cultural Foundation (Seoul, 1974).

Clark, Allen D. and Donald N.: Seoul: *Past and Present*, Royal Asiatic Society, Korea Branch/Hollym (Seoul, 1969).

Clark, C.A.: *Religions of Old Korea*, The Christian Literature Society of Korea (re-issue: Seoul, 1961).

Courant, Maurice: *Supplément à la bibliographie coréenne (jusqu'en 1899)*, Publications de l'école des langues orientales vivantes (Paris, 1901).

Cowell, E.B. (ed.): *The Jᵃtaka, or Stories of the Buddha's Former Births*, 6 vols., Cambridge University Press (Cambridge, 1895-1907).

Delaby, Laurence: *Chamanes toungouses*, Etudes mongoles ... et sibériennes: cahier 7 (Paris, 1976).

Diamond, Robert E.: "The Diction of the Signed Poems of Cynewulf", *Philological Quarterly* XXXVIII, 228-241 (1959).

Dictionnaire Coréen-francais, par les missionnaires de Corée, C. Lévy (Yokohama, 1880).

Diószegi, V. (ed.): *Glaubenswelt und Folklore der siberischen Völker*, Akadémiai Kiádo (Budapest, 1963).

Doré, H.: *Recherches sur les superstitions en Chine*, 18 vols., Imprimerie de la mission catholique à l'Orphélinat de T'ou-sè-wè (Shanghai, 1911-1938).

Dudbridge, Glen: *The Hsi-yu Chi*, Cambridge University Press (Cambridge, 1970).

Durand, M.: *Technique et panthéon des médiums Viêtnamiens (Dông)*, Ecole Francaise d'Extrême-Orient (Paris, 1959).

Eberhard, Wolfram: *Typen Chinesischer Volksmärchen*, FF Communications 120, Academia Scientiarum Fennica (Helsinki, 1937).

---: "Chinese Building Magic", *Studies in Chinese Folklore and Related Essays*, Indiana Folklore Institute Monograph Series, Vol. 23, Mouton (The Hague, 1970), pp. 49-65.

---: "Pounding Songs from Peking", *Studies in Chinese Folklore and Related Essays* (see the preceding item), pp. 147-171.

Eikemeier, D.: "Volksgodsdienstige verschijnselen in de oudste Koreaanse letterkunde", *Forum der Letteren* XIX, 284-292 (1978).

---: "Wohin gehen Koreaner nach dem Tod?", *Asiatische Studien/Etudes Asiatiques* XXXIV, 2, pp. 91-125 (1980).

Eliade, Mircea: *Le chamanisme et les techniques archaïques de l'exstase*, Payot (Deuxième ed., revue et augmentée: Paris, 1974).

Embree, John F., *A Japanese Village: Suye Mura*, Kegan Paul (London, 1946).

Emeneau, M.B.: "Style and Meaning in an Oral Literature", *Language* XLII, 2, pp. 323-345 (1966).

Eoyang, Eugene Chen: *Word of Mouth: oral story-telling in the pien-wen*, Ph.D. thesis Indiana University (Bloomington, 1971).

Findeisen, Hans: *Schamanentum*, Kohlhammer Verlag (Stuttgart, 1957).

Finnegan, Ruth: *Oral Poetry: Its Nature, Significance and Social Context*, Cambridge University Press (Cambridge/London/New York/Melbourne, 1977).

Folk Treasury of Korea (The -), ed. by Chang, Duk-soon (Chang Tŏksun), Society of Korean Oral Literature (Seoul, 1970).

Frankel, Hans H.: *The Flowering Plum and the Palace Lady*, Yale University Press (New Haven/London, 1976).

Gale, J.S.: "Han-Yang (Seoul)", *Transactions of the Korea Branch of the Royal Asiatic Society* II, 2, pp. 1-43 (1902).

---: *Korean-English Dictionary (The Unabridged -)*, 3rd ed.; ed. by Alexander A. Pieters, The Christian Literature Society of Korea (Korea, 1931).

Giles, Herbert A.: *A Chinese Biographical Dictionary*, Bernhard Quaritch and Kelly and Walsh (London/Shanghai/Yokohama, 1898).

Guillemoz, Alexandre: *Les algues, les anciens, les dieux*, Le Léopard d'Or (Paris, 1983).

---: "Les aristocrates, les moines, les femmes", *Cahiers de Litterature Orale* XVI, pp. 121-130 (1984).

Haguenauer, Ch.: "Sorciers et sorcières de Corée", *Bulletin de la Maison Franco-Japonaise* II, 1, pp. 47-65.

Harvey, Youngsook Kim: *Six Korean Women: The Socialization of Shamans*, West Publishing Company (St. Paul/New York/Los Angeles/San Francisco, 1979).

Henthorn, William E.: *A History of Korea*, Free Press (New York, 1971).

Herbert, J.: *Les dieux nationaux de Japon*, Albin Michel (Paris, 1965).

Heyman, Alan C.: see Chang Chu-keun, "Musok - the Shaman Culture of Korea."

---: "The Ritual Song of the God Sonnim", *Korea Journal* XXIII, 11, pp. 50-57 (1983).

Histoire de Dame Pak . Histoire de Sukhyang, transl. by Marc Orange and Kim Su-chung, l'Asiathèque (Paris, 1982).

Huhm, Halla Pai: *Kut: Korean Shamanist Rituals*, Hollym (Elizabeth, New Jersey/Seoul, 1980).

Hultkrantz, A.: "Ecological and Phenomenological Aspects of Shamanism", *Shamanism in Siberia*, ed. by V. Diószegi and M. Hoppál, Akadémiai Kiádo (Budapest, 1978).

Howard, Keith:*Korean Musical Instruments: A Practical Guide*, Se-Kwang Music Publishing Co. (Seoul, 1988).

---: *Bands, Songs and Shamanistic Rituals: Folk Music in Korean Society*, Royal Asiatic Society Korea Branch (Seoul, 1989).

Ikeda, H.: *A Type and Motif Index of Japanese Folk-Literature*, FF Communications No. 219, Academia Scientiarum Fennica (Helsinki, 1971).

Ilyŏn (= Iryŏn): *Samguk yusa*, transl. by Tae-Hung Ha and Grafton K. Mintz, Yonsei University Press (Seoul, 1972).

Im Sŏkchae: see Yim Suk-jay.

Iryŏn: see Ilyŏn.

Janelli, Roger L. and Dawnhee Yim Janelli: *Ancestor Worship and Korean Society*, Stanford University Press (Stanford, California, 1982).

Kendall, Laurel: "Caught Between Ancestors and Spirits: Field Report of a Korean Mansin's Healing Kut", *Korea Journal* XVII, 8, pp. 8-23 (1977).

---: "Wood Imps, Ghosts and Other Noxious Influences: The Ideology of Affliction in a Korean Village", *The Journal of Korean Studies* III, 113-145 (1981).

---: *Shamans, Housewives and Other Restless Spirits: Women in Korean Ritual Life*, University of Hawaii Press (Honolulu, 1985).

---: *The Life and Hard Times of a Korean Shaman*, University of Hawaii Press (Honolulu, 1988).

Kim, Seong Nae, "Lamentations of the Dead: The Historical Imagery of Violence on Cheju Island, South Korea", *Journal of Ritual Studies* III, 2, pp. 251-285.

---: "Dances of *Toch'aebi* and Songs of Exorcism in Cheju Shamanism", *Diogenes* 158, pp. 57-68 (Summer 1992).

Korea Newsreview, publ. weekly by the International Cultural Society of Korea, Seoul.

Ledyard, Gari: *The Dutch Come to Korea*, Taewon (Seoul, 1971).

Lee, Jung-Young: *Korean Shamanistic Rituals*, Mouton (The Hague, 1980).

Lee, Peter H.: *Celebration of Continuity*, Harvard University Press (Cambridge, Mass./London, 1979).

Lee Tae-dong: "Princess Pari" and "A Shamanistic Deity Epic (Chesŏk)", *Korea Journal* XVIII, 6, pp. 52-60 (1978).

Lewis, Geoffrey: *The Book of Dede Korkut*, translated, with an introduction and notes by -, Penguin Books (Harmondsworth, 1974).

Lord, Albert B.: *The Singer of Tales*, Harvard University Press (2nd ed.: Cambridge, Mass., 1964).

---: "Oral Poetry", *Encyclopedia of Poetry and Poetics*, ed. by Alex Preminger, Princeton University Press (Princeton, 1965), 591-593.

McCann, David: "Structural Elements of the Kasa", *Korea Journal* XIV, 6, pp. 27-34 (1974).

---: "The Korean Sijo", *Harvard Journal of Asiatic Studies* XXXVI, 114-134 (1976).

---: *Form and Freedom in Korean Poetry*, E.J. Brill (Leiden, 1987).

Magoun, F.P.: "The Oral-Formulaic Character of Anglo-Saxon Narrative Poetry", in Donald K. Fry (ed.), *The Beowulf Poet: A Collection of Critical Essays*, Prentice Hall Inc. (Englewood Cliffs, N.J., 1968), originally published in *Speculum* XXVIII (1953).

Martin, Samuel E.: Yang Ha Lee and Sung Un Chang: *A Korean-English Dictionary*, Yale University Press (New Haven/London, 1967).

Motzki, Harald: *Schamanismus als Problem Religionswissenschaftlicher Terminologie*, E.J. Brill (Köln, 1977).

Olof, A.M.: "The Story of Prince Allakkuk: *Wŏrin sŏkpo* Vol. 8", *Korea Journal* XXIII, 1, pp. 13-20 (1983).

Park, Byeng-sen: *Le récit de la "Princesse abandonnée" et les médiums à travers l'histoire de Corée*, Yonsei University Museum (Seoul, 1973).

Parry, M.: "Studies in the Epic Technique of Oral Verse-making, I: Homer and Homeric Style", *Harvard Studies in Classical Philology* XLI, 73-147 (1930).

Pihl, Marshall: "Korea in the Bardic Tradition: P'ansori as an oral art", *Korean Studies Forum* II, 1-105 (1977).
Poppe, Nikolaus: *Mongolische Volksdichtung*, Franz Steiner Verlag (Wiesbaden, 1955).
Ramsden, H.A.: *Korean Coin Charms and Amulets*, Numismatic Philatelic Publishers (Yokohama, 1910).
Redford, Donald B.: "The Literary Motif of the Exposed Child", *Numen* XIV, 209-228 (1967).
Rogers, H.L.: "The Crypto-Psychological Character of the Oral Formula", *English Studies* XLVII, 102 (1966).
Rotermund, Hartmut O.: *Majinai-uta: Grundlagen, Inhalte und Formelemente japanischer magischer Gedichte des 17.-20. Jahrhunderts*, deutsche Gesellschaft für Natur- und Völkerkunde Ostasiens, Tōkyō, Gesellschaft für Natur- und Völkerkunde Ostasiens e.V. Hamburg (Tōkyō/Hamburg, n.y.).
Ruitenbeek, K.: *Bouwbedrijf en bouwmagie in het traditionele China*, E.J. Brill (Leiden, 1984).
---: *The Lu Ban Jing: A Fifteenth Century Chinese Carpenter's Manual*, doctoral dissertation, Leiden University (1989).
Rutt, Richard (ed. and transl.): *The Bamboo Grove: An Introduction to Sijo*, University of California Press (Berkeley/Los Angeles/London, 1971).
Sandschejew, G.: "Welt-Anschauung und Schamanismus der Alaren-Burjaten", *Anthropos* XXII, pp. 576-613 and 933-955 (1927).
Schlegel, Gustave: *La loi du parallélisme en style chinois démontrée par la préface du Si-yü ki*, Brill (Leiden, 1896).
Schmitz, C.A. (ed.): *Religions-Ethnologie*, Akademische Verlagsgesellschaft (Frankfurt am Main, 1964).
Skillend, W.E.: "'Words from the Heart': An unpublished *kasa*", *Asea munhwa* V, 156-184 (1966).
---: *Kodae Sosŏl: A Survey of Korean Traditional Style Popular Novels*, School of Oriental and African Studies (London, 1968).
---: "Puritas Submersa Resurgit", *Asiatische Studien/Etudes Asiatiques* XXXIV, 2, pp. 126-139 (1980).
---: "The Story of Sim Ch'ŏng; translated from a book such as young ladies read one hundred and fifty years ago", transl. by --, in Chung Chong-wha (ed.), *Korean Classical Literature: An Anthology*, Kegan Paul International (London/New York, 1989), pp. 114-155.
Sorensen, Clark W.: "The Myth of Princess Pari and the Self-Image of Korean Women", *Anthropos* LXXXIII, 409-419 (1988).
Starr, Frederick: "Korean Charms and Amulets", *Transactions of the Korea Branch of the Royal Asiatic Society* VIII, 42-79 (1917).
Thompson, Stith: *The Folktale*, The Dryden Press (New York, 1946).
---: *Motif-index of Folk-literature*, 6 vols., Rosenkilde and Bagger (Rev. and enl. ed.: Copenhagen, 1955-1958).
Vajda, L.: "Zur phaseologischen Stellung des Schamanismus", *Religions-Ethnologie*, ed. by C.A. Schmitz, Akademische Verlagsgesellschaft (Frankfurt a. M., 1964).

Vos, Frits: *Die Religionen Koreas*, Kohlhammer (Die Religionen der Menschheit 22,1:Stuttgart/Berlin/Köln/Mainz, 1977).

---: "Tung-fang Shuo, Buffoon and Immortal, in Japan and Korea", *Oriens Extremus* XXVI,1/2, pp. 189-204 (1979).

---: "Tales of the Extraordinary: An Inquiry into the Contents, Nature and Authorship of the *Sui chŏn*", *Korean Studies* V, 1-25 (1981).

Waley, Arthur: *Ballads and Stories from Tun-huang: an Anthology*, George Allen and Unwin (London, 1960).

Walraven, B.C.A.: *De redder der armen*, Meulenhoff (Amsterdam, 1980).

---: "Blinkend als de Morgenster", *Verre naasten naderbij* XVI, 2, pp. 51-56 (1982).

---: "The Sim Ch'ŏng Kut", *Papers Presented at the 6th Annual Conference of AKSE, held in Seoul, Korea, Aug. 2-5, 1982*, Korea Research Foundation, (Seoul, 1982), 3-24 and 303-320 (Korean translation).

---: "Korean Shamanism", *Numen* XXX, 2, pp. 240-264 (1983).

---: "Tien Sasol Sijo", *Hollands Maandblad*, No. 434, pp. 36-41 (1986).

---: "The Root of Evil -as explained in Korean shaman songs", in *Twenty Papers on Korean Studies Offered to Prof. W.E. Skillend*, ed. by Daniel Bouchez, Robert C. Provine and Roderick Whitfield, Collège de France (Paris, 1989), pp. 351-368.

---: "The Deity of the Seventh Day -and other narrative *muga* from Cheju Island", *Bruno Lewin zu Ehren: Festschrift aus Anlass seines 65. Geburtstages*, Band III (Bochum, 1993), pp. 309-328.

---: "Stirring Sounds: Music in Korean Shaman Rituals", *Oideion: The Performing Arts World-Wide*, ed. by Wim van Zanten, CNWS (Leiden, 1993).

Wang, C.H.: *The Bell and the Drum*, University of California Press (Berkeley/Los Angeles/London, 1974).

Wassiljewitsch, G.M.: "Schamanengesänge der Ewenken (Tungusen)", V. Diószegi (ed.), *Glaubenswelt und Folklore der siberischen Völker*, Akadémiai Kiádo (Budapest, 1963), pp. 381-404.

Watts, Ann Chalmers: *The Lyre and the Harp: A comparative reconsideration of oral tradition in Homer and old English poetry*, Yale University Press (New Haven, 1969).

Werner, E.T.C.: *A Dictionary of Chinese Mythology*, Longwood Press (reprint of the original ed. (Shanghai, 1932): Boston, 1977).

Wu Ch'eng-en: *Journey to the West*, 2 vols., tr. by Anthony C. Yu, University of Chicago Press (Chicago, 1977).

Yim Suk-jay (= Im Sŏkchae): "Introduction au Mouïsme", *Revue de Corée* IV, 2, pp. 5-22 (1972).

Yoon, Hong-key: *Geomantic Relationships between Nature and Culture in Korea*, The Chinese Association for Folklore (Taipei, 1976).

Index

For the purpose of alphabetization no distinction has been made between aspirated and unaspirated consonants, or between vowels with or without breve or macron.